*The Problem of Human Needs and
the Critique of Civilisation*

The Problem of Human Needs and the Critique of Civilisation

PATRICIA SPRINGBORG
Department of Government, University of Sydney

London
GEORGE ALLEN & UNWIN
Boston   Sydney

First published in 1981

GEORGE ALLEN & UNWIN LTD
40 Museum Street, London WC1A 1LU

© George Allen & Unwin (Publishers) Ltd, 1981

British Library Cataloguing in Publication Data

Springborg, Patricia
 The problem of human needs and the critique
 of civilisation.
 1. Sociology
 I. Title
 301′.08   HM51

 ISBN 0-04-301133-0

Set in 10 on 11 point Times by Typesetters (Birmingham) Ltd
and printed in Great Britain
by Mackays of Chatham

For
Joan and Peter, Bob and Ziyad

Contents

Acknowledgements

In the course of my work I have incurred many debts and the greatest is certainly to my supervisor, Professor Leszek Kolakowski of All Souls College, Oxford. I thank him sincerely for his generous help and for the long and friendly letters of advice which sustained me working at such a distance.

St Anne's College offered me generous assistance of another kind and I would like to extend to them my special thanks for the award of the Herbert Plumer Bursary which provided my financial support for the year 1972 to 1973.

One of my greatest intellectual debts is to Professor John Pocock, to whose great talent and unstinting generosity as a supervisor and teacher I owe my early education in the history of ideas at the University of Canterbury, New Zealand. John Pocock read and commented on this manuscript, for which I thank him.

Mr Rom Harré, Mr Alan Ryan and the late Professor Plamenatz offered me advice and assistance in the early stages of my Oxford degree and I would like to thank them too. I have benefited greatly from the comments and criticisms of others along the way, especially Agnes Heller and Ferenc Feher of the Budapest School and now in Australia, and my colleagues at the University of Sydney, Professors Richard Spann and Henry Mayer, Carole Pateman and Michael Jackson, who read and commented on various parts of the manuscript.

I would also like to thank Professor Preston King of the University of New South Wales, Dr Ross Fitzgerald of Griffith University, Professor Charles Taylor of All Souls College, Oxford and Professor Zygmunt Bauman of Leeds University, who offered criticisms and advice in different capacities, without necessarily agreeing with my argument.

In the USA I wish to thank Professor George Kline of Bryn Mawr College, Professor Benjamin Barber of Rutgers University, Professor Nannerl Keohane of Stanford University and Professor Andreas Aschete of the University of Pennsylvania, all of whom read and commented on all or some of the manuscript. I have also benefited greatly from the comments of the Publishers' anonymous Readers, incorporating their recommendations as best I could.

My typists, Mary Megalli in Cairo, Jane Clark in Sydney and Kay Dilks in Philadelphia, and Gay Howells, who kindly checked the typescript, laboured long and hard, for which I truly thank them. And finally, but above all, I wish to thank my husband for his encouragement and support and my little son for his patience.

An early and quite different version of chapter 6 appeared as an essay, 'Karl Marx on Human Needs', in *Human Needs and Politics*, edited by Ross Fitzgerald, Sydney, Pergamon Press, 1977. Material from the later version of chapter 6 and from chapter 3 has appeared as an essay, 'Rousseau and Marx', in another collection edited by Ross Fitzgerald, *Comparing Political Thinkers*, Sydney, Pergamon Press, 1980.

1

The Problem of Human Needs

One of the things that Agnes Heller's recent excellent book on *The Theory of Need in Marx* (1976) serves to illustrate by its careful exposition of this concept in Marx's writings, is that what we have come to understand by the Marxist theory of needs has little basis in Marx's own writings.[1] Although, as she shows, the concept lurks in almost every aspect of Marx's theory, it is by no means clear that in each case this is essentially the same concept. We have been forced back by the twentieth-century, neo-Marxist renaissance of the doctrine of true and false needs to try to find its roots in Marx's own theory. But one can argue that this is a project that arises from twentieth-century imperatives more than from an essential unity in Marx's own thought on the subject. If indeed the concept of needs had represented a central concept in Marx's thought one would have expected a more systematic treatment of it, a more careful exposition of its various aspects, its range and limits. Were it even an essential underlying concept providing a key to disparate elements in Marx's thought, one would expect greater congruence in Marx's handling of the concept.

But far from this we have a rather obvious antinomy in Marx's thought on the subject in his support for the old socialist slogan 'to each according to his needs', on the one hand, which seems to suggest that socialism is a condition in which all needs can be met, and his espousal of the stoic doctrine of true and false needs, on the other, which suggests the opposite. It is true that Marx only makes explicit his support for the doctrine of true and false needs in a fleeting reference, mainly confined to footnotes in *The German Ideology* and, as some have suggested, one could make too much of this (*Collected Works*, Vol. 5, p. 255).[2] Nevertheless, most of Marx's toss-away remarks are symptomatic of something and this is no exception. Indeed, throughout the *Economic and Philosophic Manuscripts* as well as *Capital* itself we find ourselves constantly reminded that capitalism perpetuates itself precisely by treating articles of use as bearers of wealth, thus persuading people to produce, exchange and accumulate them in a volume and at a rate quite unrelated to their genuine needs. Although this argument is nowhere to my knowledge explicated in these terms, Marx's critique of capitalism would be meaningless if we did not assume it. In other words, the whole thrust of his distinction between use value and exchange value serves to remind us that whatever the mechanisms may be that allow us to inculcate a demand for the ever-increasing flow of commodities that capitalism produces, they stand in stark contrast to the needs of man under socialism.

And this really is the central thrust of Marx's distinction between true and false needs: it serves not so much to condemn the ever-proliferating needs of man under capitalism, as to set a criterion of genuine needs as the basis for justice under socialism. Marx believed that capitalism, despite its omnivorous appetite for commodities, had an all-round civilising influence. He did not advocate a return to the parsimoniousness of the man of few needs, that stoical fellow portrayed by the early socialists. In fact he explicitly condemned utopian primitivism, 'the abstract negation of the entire world of culture and civilisation, the regression to the *unnatural* simplicity of the *poor* and crude man who has few needs and who has not only failed to go beyond private property, but has not yet even reached it' (*CW*, Vol. 3, p. 295). Man under socialism will be for Marx a man rich in needs, but these will spring from the unfolding of his latent powers and potentialities and not from the dictates of an economic system.

This brings us to perhaps the most interesting aspect of Marx's use of needs as a concept. By this I refer to the role needs play in Marx's ontology, his theory of human nature. Here we have the most appealing and most humane aspects of Marx's thought: his vision of man as a creature of unlimited reach, whose powers will bloom given the construction of a humane environment, whose artistic and creative powers will be unleashed, and whose conquest of nature will bring him to heights of human perfectibility that were formerly undreamed of. Marx sees this process as one of dialectical interchange, of a ceaseless striving in which needs represent both a teleological imperative and a motivational mechanism. That is to say, needs represent both an *ought* and an *is* simultaneously. Thus we find the concept used sometimes as a synonym for 'powers' to indicate that such capacities spring from an impulse deeply embedded in human nature. At other times the term is synonymous with values, and here it represents an ethical imperative. So, for instance, we find Marx insisting that what distinguishes man from an animal is that while animals produce 'one-sidedly', man produces 'universally'; animals produce 'only under the domination of immediate physical need, whilst man produces even when he is free from physical need and only truly produces in freedom therefrom' – clearly a statement of value (ibid., p. 276).[3]

It is just this value criterion by which capitalism stands condemned, for under its alienating conditions the needs of the workers are constantly being driven to mere subsistence level, limited in form and range to mere animal functions. Alienated man is reduced to the crudity of raw needs, so he eats solely to stave off hunger, drinks only to slake his thirst, sleeps to replenish his strength to work, procreates in order to reproduce his labour power and is, in this way, reduced to an animal existence, oblivious to the human form that needs may take. Since alienation violates the fundamental distinction between man and animals – concerning the form and content of needs and their mode of gratification — the imperatives of dealienation are to be found in precisely this area. Marx draws an evocative picture of the dialectical unfolding of human needs and their objects reminiscent of the spirit of the German Romantic movement of the nineteenth century and Hegel himself. In Marx's summation of the history of civilisation as progress in the development of man's five senses, we see brought to fruition the expressivist theory of the *Sturm und Drang* period and its distillation in the philosophy of Georg Wilhelm Friedrich Hegel.[4]

It was the mark of expressivist theory to place priority on the emotions as the vehicle through which man's essential relations to the world are revealed. As pre-theoretical, spontaneous impulses, the emotions are seen to affirm man's physical dependence on nature but, at the same time, in their variety and range and in the scope of the human imagination, the emotions indicate his ability to transcend the limits of physical existence. All of man's characteristic strengths and weaknesses are prefigured in his capacities for love, hate, fear, trust, pleasure, pain, joy, anger, sadness and happiness. The impulse of impulses or emotion of emotions is seen to be desire itself. Desire supplants the Cartesian *cogito* as the fundamental relation of man to reality, for, prior to thought, from the moment of birth itself, desire is the first and most urgent experience of the self. It is in desire that man comes to know himself, at first negatively, as a being to which what it needs is lacking; and then positively as he becomes aware of the being that he is and what it means to complete the lack and satisfy his needs.[5] In this way, these physical needs which he shares with the animals become the opportunity for him to distinguish himself from other animate existence by his capacity for self-consciousness and rational thought. It is from reflection on the significance of desire and the nature of his needs that emerges the capacity for reasoning that produces the highest forms of abstract thought.

Although it has its roots in the nature philosophy and pantheism of the romantic period, this orientation to needs embraces rationalism in its purest form. It is a conception of the world that remains organic without, however, being strictly materialist. While needs and desires are seen as the primary orientation of man to the world they do not describe that relation in their finitude. For thought as a response to needs is more than a need itself and man as body is also spirit. It is not with Hegel but with Marx that this line of reasoning is taken to its ultimate conclusion and the concept of needs is expanded to encompass all aspects of human nature, both man's physical and cognitive powers. Thus it is that Marx can refer to thinking, willing, loving, feeling, observing and experiencing as 'mental senses', analogous to the five physical senses in their dependence on the world of objects (*CW*, Vol. 3, pp. 299–300).

It is this attempt to establish a materialism that arrogates without necessarily extinguishing the spiritual realm that stamps the Marxian project. In the vicissitudes of the concept of needs we see one aspect of the career of this project. The concept of needs represents the attempt to embrace both freedom and necessity according to the principle of dialectical materialism. In his emphasis on the ontological significance of needs, Marx is concerned to give an account of the human essence, man's species-being, such that both the material and physical constraints of human existence, as well as man's immanent capacity to transcend these limits, are included. Not only are 'seeing, hearing, smelling, tasting, feeling, thinking, observing, experiencing, wanting, acting, loving' (ibid.) human needs every bit as much as eating, sleeping, breathing and procreating, but it is as 'needs' that man experiences these propensities of his nature. And it is only a question of whether his social environment affords the satisfaction of such truly human needs whether man's nature is realised or not.

This ontological conception of needs raises most precisely the unique features of expressivist theory in Marx's thought: the attempt to provide a non-essentialist, non-theological, and materialist theory of human nature which nevertheless escapes the reduction of man to the dry bones of eighteenth-century Humean empiricism or French materialist *homme-machine* theories. And in this one respect almost all subsequent versions of need-theory agree: that an explanation of human motivation and conduct is to be sought not in the metaphysical realm of the soul, divine will, or spirit, but in certain instincts, drives, propensities or powers which bespeak man's predicament as a physical being in the world of things whose capacities nevertheless include certain cognitive and intellectual inclinations which far exceed these material limits. How to assess the successes and failures of this project to create a secular and materialist theory of human nature that nevertheless tries to take full account of man's spiritual, intellectual and artistic powers? We cannot do more here than indicate the kind of questions that it raises. Does this theory arrive at a concept of the self that is in any way adequate to our own experience? To what degree do we understand, or can we understand ourselves as need-governed creatures, and what then counts as a need? Is it possible to arrive at a theory of human nature that can account for the path of history as an objective process and at the same time do justice to our subjective understanding of human behaviour? In other words, can the problem of freedom and determinism be resolved through the doctrine of needs? And can the problem of evil, or the phenomenon of alienation be explained in terms of true and false needs?

As we shall see, need theory pulls in both directions. The writings of the early Marx, in which the concept of needs figures in an important way, lean in the direction of freedom. Needs are seen much more as an expression of man's capacity for free, spontaneous, creative activity, than as the constraints which the material world imposes on man as a physical being. And yet, of course, a certain tension remains since both these considerations reflect the truth of man's existence. In the writings of Hegel and of twentieth-century existentialists, particularly of Sartre, we see both the ancestry and the legacy of the ontological conception of needs for which Marx's early writings are a watershed. Meditations on the concept of needs in these works have produced a new focus on the problem of freedom and necessity that does much greater justice to the ambiguities and subtleties of the problem than one found hitherto.

In the writings of the later Marx and his attempt to explore the dynamics of economic determinism, we see a thrust in the other direction. From *The German Ideology* on we see in the expansion of human needs, a link between the production of commodities, and the motivations peculiar to capitalist man. The idea grew out of Marx's attempt to give his theory of dialectical materialism greater specificity. Intent as it is on establishing both a non-theological conception of human nature and an account of history as a dialectical unfolding which involves a mutual interchange between subject and object, historical materialism found in the concept of needs a suitable vehicle to explain the dynamics of this process. If needs arise both as a consequence of man's physical relation to the material world and are, in turn, shaped by the way in which he brings his cognitive powers to bear on that world, then one can see in needs a reflection both of the powers of man as subject and of the material world as object whose resistance creates the field in which these powers have their play. Ever-expanding needs have an intimate role in the theory of historical materialism as the motor of progress and as a way to account for the motivations that one had to presuppose of capitalist man in order to explain this progress. But this is a link that remains largely unexplored in Marx's own theory, and whatever gains in the rigour of dialectical materialism have been made by forging it in the doctrine of true and false needs, have been bought at a great loss in the subtlety and persuasiveness of the Marxist theory of human nature and the role that needs play there. In addition it gives rise to outright contradictions.

The doctrine of true and false needs is by now so ubiquitous that it hardly needs an introduction. It has given the concept of needs such currency that suddenly, as if out of nowhere, this new criterion has appeared that is being applied everywhere. For instance, in education theory, social work theory, urban planning, environment theory, we have talk of programmes geared to needs, distribution according to need, resource use according to need, as if this concept supplied the magic talisman that will solve these complex problems. The concept makes such a direct appeal to common sense that it seems to require no further justification and, indeed, one wonders why it had not been thought of before. And yet philosophic and social science dictionaries, encyclopaedias and indexes yield almost no reference to the concept which seems to have been absent from the writings of most of the classical political thinkers as well. In a field where there is nothing new under the sun this appears to be a real philosophical innovation. Earlier thinkers simply failed to appreciate the possibilities of this concept and its explanatory power − or at least so it would seem.

As it turns out there are indeed historical antecedents in a rather subordinate philosophical tradition that runs from the Stoics through Rousseau, Locke and Enlightenment materialists, to the early socialists, where a doctrine of true and false needs is to be found in rudimentary form. But until the advent of dialectical materialism, this doctrine was without the epistemological foundation that it needed to establish itself in its own right. In other words, without the addition of Marxist principles it would never have acquired the air of certitude which has given it its cutting edge.

Now one of the great appeals of the doctrine is precisely its apparent breadth of explanatory power, which accounts no doubt for why it comes up in so many different fields. It manages to combine a critique of modern culture with a description of the motivational and economic mechanisms which account for the dynamics of the system, thus explaining consumerism, the longevity of capitalism and the psychic and social effects of alienation in the most economical way possible. Briefly the doctrine of true and false needs asserts that capitalism has developed the unique capacity to perpetuate itself by introjecting into the psyche of its subjects those needs that it requires them to have in order for it to survive. It is only by being able to create a demand for new products that keeps pace with the volume at which these commodities are produced that capitalism has been able to stave off the effects of the law of the declining rate of profit, overproduction, and so on which would otherwise have brought about its collapse. At the same time, the cost to its subjects has been enormous so that, it is argued, the corruption of capitalist man, his willing compliance as an insatiable consumer, produces a more gross form of alienation than that produced by the outright exploitation of capitalism in its earlier phases.

Herbert Marcuse is the foremost exponent of this doctrine which is to be found in its most explicit form in *One Dimensional Man*. The whole notion of marrying Marx and Freud in this way is in fact an innovation of Wilhelm Reich that was adopted by members of the Frankfurt School as early as Erich Fromm's essay on 'The method and function of an analytic social psychology', of 1932. The concept of true and false needs is found in Marcuse's work as early as the essay 'On hedonism' of 1938, and one may see his work on Marx and Freud in *Eros and Civilization* as an attempt to lay the psychological basis for needs as a major explanatory variable. In its fully developed form the doctrine constitutes a synthesis of three major bodies of theory which were already to hand when Marcuse wrote *One Dimensional Man* and which he more or less acknowledges as his sources. They are (1) Freudian theory where needs and drives are seen as basic psychological mechanisms, and culture is held to be a process by which these instinctual drives are mitigated through societal repression; (2) the critique of mass society in the works of Vance Packard, C. Wright Mills, William H. Whyte, Fred J. Cook, and so on; and (3) the theory of Marx.

In a quite literal sense the doctrine of true and false needs is a revisionist Marxist theory. Its major exponents, Marcuse, Reich, Fromm and Sartre have taken pains to trace the doctrine back to Marx and, indeed, quite a lot has been written on Marx's theory of needs. But it takes only a moment's reflection to see that this new theory of alienation in the form of the doctrine of true and false needs and Marx's theory of alienation are more or less mutually exclusive.

Marx, for all that he made enormously perceptive comments on the psychic and social effects of alienation, was nevertheless primarily concerned with alienation as an economic phenomenon. Alienation was, above all, and from his earliest writings a function of alienated labour: the fact that the proceeds of labour are appropriated by the owners of the means of production. From this central fact flowed all other consequences: the ability of the capitalist to extract surplus value, or make a profit, and thus the unique capacity of capitalism for economic growth, as well as the relative and increasing deprivation of the worker who is exploited in direct proportion to the rate at which capital accumulates.

The intimate link between Marx's theory of alienation and the labour theory of value has not, incidentally, been impaired by any of the several attempts to establish a major break in Marx's work − an essential difference between his critique of capitalism in the early and later works. Whatever the undoubted differences between his early and mature theory, Marx's account of alienation from the beginning involved a specific notion of economic causality. It was this specificity that made it a limited and therefore a viable theory within the context of Marx's work as a whole. Alienation with Marx was not meant to cover everything from the malaise of the suburban housewife to why X is having problems with his girlfriend − or boyfriend.[6] Alienation for Marx had specific roots in the exploitation of the worker and was, given the right conditions, a social evil for which there was an end in sight; it did not encompass all the discontents with the human condition in general.

The doctrine of true and false needs offers an account of the roots of alienation in quite different terms, so that it more or less supersedes the labour theory of value as the central explanatory principle in the critique of capitalism. It is for this reason that it is termed revisionist. But by putting it this way the problem is in a sense falsely posed, in that it can be quite convincingly argued that the doctrine of true and false needs was deliberately formulated to account for a shortfall in classical Marxist theory − its failure to foresee the longevity and tenacity of capitalism as a self-perpetuating system. Marx had argued for the inevitable and imminent collapse of capitalism in terms of the exploitation of the worker which vitiated his role as consumer. In order to cover rising capital costs, the capitalist had to extract surplus value from the worker at a constantly increasing rate to maintain a constant rate of profit. This meant a real decline in the wages of the worker proportionate to the growth of capital. By thus exploiting the worker, the capitalist was at the same time depriving himself of a domestic market for his goods which required of the worker a dual role both as efficient consumer and efficient producer. These tensions were considered by Marx to be sufficient to cause the internal collapse of the system, at which point leadership would pass to the proletariat.

The doctrine of true and false needs represents a *deus ex machina* to explain why this has not come about, and as such it involves a radical revision of Marxist theory itself. Under this new theory alienation is construed not in terms of the exploitation of man as producer, but rather in terms of his manipulation as a consumer. It is not the scarcity of goods to satisfy his human, and even his physical, needs that constitutes alienation according to this theory. Rather, alienation is due to a surfeit: it is because man under capitalism is forced to consume in greater and greater quantities commodities that he really does not need. Now there is no way to explain how the consumer comes to be able to purchase these commodities that is congruent with the labour theory of value and its principle that the disposable income of the worker is being constantly reduced to nil by the necessity of the capitalist to make a profit. The doctrine of true and false needs, to the extent that it offers a theory of exploitation, means by that something entirely different.

It is precisely here that the doctrine encounters major difficulties. It is one thing to argue a theory of alienation and exploitation in specific terms for which there are readily identifiable criteria — that is a declining standard of living in real terms, poverty, malnutrition, high infant-mortality rates, low life-expectancy rates, unemployment, child labour, and so on. Marx's theory was indeed specifically in these terms. It is altogether more difficult to establish the presence of alienation and exploitation where the opposite conditions prevail: a surfeit of commodities, overindulgence, boredom due to satiation and so on. (We shall leave aside the fact that the theories of Marcuse and Fromm by focusing on these features of the buoyant economies of the 1950s and 1960s have been more or less surpassed by events under the recession of the 1970s.) By framing a theory of alienation in terms not of deprivation, but of a surfeit, the doctrine of true and false needs meets peculiar difficulties. What it really asserts is that men under capitalism are alienated not because their fundamental human needs have not been met, but because the needs they exhibit are not genuine ones. Exploitation then consists not in the failure to meet basic needs so much as in the creation of false needs.

Precisely because of this difference, the doctrine of true and false needs puts a burden on the concept of needs that is not presupposed by the old Marxist theory of exploitation, and one that it cannot easily carry. According to the old theory, the worker is forced to sell his labour power at a price which will not even guarantee the satisfaction of his basic needs, that is the prerequisites of survival. In this case the needs of the worker as a criterion for exploitation are readily understood: that is they involve his basic needs for food, warmth, shelter and the protection of his family.

In the case of the doctrine of true and false needs the criteria are by no means as readily identifiable. This is after all a theory that specifically concerns those needs which are in excess of basic human needs. But while it is possible in principle to set a *minimum* limit for basic human needs — survival is an obvious threshold — it is much less easy to set a *maximum* limit. The work of social psychologists who have set out to study the range of human needs has proven, if nothing else, that a list of what might count as genuine needs is inexhaustible. Needs for security, affection, self-esteem, the esteem of others, creativity, and so on, may take any conceivable form. If the severity with which they are felt is a measure of their genuineness, it is, I think, quite true to say that suicides are more frequently prompted by needs such as these than they are by an insufficiency of basic subsistence needs, where some sort of survival instinct seems to be triggered — perhaps one could even say that this is tautological and that to feel one's subsistence needs are not being met presupposes a will to survive.

Now the advocate of the doctrine of true and false needs may very well respond that what the suicide indicates is not the genuineness of the need but the conditions of alienation which permit such needs to arise. And there is no easy answer to this argument, except to point out that a theory which requires us to set aside individual human experience as evidence for phenomena (needs) which seem to make a direct appeal to subjective experience, must offer great explanatory power in other terms in order to persuade us to do so. Proponents of the doctrine of true and false needs do in fact rule out the appeal to subjective criteria by the terms of their own argument: the severity with which a need is felt is not a guarantee of its genuineness, precisely because their theory stipulates the creation and inculcation of false needs as a systemic effect of capitalism. This involves, of course, the attribution of false consciousness to the individual, which is only permissible if, as an account of the longevity of capitalism and the phenomenon of consumerism, the doctrine is sufficiently compelling to invalidate the subjective experience of the individual. That is to say, the compellingness of the theory is to be construed not in terms of a convincing account of individual experience, but in terms of a theoretical precision such that individual experience can be set aside. As I shall try to show later, however, this precision is more apparent than real. The appeal of the doctrine of true and false needs lay in its simplicity, as a very neat and economical answer to the problem of the longevity of capitalism, and consumerism as a characteristic feature of late capitalism. This simplicity is altogether lost once the concept of false consciousness is invoked, involving as it does a regress and the appeal to hypothetical intermediary states to explain false needs. But without this device the doctrine of false needs suffers from a circularity that it cannot otherwise escape: that is it seems to be both explaining the persistence of capitalist structures in terms of true and false needs, and explaining true and false needs in terms of the persistence of capitalist structures.

There is a way in which we typically invalidate subjective experience with respect to needs or desires and that is on moral grounds: that is the assertion that 'X needs Y even where X does not *feel* the need for Y', is familiar as a value assertion. In this case, however, its normative status is quite clear, although we would perhaps be better to rephrase it as: 'X should have Y, even if he does not want it.' We can also make the same kind of claim in reverse: 'X wants Y but he does not really need it.' This is in some senses an attribution of false needs, but it is once again a moral claim: that X feels he needs Y but that he really should not have it.

Now the doctrine of true and false needs may seem at first glance to be a normative theory of this kind. As a theory of moral corruption it is not so different from the arguments of Plato, Aristotle, the Stoics and Epicureans, all of whom argued that a man's character and the moral condition of the culture from which he sprang could be judged by those values which were raised to the level of needs. The difficulty is, however, that if it is to be construed in this way, the doctrine of true and false needs turns out to be an ethical theory which (1) does not recognise its status as such, and (2) does not admit of ethical solutions. Dialectical materialism specifically rejects the fact/value distinction, on the grounds that moral imperatives merely reflect the presuppositions and require-ments of an economic system. The doctrine of true and false needs is advanced not as an ethical or normative but as a scientific theory, whose laws hold with the same necessity as the laws of the physical world. In other words, in so far as it supplants the labour theory of value as an explanation of the underlying mechanisms by which the capitalist system maintains itself, the doctrine of true and false needs is understood as having the same force: as an empirical and not as an ethical theory.

Let us take (1) or the claim that this doctrine is an ethical theory in the disguise of an empirical theory. Even if we grant for the moment that a rigorous distinction between normative and empirical theories is impossible to maintain and that there is an inescapable value dimension to all descriptive theories, we still have problems. This is because the doctrine of true and false needs as a 'scientific' theory makes claims for which the laws of evidence do not apply. In its strongest form, in Marcuse's latest works, the claim is made that false needs are internalised in the psyche to the point of becoming embedded in the instinctual structure. If we took Marcuse quite literally this would mean that these false needs could be genetically transmitted. Certainly he intends us to think of them as having passed from the moral realms of intentions to the biological realm of physiological impulses, and he several times talks of a 'new morality' as taking the form of a 'new biology', or an instinctual transformation (Marcuse, 1972*a*, pp. 15, 19, 56–7, etc.). Because, as he argues, these needs have become instinctual, they now belong to the irrational impulses of the unconscious, beyond the rational scrutiny of the ego.

But this idea that false needs ineluctably determine human behaviour as physiological mechanisms, unconscious and inbuilt impulses or instincts, is a fantastic empirical claim. After many decades of scientific research very little is still known about physiological mechanisms, how genetic transmission works, and so on. Even the most rigorous behaviourists in this field are willing to concede that even if a physiological structure of causation parallels all psychic phenomena, it does not necessarily supplant these phenomena in their own right. That is to say, even though one can trace a direct line of causation in physiological terms, this does not mean that physiological phenomena *generate* psychic phenomena: physiological mechanisms are more probably literally just that; that is, the form in which psychic and cognitive phenomena are experienced and transmitted.

The doctrine of true and false needs poses the mind/body or mind/brain problem in an unacceptable form. In addition, it places an emphasis on the instincts that runs counter to the dominant trend of modern biological theory which argues that man is relatively instinct-free and that the development of his cognitive and social skills is in large part due to his need to compensate for weak instincts. This is an assumption, curiously enough, on which Marxist theory, with its assumption of man's infinite malleability and the self-creation of human nature through *praxis*, depends. For instance, Marx's claim in the *Economic and Philosophic Manuscripts*, that it is man's ability to create freely, rather than under the domination of instinct, to 'make his life activity the object of his will and of his consciousness' that marks him as a singular creature, makes this very assumption on which the expectation of a transition to socialism is predicated (*CW*, Vol. 3, p. 276).

Now it may seem only a small step from here to claim that it is this freedom, as opposed to the instinct-governed behaviour of animals, that has been lost under alienation. The exigencies of monopoly capitalism, modern advertising, and so on have conspired to whittle away this freedom so that people spend their lives in the pursuit of this or that false need. The problem is, however, that such a theory of alienation puts out of reach the very solution that it seeks. If, in fact, people were subject to total conditioning through the introjection of false needs, the belief that the proletariat will transcend conditions of alienation and establish a new society under socialism would be without foundation. Thus the doctrine of true and false needs involves a hidden contradiction, a practical antinomy. It makes a judgement on capitalism as a system which does not permit man to realise his latent powers and his full development as an individual, on the tacit assumption that under other conditions or another system these powers can flourish. But to find his way out of the condition of alienation presupposes that man still has the critical judgement and moral capability to transcend the constraints of his condition. And yet it is precisely this critical judgement and moral capability that the doctrine denies by arguing that false needs have been introjected into the psyche of the individual, so that behaviour is predetermined.

Now the problems that we have suggested here for the doctrine of true and false needs admittedly apply to that doctrine in its strong form, or its extreme form as a theory of psychic or instinctual determinism. Is it still not possible to preserve some weaker form of the doctrine, by arguing, for instance, that the false needs generated by the consumer society, although they do not necessarily do so, nevertheless, on empirical evidence, do for the most part determine behaviour? This seems plausible enough. It is certainly true that most of us in one way or another have been seduced into a desire for the kind of lifestyle we can not quite afford. It is certainly true, in addition, that capitalism depends on a constant demand for its commodities, or the kind of perils which are endemic − overproduction, unemployment, etc. − set in. It does seem reasonable to argue then that these two factors reinforce one another.

The difficulty with the argument in its weak form is that it does not yield the kind of conclusions that those who argue it wish to draw. It does not suggest an alienation so complete that revolution becomes an imperative. In fact the theory is doubly hampered by trying to make two incompatible arguments. On the one hand, it is arguing that people have been so completely bought off by the false goods of capitalism that they are deliriously happy to be its dupe (Marcuse's idea of repressive de-sublimation). On the other hand, it claims that capitalism produces an alienation so severe that revolution and the transition to socialism become an ineluctable necessity. But we can see that this second, and classically Marxist conclusion, can only be drawn from a much different concept of alienation − one in which the incentive for revolution and a more equitable society flows from misery and deprivation, and not from satiation and the satisfactions of a fool's paradise.

Now that we have established that the conclusions of the doctrine of true and false needs do not follow from its premises, where does this leave us? As long as it is merely suggesting that capitalism is a system which thrives off the weaknesses of its subjects for material wealth, the theory simply tells us something we already know. As Marx pointed out succinctly, capitalism is a system unique for its capacity to generate wealth; this presupposes that the creation of wealth is a high priority in that society, maybe too high. On the other hand, as Marx also emphasised, wealth must be created before it can be distributed, and in this sense and for this reason, capitalism blazed the path for socialism as an economy of abundance.

In its weak form, then, the doctrine of true and false needs is no more than a theory about man's susceptibility to corruption. As such it is a variation on an old theme. The Stoic critique of civilisation from the time of Seneca and Lucretius, down through Rousseau and the early socialists, was in terms of the tendency of needs to proliferate with the progress in ideas. From the decline of the Roman Empire on (for this theory seems to have been an innovation of the Roman Stoics), there has been a long tradition of critics of civilisation who have argued that for all the benefits of culture, we have paid too high a price in moral and psychic terms. As the opportunities and goods that society promises expand, the range of possible satisfactions and dissatisfactions expands accordingly. Since every new need offers the possibility of pain just as readily as pleasure, an expansion of possible satisfactions makes happiness and peace of mind a lot more difficult than the simple life of a subsistence economy.

It is not difficult to think of a half-dozen classical treatises on just this subject: from Seneca's 'Ninetieth letter on philosophy and progress', to Lucretius's *On the Nature of Things*, Rousseau's first and second Discourses, Diderot's *Supplement to Bougainville's Voyage*, down to Freud's *Civilization and Its Discontents*. Marcuse's *Eros and Civilization* may seem to be nothing but a modern variant — which in a sense it is. The difficulty is, however, that the neo-Marxist critique of culture in terms of the doctrine of true and false needs brings together not only heterogeneous but incongruous elements. Marxist conclusions about socialism as the society of the future can only be yielded by some very odd assumptions. It is argued that capitalism produces complete alienation by the enslavement of its subjects to the commodities it produces, through the introjection of false needs. Yet it cannot explain how the goods of capitalism, which on its own account become shoddier and shoddier, could have sufficient attraction to bring about this result. It must resort to the concept of ideology to show how not the goods themselves but all the social forces that can be mustered conspire to produce false-consciousness, under whose conditions these goods acquire a compelling power.

But as we can see, what on first glance was a very economical theory, compelling for its simplicity, has now become unduly complex, involving a regress and the postulation of hypothetical intermediary states to explain the problem it diagnoses. By postulating false consciousness as a source of false needs in this way, it appeals to a concept that cannot be vouched for in any terms other than the internal necessity of the theory. And it takes only a little reflection to see what a risky policy it is to call on the theory to be an advocate in its own cause — especially where this involves setting aside much more tangible evidence in the experience of the individual.

The concept of needs, if not one of Marx's central categories, is, as we have suggested, important enough to have been elaborated time and again by neo-Marxists. Marx's own treatment of needs, as I try to show in Chapter 6, is more often elliptical than explicit, but he makes reference to the concept at crucial points in his major arguments: human nature as a totality of powers that are actualised under the pressures of material existence through needs; a critique of bourgeois society in terms of true and false needs; false needs as a feature of alienation; needs as the criterion underlying use value; the substitution of needs for 'bourgeois rights' as the measure of justice under socialism; the elimination of false needs through the destruction of their economic roots in a reconstituted socialist society, to name the most important. A theory of needs can be reconstructed from Marx's dialectical materialism, his psychology and anthropology, the labour theory of value and his theory of distributive justice. Or at least this is what a number of neo-Marxists have tried to do. The various aspects of the doctrine of true and false needs as it is reconstituted by these thinkers are discussed in Chapters 7 to 12.

The focus on needs was not new with Marx; it has been characteristic of socialist theory from the beginning. A doctrine of true and false needs and the maxim 'to each according to his needs', representing the vision of a society in which only true needs will prevail, are first found together in the writings of the early socialists of the period following the French Revolution of 1789 and before the débâcle of 1848. They were the earliest thinkers to put together elements that have now become characteristic of a certain tradition of Marxist thought: the distinction between true and false needs, developed on the basis of sensationalist psychology and Enlightenment materialism; the labour theory of value, derived from the addition of political economy to natural law principles; and a theory of progress, inherited from the Idéologues and later modified by German Idealism. (The concept of needs in the early socialist writings is discussed in Chapter 4.)

In fact, a theory of true and false needs dates back to the Stoics who praised frugality and the simple life and appealed to nature as the source of uniform laws of cosmic order and human behaviour. According to them, the disjunction between subjective desires and objective needs had to be restored by bringing the will into conformity with the dictates of nature, and they praised as their ideal 'the man of few needs'. The relation of needs and wants was also much discussed by the Epicureans who advanced an early theory of utilitarianism based on man's universal attraction to pleasure and avoidance of pain. Enlightened hedonism suggested that if, indeed, men are motivated by their self-interest above all, then it is only necessary for them to take a sufficiently long-range view, for their desires to coincide with their true needs.

These two ancient positions were raised to prominence again under the European Enlightenment, a period of unprecedented scepticism and inquiry, in which Christian views on the problem of evil, the boundaries of legitimate human activity, the satisfaction of natural wants and drives, terrestrial happiness and the ethics of progress, were all called into question. During this period ideas of classical antiquity received a high degree of elaboration. The rudimentary sensationalist psychology of the Greek atomists found its counterpart in the highly developed system of Locke and his followers, the French materialists, Condillac, Helvétius, d'Holbach, La Mettrie, and so on. The Lockean sensationalist psychology opened up two paths, utilitarianism, the one that Locke himself took, and socialism, the one towards which the French materialists were inclined.

The utilitarians tried to resolve the dilemma of needs and wants in a more elaborate version of Epicurean enlightened self-interest, arguing that man's sensory perceptions and deliberations thereon can lead to the choice of remote over proximate goods through the faculty of judgement. Since no real distinction was made between the pleasurable and the good, the dichotomy between subjective desires and objective needs was removed, and needs and wants were considered to be long- and short-range sources of the same thing: pleasure.

The socialists drew different conclusions from the same premises. Refutation of the doctrine of innate ideas and the assertion of man's unlimited susceptibility to environmental influence had raised the possibility of changing human nature by manipulating social conditions. This was the inference that the socialists drew, and what distinguished their position from that of the utilitarians was a more radical materialism which dispensed with even a token concession to the concept of the will in the faculty of judgement. The power that they attributed to material conditions was inversely proportionate to their diminution of men's own faculties of control — judgement, will, choice, etc. If, in fact, men experience the world through the senses and develop all their ideas on this basis, they reasoned, then the problem of bringing their wants in line with their needs can be resolved by arranging their experience so that they find only their true needs in it. This means eliminating the economic roots of false needs, property, capital and those institutions which encourage acquisitiveness, competition for material goods, consumerism, and so on.

It was Rousseau who made the theory of true and false needs most famous in this period. Scholars have argued convincingly that he owed much to the Roman theorists, the Stoic Seneca and the Epicurean Lucretius, for his account of human nature and the growth of false needs with the progress of civilisation. With Rousseau, the Enlightenment debate over nature and culture, nature and convention, natural and artificial needs, was intensified and the ambiguities in his writings reflect the pull of materialist environmental arguments against the resistance of natural law ethics and a belief in the human capacity of self-determination through the will. This tension in Rousseau's writings was a source of inspiration to Kant in his treatment of these questions.

The thesis advanced here, that socialism developed out of the marriage of English empiricism and French materialism, is not really new: Marx himself made such a claim in his brief history of socialism in *The Holy Family* (*CW*, Vol. 4, pp. 124–34). The first four chapters of this work are an attempt to follow this argument through with particular reference to the doctrine of needs, showing the presuppositions that the doctrine carries over from earlier forms of thought. For instance, Chapter 2 will deal with the appeal to nature as norm, inherited from Hellenistic philosophy;

primitivism; notions of progress as evil and of evil and discord as socially created, which are associated with it; along with the ideal of self-sufficiency as the basis of a natural harmony between man and nature. The concepts of *amour-propre* and *amour-de-soi*, natural and artificial needs to be found in the work of Rousseau are the subject of Chapter 3. Chapter 4 deals with Lockean sensationalist psychology and its contribution to the socialist doctrine of needs in the materialist theory of environmental conditioning, emphasis on physiological determinism, psychologism and utilitarianism. The history of these ideas can be convincingly documented, since the linkages between ancient, Enlightenment and Marxist thought are fairly explicit. But merely to trace the genesis of the doctrine of needs is not enough. By analysing the concept (Appendix) and examining the various forms the distinction between true and false needs took, one must try to show the difficulties its advocates faced when attempting to give coherent philosophical justification for the distinction.

The context in which the discussion of needs arose both in the ancient world and the Enlightenment had to do with the problem of evil. In the case of the Epicureans, Stoics and Sceptics, as Marx in his doctoral dissertation suggests, rejection of the universal systems of Plato and his followers took the form of a return to nature and more elemental questions concerning the natural basis of human behaviour and the practical relation of philosophy to reality. The European Enlightenment presents a parallel case: rejection of the mediaeval system of scholasticism led to a reinvestigation of the relation between nature and culture and a naturalistic account of human nature. It is not too much to postulate Marx's case as a third example, since he in fact considered himself, following on Hegel, to be placed like the Stoics, Epicureans and Sceptics in the wake of Plato — forced back from the 'rich intellectual forms' and 'universal range' of the great systematisers, to confront the primary question of man's relation to nature ('The difference between the Democritean and Epicurean philosophy of nature', *CW*, Vol. 1, pp. 35 and 491). How, in the absence of the great ethical systems, was evil to be accounted for?

The answer is that it was accounted for in terms of 'false needs'. The dilemma of the coexistence of evil with the idea of a beneficent God was first posed by Epicurus. As Bayle, who took his formulation from Vanini, who took it from Epicurus, succinctly put it: either God is incapable of preventing evil, and so is not God; or he does not will to do so and is not good (Crocker, 1959, p. 38). One might speculate that it was indeed this dilemma that was a catalyst for the abandonment of the theological monism of Plato and Aristotle for a philosophy of nature by Epicurus and the Stoics. Enlightenment thinkers subsequently turned to these pagan sources to explain the problem of evil which posed such a challenge to Christianity. That they found in nature an acceptable substitute for the traditional metaphysical systems, was because nature revealed order, rationality and harmony, which made possible a 'scientific' account of human behaviour. Evil was from this perspective identified with disorder, conflict and destructiveness. Whence did these negative characteristics derive? They were the product of false needs which accompanied the growth of luxury and vice and departure from the 'life according to nature'. Primitivism in social theory was a distinguishing feature of this theory of evil and Seneca's 'Ninetieth letter on philosophy and progress', a signal example, contained a theory of true and false needs, while Lucretius in *De Rerum Natura* gave a classic account of the simultaneous rise of civilisation and corruption.

The doctrine of true and false needs thus characterised a certain configuration of ideas that included primitivism, the tendency to see evil as a social and therefore artificial product, and to see man's relation to nature and his fellows as one of harmonious symbiosis. But whereas in ancient philosophy social harmony came from the self-sufficiency of the individual, his willingness to confine his appetites, in the socialist version of these ideas – from the early socialists, Saint-Simon, Fourier, Owen, Cabet, Weitling, and even earlier Morelly, Mably, Meslier, Babeuf and Buonarroti, to Marcuse, Fromm and Sartre – the notion of a spontaneous unity between the individual and the collectivity is the distinctly modern feature. It is a mark of socialist doctrine that this unity does not depend on the exertion of individual wills, but on conditioning mechanisms. By postulating man's unlimited malleability and a theory of environmental conditioning, socialists argued that all fundamental questions relating to the individual and the totality, such as, for instance, the question of human needs, are in principle uncontentious.

It is interesting, but hardly surprising, that these materialist ideas should have been accompanied from the beginning by a bias towards 'scientific' solutions to philosophical problems. Lucretius, for instance, claimed that science was enough 'to loosen the hold of religion on men's minds': 'This dread and darkness of the mind therefore need not the rays of the sun, the bright darts of day; only knowledge of nature's forms' (*De Rerum Natura*, I, pp. 146–8).[7] The scientific basis greatly increased under the modern version of the constellation of ideas we have been discussing. One of the reasons for this belief in the uncontentiousness of most fundamental questions is the fact that these socialists took as their model for decision-making the resolution of technical problems. Politics, Saint-Simon was the first to declare, can be handled as a strictly administrative problem. It was consistent with the conception of truth and falsity that these socialists held, to believe needs, like values, to be uncontroversial, ultimately reducible to matters of scientific fact.

In the form in which the problem of evil was raised by seventeenth-and eighteenth-century thinkers, Pascal, Spinoza, Leibniz, Bayle, Voltaire, Diderot, Shaftesbury, Rousseau and others, this scientific orientation is already evident. This period saw the first serious psychological investigation of the problem of evil, and a richer feast of psychological speculation was not offered again until Freud, whose critique of civilisation it in many respects anticipated.

A plethora of positions emerged, from the Manichean determinism of Bayle, who believed that man's power over his actions is so limited that they should be judged entirely by intentions, regardless of whether or not these are carried through; to the hedonism of the utilitarians who believed that behaviour is motivated exclusively by self-interest; and the cynicism of the nihilists, such as Sade, for whom irrationality and malevolence were endemic human characteristics. The question of human needs was central to a naturalistic or a psychological account of human behaviour, and needs were treated from every conceivable point of view. Distinctions were made between needs, desires, passions (Condillac); between subcategories of the faculty of desire; propensities, inclinations, passions (Kant); and one thinker even constructed a 'Great Order of needs' (Court de Gebelin). While more traditional, natural-law oriented theorists found in the *similarity* of human needs the basis for a universal human nature, a number of more radical materialists who subscribed to associational psychology and environmental arguments found only the desire for well-being common to all men, who were otherwise as *various* as their needs made them.

It is not my purpose to elaborate on all the alternatives that were advanced.[8] The specific contributions that ancient and Enlightenment thought made to the early socialist doctrine of needs were, on the one hand, the doctrine of materialism and its ramifications in a primitivist theory of society, and, on the other, sensationalist psychology and conclusions drawn from it about the modifiability of human nature through environmental influence. These are the questions to which we now turn.

NOTES

1 Heller is not suggesting this but it is an inference that can be drawn from her work.
2 All references to Marx's works are to the *Collected Works* (*CW*) cited in bibliography, unless otherwise noted.
3 The value dimension of the concept of need has been ably discussed by Agnes Heller (1972).
4 I have borrowed the term 'expressivist theory' from Charles Taylor's excellent book on Hegel, which contains an extended and penetrating treatment of this aspect of Hegel's thought (Taylor, 1975, esp. pp. 13–29). Taylor acknowledges a debt to Isaiah Berlin for the concept developed in Berlin's discussion of 'Herder and the Enlightenment', in Wasserman (ed.) (1965) (see Taylor, p. 13).
5 If this consideration of desire is reminiscent of the language of the existentialists, this is indeed no accident. Sartre, in particular, is heir to the Hegelian concept of desire which was transmitted through the teachings of Alexandre Kojève; Jean Wahl and Jean Hyppolite, who were largely responsible for the Hegel revival of the 1930s in France. In Kojève's highly interpretive commentary on Hegel's *Phenomenology* we find desire as that which reveals the subject to himself; desire as that by which 'man is formed and revealed – to himself and to others – as an I'; desire as 'the Sentiment of Self'; desire as the challenge to man to transcend the limits which the material world imposes on man; and desire as that which reveals the I 'to itself and to others as Self-Consciousness' (Kojève, 1969, pp. 3–5).
6 Marcuse, too, is now willing to recognise that Marx's theory of alienation was a specific and a limited theory. See his BBC radio broadcast on 'The need for an open Marxist mind' (1978). Quite what the implications are for Marcuse's own theory he does not make clear.
7 1937 Loeb edn, p. 13: but I have used the more literal translation of Peter Gay (1966), Vol. 1, p. 101.
8 Until recently, the ancestry of Enlightenment theories of human nature and specifically the influence of the Stoic and Epicurean schools have been very little studied. Quentin Skinner in his magisterial work, *The Foundations of Modern Political Thought* (1978), emphasizes the degree to which Stoic influences on modern political thought have been underestimated. One of his dominant concerns, he declares, is 'to emphasize the remarkable extent to which the vocabulary of Renaissance moral and political thought

was derived from Roman Stoic sources . . . I do not think it has been fully appreciated how pervasively the political theorists of Renaissance Italy and of early modern Europe in general, were . . . influenced by Stoic values and beliefs' (Vol. 1, p. xiv). Other references to Stoic influences, in particular of Cicero, Sallust, Juvenal and Seneca are to be found in Vol. 1, pp. 42–3, 44, 87–8, 162–3; and Vol. 2, pp. 276–8, 279–84, 340–1, 343 and 346.

For a specific treatment of the concept 'luxury', central to the discussion of needs in Epicurean, Stoic and Enlightenment thought, see John Sekora's masterful study, *Luxury, The Concept in Western Thought* (1977).

2
Needs in Hellenistic and Enlightenment Materialism

It is not difficult to see that the concept of true and false needs is quite closely related to the question of true and false pleasures that Plato posed in the *Philebus*. Both questions seem fraught with the same difficulty: neither needs nor pleasure are judgements on things and how, therefore, can they be true or false? Either I have or do not have a need, or I feel or do not feel pleasure. If I have a need or feel pleasure, these experiences are in a sense self-authenticating and it is only really if I think I have a need but do not have it, or think I feel pleasure but do not feel it that these are usually understood as false or mistaken judgements. Would it not, therefore, be truer to say that there are genuine as opposed to mistaken needs, real as opposed to ephemeral pleasures?

One of the interesting things about Stoic philosophy is the fact that the Stoa believed that to feel a need or a pleasure did involve a judgement and that the specific pleasures and needs that the individual felt or sought were a reflection of his moral character or the disposition that he had developed. We are rather accustomed to thinking of the personality in Platonic terms as a complex phenomenon with different and competing parts: reason set over against the appetites or desire, and the constant conflict between them. The Stoic philosophers, Zeno, Chrysippus, Epictetus, and so on, did not hold with this dualistic or Platonic concept of character but subscribed to a unitary theory of the personality. They argued against the idea that the passions are some kind of involuntary impulse that sweeps over us, threatening to carry us away if reason does not intervene to check them. According to them, there was no such thing as purely involuntary behaviour and all behaviour, even of a highly muscular kind, was seen to involve varying degrees of 'assent'.[1] It is not, then, as if people are all susceptible to the same desires, passions or needs, but that some have a better-trained will than others and are more virtuous in conquering these appetites. The Stoics actually maintained that for the wise man the temptations of forbidden desires or pleasures do not arise. The wise man has some kind of moral veto over his own desires and pleasures such that the only desires and pleasures he actually feels are those consistent with virtue. Epictetus, for instance, argued that when a wise man sees a pretty woman who is another man's wife, he simply does not feel attracted to her and so he has no improper desires.

To maintain, as the Stoics did, that all feelings of pleasure or desire involve varying degrees of assent opened up the possibility that needs and desires like other forms of judgement were susceptible of truth or falsity. But with respect to what criteria? The wide difference between reflections on these questions in antiquity and in the modern period has to do with a change in the ordering of moral priorities. From the pre-Socratics, Plato, Aristotle, through to the Epicureans, Stoics and Sceptics of the Hellenistic period, the whole orientation of ancient philosophy was concerned with the problem of the good for man and how to achieve it. Various possibilities were explored: happiness as the good for man (Aristotle); wisdom as the good for man (Plato and the Stoics); pleasure as the good for man (the Epicureans); and so on. The questions of permissible desires, material goods, relations to other men, duty, etc., were all related back to this central problem.

Under Christendom, the question of needs and desires and permissible gratifications was not an open question and people were urged to eschew the world, the flesh and the devil. Christian virtues of poverty, humility and asceticism suggested that people should restrict their needs as much as possible and conquer their desires as marks of holiness. One of the most interesting and enduring features of Christianity was a new emphasis on equality and social justice, which related in a rather obvious way to the problem of needs, foreshadowed to some extent by the Stoics. If, in fact, resources are scarce and one at the same time subscribes to the value of equality, then in the name of social justice people must be called on to restrict their needs so that they are compatible with the welfare of others.

Plato and Aristotle had also been concerned with the problem of justice, and specifically with the question of distributive justice, but they did not associate justice and equality. On the contrary, justice to Plato meant a distribution of goods and powers consistent with the maintenance of important differences between individuals and social classes. For Aristotle the problem of justice was posed for the very reason that a strict equality would not do. When under the Enlighten-ment and in the period of the early socialists talk about needs was revived, one of the important legacies of the Christian tradition that was maintained was the association between justice and equality. The early socialist slogan 'to each according to his needs', which meant that a distribution of goods should be made not on the basis of the social contribution people made, but on the basis of their individual require-ments, had a very Christian ring to it. Such a notion appealed to Christian virtues of charity, equality and fraternity.

This concern with social justice and equality has characterised need theory ever since. It is perhaps typical of our production-oriented culture that we are in general more concerned with the equitable distribution of the goods that we create and the benefits that they produce, than we are with the question of the good life defined from a moral point of view, which might suggest giving up these so called 'goods' altogether. This is a legacy of the doctrine of progress to which Marx helped contribute.

The difference could not be illustrated better than with reference to the Stoic Epictetus. The axiom of Epictetus's philosophy is the classic Stoic slogan: 'Man's good and evil lies in moral choice, and all other things are nothing to us' (*Discourses*, 1925 Loeb edn, Vol. 1, p. 157). 'Externals', he maintained, 'are not under my control; moral choice is under my control' (p. 239). The famous opening lines of Epictetus's *Encheiridion* run:

> Some things are under our control, while others are not under our control. Under our control are conception, choice, desire, aversion, and, in a word, everything that is our own doing; not under our control are our body, our property, reputation, office, and, in a word, everything that is not our own doing. Furthermore, the things under our control are by nature free, unhindered, and unimpeded; while the things not under our control are weak, servile, subject to hindrance, and not our own. Remember, therefore, that if what is naturally slavish you think to be free, and what is not your own to be your own, you will be hampered, will grieve, will be in turmoil, and will blame both gods and men; while if you think only what is your own to be your own, and what is not your own to be, as it really is, not your own, then no one will ever be able to exert compulsion upon you, no one will hinder you, you will blame no one, will find fault with no one, will do absolutely nothing against your will, you will have no personal enemy, no one will harm you, for neither is there any harm that can touch you. (1928 Loeb edn, Vol. 2, p. 483)

Epictetus is not advocating asceticism for its own sake, but only in so far as moral purpose and prudence require it. The Stoics were famous in later epochs for their ideal of the 'man of few needs', but as we can see, this was less a moral principle than a strategy. Since tranquillity and peace of mind (*ataraxia*) could only be attained by distinguishing carefully between those aspects of life over which we have little control (health, fortune, fame, death) and those we control and for which we bear responsibility (choice, aversion, moral purpose), man's good required transferring importance from things external to those things related to choice and moral purpose. This entailed making oneself as little vulnerable as possible to misfortune and disappointment. The man with few needs or desires was also the man who had few opportunities for frustration and dissatisfaction.

The Epicureans held a similar view even though they came to it from a quite opposite perspective. Like the Stoics they advocated a life according to nature and the strategy of the man of few needs, even though they considered the good for man to lie not in freedom or virtue, but pleasure. We do not usually associate pleasure or hedonism as a governing principle with the restriction of desire, but this is exactly what the Epicureans did. For their concept of pleasure was one that was compatible with peace of mind or tranquillity and they, too, argued that the proliferation of needs and desires could only result in excessive pain for the small margin of extra pleasure it afforded. One of the aspects of Epicurean thought that had surprising ramifications in history was their utilitarian doctrine that man's nature is such that his primary motivations are pursuit of pleasure and the avoidance of pain and that the good for man entailed the maximisation of pleasure. This principle, and the theory of sensationalist psychology in which it was embedded, constituted the main contribution of the Epicureans to Enlightenment thought where it found its apogee in the philosophy of Jeremy Bentham.

In fact, Epicurus and the Epicureans in general enjoyed a considerable revival in the European Enlightenment precisely because they had developed a rudimentary theory of human motivation that was in some sense 'scientific' or secular rather than theological. The eighteenth-century Enlightenment saw a revival of interest in the scientific explanation of behaviour. The ethical orientation of ancient philosophy came under attack, as did theology and religion in all its forms, and for the first time on a large scale all the classic positions on human nature were put under review. The Enlightenment theorists favoured explanations that put emphasis on the causal determinants of behaviour and they investigated the question of needs and desires in relation to conduct and whether these supplied the reasons or causes of action. They raised again the old Stoic and Epicurean questions of whether men were able to control their desires and choices, or whether the stimulus of desire was a determining mechanism.

The Epicureans had developed a theory of behaviour based on atomistic determinism that gained favour but, as we shall see, it was not without its peculiarities. Although, as they argued, man is predisposed to seek pleasure and avoid pain, they nevertheless made room for the insertion of judgement and choice in their idea of the atomic swerve. (This idea had taken care of randomness and chance as features of the physical world, but became the basis for a notion of moral direction in the field of ethics.) It was this aspect of Epicurean theory that found its elaboration in the philosophy of John Locke who, in his *Essay Concerning Human Understanding*, developed the concept of man as a creature governed by pursuit of pleasure and avoidance of pain and thus susceptible to environmental conditioning, whose only control over his own fate lay in the faculty of judgement. Locke was the true precursor of all later theories of environmental conditioning and, in particular, the theories of the early socialists. Locke rejected the concept of innate ideas, arguing that all our ideas come from experience and our judgement on sense impressions. Whether a man attains his potential or not, and the kind of character that he develops, are conditioned by the environment and the way in which its stimulus comes to bear on his faculties. It was not difficult for the early socialists to conclude from this that the social world had only to be rationally organised in order to produce entirely rational creatures and to eliminate social conflict altogether. Evil and discord were therefore considered to be artificial or social phenomena, not endemic to human nature as such. This notion of the artificiality of evil tended to be tied to a concept of false or artificial needs and the idea that it was civilisation, through progress and the creation of luxury, that had permitted the rise of evil, social conflict and injustice. This critique of civilisation had its roots in Stoic and Epicurean philosophy and the valorisation of nature to be found in it.

In the materialism of the Stoics, Epicureans and Sceptics, who succeeded Plato and Aristotle and launched the first major attack on the philosophy of idealism, we see in an early form a constellation of ideas that came to characterise dialectical materialism. It is no accident, as we shall see, that Marx wrote his doctoral dissertation on the atomism of Democritus and Epicurus, and that in his early career he planned a full-scale history of these Hellenistic schools. In each of these forms of the philosophy of materialism, the principle of determinism was the driving idea. From this followed the distinctions between objectivity and subjectivity, or reality and appearances; a philosophy of nature; needs as a motivational principle; and the distinction between natural and artificial needs as the basis for an ethics. The concept of needs had an obvious suitability for the philosophy of materialism because it explained human behaviour deterministically, in terms of stimulus and response, or the power of instinctual drives. Of course, there were important variations in how motivation was explained by these schools, and while the Epicureans postulated a fundamental drive to seek pleasure and avoid pain which underlay specific needs, the Stoics saw in needs a strong but not unconquerable attraction. A tendency to cultural primitivism, or the belief that those early forms of society which were closest to nature were also the most authentic, accompanied these materialist ideas and the emphasis on needs. While this had its legacy in the thought of Enlightenment materialists, primitivism is one aspect of the materialism of antiquity that Marx rejected.

Hellenistic materialism and cultural primitivism are conceptually related to the development in Greek thought of certain normative connotations of the term 'nature'. According to its etymological derivation, nature meant birth or genesis; it came subsequently to be associated with innate characteristics, 'what things are really made of', as the basis for the distinction between reality and appearances. This distinction was most explicitly defined in the atomism of Democritus who declared that only atoms have objective reality and that all other qualities, because they appear different to different people, are merely subjective appearances: '. . . conventionally things possess colour, conventionally they are sweet, conventionally they are bitter, but in reality there exist only atoms and the void'.[2] The term 'conventional' was the same term as that for 'by law' or 'according to accepted mores', which were its usual meanings, and it was by no means insignificant that human laws and mores came at this point to be associated with subjectivity and error. Interestingly, the notion of the subjectivity of convention went along with nominalism (again etymologically related) and the assumption that names are conventional and indifferent. On these grounds the Sophist Prodicus had attacked the dialectical method of Socrates for pretending to elicit something more than a collection of linguistic facts, and for assuming that something real, as distinct from conventional, underlies the meaning of words.

The impact of nominalism and ethical relativism associated with the distinction between nature and convention, in combination with external pressures on the traditional moral values of the polis, had been considerable enough by the second half of the fifth century for Aristotle to remark in the *Nicomachean Ethics*: 'Instances of morally fine and just conduct . . . involve so much difference and variety that they are widely believed to be such only by convention and not by nature' (I. 1094b 14. 1976 Penguin edn).

It was from just this disillusionment with tradition and convention and the search for new objective moral criteria, that the Greek materialist philosophies of the sixth to the fourth centuries emerged. By the end of the fifth century 'nature' had already come to be associated with the cosmic system as a whole, its laws and properties, as opposed to the laws which man made. In the moral sphere, where objectivity was also measured 'according to nature', the test was universality or *consensus gentium*. Of course, such a criterion for ethics was a double-edged sword and it was possible to argue like the Pyrrhonic Sceptics that on the grounds of universality 'there is nothing good or bad by nature, for if there is anything good or bad by nature, it must be good or bad for all persons alike, just as snow is cold to all. But there is no good or bad which is such to all persons in common; therefore there is no such thing as good or bad by nature' (Diogenes Laertius, IX. 101).[3] Montesquieu and other *philosophes* who some twenty centuries later canvassed the customs of different nations for universal moral laws, reached similar conclusions.

But scepticism was not the most significant product of the distinctions between nature and convention, nature and culture that philosophers of the Hellenistic period drew. The positive result was the development of a primitivist ethic and a theory of history as progress on materialist and naturalistic principles. The primitivism of these schools, in particular of the Stoics, was largely derived from the Cynics, whose main tenets are to be gleaned from later commentators. The Cynics juxtaposed the Socratic ideal of self-sufficiency to the principle of nature as norm and on this basis elaborated an ethic of the simple life that had much to say about human needs and their true limits. They interpreted self-sufficiency to mean that happiness implies controlling the irrational multiplication of wants, asserting that acquisitiveness and the insatiable and ever-expanding desire for economic goods are both the root of evil and the impetus to technological development. They deplored the psychological, and in their eyes almost pathological, dependency on superfluous goods that men exhibited and extolled nature against artifice and civilisation, calling for the satisfaction of natural needs but the elimination of artificial needs and their economic basis. Consistent with their line of argument, they defined natural needs as 'primary, universal, instinctive and irrepressible, spontaneous rather than factitious, not prompted by emulation or vanity or the lust of possession for possession's sake . . . easily and equally gratified by all men', and few (Lovejoy and Boas, 1935, p. 120). While artificial needs, which bore the marks of artifice and subjectivity, were to be eliminated, natural drives such as sex and hunger could be repressed only at great cost and with harmful consequences, they believed.

After the Stoics, the rigours of the primitive ethic of the Cynics were most closely approximated by the Epicureans, for all that popular wisdom has it otherwise. Epicurus, deriving from atomistic materialism a sensationalist form of psychology which postulated pleasure and pain as the primary motivations of behaviour, reiterated the Socratic principle of self-sufficiency as the only route to inner tranquillity. Happiness came from the limitation of desires to those parsimonious needs which were both natural and necessary, and the scorning of such fictitious benefits as luxury, fame and wealth, he argued.

Among the followers of Epicurus, the Roman Lucretius exerted perhaps the greatest influence on the materialists of the French Enlightenment, both through his theory of progress and his attack on religion. *De Rerum Natura*, published posthumously in 55 BC, gives an account of the historical development of civilisation from the state of nature, an idyllic condition where men lived in harmony, hardy and self-sufficient, their few needs easily satisfied, to a very modern-sounding state of corruption. It has been argued that Rousseau's account of the 'Origins of inequality' in the second 'Discourse' owes much to Lucretius, and the similarities are striking. The first stage in the process of emergence from the state of nature is in each case the institution of monogamous cohabitation, the family and language. Both postulate incipient conflict, a softening of the rigours of existence with the multiplication of needs and their means of satisfaction, but nevertheless conclude that this period of *la société naissante* constituted a golden age. Lucretius, like Rousseau, rejected strict chronological primitivism. The happiest period for man was not the state of nature where he lacked social ties, morality, and any intellectual development, but the period of rudimentary agriculture, the simple arts and a primitive form of social organisation where goods were distributed according to strength and merit. Departure from this golden age was heralded by the discovery of gold and the introduction of wealth 'which easily robbed both the strong and the handsome of their honour' and led to the substitution of artificial for natural criteria of merit, as well as envy, competition for riches and so on (*De Rerum Natura*, v. 1113–4, 1937 Loeb edn, p. 419). The development of metallurgy furnished the materials for war now that incentives had been provided. Rousseau, probably with reference to Lucretius, declares: 'pour le poëte c'est l'or et l'argent, mais pour le philosophe ce sont le fer et le blé qui ont civilisé les hommes et perdu le genre humain' (*Discourse on Inequality*),[4] reflecting the influence of Locke who also saw in the more general phenomenon of property, rather than money, the source of evil and the epitome of false needs.

Most extraordinary among the similarities in the two accounts is the fact that Lucretius foreshadows the much celebrated doctrine of alienation in his description of the psychological corollaries of the institution of wealth. Among these are envy, competition for material goods in the pursuit of honour and esteem – which produce alienation from one's fellows – and, most damaging of all, desires for self-esteem, measured by projecting these spurious criteria back on oneself. By this measure, psychological equilibrium can only be gained by the gratification of an increasing proliferation of fictitious needs – which constitutes self-alienation. Lucretius sees the same long-term political consequence as Rousseau: the institution of the state and of positive law, made necessary by the fact that men cannot be induced to keep peaceful covenants otherwise (Lovejoy and Boas, 1935, p. 240).[5]

It was with later Roman Stoics, Seneca and Diogenes Laertius, that the rigours of the Cynic regimen were reintroduced in a communistic form. Zeno's teachings, which were said to appeal to the poorest classes, prescribed frugality in diet and clothing, communality of wives, the permissibility of incest (since it was not universally proscribed), that the use of money should not be considered necessary either for exchange or for foreign travel, and that reputation and the esteem of others were not goods (ibid., pp. 260–1). The dictum 'to live according to nature' received a more pantheistic interpretation, with emphasis on cosmic piety and mysticism. But at the same time room was made for the relaxation of Cynic asceticism by the introduction of a class of things which were neither good nor bad but which were in themselves indifferent, such as health, pleasure, beauty, wealth, fame and good fortune, which could all be legitimately enjoyed as long as they did not threaten the attainment of tranquillity.

A recent study (Furley, 1967) has shown that Epicurus held similar views to Aristotle on moral activity and individual responsibility, in which, as we shall see, the concepts of need and desire played a crucial role. Marx in the notes for his doctoral dissertation actually excerpted the passages on which the new study bases its case, although he made no further reference to them. The point of departure of Epicurus's ethical theory, like that of the Stoics, was with the problem of pleasure and pain. The Greeks did not conceive of 'free will' as such, and actions were subject to moral appraisal in the context of 'excuses'. Action for which one had an adequate excuse was action for which one could not be blamed. As one would expect, an atomistic account of the human psyche, such as that to which Epicurus subscribed, laid emphasis on behaviour as a response to stimulus: the stimulus of pleasure or pain. Were there pleasurable experiences for which one could be blamed, or experiences causing pain for which one could be excused? It has been conventional to assume that the 'atomic swerve' had its counterpart in the constitution of the psyche, and that as in the case of the movement of physical bodies, intervention between stimulus and response may allow for unpredictable behaviour, which is nevertheless determined by some exogenous atomic complex. But the atomic swerve may also be interpreted as a concession to the idea of human self-determination, as Marx in fact suggested, and as Furley and more recent commentators have argued.

There were counter-tendencies in Epicurus's work which considerably modify his initial determinism, to be seen for instance in his doctrine of three classes of desire: the first natural and necessary, the second natural but not necessary, and the third neither natural nor necessary.[6] Epicurus argues that all desires do not have the compelling force of basic physical needs, and that different criteria apply to higher needs which are subject to our control. This suggests, of course, that pleasure and pain are not after all ineluctable determinants of behaviour, but can be resisted with sufficient strength of mind.[7] Cicero, one of the most reliable authorities on Epicurus, paints a picture of Epicurean moral doctrine and suggests striking similarities with that of the Stoa:

. . . Epicurus thus presents his Wise Man who is always happy: his desires are kept within bounds; death he disregards; he has a true conception, untainted by fear, of the immortal gods; . . . it is a fine saying of Epicurus that 'the Wise Man is but little interfered with by fortune; the great concerns of life, the things that matter, are controlled by his own wisdom and reason. ('On the highest goods and evils', I. xix. 62)[8]

The 'Wise Man' thus equipped, was believed to enjoy the 'perpetual pleasure' of a soul in harmony, undivided by the discord created by conflicting and frustrated desires and fears. Marx, in *The German Ideology*, commends Epicurus as the radical activist of antiquity who dares openly to attack the Gods. He does not add the qualification that so reluctant was Epicurus to be associated with the determinists that he even declared, 'It was better to follow the myth about the Gods than to be a slave of the fate of the physicists, for the former suggests a hope of forgiveness in return for honour, but the latter has an ineluctable necessity.'[9]

The Epicurean, Lucretius, devoted attention in *De Rerum Natura* – from which Marx quotes extensively in his notes (*CW*, Vol. 1, pp. 466–78 and 489–90) – to the question of voluntary and involuntary behaviour, making the observation that in the case of a voluntary action, the perceptible behaviour which we call 'the action' is the last thing to happen, and that there is an interval between the stimulus and the response which represents the time it takes for the individual to decide on his movements. In the case of forced behaviour, the opposite is true, for instance, 'under the impulse of a blow, or when another man uses great strength or compulsion on us', then the physical reaction is immediate and only gradually is the body brought back under the control of the will (cf. Furley, 1967, p. 176). Aristotle also discussed voluntary and involuntary behaviour in the context of the claim that pleasure and pain exercise a compelling power over us, and he drew the sensible conclusion that if that were the case, since most actions are done with pleasure and pain in mind, *all* objects would be compelling, and that 'it is absurd for the agent to lay the blame on external factors and not on himself for falling an easy prey to them' (*Nicomachean Ethics*, III. 1110b 9–15. 1976 Penguin edn).

Epicurus, in his *Letter to Menoeceus* declared 'that which is in our power is free, and blame and its opposite are applicable to this' (para. 133, cited Furley, 1967, p. 184). He saw three challenges to the power of the will: (1) external force (such as Lucretius described); (2) internal necessity, constituted by the disposition or character of the individual; (3) external necessity, or the attractions of pleasure and pain. Epicurus's general argument is similar to Aristotle's: the receipt of a stimulus must be taken in conjunction with an established disposition on the part of an individual, to account for the cause of an action. How then is behaviour voluntary? Epicurus implied what Aristotle stated: that habit and inclination, the perception of need, pleasure and pain, are all relevant considerations in deciding whether an action is voluntary or not, but that when it comes to the question of accountability, people are ultimately responsible for the way in which they have permitted their characters and habits to develop. A disposition to virtue requires that people train their characters so that they no longer feel harmful or unnecessary pleasures as needs (*Nicomachean Ethics*, III. i–v. 1110a–1115a 5. 1976 Penguin edn).

Epicurus's distinction between different kinds of desires, points up something of which Marx, for instance, is guilty, and that is that to talk in the same breath of physiological needs whose satisfaction is compulsory for survival, satisfying the double criteria that they are both needed and wanted, and conditions for the actualisation of the human essence as 'needs' or 'wants' of the same order is illegitimate. To say that higher needs are necessary can only mean that they are subjectively, rather than objectively, necessary. That is to say, individuals are convinced, rightly or wrongly, that they are necessary, which is not necessity at all, strictly speaking. This is in no way to call into question how strongly the person feels about his wants or needs, but rather to point out that these needs are the product of his judgement or will and are not materially or physiologically dictated.

If Epicurus made room for the concept of voluntary behaviour, something which his successors in the eighteenth century tended to overlook, in Stoic philosophy, despite its materialism, freedom was a central concept. As the belief that men can transcend circumstances by choosing the good, freedom was considered by most later materialists, including Marx, to be a characteristically idealist notion. In the Stoic belief in the conquest of desires through the will they saw passive quietism of the worst sort. And yet the Stoics were among the first to embrace an active freedom that came from a rejection of the things of this world and the belief that only spiritual goods were real. This indeed was the rationale for their advocacy of the 'man of few needs'. That happiness is within our individual reach, is precisely because we can reject pleasure in favour of tranquillity. True and false needs, because they were judged in terms of freedom versus dependence, happiness versus pleasure, therefore meant something more to the Stoics than the distinction between natural and artificial needs. For such rigorists as Epictetus even basic physical needs were surpassable – hence the bold boast of the Stoics that a wise man is perfectly happy even inside the bull of Phalaris.[10] They argued that since all needs and desires are an unavoidable source of pain, even physical needs should be reduced as far as possible. A direct lineage between the concept of freedom of the Stoics and that of Spinoza can be traced, and both turned on a choice of good over evil that was indifferent to 'needs'.

Some things also need to be said about the concept of self-sufficiency (*ataraxy*) as the lynchpin of Epicurean ethics. While the 'life according to nature' made limitations on the expansion of needs and desires necessary to establish physical and psychological equilibrium, it imposed no limits on intellectual curiosity. Quite the contrary, the true basis of self-sufficiency was knowledge, or better still science – an understanding of nature and her laws which would dispense with the prejudice and superstition of religion and myth. From Virgil, Voltaire and Diderot to d'Holbach, Hume and Marx, Epicurus and Lucretius were read as the radical enlighteners of antiquity (see Gay, 1966, Vol. 1, pp. 98–105). Lucretius, author of a materialist account of human nature, was the declared enemy of religion and his celebrated lines to the effect that the solvent of fear and darkness is not light but knowledge of nature's forms, were often quoted. Through science he hoped to loosen the hold of religion on men's minds and in book 5 of *De Rerum Natura* he attributes the force of religion and superstition to the projection of human anxieties into an otherworldly realm and of frustrated human powers on to omnipotent creatures of the imagination, in a way that looks forward to Feuerbach. It is in this spirit that Marx in the foreword to his doctoral dissertation praises Epicurus's claim that 'Not the man who denies the gods worshipped by the multitude, but he who affirms of the gods what the multitude believes about them is truly impious' (*CW*, Vol. 1, p. 30).

The Hellenistic ideal of self-sufficiency had its epistemological corollary in the belief that direct access to nature is given to man through perception. '"If you live according to nature", Epicurus declared, "you will never be poor; if you live according to opinion, you will never be rich." Nature's wants are slight; the demands of opinion are boundless', Seneca, his commentator, added (*Epistle* XVI. 7–8).[11] From this distinction between truth and opinion flowed an attack on religion and superstition in the name of 'science', through whose agency the transparence of reality was thought to be guaranteed, which was characteristic of a certain tradition of materialism that carries through Marx and beyond. Associated with it was a theory of human behaviour in which needs and desires, the attraction of pleasure and repulsion of pain, were seen to be the primary motivations. In order to avoid exaggerating the significance of its antique origins, however, it is important to bear in mind the way in which Lockean sensationalist psychology and its derivatives impinged on this tradition, adding the distinctly modern dimension of radical environmentalist theory. This was a crucial element for the development of the socialist theory of needs.

It is not surprising, as Marx was to remark, that when a metaphysical system is seen to have run its course, philosophers should turn back to a more material and tangible conception of reality and seek in nature the basis for a new understanding of the world of men and things (*CW*, Vol. 1, p. 491). Just as the Hellenistic determinists rejected Platonic and Aristotelian idealism, so the seventeenth- and eighteenth-century rejection of scholasticism and the doctrine of final causes took the form once again of a reinvestigation of materialism and determinism. In their haste to overturn Aristotelian metaphysics and the doctrine of essences, these determinists also rejected the notion of freedom of the will, substituting desires or needs as causes.[12] Human action was once again conceived of within the limits of voluntary and involuntary behaviour, while the concept of judgement, as the basis for a theory of responsibility, was the only concession to freedom that was admitted. For Hobbes and his successors, the scope of freedom concerned only the compatibility of a more or less kinetic freedom of motion with the principles of determinism. Moral judgements were seen as relative and conventional, ultimately reducible to basic human needs and drives and the twin forces of attraction and repulsion, pleasure and pain. Freedom under these conditions came to mean nothing more significant than the absence of impediments and the unobstructed exertion of human powers on their objects. Adherents to the new science of Newton were concerned to locate human behaviour in the mechanistic and material world of nature and this meant evaporating the world of moral experience into a set of natural determinants, needs, instincts, motives, and their material objects plus the push and pull of pain and pleasure.[13]

The debate over freedom and determinism in this period moved within characteristic limits and turned on the question of whether behaviour is ineluctably determined by the force of natural drives as they translate into desires, or whether there are intervening factors: randomness and chance, on the one hand, or the ability of the individual to generate new ideas out of the data of sense and experience, on the other. The first alternative, allowing for randomness and chance, involved a modification of strict determinism through the concept of freedom of indifference on the model of the Epicurean atomic swerve. Human action was seen to result from a complex of motives which are themselves in turn the product of material and sensual stimuli. An aggregative function was ascribed to the will in balancing off conflicting motives and producing a resolution in one direction or another. (Proponents of this view often used Cicero's model of the will as a scales which tips in the direction of the strongest motive.) That behaviour was not predictable was due to the complexity of conflicting motives, but this did not mean that it was free, for to be free would, on this view, be to act without motives, which is inconceivable. Freedom was categorically ruled out by the assumption that action is governed by the will but that the will is determined by motives which in turn reflect the attraction of objects. (Interestingly enough, Leibniz turned against the notion of freedom of indifference the damning criticism that having distinguished between motives and causes it then empties the distinction of all content.)

The distance between the first alternative to strict determinism, or the theory of freedom of indifference, and the second, according to which the individual is credited with the ability to determine his behaviour on the basis of ideas that he himself generates out of the data of sense and experience, is not necessarily great. Both postulate the primacy of sense, the aggregative function of the will and make freedom dependent on the intervention of judgement and its faculty to deliberate on competing motives. The most penetrating and influential treatise on sensational psychology was John Locke's *Essay Concerning Human Understanding* of 1690.

Concerned to establish that there are neither innate principles in the mind which direct man towards truth, nor innate moral principles which incline him towards virtue, Locke turned to the Epicurean motivations of pleasure and pain as the foundation of a naturalistic theory of human behaviour. He remarked on the superiority of practical principles derived from nature which 'must produce Conformity of Action not barely speculative assent to their truth', postulating attraction to happiness and aversion to misery as universal and 'innate practical Principles, which (as practical Principles ought) do continue constantly to operate and influence all our Actions, without ceasing' (Locke, 1975 edn, I. iii. 3, lines 14–15 and 18–20, p. 67). 'Principles of Actions indeed there are lodged in Men's Appetites, but these are so far from being innate Moral

Principles, that if they were left to their full swing, they would carry Men to the over-turning of all Morality' (ibid., I. iii. 13, lines 11–14, p. 75). But despite the universality of attraction to pleasure and avoidance of pain as the law of the appetites, religion as a system of sanctions can hold the appetites in check by promising greater, though more distant, rewards and punishments. Action ordinarily arises at the instigation of desire. Men are impelled by the constant pressure of needs both natural and artificial which leave little room for the contemplation of remoter goods (ibid., II. xxi. 45, pp. 261–2). Nevertheless, Locke distinguished between desire and will in the determination of behaviour. Men desire what is conducive to their happiness and call that 'good'. Will is the power to direct or suspend the operations of desire which allows the individual to lay aside the pursuit of ephemeral pleasures in favour of moral rectitude, by applying reason to ascertain moral laws and the sanctions of religion to follow them.

The essence of liberty, what is in Locke's eyes 'improperly called free will', is this ability to suspend desire before the will is determined to action, and to subject our motives to a fair examination (ibid., II. xxi. 47, lines 27–8, p. 263). Like Aristotle, he believed that the efficacy of moral judgement depends on being able to raise in oneself a desire for moral goods sufficiently strong to be able to counteract the force of the instincts (ibid., II. xxi. 57, lines 2–7, p. 272). He suggested that the understanding, as long as it is not in the grasp of the passions, is capable of arriving at 'the true intrinsik good or evil that is in things', foreshadowing the role of the impartial spectator in later utilitarian theory, especially Adam Smith's *Theory of Moral Sentiments*. Locke exhibits the same propensity as the utilitarians to judge actions as good or evil by an appraisal of their consequences rather than their intentions. (Here, as Kant was to demonstrate, lies the subjectivity of a doctrine which depends for its validity on the calculation of the empirical and contingent.) And he laid the foundation for later moral sense theories, even though, by the insertion of the faculty of judgement between desire and volition, he tried to rescue man from the subjectivity of appetite and sensuous need.

Although Locke's theory of judgement, his insistence that '*Morality is the proper Science and Business of Mankind*' (ibid., IV. xii. 11, lines 12–13, p. 646), and that practical reason is of superior status to knowledge of the natural world, put him closer to Kant and Rousseau than to the radical materialists, his historical influence was in the direction of the latter. There is some justice in this, as we have seen, for Locke explicitly rejected what for Descartes and Kant constituted the necessary condition for morality: man's ability to choose the good against his own interests. With Locke, freedom is still essentially the freedom to do what one wants, even though what one wants is properly arrived at by an enlightened judgement which takes account of both proximate and remote goods. In most cases, men are not free in their volitions, according to Locke, because of the force exerted by natural and acquired needs. Nevertheless, they may be held responsible for their actions on the grounds that they failed to suspend choice until all possible options had been deliberated. And if they are psychologically disposed to precipitate action they are held responsible for failing to habituate themselves to deliberation. This responsibility holds and punishment may be incurred even where men *will* what they judge to be good but where because of a hasty choice the measure of good and evil is erroneous.

Consistent with his commitment to the Epicurean principles of pleasure and pain, Locke sees human behaviour as necessarily motivated to pursuit of good and avoidance of evil. He tends to subsume the principle of enlightened self-interest under the concept of desire. Thus, in the second edition of the *Essay Concerning Human Understanding*, in the chapter 'Of Power' (ibid., II. xxi. 28–66, pp. 248–78). Locke revises his argument that the will is ultimately determined 'by the greater good in view' in favour of the claim that desire is the true cause of willing (Locke, ed. von Leyden, 1954, p. 264). 'Desire', he argued in his notebooks, 'is nothing but a pain the mind suffers in the absence of some good' and 'is increased and varied by divers considerations', ease of attainment, 'greatness or smallness of the good', not only in relation to the actual pleasure it produces, but also in relation to other 'enjoyments' or goods (ibid., p. 270). And in his entry on 'The passions', Locke lapses into Hobbesian mechanistic language claiming of pleasure and pain that they are 'the two roots out of which all passions spring and a centre on which they all turn' (ibid., p. 265). 'Where they are removed', he goes on to say 'the passions would all cease, having nothing left to wind them up or set them going.' Locke shows a familiarity with Gassendi's *Philosophiae Epicuri Syntagma* and Gassendi, as even Marx was to note, was, together with Hobbes, a crucial figure in the development of mechanistic materialism which received its full development in the eighteenth-century, man-machine theories of Condillac and La Mettrie, Locke's most famous successors.

Although Locke emphasises the active power of the mind to generate new ideas out of the data of sense experience (*Essay*, 1975 edn, II. xxi. 72, p. 286), he provides no sound basis for a conception of moral activity. His appeal to natural law provides no anchor for morality as something which might require the sacrifice of personal interest. Although subscribing to the Stoic notion that natural law represents the principles constitutive of the universe and that these laws, like those governing the physical universe, are the same for all men in all times, natural law is said by him to be transmitted through man's natural faculties, sensation and judgement which, in their ordering operations, are held to reflect 'the light of nature'. But if these faculties are governed by the principles of pursuit of pleasure, avoidance of pain and enlightened judgement on these, what independent content could natural law, as such, be said to have? The 'life according to nature', as a Stoic principle to which Locke several times refers (Locke, ed. von Leyden, 1954, pp. 111, 109, 223), loses its moral content in his version of it. The distinction between things according to nature, as it is properly constituted, and things as they are naturally found, once made, was quickly forgotten, as in the case of Rousseau somewhat later.

The impasse Locke reaches is reflected in the subsequent course of the debate over free will and determinism which tends, on the one hand, to voluntarism with the theory of indifference and, on the other, to naturalistic conditioning theory, with the further development of sensationalist psychology. The belief that judgement constitutes moral activity, which Locke found difficult to explain, is gradually abandoned by his followers. Although d'Alembert and Condillac, in his early work, popularisers of Lockean psychology, ascribe to the higher functions of the mind a creativity which is distinguished from the passive registration of sensation, nothing more than an aggregative function is ascribed to the will. Condillac, in his early *Essai sur l'origine des connaissances humaines* (1746), develops the concept of 'attention', which looks forward to vitalist theories of the nineteenth and twentieth centuries, to show how the stamp of personality and the particular configuration of temperament, needs, passions, memories and ideas of an individual bear on the selection of his motives (Crocker, 1959, p. 120). But in his *Traité des sensations* (1749) he turns from an active to a passive conception of the mind, as the operative mechanism to process sensations according to the principles of pleasure and pain (ibid., pp. 120–1).

With Helvétius and La Mettrie the concept of the man-machine was born and the conviction that man's susceptibility to the environment through sense-experience makes him a completely modifiable creature. Diderot fought a rearguard action against this crude naturalistic view by pointing to the logical fallacy of mistaking conditions for causes ('Réfutation d'Helvétius', *Oeuvres*, Vol. 2, pp. 335–7).[14] Although sensations and the pleasure principle constitute necessary conditions, they are insufficient to account for the causation of behaviour. Diderot was interested in the psychic structures which account for a basic intractability of the human personality and explain why men are not infinitely malleable or subject to unlimited environmental conditioning. Nevertheless he was a determinist too, although concerned to establish the causality of motivation on non-physiological grounds. Choice is merely the power to select ideas, 'the last impulse of desire and aversion, and the last result of all one has been from his birth until the present moment' (*Le Rêve de d'Alembert*, pp. 136–8).[15] As for will, it sums up the complexity of the personality which as an entity nevertheless constitutes the single cause of actions. It is only with Rousseau that the materialism of the *philosophes*, including Diderot, is called into question in the name of an autonomous moral will, and certain materialist contradictions live on in his writings as well.

Notes

1   J. M. Rist's *Stoic Philosophy* (1969), gives a very good account of the Stoic position on the emotions, pleasure and pain and the nature of the good. See especially chs 1 to 3.
2   Quoted by Marx in *CW*, Vol. 1, pp. 39 and 458, and by Lovejoy and Boas (1935), p. 106. I am indebted to Lovejoy for the following account of Greek primitivism.
3   1931 Loeb edn, Vol. 2, p. 513. Quoted by Lovejoy and Boas (1935), p. 109n.
4   *OC*, Vol. 3, p. 171, cited by Lovejoy and Boas (1935), p. 241. See also Lovejoy's essay, 'The supposed primitivism of Rousseau's *Discourse on Inequality*' (1948), pp. 14–37.
5   Lovejoy's account of the essential similarities of Lucretius's and Rousseau's position is given in pp. 240–2.
6   Marx in the notes for his doctoral dissertation excerpted passages from Cicero's commentary on Epicurus's three classes of desire: 'Nothing could be more useful or

more conducive to well-being than Epicurus' doctrine as to the three classes of desire. One kind he classified as natural and necessary, a second as natural without being necessary, and a third as neither natural nor necessary: the principle of classification being that the necessary desires are gratified with little trouble and expense: the natural desires also require but little, since nature's own riches, which suffice to content her, are easily procured and limited in amount, but for vain desires no bound or limit can be discovered' (Cicero, 'On the highest goods and evils', I. xiii. 45, quoted in Marx, *CW*, Vol. 1, p. 508).

7 The recent fine study of Lucretius by James Nichols (1976) emphasises these aspects in the thought of the most famous Roman Epicurean, dealing also with Lucretius's influence on Rousseau, and his relation to early modern political thought on questions of virtue, power, corruption and the nature of desires.

8 Cited by Marx, *CW*, Vol. 1, p. 508.

9 Epicurus, *Letter to Menoeceus*, para. 134, quoted by Furley (1967), pp. 174–5, from whom this translation is taken, was also excerpted by Marx in his doctoral notes (*CW*, Vol. 1, p. 408), although he never commented on it.

10 I am indebted for this discussion of the Stoic concept of freedom to a private communication from Professor Kolakowski.

11 Excerpted by Marx in his doctoral notes (*CW*, Vol. 1, p. 481).

12 The mechanistic nature of such a concept of motivation is evident in Hobbes's statement: 'These small beginnings of motion, within the body of man, before they appear in walking, speaking, striking and other visible actions, are commonly called ENDEAVOUR. This endeavour, when it is toward something which causes it, is called APPETITE, or DESIRE, the latter being the general name' (*Leviathan*, I. vi).

13 I am indebted for the account that follows of the freedom of indifference and the materialist onslaught on ethical theory in the Enlightenment to Lester Crocker's excellent analysis in *An Age of Crisis* (1959).

14 See Crocker (1959), pp. 123–4.

15 Cited in Crocker (1959), p. 126.

3

Rousseau on Natural and Artificial Needs

The debate over the problem of evil, often referred to as 'the Epicurean dilemma', lay at the heart of the Enlightenment investigation of the psychological bases for behaviour, and in this the concept of needs was crucial. For the first time on such a scale, men addressed themselves to the moral and social function of the passions, those admittedly irrational aspects of human behaviour, in an open-minded way. They considered the relation of the appetites to needs as both an instinctual and cognitive stimulus. They compared natural physiological needs with those which are socially produced, considering their moral effects both on the individual and in society. Some saw in social, or artificial, needs the source of evil, but others considered them morally indifferent, perhaps even the source of social solidarity. Among the former a distinction was made between the needs for self-esteem, which were considered the cause of pride, envy, competition and social conflict, and genuine self-regarding needs, which were considered legitimate for the self-preservation and integrity of the individual. This distinction was expressed in terms of a contrast between *amour-propre* (selfishness) and *amour-de-soi* (self-regard), and in it we see implicit the distinction between natural and artificial needs, the idea that evil is socially created and may, given the right procedures, be socially eliminated.

One of the reasons for the deep dissatisfaction with Christianity among Enlightenment thinkers had to do with the way in which it was seen to repress ego-centred impulses which were sublimated in the desire for an eternal hereafter. Spinoza and Pascal had already laid the basis for a secular discussion of this very contentious issue by considering the source of destructive urges not in a fall from grace but in certain ego-needs, foreshadowing Freud's concepts of the life and death instincts. The ego, they maintained, in its love of being and desire for protection strives to perfect itself and this is the source of its greatness and of those positive emotions which truly enlarge the personality – love, honour and so on. However, its fears of weakness and diminution lead the ego to inflate itself and to seek self-esteem in the opinions of others, the approval of one's peers producing exultation, their disapproval shame. The desire to avoid feelings of weakness, humility and shame, encourages the ego, then, to enlarge the self by belittling others and this is the source of the negative emotions – pride, anger, vengeance, cruelty, hatred. Spinoza concluded that 'men are by nature inclined to hatred and envy', painting a picture of the competition for reputation, esteem and their evil social consequences as black as Rousseau's famous passage in the *Discourse on Inequality* (although he believed that the striving for rationality is part of man's nature too) (Spinoza, *Ethic*, pt 3, prop. 55).[1]

Hobbes and the Jansenist Nicole had emphasised how the desire to be loved may turn into a desire for power, pointing to the social bond of dependence which the need for self-esteem creates. (Rousseau footnotes Hobbes in his own account of *amour-propre*.) Malebranche, Abbadie, Fontenelle, Bayle and Mandeville, all took up the distinction between positive and negative forms of self-love, *amour-de-soi* and *amour-propre*, considering the ego-needs of the individual and their social consequences. Not only did they see evil and irrationality as endemic to human nature, but some even saw them as socially necessary. The desire for pleasure, comfort and the esteem of others created a social bond which favoured peace over discord, according to Hobbes and Nicole. Vanity, emulation and greed were also a stimulus to the creation of wealth and prosperity, according to Fontenelle. The reason why evil, atheism and moral anarchy were not obstacles to social order was, according to Bayle, because 'Human nature itself produces the *repressive principle* which . . . [men] need' in the very pursuit of reputation; for, esteem can only be bought at the cost of conformity to prevailing social values (*Oeuvres diverses*, Vol. 3, p. 358).[2] And Mandeville went so far as to argue openly for the social utility of vice: pride and shame are the 'two passions in which the seeds of most virtues are contained', and the urge to conform is the very source of social solidarity (*The Fable of the Bees*, Vol. 1, p. 56).[3]

The distinction between *amour-propre* and *amour-de-soi*, between ego-centric love and self-regarding love, was a major source for the distinction between true and false needs, and on this question the ancient lines of demarcation between Epicurean and Stoic philosophy, which had been minimised from the time of the Roman eclectics on, were redrawn. The Epicureans and their Enlightenment advocates believed that evil and irrationality were ineradicable features of the human condition. The Stoics believed that they were not. We see this important difference in the sanguine Epicureanism of those hard-headed realists, Bayle, Hobbes and Mandeville, who had an almost clinical interest in the social consequences of evil, compared with the Stoicism of Rousseau and the utopian socialists, who were intent on eradicating it.

Rousseau explicitly attacked Mandeville's thesis of the social utility of the passions, or the public benefits of private vices.[4] Pride, *amour-propre*, competition for honour and wealth were unambiguously evil, he believed, and so was the relationship of social dependence which they create. He made a distinction between social mores and moral values (which, incidentally, Mandeville and most of the former group upheld), declaring that socially created needs and mores must be resisted. Here we catch an early glimpse of the eschatological element which was to distinguish socialist thought: the demand for the purification of society and the restitution of a natural harmony between the social and moral orders. Many of the salient features of this critique of society are specifically Stoic: the distinction between true and false needs; the elimination of corruption through the rule of equality; disparagement of luxury and wealth and the insistence on frugality and self-denial.

Rousseau took over the distinction between *amour-de-soi* and *amour-propre* from Abbadie and Vauvenargues, characterising the former as a natural feeling, common to all animals which tends to their self-preservation but which in man, directed by reason and modified by pity, produces humanity and virtue (*OC*, Vol. 3, pp. 219 and 1,376). *Amour-propre*, on the other hand, 'is a relative feeling, artificial, and born in society', which serves men to raise themselves above others, and which is the source of all evil, particularly pride. In 'our primitive state, in the true state of nature *amour-propre* did not exist', for each man was his own sole observer, the sole judge of his own merit, and since 'it is not possible that a feeling which owes its source to comparisons which he is not disposed to make, could take root', man would know neither hatred nor desire for vengeance (Note 15, ibid., p. 219). That Rousseau should make social comparisons and the opinion of others the source of evil is consistent with his doctrine of true and false needs. He saw the desire to impress, competition for honour and the pursuit of reputation giving rise to all the artificial needs from which he hoped to shield the young Emile by isolation.

Since the doctrine of needs, derived by the early socialists principally from Rousseau, has continued to be surprisingly durable, it is important to consider the significance of the transition from *amour-de-soi* and *amour-propre* to true and false needs. We have in *Emile* perhaps the plainest statement of it:

> A self-love [*amour-de-soi*] which concerns itself only with ourselves, is content when our true needs are satisfied but selfishness [*amour-propre*], which is always comparing self with others, is never satisfied and never can be; for this feeling, which prefers ourselves to others, requires that they should prefer us to themselves, which is impossible. Thus the tender and gentle passions spring from self-love, while the hateful and angry passions spring from selfishness. So it is the fewness of his needs, the narrow limits within which he can compare himself with others, that makes a man really good; what makes him really bad is a multiplicity of needs and dependence on the opinions of others. (*OC*, Vol. 4, p. 493)[5]

In the early *Dialogues* Rousseau had asked the question: '. . . how is this disposition to compare, which changes a natural and good passion into an artificial and false one, arrived at?' He answered it himself: '. . . it comes from social relations, the progress of ideas and cultivation of the mind' (ibid., p. 1,457). In other words, false needs require fertile ground and this can only be provided by social development and the proliferation of objects for which needs are created.

The history of this progress is precisely what he set out to trace in the *Discourse on the Origins of Inequality*, where he outlines the social and economic conditions for the development of false needs, locating the same stages Lucretius described so much earlier. Rousseau, like

Lucretius and unlike Seneca, was not a chronological primitivist and he postulated a point in the emergence of civilisation from the state of nature at which needs and their means of satisfaction would have been in equilibrium, the golden age of primitive agriculture and domestic harmony − a state far removed from the life of 'the noble savage'.[6]

Rousseau set great store by an equilibrium of human needs and powers as a condition of happiness. One of the guiding principles of Emile's education was that he should not be confronted with new needs, demands or temptations until he had developed the strength of character and self-discipline to handle them:

> The closer man remains to his natural conditions the less difference there is between his desires and powers, and consequently the less he is remote from happiness. He is never less miserable than when he appears deprived of all: for misery does not consist in the privation of things but in the need which they arouse. (ibid., p. 304)

One cannot fail to notice an old set of ideas resurfacing: the Epicurean notion of the attraction to pleasure and avoidance of pain as primary human motivations, in conjunction with the Socratic ideal of self-sufficiency, which characterises classical primitivist thought. As Rousseau puts it:

> The feeling of pain is inseparable from the desire to escape it, pleasure from the desire to enjoy it. All desire implies a want and all wants experienced are painful; hence our misery consists in the disproportion between our desires and our powers. A conscious being whose powers were equal to his desires would be perfectly happy. (ibid., pp. 303−4)

True to this particular Hellenistic tradition, Rousseau appeals to nature, 'who does everything for the best', and the condition in which she placed man from the first, to defend the ideals of harmony, equilibrium, tranquillity. At first nature gave man 'only such desires as were necessary for his self-preservation and such powers as were required for their satisfaction . . . It is only in this primitive condition that we find equilibrium between desire and power and only then is man not unhappy' (p. 304). Of course, man's potential exceeds natural bounds and as he comes closer to realising it his imagination outstrips his powers, his desires their means of satisfaction. What is to be done? The mere limitation of desire would leave newly awakened powers idle, but the extension of man's powers brings an escalation of desires. True happiness consists 'in decreasing the difference between our desires and powers, in establishing a perfect equilibrium between the power and the will. Then only, when all forces are employed, will the soul be at rest and man . . . find himself in his true position' (p. 304). The Greek ideal of *ataraxia* or tranquillity is married to the Christian notion of man's place in the scale of being.

Rousseau shares much in common with the ancient primitivists taking from the Epicureans the emphasis on pleasure and the absence of pain as conditions of happiness, and from the Stoics self-denial and self-control as means to stem the growth of needs which the imagination unchecked produces. He goes some distance towards the rigours of the Cynics, quoting Favorinus: 'Great needs . . . spring from great wealth; and often the best way of getting what we want is to get rid of what we have' (p. 305). He follows the Stoics, in particular Seneca, in his wholesale condemnation of progress, civilisation and the arts. Despite his emphasis on the role of the will there is an underlying materialist and utilitarian strain in Rousseau: the same preoccupation with the external conditions of happiness, gratification and the avoidance of pain, the disproportion between capability and desire, that we find in Locke and the French materialists.

In fact, Rousseau goes a long way with Locke and the proponents of sensationalist psychology. In book 3 of *Emile*, where he summarises the progress his pupil has made so far, he gives an account of the learning process in precisely Lockean terms. At first a child experiences sensations, from which he comes by the comparison of successive and complex sensations to have ideas, which are in themselves a complex form of sensation. The way in which ideas are formed also moulds the character of the mind. Ideas derived from real relations are true and the mind thorough; ideas derived from apparent relations are false and the mind superficial. Simple ideas register sensations and like all forms of sensation they involve judgement. The difference between a sensation and an idea lies in the fact that in the former judgement is passive, while in the latter it is active: it connects, compares and discriminates between relations not perceived by the senses. 'That', Rousseau declares, 'is the whole difference, but it is a great one', and he goes on to conclude from this that 'Nature never deceives us; it is we who deceive ourselves' (*OC*, Vol. 4, pp. 481–2).

In other words, sensations cannot be false, only the judgements we make on them. He invokes the concept of experience to show how a child who burns his mouth on something cold cannot distinguish his pain from a burn caused by something hot. It is not the sensation that is wrong but the judgement on its cause. Experience enables us to correct such a mistake – here the emphasis on sensation, judgement, experience and learning is in line with orthodox sensationalist psychology. He then gives another example, the classic one of the stick in the water appearing bent or broken, and in this case his inference is idiosyncratic but not incompatible with Lockean principles. Science may appear to correct such optical illusions, he declares, but in fact science is no palliative for human error. The learned get further and further from the truth because pride in their judgement increases more rapidly than their progress in knowledge.

Once again his conclusion is simply Stoic; the more we know the more mistakes we make, and ignorance is the only guarantee against error. Form no judgements and you will never be mistaken; it is the teaching of nature as well as reason. 'Beyond the few immediate contacts we have with sensible things, for the rest we have naturally only a profound indifference. The savage would not turn his head to see a fine machine at work or the wonders of electricity' (p. 483). What is it to him? Now, of course, civilised man no longer has the option of ignorance. He is dependent on everything, curiosity has increased his needs and his artificial needs have increased his dependency. But still it remains true that when it comes to confirming his judgements he must do so by reducing his experiences to sense data and verifying the experience of one sense in terms of another. 'Then each of our sensations will become an idea and this idea will always correspond to the truth' (p. 484). This, in fact, constitutes the method of inductive reasoning, Rousseau claims.

It is interesting to see that in one of the variants of *Emile*, 'Manuscript P'[7] Rousseau discussed the question of whether or not our senses deceive us, with direct reference to the Epicureans. He believed that they were correct in holding that the senses cannot deceive us, but mistaken in believing that judgements are also sensations and therefore cannot be false: 'It is here that the Epicureans are mistaken, claiming that the judgments that we make on our sensations can never be false. We feel our sensations but we do not feel our judgments, we produce them' (*OC*, Vol. 4, p. 1,447).

Rousseau in the same 'Manuscript P', emphasised the active power of judgement and the fact that through it men are capable of deriving ontological propositions from sensations:

There is in the human understanding an active force which aggregates and judges, which compares two images, which brings together two ideas, which infers from two propositions, which counterposes, so to speak, two objects, one against the other, in order to pronounce on what they have in common and where they are different. According to me the distinctive faculty of every active or spiritual being is the power to give meaning to the word 'is'. I seek in vain this unifying force in a purely sentient being and I do not see it in nature. This passive being would sense each object separately or even experience the total object formed from two others, but it would never compare them. (ibid., p. 1,447; see also pp. 571–2)[8]

It is this notion of the active power of judgement that Rousseau turns against the radical materialists – particularly the man-machine theorists, La Mettrie, d'Alembert, Helvétius, d'Holbach, and so on – in book 4 of *Emile*. There is no doubt that Rousseau's account of sensationalist psychology in book 3 excludes moral and metaphysical considerations for pedagogical rather than philosophical reasons. In the 'Profession of Faith' in book 4 he adds them back in. Sensation, or feeling, already includes an innate sense of right and wrong which Rousseau associates with conscience, natural law and the moral order. Here he comes close to the moral sense theories of Shaftesbury and Hutcheson, but he saves himself by his concept of the will and the active power of judgement through which man can transcend the senses and go against his instincts. He manages in this way to steer a course between the Charybdis of French Enlightenment materialism, as it descended from Locke, and its image of man as a need-governed creature, and the Scylla of moral-sense theories and their glorification of natural man and his innate sensibilities.

In fact, Rousseau parries thinkers on all sides. He attacks Locke and the materialists for taking no account of man's capacity to think and reducing him to an entirely passive and sentient existence in the world of natural things. He claims to refute them on their own grounds: if man cannot think then he cannot feel either; it is equally impossible to locate 'a sensitive unit, the individual ego' as it is to locate the mind, in a collection of molecules (ibid., p. 58). 'I know not how the materialists understand it', he claims, 'but it seems to me that the same difficulties which have led them to reject thought should have also led them to reject feeling; and I do not see why, having taken the first step they do not take the next, what more would it cost them, and since they are certain that they do not think, how do they dare to assert that they feel?' (pp. 584–5).

On the other side, he attacks 'modern philosophy' which he claims entirely neglects instinct and reduces man to the dry bones of reason and absolute dependence on learned behaviour. If it is true that instinct, sensations and conscience are so negligible, how does man come to acquire knowledge and the ability to learn and reflect it all? (p. 595).

Rousseau maintains, on balance, a form of the Cartesian mind/body duality which he translates into practical philosophy as the option that is always open to man to choose either to transcend his instincts through the will, or to permit himself to be entirely overrun by his needs, wants, instincts and appetites (ibid., p. 1,540).[9] It is for this reason that he attacks thinkers who close off either one or the other of these alternatives, by strict materialism on the one hand, or strict rationalism, on the other. He himself leans so far in both directions that he involves himself in inevitable contradictions; for instance, the concept of instinct is at one time synonymous with appetite and the senses, at another with conscience; the belief that nature is morally neutral and the natural life one of mere animal existence, on the one hand, but his insistence on 'natural needs' as the criterion of the good life, on the other. It is hardly surprising that thinkers as diverse as Kant and the early socialists should claim to be his heirs. Kant takes up certain themes of his moral philosophy, but it is Rousseau's naturalism that is amplified in the writings of the early socialists.

In Rousseau's first and second 'Discourses', although among his earliest works, the doctrine of true and false needs, latent in the thought of the Stoics, is fully articulated. Apart from obvious references to various Stoic philosophers such as Diogenes, Cato, Epictetus, Seneca, and so on, in his writings, Georges Pire (1953–5) and Peter Jimack (1960) have shown conclusively through their researches that Rousseau's moral philosophy as a whole is greatly influenced by the Stoa and, in particular, by Seneca (see also Roche, 1974, ch. 1). 'The theses of the two Discourses are already completely those of Seneca', Jimack claims (1960, p. 350), and according to Pire (1953–5, p. 73) the two authors share 'principles fundamentally identical'. One could easily exaggerate this influence, but as Pire is careful to point out (pp. 83 ff.) Seneca is only one bibliographic source among a host of others. The work of Pire, Jimack and Jean Morel alone has documented Rousseau's indebtedness to the Epicurean Lucretius on progress from the state of nature to advanced civilisation (Morel, 1909, p. 163 ff.); to Diderot on the infinity of possible fictitious needs compared with limited natural needs (ibid., p. 140); to Condillac on the growth of needs and desires due to the ability to make comparisons (ibid., p. 146); his indebtedness to Locke for his account of the genesis of ideas in the individual (Jimack, 1960, p. 289); to Condillac, Buffon and Helvétius for elements of sensationalist psychology taken in turn from Locke (ibid., ch. 13); and his indebtedness to Plutarch, Montaigne, Grotius and Pufendorf on natural law (Morel, 1909, p. 160 ff.). All of these were important themes in the second 'Discourse'.

As the watershed of so many influences, and indeed as a powerful critique in its own right, the *Discourse on the Origins of Inequality among Men* is worth careful attention for the role that the concept of needs plays. The first *Discourse on the Arts and Sciences* makes in general and without too much theoretical rigour, as Rousseau subsequently admits, the argument that he develops in specific form in the second 'Discourse'. Although relentless enough in its criticism of civilisation and the corruption of morals through the cultivation of the arts and sciences, the first 'Discourse' nevertheless contains the seeds of an ambivalence on the relation between man and society that becomes very apparent in the second. Although Rousseau argues in general that 'Before art had moulded our behaviour, and taught our passions to speak an artificial language, our morals were rude but natural' (first 'Discourse', 1913 Everyman edn, p. 122),[10] he nevertheless concedes that 'The mind, as well as the body, has its needs; those of the body are the basis of society, those of the mind its ornaments' (p. 120). It seems that in man's natural needs, if one includes the needs of the mind, Rousseau already postulated a basis for sociability.

The subject proposed by the Academy of Dijon, to which the second 'Discourse' is addressed, 'What is the Origin of Inequality among Men and is it Authorized by Natural Law?', poses more directly the question of whether society, as it has developed, has a basis in human nature as such. Rousseau's choice of the text by Aristotle on the title-page is revealing enough: 'We should consider what is natural not in things which are depraved but in those which are rightly ordered according to nature.' In other words, he hopes to distinguish those fundamental attributes constitutive of human nature from the accretions or deviations which a certain form of social development had produced. The quotation from Aristotle could well have been a Stoic text suggesting, as it does, the valorisation of nature in the concept of 'the life according to nature' and the possibility of distinguishing between things to be found in nature which are 'indifferent' and those which represent the uniform and universal features constitutive of the structure of the physical and moral universe. This text alerts us to the necessity to see Rousseau's concept of 'natural needs' in a special light: they are not to be read as needs found in nature in the loose sense, since these may well be morally indifferent, but rather as those which are constitutive of human nature. True, Rousseau constantly obscures this distinction himself, by talking about the natural needs found in primitive man, moving from descriptions of the chronological state of nature to hypothetical statements about universal tendencies of human nature. This represents a basic and unresolved ambivalence in his thought, to which we have already referred. On the one hand, we have Rousseau the primitivist who, assuming that the natural state of affairs was the true state of affairs, draws the unwarranted inference that this was therefore the uncivilised state, confusing the two concepts of nature that he had already distinguished. On the other hand, we have the Rousseau who is insistent on distinguishing between nature in a descriptive sense (whatever may be found in nature), and nature in a normative sense (things in accordance with nature rightly ordered), and who is careful to distinguish between the attributes of man in the natural state and those which are constitutive of human nature as such. This latter Rousseau it is who in the end prevails, I think, for two reasons. First of all, Rousseau does ultimately conclude that the golden age of mankind, or that in which man most closely approximated his true nature, was not that of the essentially solitary primitive, but rather that of the early community of households. And secondly because, despite himself, Rousseau admits a mutual dependence between the development of man's innate potentialities and the creation of society.

What is it that distinguishes man from the animals after all? As Rousseau notes, whereas 'an animal is at the end of a few months all he will ever be during his whole life, and his species, at the end of a thousand years, exactly what it was the first year of that thousand' (ibid., p. 170), man through the faculty of self-improvement (perfectibility) has become so changed, and in changing himself has so completely covered the tracks of his own development, that one can only uncover with difficulty the 'lost and forgotten road by which man must have passed from the state of nature to the state of society' (p. 219). Nevertheless, if we try to retrace these steps we 'cannot fail to be struck by the vast difference which separates the two states'. We shall see 'how the soul and passions of men insensibly change their very nature; why our wants and pleasures in the end seek new objects; and why, the original man having vanished by degrees, society offers to us only an assembly of artificial men and factitious passions, which are the work of all these new relations, and without any real foundation in nature' (p. 220). So far removed are we from the original 'peace and liberty' of the primitive man that 'even the *ataraxia* of the Stoic falls short of his profound indifference to every other object' (p. 220).

Strictly speaking this conclusion of Rousseau's does not follow from his premises. If, as he shows, perfectibility means the progressive development of the species, and if the creation of society constitutes a precondition for this development, then he is not in a position to argue that the attributes of civilised man, as the outcome of this process, are artificial and have no basis in nature. Even if we interpret the claim that the attributes of civilised man have no basis in nature favourably to mean that they are not in accordance with the laws of nature (rather than that they are not to be found in the state of nature, which would not tell us much), the claim is still not easily vindicated, since if perfectibility entails progress, there is in Rousseau's description of human nature a basis for whatever the hazards of progress produce. Rousseau spells out the mutual dependence of man's cognitive development and the growth of new needs and their objects, as well as the development of such societal institutions as language, the family and co-operative labour. That the dynamics of progress once set in motion cannot be easily stopped is a conclusion that even he is reluctantly forced to concede. The state of nature saw an equilibrium between man's needs and their objects; for this reason men were not disposed to exercise their wits, 'for we desire knowledge only because we wish to enjoy'. But 'the passions too originate in our wants and their progress depends on that of our knowledge; for we cannot desire or fear anything except from the idea we have of it, or from the simple impulse of nature' (p. 171). 'Now the savage man', Rousseau argues, 'being destitute of every species of intelligence, can have no passions save those of the latter kind: his desires never go beyond his physical wants.' Like an animal, his instincts adapt to, and are restricted by, the means of satisfaction that his environment naturally provides. Only the growth of new (and artificial) needs could have permitted this vicious circle to be broken. Were it not for these, man would never have departed from his 'stupid' and 'brutish' state where 'the only goods he recognized in the universe were food, a female and sleep; the only evils he feared were pain and hunger' (p. 171).

The development of society was, therefore, far from being an accidental aberration. Whatever concatenation of circumstances occasioned its specific emergence (growth of population, which put pressure on resources, the necessity for larger units for self-defence, and so on) merely brought about a tendency already latent in the constitution of things, if we take the idea of perfectibility seriously. It is interesting that Rousseau should argue the mutual dependence of ideas, new needs and language. In accordance with the principles of sensationalist psychology, which he takes over from Locke, Condillac, Helvétius and others, Rousseau argues that intellectual curiosity arises at the behest of need or desire, that is to say the passions, but that the passions are, in turn, only developed simultaneously with the availability of objects for their satisfaction. This suggests the interdependence of the progress of ideas, technological innovation and the production of new needs, which has been a feature of the account of the progress of civilisation from the Epicureans and Stoics down to Marx, and which owes something to underlying principles of materialism common to them all. Seneca himself had argued:

> Nature suffices for all she asks of us. Luxury has turned her back on nature, daily urging herself on and growing through the centuries, pressing men's intelligence into the development of the vices. First she began to hanker after things that were inessential, and then after things that were injurious, and finally she handed the mind over to the body . . . All those trades that give rise to noise or hectic activity in the city are in business for the body . . . This is the starting point for textile and engineering workshops, for the perfumes used by chefs, the sensual movements of our dancing teachers, even sensual and unmanly songs. And why? Because the bounds of nature, which set a limit to man's wants by relieving them only where there is necessity for such relief, have been lost sight of; to want simply what is enough nowadays suggests to people primitiveness and squalor. ('Ninetieth letter', *Letters From a Stoic*, 1969, p. 168).

Part 1 of Rousseau's *Discourse on the Origins of Inequality* represents a general answer to the question of whether inequality is constitutive of human nature as such, or not. His answer is that it is not. Distinguishing between natural or physical inequality, which comes from differences of strength and ability, and moral or political inequality, which he argues is conventional, he asserts that only the first is natural and that it is generally insignificant and far surpassed in importance by the artificial inequalities that society itself establishes. These inequalities are a direct consequence of the growth of artificial needs and the monopoly of resources through the institution of property that allows the needs of some to proliferate without limit and the basic needs of others to go unsatisfied. True to his characterisation in the first 'Discourse' of needs of the mind and needs of the body, Rousseau distinguishes between physical needs, or the need for commodities to satisfy the physical appetites, and psychological needs, or the need for goods for purely symbolic purposes in the competition for status and honour. The latter are far more insidious, he thinks.

Rousseau's specific indictment of modern society and where it went wrong focuses not so much on the waste, injustice and physical hardships which inequality produces, as on the moral corruption that stems from abandoning the 'life according to nature' and the voice of conscience in favour of conventional mores and popular opinion as a guide to behaviour. Social life generated reciprocal needs and of these the need for approbation or *amour-propre*, the recognition of others, which Rousseau describes in note 15 of the *Discourse on Inequality* as 'relative, artificial, born in society', is the root of evil. For Rousseau shows that by expanding their range of commodities and physical comforts men lost their natural hardiness and even allowed these luxuries 'to degenerate into real needs'. But becoming soft in this way was by no means as dangerous as becoming morally corrupt through a dependence on psychological needs for self-esteem and approbation. Goods then acquired a surrogate value as currency in the competition for honour and power which became all-consuming and which destroyed the natural basis for morality, compassion and set egoism and the pursuit of gain in place of all other considerations.

In the preface of his comedy *Narcissus, or the Love of Self*, written in 1753, a year before the *Discourse on Inequality*, Rousseau painted a graphic picture of the hazards of 'fastening the knots of society by personal interest' putting men 'in mutual dependence, giving them reciprocal needs and common interests and obliging each of them to contribute to the good of others in order to ensure his own' (*OC*, Vol. 2, p. 968). The satisfaction of needs becomes subject to competition, which encourages dissembling, cheating and betrayal. It becomes necessary

> . . . to take care that no-one sees what we are like; because for every two men whose interests agree, those of ten thousand perhaps are opposed, and there is no other way to succeed than to cheat or ruin all those people. Here is the fatal source of violence, cheating, lies and all the horrors necessarily brought about by a state of affairs where each pretending to work for the fortune or reputation of others can only raise his own above theirs at their expense.

In the second 'Discourse' Rousseau embellishes this picture of the servitude to which men are subjected by 'a multiplicity of new wants' by which they are 'brought into subjection . . . to all nature, and particularly to one-another'. Whether victor or vanquished in the competition for power their dependence is just as great. 'Insatiable ambition, the thirst of raising their respective fortunes, not so much from real want as from the desire to surpass others, inspired all men with a vile propensity to injure one another, and with a secret jealousy, which is the more dangerous, as it puts on the mask of benevolence' (1913 Everyman edn, p. 203). What were these evils but 'the first effects of property, and the inseparable attendants of growing inequality', Rousseau concludes (p. 203). This emphasis on property as the foundation of civil society has led a number of recent scholars to see in Rousseau a precursor to Marx. Lucio Colletti in his excellent essay 'Rousseau as critic of civil society', (1972) and a number of contributors to the 1962 Dijon Studies on the Social Contract, have seen in Rousseau's condemnation of the specific evils of modern society and his distinction between *bourgeois* and *citoyen*, the argument that what has gone wrong with Western European society has to do with the exigencies of co-operative labour, the institution of property, government as the guarantor of property rights and class divisions, the arts and sciences as class phenomena, and so on.

There is, indeed, a basis in Rousseau's writings for such a reading. Since Rousseau does show in his account of human nature the need for society as the precondition for perfectibility, we are forced to conclude that it is not society as such that he condemns so much as a specific form of society: that governed by the pursuit of luxury and ephemeral goods, characterised by inequality, consumerism, corruption, and so on. Indeed we know from a careful reading of the second 'Discourse' that it was not the primitive, asocial condition of man that Rousseau identified as the golden age of mankind − and that which, therefore, most closely realised the propensities of human nature − but rather the community of self-sufficient households. The causes for a departure from this happy condition are given as the growing awareness of the possibilities offered by co-operative labour:

> . . . from the moment one man began to stand in need of the help of another; from the moment it appeared advantageous to any one man to have enough provisions for two, equality disappeared, property was introduced, work became indispensable, and vast forests became smiling fields, which man had to water with the sweat of his brow, and where slavery and misery were soon seen to germinate and grow up with the crops. (1913 Everyman edn, p. 199)

In *Emile* Rousseau explicitly linked the expansion of needs with the generation of a surplus and the problems of the division and distribution of labour:

> So long as only physical needs are recognised man is self-sufficient; the introduction of a surplus necessitates the division and distribution of labour; for although one man working alone earns only one man's subsistence, a hundred working together can earn enough for two hundred to subsist. (*OC*, Vol. 4, p. 456)

Metallurgy and agriculture, 'the two arts which produced this great revolution', were by no means accidental discoveries: they presupposed a disposition to co-operative labour that was already postulated by Rousseau in the initial undertaking to live and work together in communities, that were by this stage well established. The development of metallurgy and agriculture permitted a division of labour that increased the efficiency of co-operative labour while bringing in train the perils of exploitation of the individual and tightening the knots of dependence between the individual and the group. While the toolmakers were indispensable for the development of agricultural implements, they were also dependent on the farmers to produce a surplus so that they could eat. Dependence of the individual on the group was increased at the very point at which individual property through enclosure of the land came to be introduced, bringing a tension that was to become a major source of social conflict. As Rousseau showed, the concept of property had already been established in the community of households, but this was property on the basis of use, which neither permitted the unlimited accumulation of goods, nor was the source of much contention as long as it was kept on this basis (1913 Everyman edn, p. 195). It was with the enclosure of land and the development of a surplus, made possible by the technologies of metallurgy and agriculture, that individual property, the peculiar basis of civil society, was instituted and all its attendant evils came into play.

In his glorification of manual labour; his claim in *Emile* that 'the value set by the general public on the various arts is in inverse ratio to their real utility' (*OC*, Vol. 4, pp. 456–7); his suggestion in the second 'Discourse' that labour is the source of value (*OC*, Vol. 3, p. 173); that wages are driven down to the barest minimum for subsistence because of the exigencies of supply and demand (*Emile, OC*, Vol. 4, pp. 456–7); Rousseau enumerates elements of the labour theory of value. There is a conceptual connection between the emphasis on needs as an objective category and utility as an economic criterion that is already made by Rousseau. Interestingly enough, he, too, relates the distinction between true and false needs to the propensity of men to seek happiness in appearance rather than reality. And because, after the Greeks, he associates true needs with the requirements of nature, he feels safe in referring to them as an objective standard in economics.

Despite the striking similarities between this picture which Rousseau paints of the dialectic of civilisation and the critique of bourgeois society of Marx, we should not be blind to its antecedents. Surprisingly enough we have in both Seneca and Lucretius, known to be formative influences on Rousseau, an account of the development of civilisation and its evils which also focuses on the development of metallurgy and agriculture, the institution of individual property, and so on. The Stoics were known advocates of proto-socialist principles: the essential equality of man, the ideal of communally owned goods, the exhortation to treat all men as brothers; tenets of Cynic philosophy which had been handed down to them through Zeno. In Seneca's account of the life according to nature which was also, incidentally, that of primitive man, in his 'Letter on philosophy and progress', we see these principles implicit:

> The earth herself, untilled, was more productive, her yields being more than ample for the needs of peoples who did not raid each other . . . All was equally divided among people living in complete harmony. The stronger had not yet started laying hands on the weaker; the avaricious person had not yet started hiding things away, to be hoarded for his own private use, so shutting the next man off from actual necessities of life; each cared as much about the other as about himself . . .
>
> What race of men could be luckier? Share and share alike they enjoyed nature. She saw to each and every man's requirements for survival like a parent. What it all amounted to was undisturbed possession of resources owned by the community . . . Into this ideal state of things burst avarice, avarice which in seeking to put aside some article or other and appropriate it to its own use, only succeeded in making everything somebody else's property and reducing its possessions to a fraction of its previously unlimited wealth. (*Letters from a Stoic*, 1969 edn, pp. 174–5)

Lucretius's account of the development of society out of the state of nature follows the same successive stages as Rousseau's: from the hardiness of a solitary existence in nature, to the institution of the family group, and the development of language and covenants. As Rousseau notes, for the poet it was gold and silver 'which first civilized man and ruined humanity', where for the philosopher it was iron and corn (1913 Everyman edn, p. 199), referring undoubtedly to Lucretius (*De Rerum Natura*, v. 1113–14. 1937 Loeb edn, p. 419). Nevertheless, for Lucretius too, metallurgy and agriculture were significant developments in the history of progress, precisely because of the growth of needs that attended them:

> For what is ready to hand, unless we have known something more lovely before, gives pre-eminent delight and seems to hold the field, until something found afterwards to be better usually spoils all that and changes our taste for anything ancient. So men grew tired of acorns, so were deserted those old beds strewn with herbage and leaves piled up . . . Therefore mankind labours always in vain and to no purpose, consuming its days in empty cares, plainly because it does not know the limit of possession, and how far it is ever possible for real pleasure to grow; and this little by little has carried life out into the deep sea, and has stirred up from the bottom the great billows of war. (v. 1412–35. 1937 Loeb edn, p. 489)

For Lucretius, the source of evil was not so much progress as such, as the intentions of men who allow themselves to be overridden by insatiable desires which they have the capacity and the duty to hold in check. Even though Rousseau, like Epicurus and the Stoics, linked needs and the expansion of knowledge as mutually determining facts, he, like them, was unwilling to argue that needs were therefore socially *determined*, their ineluctable expansion something over which we have no control or for which we bear no responsibility. A number of recent authors have argued that Rousseau sees in society the source of evil, shifting the theodicy problem from man, and his individual fall from grace, to society and its peculiar propensity to develop in him false needs (cf. Colletti, 1972, pp. 144–5).

But Rousseau subscribes to certain Stoic axioms that make such a simple position impossible for him. As Epictetus claimed, it is not things themselves that disturb men, but their judgements about them (*Encheiridion*, 1928 Loeb edn, Vol. 2, p. 487), and Rousseau, too, upheld the role of the faculty of judgement, admitting the intervention of the human will between sensation and desire. In *Emile* we have a number of reflections on the subject, some with explicit reference to the Epicurean view of sensation, where he insists that the sensationalist psychology of the Epicureans, which sees judgement itself as a species of sensation and that our judgements are therefore naturally determined, is false. In the *Discourse on Inequality* Rousseau argues quite specifically against deterministic theories of human motivation. What distinguishes men from animals is not intelligence as such, he insists, but 'the . . . quality of free agency':

> Nature lays her commands on every animal, and the brute obeys her voice. Man receives the same impulsion, but at the same time knows himself at liberty to acquiesce or resist: and it is particularly in his consciousness of this liberty that the spirituality of his soul is displayed. For physics may explain in some measure, the mechanism of the senses and the formation of ideas; but in the power of willing or rather of choosing, and in the feeling of this power, nothing is to be found but acts which are purely spiritual and wholly inexplicable by the laws of mechanism. (1913 Everyman edn, p. 170)

Rousseau, interestingly, links the capability of free agency to the ability of man to vary the form that his needs take. He sees 'nothing in any animal but an ingenious machine, to which nature hath given senses to wind itself up' – language which bears a striking similarity to Locke's account of the human instincts. The difference between the animal who 'chooses and refuses by instinct' and man, who chooses 'from an act of free will', is that 'the brute cannot deviate from the rule prescribed to it, even when it would be advantageous for it to do so; and, on the contrary, man frequently deviates from such rules to his own prejudice' (p. 169). Rousseau gives his famous, and inaccurate, example of the pigeon who would 'starve to death by the side of a dish of the choicest meats, and a cat on a heap of fruit or grain; though it is certain that either might find nourishment in the foods which it thus rejects with disdain, did it think of trying them' (pp. 169–70). Man, by contrast, is able not only to vary the form that his basic physiological needs takes, but invents fictitious needs to take over where these leave off: 'Hence, it is that dissolute men run into excesses which bring on fevers and death because the mind depraves the senses and the will continues to speak when nature is silent' (p. 170).

But whatever Rousseau has to say about the natural needs of primitive man cannot lead us to associate innocence with virtue. Man's nature is such that once his cognitive and moral faculties have been developed (which already involves a departure from the natural state), all needs and desires involve a degree of assent, an element of judgement. Morality depends not on nature but on how we bring our will into accordance with its principles. The 'life according to nature' in this sense is far from being the life of the primitive in which, as for the brute, instinct rules. Rousseau, like the Stoics, defined freedom as the ability to adopt a rule of behaviour and follow it: the ability to subjugate superfluous desires. This is a moral act that can only be undertaken by man already aware of choice and the range of options of which primitive man is innocent. Virtue is not a product of nature but of moral capability. No one expressed this better than Seneca in the closing lines of his 'Ninetieth letter'. Speaking of the primitive man he declares:

> But however wonderful and guileless the life they led, they were not wise men; this is a title that has come to be reserved for the highest of all achievements . . . though they all possessed a character more robust than that of today, and one with a greater aptitude for hard work, it is equally true that their personalities fell short of genuine perfection. For nature does not give a man virtue: the process of becoming a good man is an art . . . the fact remains that their innocence was due to ignorance and nothing else. And there is a world of difference between, on the one hand, choosing not to do what is wrong and, on the other, not knowing how to do it in the first place. They lacked the cardinal virtues of justice, moral insight, self-control and courage. There were corresponding qualities in each case not unlike these, that had a place in their primitive lives; but virtue only comes to a character which has been thoroughly schooled and trained and brought to a pitch of perfection by unremitting practice. We are born for it, but not with it. And even in the best of people, until you cultivate it there is only the material for virtue, not virtue itself. (*Letters from a Stoic,* 1969 edn, pp. 176–7)

Rousseau's thesis in the first and second 'Discourses' that evil is a social phenomenon related directly to the emergence of artificial needs which accompanies the expansion of inquiry, technological innovation and economic development belongs to a genre of writings that we have argued was well established by the time he wrote. This genre, the critique of civilisation, may claim such works as Lucretius's *De Rerum Natura*, Seneca's 'Ninetieth letter on progress', Diderot's *Supplement to Bougainville's Voyage* and various Cynic and Stoic writings that are less famous. There is in these works a primitivist tendency, the propensity to judge the evils of civilisation by comparing the life of advanced society with that of the simple life, which dates back as far as Plato's *Republic* and his nostalgic portrayal of the 'genuine and healthy society' (372e, 1974 edn, p. 122) where men limit their desires to the real 'necessaries' of life (373a, ibid., p. 123). (As Lovejoy points out, commentators frequently lose sight of the fact that Socrates does not appear to agree with Glaucon that such a city is suitable only for pigs; possibly he still considers it to have been the most enviable society; and certainly he turns to examine a 'luxurious' city rather than a healthy one on the grounds that 'by considering that sort of city we may the more easily see how both justice and injustice grow up in cities' (372c–73).[11]

The appeal of the life 'according to nature', as we have tried to show in the case of Rousseau, has two senses which are often confused: it may be an appeal to nature in the descriptive sense, that is to say nature before man's influence through society was brought to bear on it, which is associated with the earliest chronological period of man's development. Or it may be an appeal to nature in the normative sense, that is to say to the principles of nature, or the laws constitutive of man's nature and the physical universe at large. These principles as uniform and universal tendencies operate in all historical epochs and are always accessible to man through reason, and so an appeal to the life according to nature in this sense is not necessarily associated with the 'state of nature' or primitivism at all. Rousseau, like the Stoics, tended to vacillate between these two meanings, the reason being that although capable of distinguishing between them, they were nevertheless disposed to think that the simple life of primitive man did accord better with the correct ordering of nature than the life of advanced civilisation.

Even though the primitivist tendency is strong in these writings it did not entail naturalism. Both Rousseau and the Stoics were doubtful whether the life of the primitive man, the man who knew nothing but his natural needs, was in itself virtuous, because virtue involves moral choice and innocence is a natural goodness that knows no choice, assuming as it does ignorance of evil. Their position is therefore considerably more sophisticated than at first appears: not only is it not the life of natural man as such to which they appeal as the most perfect form of existence. Nor do they recommend man in advanced society to return to that form of existence. Rather, what they are advocating is that civilised man should re-establish the harmony and tranquillity that primitive man enjoyed naturally, by consciously ordering his life according to the principles constitutive of human nature through exercise of his reason and will. This is a moral project and not the restitution of some primitive state and, as a consequence, even the 'natural' needs of man can no longer be seen simply as those basic needs for survival found in primitive man. Thus Rousseau made it clear that to want to abandon advanced society and return to the primitive state is a conclusion that only his detractors would wish to draw from what he has said (second 'Discourse', note 9). Not only is it not feasible to put back the clock, as Seneca and most other critics of civilisation realised, but it would achieve nothing. The problem of evil was the responsibility of the individual and his moral choice. Although having historical origins these were not problems susceptible to an historical solution.

Notes

1   Quoted by Crocker (1959), p. 289. I am indebted to Crocker for his account of reason and the passions in his two-volume history of ethical thought in the French Enlightenment. See also, Lovejoy, *Reflections on Human Nature* (1961), and Hirschman, *The Passions and the Interests* (1976). Horne in his study *The Social Thought of Bernard Mandeville* (1978) gives a useful survey of Jansenist moral philosophy, moral sense theories and mercantilism as they relate to Mandeville and his views on the expansion of needs, virtue and commerce.
2   Quoted by Crocker (1959), p. 294.

3 Quoted by Crocker (1959), p. 297.
4 'Discours sur l'origine et les fondements de l'inégalite', *OC*, Vol. 3, pp. 154–5. All references to the *Oeuvres complètes* (*OC*) are to the Gallimard, Bibliothèque de la Pléiade edn cited in the bibliography.
5 Translation from the Everyman edn (1911), pp. 174–5, with some changes.
6 This is the significance of the rather misleading title to Lovejoy's article, 'The supposed primitivism of Rousseau's *Discourse on Inequality*' (1948).
7 Bibliothèque de l'Assemblée Nationale, Paris, Ms. 1428.
8 Pierre Burgelin in his annotations to the 1969 Gallimard Bibliothèque de la Pléiade edn of *Emile* argues (p. 1,522) that in this passage cited Rousseau is following Locke's *Essay Concerning Human Understanding* (II. i. 4), specifically.
9 Annotation by Pierre Burgelin. See also Cassirer (1963 and 1970).
10 Translations of the first and second 'Discourses', except where noted are taken from the 1913 Everyman edn of *The Social Contract and Discourses*, cited in the bibliography.
11 Cited by Lovejoy and Boas (1935), p. 155. In *The Laws* (III. 676–9. 1970 Penguin edn, pp. 118–23) Plato also argues that in order to investigate society's 'moral progress or decline' (676, p. 118) one should undertake a reconstruction of primitive society, which was, on his account, free of the guile and sophistication of the 'modern' state (677, p. 119). It was under the pressure of population, Plato argues, that men departed from an agricultural subsistence economy, in which their basic needs were met, and by means of technological and organisational development, in which metallurgy played an important role (678, p. 121), created the superstructure of the state and the resources for competition, envy, violence and crime (679, p. 122). Plato, interestingly enough, maintains, like Seneca and Rousseau after him, that this primitive society, conspicuous for its lack of vice, was nevertheless a state in which true virtue was also absent (678, p. 121): men in this society 'were *good* . . . partly because of what we might call their naïveté' (679, p. 122).

4

The Early Socialists on Needs and Society

Although the Stoic and Epicurean doctrine of the life according to nature and the ideal of the man of few needs were enormously influential in the period of the European Enlightenment, it is true to say that these philosophers were not read by Enlightenment and early socialist thinkers as moral philosophers so much as exponents of materialism. Marx, in a very interesting short history of the origins of socialism in *The Holy Family* (*CW*, Vol. 4, pp. 124–34), argues that socialism was born of a peculiar marriage of French and English materialism and that 'French and English materialism was always closely related to *Democritus* and *Epicurus*' (p. 126). But, as we shall try to show, eighteenth-century materialism was a theory of the power of the object in a way that Hellenistic philosophy was not. Eighteenth-century materialism was deterministic while Stoic and Epicurean materialism, although postulating universal laws of nature and the operation of atoms as con- stitutive of the physical world, nevertheless held that the correct ordering of the human and moral realms depended on reason and the will to bring human nature into accordance with nature's laws. The positions could hardly have been further apart, in fact.

Socialism, with all its apparent Stoic similarities: the ideals of liberty, equality and fraternity, common ownership of goods, the ideal of the man of few needs, and so on, was the natural offspring of materialism, as Marx himself saw. And the achievement of eighteenth-century materialism was to discredit metaphysical explanations of human nature in favour of scientific ones. In its development, refutation of meta- physics was not enought:

> . . . a *positive, anti-metaphysical* system was required . . . *Locke*'s treatise *An Essay Concerning Humane Understanding* came from across the Channel as if in answer to a call . . . Hobbes had systematised Bacon without, however, furnishing a proof for Bacon's fundamental principle, the origin of all human knowledge and ideas from the world of sensation. It was *Locke* who, in his *Essay on the Humane Understanding*, supplied this proof. (*CW*, Vol. 4, pp. 127–9)

It was not Bacon, as we know, but the Epicureans who had pioneered the theory of sensationalist psychology, to which Locke was a direct heir, whether knowingly or not. The peculiarity of this doctrine is the distinction it draws between sensation and judgement. Generally, the argument goes, we are attracted to objects which are pleasurable, repelled by objects that are painful, and we select among options on this basis in a more or less automatic fashion. However, both the Epicureans and Locke argued that although human behaviour can, for the most part, be explained deterministically in this way, it is not always the case. The Epicureans, in the notion of the atomic swerve, allowed for the intervention of human judgement and, for Locke too, judgement was an intervening faculty that allowed men to insert the operation of the will between the stimulus of sensation and the normal automatic response. Through deliberation the individual was able to bring reflection to bear on conduct, and judgement represented choice and not the determining mechanism of the instincts. Locke was unwilling to admit that this constituted free will, as such, because, he argued, the will was then determined by deliberation itself. This involved a confusion of reasons with causes which has been the subject of much twentieth-century controversy. Basically, Locke misunderstood what 'free will' was usually considered to mean. Since this amounted to the distinction between behaviour for which one has reasons, arrived at by deliberation, in contrast to behaviour which is unreflected and habitual, simply a stock response to a certain kind of stimulus, Locke's concept of deliberation and judgement corresponded in all important respects with the usual theory of free will. Most of us would agree that for much of the time our behaviour is unreflected, habitual, routine and a stock response to situations, while admitting that we are in principle capable of changing the course of our behaviour at any juncture by bringing deliberation to bear. This was Locke's point.

But it is not his concept of judgement for which either Locke or Epicurus is famous in the Enlightenment and early socialist period. Even Rousseau associated Epicurean sensationalist psychology, like that of Locke, with the principle of determinism, accusing them of failing to distinguish between sensation and judgement, as we have seen. While Locke and the Epicureans, unlike the Stoics, were not prepared to argue that all sensations involve a degree of assent, they nevertheless reserve the possibility that judgement may be brought to bear on sensation to alter the response. This Rousseau overlooks in their theories in the same way that Enlightenment and early socialist thinkers generally overlooked this element in Locke.

Who, after all, were Locke's most famous successors if not Condillac, who in his *Traité des sensations* (1749) simply sees the mind as a sorting machine for sensations which operate according to the principles of pleasure and pain; and the man-machine theorists, Helvétius, d'Holbach, d'Alembert and La Mettrie, who see the mind as nothing but the black box which converts stimulus to response in a predetermined fashion? Marx traced just such a line of descent in his brief history, distinguishing two trends in Enlightenment materialism, the first pointing towards a mechanical natural science, the second towards a new theory of society. He noted the contributions to the former of Gassendi, the reviver of Epicurean atomism, Le Roy and Cabanis, whose physiological theories later influenced Saint-Simon; and the influence of Locke, Condillac, Helvétius, La Mettrie, d'Holbach, on the latter, singling out the development of the environmental argument on the basis of sensationalist psychology as being of special importance. Belief in the natural equality of man, his innate goodness, his disposition to self-love and enjoyment through the senses, the 'omnipotence of experience, habit and education, and the influence of the environment on man', all pointed to socialism as a natural conclusion (*CW*, Vol. 4, p. 130).

Although the term 'socialism' was not coined until the 1830s, we can see immediately its etymological significance in the implication that evil is socially created rather than natural and that society is the unique mechanism for the realisation of human powers. Marx quotes from the radical Enlightenment materialists, conclusions that already pointed in this direction. According to Helvétius

> 'Man is not wicked but he is subordinate to his interests. One must not therefore complain of the wickedness of man but of the ignorance of the legislators, who have always placed the particular interest in opposition to the general interest . . . Human beings are born neither good nor bad but ready to become one or the other according as a common interest unites or divides them . . .'

D'Holbach declared in the same vein: 'True morality, and true politics as well, is that which seeks to bring men nearer to one another to make them work by united efforts for their common happiness. Any morality which separates *our interests from those of our associates*, is false, senseless, unnatural'.[2]

Marx shows, with extensive quotations (*CW*, Vol. 4, pp. 132–3), how, in the propositions of the old French materialists, d'Holbach, Helvétius, and so on, the connection between materialism and socialism is already made. 'The apologia of vices by *Mandeville*, one of Locke's early English-speaking followers, is typical of the socialist tendencies of materialism', Marx points out (p. 131), and then, tracing other links between materialism and the theory of environmental conditioning, he goes on to say:

> *Fourier* proceeds directly from the teaching of the French materialists. The *Babouvists* were crude, uncivilised materialists, but developed communism too, derives *directly* from *French materialism*. The latter returned to its mother-country, *England*, in the form *Helvétius* gave it. *Bentham* based his system of *correctly understood interest* on *Helvétius'* morality, and *Owen* proceeded from *Bentham's* system to found English communism. (*CW*, Vol. 4, p. 131)

In these theories of communism which Marx outlines, the theory of environmental conditioning is central:

> There is no need for any great penetration to see from the teaching of materialism on the original goodness and equal intellectual endow-

ment of men, the omnipotence of experience, habit and education, the influence of environment on man, the great significance of industry, the justification of enjoyment, etc., how necessarily materialism is connected with communism and socialism. If man draws all his knowledge, sensation, etc., from the world of the senses and the experience gained in it, then what has to be done is to arrange the empirical world in such a way that man experiences and becomes accustomed to what is truly human in it and that he becomes aware of himself as man. If correctly understood interest is the principle of all morality, man's private interest must be made to coincide with the interest of humanity. If man is unfree in the materialistic sense, i.e., is free not through the negative power to assert his true individuality, crime must not be punished in the individual, but the anti-social sources of crime must be destroyed, and each man must be given social scope for the vital manifestation of his being. If man is shaped by environment, his environment must be made human. If man is social by nature, he will develop his true nature only in society, and the power of his nature must be measured not by the power of the separate individual but by the power of society. (pp. 130–1)

A conclusion that Marx claims the Babouvists, Owen, Cabet, Fourier, Dézamy and Gay all drew.

His claim can be readily vindicated. The pre-socialist socialists, Morelly, Mably, Meslier, drew such conclusions from the same premises. Evil was the artificial product of civilisation, that is to say of society falsely constituted. Once human psychology was plumbed and the orientation of behaviour to fulfil interests formed on the basis of sense experience was understood, education and socialisation would eliminate tension between the public and the private good. In one of the most early and remarkable statements of this position, Morelly's *Basiliade* of 1753, we already see the socialist extension of these ideas in the imputation that a spontaneous identification of the individual with society through a united will guarantees the elimination of social evils such as poverty, promising the satisfaction of all those needs which have hitherto been frustrated by false ideas and 'foolish prejudice'.

> And thou, Humanity, be now free and rest at ease. Be for the future one united body, closely joined together by perfect unanimity. Let all varieties of desire, sentiment, and inclination be concentred on one united will, which shall direct the efforts of all mankind towards one single end, the common welfare. As light sheds its rays equally upon all, so let happiness be equably diffused over all . . . Let myriads of active hands heap up in thy common treasure-house the fruits of abundance and the uncounted products of universal industry, adding, without ceasing, more than ever the needs of nature shall be able to exhaust. Then, oh Humanity! thou shalt no more be subject to uncertainty, made uneasy by unwise thoughts nor beset by a multitude of foolish prejudices, no longer restrained tyrannically from revolting contrareities . . . Henceforth let there be mutual love and support as among sons of the same common father.[3]

The origins of the belief of the identity of the individual and society through the uncorrupted will are Stoic. It was Seneca who declared: 'He who would do nothing but what he ought may safely be allowed to do what he wills.'[4] The development of the concept in the unity of civil society and the state under socialism arose from the addition of Epicurean utilitarian principles elaborated on the basis of Enlightenment sensationalist psychology. Out of the old elements something peculiarly new was created: the theory that individual and social needs can only be met by a transformation of the social environment to produce a state of natural harmony in which institutions to differentiate social groups and to mediate between individuals and the totality will be superfluous. The possibility that individuals would baulk at such an identification of their interest with the needs of the group was ruled out by the theory of environmental conditioning. Education would eliminate unruly elements, and where it did not these humanists had no hesitation in prescribing severe punishments as a deterrent. 'Penal laws are motives that experience shows us to be capable of containing or annihilating impulses that passions give to men's will', d'Holbach claimed. The legislator, in 'decreeing gallows, tortures, various punishments for crimes . . . does nothing different from the person who, in building a house, places gutters to prevent the rain water from eating away the foundations of his dwelling'.[5]

The radicalising influence of Lockean sensationalist psychology when brought to bear on old Epicurean and Stoic ideas can be easily seen if one reflects for a moment on the ramifications of the environmentalist argument. The principle of equality is arrived at through the refutation of the doctrine of innate ideas. If heredity does not stigmatise some from birth, then all men are indeed equal. Since ideas are formed from experience, men's experience has only to be so arranged that their ideas are correct. The Epicurean and Stoic belief in nature as norm and that men are naturally inclined to seek happiness through pleasure, provided justification for the utopians in their attempt to bring society to a condition of natural unity. Lockean theses that man is a compound and malleable being, equipped at birth with a capacity for feeling which is independent of the will, that feelings and convictions are a product of experience and that the will is a synthesis of these which provides the motive and stimulus to action; and that pleasure and pain are the levers of power for the social reformer, were reiterated by Robert Owen, William Godwin and many others. It was typical of utopian socialists to elevate feeling and denigrate the will since they appealed to a natural and not a conventional social harmony.

Owen's *The Book of the New Moral World* of 1836 is entirely devoted to the systematic elaboration of these principles of sensational psychology. He advances as 'the *Great Truth*' of the 'new Moral Science of man', the knowledge 'that all physical and mental feelings are instincts of human nature, and that these instincts create the will', claiming that 'the Cause of past evils . . . the Source of disunion, of crime, and their Consequent misery' was 'the mistaken notion that instincts were free-will, while all facts prove that the will of man is the necessary result of those instincts' (Owen, 1836, pp. 95–6). This error, perpetrated by religion, was similar in magnitude to the universal error of the physical sciences that the earth was flat and that the sun revolved around the earth. Owen works through the typical arguments: that the individual is as equally receptive to false notions as true ideas; that false ideas produce irrational behaviour, true rational; that good character is formed by the conjunction of favourable circumstances, producing 'superior sensations', and a good physical and moral constitution. His ultimate claims for the 'harmony, unity and efficiency' of this new moral science, involve a leap from the premise of instinctual behaviour to socialist conclusions about natural unity, the elimination of competition and the satisfaction of all needs:

> It is the general knowledge of this invaluable Truth [the instinctual basis of behaviour], that is alone wanting to complete the great change in humanity, from irrationality, pain and misery, to the most delightful state of existence. For men of experience know, that all the materials to over-supply the inhabitants of the world now and for ever, with all that is necessary for their happiness, superabound, and that there is also far more power in the labour and skill of man, were they wisely directed, than is necessary to work up these materials into the most valuable products, and that all contests for their use and enjoyment will be unnecessary. (p. 96)

Without, it seems, any awareness of the dangers of such a position, Owen had already, in the earlier *New View of Society*, advanced the broad general principles that 'any general character from the best to the worst, from the most ignorant to the most enlightened, may be given to any community, even to the world at large, by the application of the proper means; which means are to a great extent at the command and under the control of those who have influence in the affairs of men' (Owen, 1970, edn, p. 101). He outlined here the principles of sensationalist psychology and utilitarianism that he was later to elaborate at length.

The environmental argument ran into a trap that naturalism in any form cannot easily avoid. And that is an inability to distinguish between good and evil and therefore to justify its own position. If all behaviour is the product of external conditioning, then, in the absence of a will free to implement it, it makes no sense to set up a code of correct conduct. Good and bad behaviour presuppose the moral autonomy of the individual. As Marx pointed out in the *Theses on Feuerbach*, the problem with theories of environmental conditioning − and specifically Owen's − is that they overlook the fact that the educator must himself be educated, if any good is to come of them. But how can he be if he is also subject to the conditions which the theory describes? Not only does the argument lead to an infinite regress, since educating the educator simply pushes the problem back another step, but the notion of education is itself entirely inappropriate in a theory in which the natural is the good.

It is precisely in the context of theories of environmental conditioning that the doctrine of true and false needs, this time as a scientific and not a moral theory, comes to have such an important role in early socialist theory. 'Correctly understood interest' as 'the principle of all morality' under the materialists, gave way to 'needs' as the basis of the socialist critique. The concept of 'interest' added little, after all, to the principle that all behaviour is motivated by the pursuit of pleasure and the avoidance of pain; but the concept of 'needs' provided a criterion in terms of which interests could be evaluated. Almost all the socialists that one can think of began from the assumption that men have certain natural needs which can be distinguished from the artificial needs of man in modern society, but also that these natural needs made a collective life necessary. Not only were false needs seen to be inextricably bound up with technological innovation and progress that had got out of control, but they perpetuated the evils of a society falsely constituted. As such they were seen as a good point at which to begin social reform. This would involve nothing less than the elimination of artificial needs and restitution of the common life that had been lost. Thus Babeuf, quoting Morelly's *Code de la Nature*, declared: '"Nature" has impressed upon men, by means of their common human needs and human feelings, their equality in fact and in right, the necessity for a collective life' (Babeuf, ed. Scott, 1967, p. 72). As long as men restrict their desires to those needs that they have in common, he argued, equality will prevail − tautological, but undoubtedly true! It is by virtue of 'the insane value distinctions between one of its members and another' that society makes, that 'the human species alone has been obliged to experience misery and want. There is no need for men to lack those things which Nature has provided for all . . .' (p. 56).

Out of the elements we have so far elaborated: the primitivism of antiquity and its emphasis on nature as norm; Enlightenment environ-mentalist arguments; and the writings of Rousseau, Morelly and Mably, who were important transmitters of these ideas, the early socialists developed their doctrine of needs. It is no exaggeration to attribute the genesis of their theories explicitly to these sources. Under constant pressure, as they were, to defend their attack on property and established institutions, they made their case by appealing to the authority of their predecessors. Gracchus Babeuf, on trial for his life for the part he played in the Conspiracy of Equals, in his defence before the high court of Vendôme of 1797, made a classic statement of the socialist case, citing Rousseau, Morelly (Diderot as he thought), Mably and Helvétius as his authorities, along with Lycurgus, the Gracchi and others, often quoting long passages from their works.

His line of argument, quite typical of later utopian socialists, begins (p. 67) with the claim that: '"Nature decrees equality"' (Mably); that in the state of nature goods are held in common, the fruits of the earth belong equally to all, and that all natural needs and their means of satisfaction are in equilibrium. The institution of property was a piece of trickery, and the principles which proceed from it − the law of inheritance, the law of alienability, along with 'the difference in value and in price that arbitrary opinion attaches to the diverse products of toil and manufacture' are the precise sources of inequality and human misery. Citizens lack for the satisfaction of their basic needs because their 'natural rights' to the earth and its fruits are legally usurped − Babeuf long preceded Proudhon in his claim that 'all property is theft' (pp. 52−4). The arbitrary values which society assigns to various social products exacerbate inequalities, he maintained.

This very argument for an equality of basic needs is echoed constantly in socialist thought and frequently in almost the same words. It is, of course, a very old theme and one of the earliest examples is to be found in 'A debate on the simple life', between Lycinus and a Cynic, for a long time attributed to Lucian, but now said to be written later by a Cynic of Byzantium.[6] Although certainly not a socialist treatise this work is classic on the theory of true and false needs. The Cynic wants to establish that man's basic needs are equal and few, that there is a 'sufficiency' where these basic needs have been satisfied, and that God, 'the generous host', by spreading before man a feast, challenges him to exercise his self-control 'since [man] has after all only one stomach and needs but little to nourish him, it is quite certain that he will come to grief from partaking so liberally' (Lovejoy and Boas (1935), p. 142). The Cynic then recounts the ineluctable progression of wants of the 'greedy and insatiable guest' who 'helps himself to everything':

> Not content with what is near at hand, you reach out everywhere; your own soil and seas are quite insufficient; you purchase your pleasures from the ends of the earth, always preferring the imported to the domestic article, the dear to the cheap, things that are hard to come by to those that can be had without trouble; in fact you prefer to have troubles and annoyances rather than to live without them. For all that costly array of means of enjoyment which you so gloat over is obtained only at the price of labor of the body and vexation of the mind. Consider, of you please, the gold that is so sought after, the silver, the luxurious houses, the elaborate clothing – and remember through how much toil and trouble and danger these have been acquired – yes, and through how many men's blood and death and ruin. To bring these things to you many seamen must perish; to find and fashion them, many laborers must endure misery. Nor is that all: conflicts often arise because of them, and the desire for them sets friend against friend, children against parents, wives against husbands . . . And all this goes on in spite of the fact that embroidered clothes are no warmer than others, houses with gilded roofs keep out the rain no better; a drink out of a silver cup – or a gold one, for that matter – is no more refreshing, and sleep is no sweeter on an ivory bed – the reverse, in fact, is true; your 'happy' man, between the delicate sheets on an ivory bed, is often unable to sleep. As for all the trouble that is devoted to the preparation of fancy dishes, it is needless to say that it contributes nothing to our nourishment; on the contrary, such dishes injure the body and breed diseases in it. No need, either, to mention all the things that men do and suffer for the sake of sexual gratification – though the desire is easy enough to satisfy, if one is not too fastidious about it. But it is not only in this that men show their madness and corruption; nowadays they pervert everything from its natural use . . . (pp. 142–3)

This strain of primitivism is also to be found in the writings of the medieval scholastics (see Boas, 1948; Schumpeter, 1954, ch. 2, pp. 73–142) who appeal against the use of 'gifts of God in ways contrary to nature' just like this Cynic (Lovejoy and Boas, 1935, p. 143); and in countless examples of utopian writings where the same distinction between true and false needs is drawn.

Babeuf is the one who is given credit for having coined the slogan 'to each according to his needs' that was taken up later by Louis Blanc, Etienne Cabet, Marx, and others. What this slogan meant was that the rewards of labour, that is to say wages or profits, should be redistributed on the basis of those common needs of men given by nature. Rousseau in the *Discourse on Political Economy* had pointed to the objection that since society had already created distinctions between men, and since the privileged had got used to their expanded needs, there were good grounds for saying that these were real needs in every sense. Nonsense, he retorts, can one seriously argue that a grandee has greater needs than an ordinary man? No, a grandee has two legs and a stomach just like a cowherd (1913 Everyman edn, p. 262). Rousseau, in the third book of *Emile*, also claims that 'since man is the same in every station, the rich man's stomach is no bigger than the poor man's . . . and indeed the natural needs are the same for all . . . the means of satisfying them should be equally within reach of all' (*Emile, OC*, Vol. 4, p. 468).

Babeuf, who probably took the idea from Rousseau, Marx and countless others, echoes these words. No social distinctions, no greater intellectual capacity, or even skill warrant the greater regard of some over others because social distinctions 'do not expand the capacity of the stomach', Babeuf argued, so 'no wage can be defended over and above what is necessary for the satisfaction of a person's needs' (1967, p. 55). 'Difference of *brain* and of intellectual ability do not imply any differences whatsoever in the nature of the *stomach* and of physical *needs*', declared Marx, 'therefore the false tenet based on existing circumstances, "to each according to his abilities", must be changed . . . into the tenet, "*to each according to his need*"' (*CW*, Vol. 5, p. 537). Marx went on to argue that, 'One of the most vital principles of communism, a principle which distinguishes it from all reactionary socialism, is its empirical view, based on a knowledge of man's nature that . . . a *different form* of activity, of labour, does not justify *inequality*, confers no privileges in respect of possession and enjoyment' (p. 537). This claim to 'empirical' knowledge of human nature has come to be the classic justification of need theory. We see it even in the recent assertions of Alasdair MacIntyre, Charles Taylor and the descriptivists, for whom human nature is a substantive concept about which quasi-factual statements can be made.

Babeuf, like Rousseau, Helvétius and proponents of the environmental argument since Locke, believed that men are born equal but made unequal by education and socialisation, arguing that the malleability of man's nature gives ground for hope that inequality and evil may be totally eradicated, if only social conditions are sufficiently altered:

> Society must be made to operate in such a way that it eradicates once and for all the desire of a man to become richer, or wiser, or more powerful than others. Putting this more exactly, we must try *to bring our fate under control*, try to make the lot of every member of society independent of accidental circumstances, happy or unhappy.

> We must try to guarantee to each man and his posterity, however
> numerous, a sufficiency of the means of existence and nothing more.
> We must try and close all possible avenues by which man may
> acquire more than his fair share of the fruits of toil and the gifts of
> nature. The only way to do this is to organize a communal regime
> which will suppress private property, set each to work at the skill or
> job he understands, require each to deposit the fruits of his labour in
> kind at the common store, and establish an agency for the
> distribution of basic necessities. (Babeuf, 1967, p. 57)

Morelly, whom Babeuf quotes with approval, was also convinced that
justice was simply an administrative problem. Greed, the mother of all
vices was responsible for the establishment of private property, he
argued, the abolition of which, if accompanied by the appropriate social
planning, would eliminate all obstacles to equality. The articles of
Morelly's Code include: (1) the right to appropriate only in accordance
with need, (2) turning 'every citizen into a public servant employed at
public expense', (3) having every citizen contribute to the state 'in
accordance with his strength, ability and age' (Babeuf, 1967, p. 78, citing
the Code). '"The practical difficulties", he assures us "involved in
putting into effect the laws on the allocation of jobs, public services, and
the fair and orderly distribution of goods, are very minor"' (p. 76).

It is not difficult to demonstrate the degree to which sensationalist
psychology, belief in environmental conditioning, needs as an objective
criterion and the socialist critique of society hung together. Morelly, for
instance, in the *Code de la Nature*, gives an account of human nature
which reads like a compendium of Lockean psychology, emphasising, as
it does, the absence of innate ideas; the formation of ideas through the
excitation of the senses by basic needs; the necessity of a balance of needs
and powers such that the former slightly exceed the latter to prevent man
from falling into a state of indifference; the natural inclination to self-
preservation; the frustration of this natural drive by 'artificial
institutions'; the weakness and sensibility of man as the source of his
sociability and need for solidarity (Lichtenberger [1895] 1967, pp.
114–15).

Those among the early socialists who used the distinction between true
and false needs unquestioningly, did so because a natural-law tradition
which dated back to the Stoics, taken in conjunction with the premises of
sensationalist psychology, had them convinced that men's needs and
powers were in principle equal. Babeuf, too, had insisted, 'everything is
superfluous above and beyond the sheerest of physical necessities. Everything beyond this is a source of evil' (1967, pp. 62–3), which led him, on
Rousseau's good authority, to condemnation of science and the arts.
Weitling was another, making the bold claim: 'If one wishes to attain a
state of general felicity, one must wish each to possess and enjoy all that
he needs and nothing more'; it turns out that all that he *really* needs are
clothes, food, lodgings.[7] Weitling castigates the *'ordre bourgeois,
artificiel et imposteur'* of the exploiters who use the physical and mental
energy of the workers, while depriving them of the necessities for
existence (Bravo, 1970, Vol. 2, p. 75). He refers to market conditions
which drive wages down to the minimum for subsistence; the disadvan-

tage of the worker who as a purchaser can only buy in small quantities from small outlets (p. 76). He attacks mechanisation which causes workers to be made redundant, while at the same time 'the needs of each grow in number and volume to a considerable extent' (p. 77).

Certain as they were that true needs were the basic needs for subsistence common to all, the early socialists attributed to false needs all the evils of modern society. For instance, the Babouvist Jean-Jacques Pillot in his tract of 1840, *Ni chateaux ni chaumières* (Neither chateaux nor thatched huts), talks of the 'vices and artificial needs . . . bizarre fantasies . . . extravagant desires . . . [and] depraved tastes' of the rich which are what condemn the poor to their hovels (Bravo, 1970, Vol. 2, p. 246). Most of the early socialists assume on good Stoic principles that if men confined their needs to those common needs endowed by nature there would be more than enough for all.

Some, it is true, saw it as being perhaps a bit more complicated than this, and that strict equality might become unpalatable. Weitling himself had reservations; as he graphically put it: 'A uniform and severely measured equality would be like a dish without salt, to which the stranger, famished and exhausted by the journey, eagerly extended his hand only to find it more and more unpalatable and finally disgusting' (Bravo, 1970, Vol. 2, p. 96). The growth of needs is in itself natural, he says, 'each has his desires and longings . . . and these appetites are growing constantly, thanks to the indefatigable activity of the mind . . . This is why the principle of social equality ought to be intimately mingled with that of individual liberty' (p. 97). He admits that under this principle 'the numerous needs of which we already have knowledge would find themselves augmented still further', but concludes that 'this growth would not be harmful to society and would only be a burden to those who would wish to have superfluous goods'. After all, why allow the just regime of socialism to be destroyed just because 'one man suddenly does not wish to work this or that day. Another likes the clothes furnished by the administration but not the furniture. Another has a desire to eat something that is not on the collective list . . .'? (p. 97).

Although Weitling and some others expressed an unease at the assurance of some socialists that true needs could so easily be catalogued and enforced, their reservations were expressed against a background of general unanimity that the discovery of true needs was a scientific question fundamental to the rational ordering of society. For instance, Morelly, an early advocate of the scientific approach, had claimed on the distribution of goods: 'All this adds up to is a simple question of listing *things* and *people*; a matter therefore of simple mathematical calculation, it admits of easy solution. Social planners, both ancient and modern, have conceived and carried into effect projects of incomparably greater difficulty . . .' (cited by Babeuf, 1967, p. 76).

Of course, if the problem of justice were simply a question of arithmetical equality it would not be a philosophical problem, as Aristotle and others have seen. In the same way, to assume that the problem of needs is just a question of deciding what common requisites for survival people in a given society share is to assume that this is not a philosophical problem either. Although some were worried that false needs and capricious desires might survive into the new socialist regime and provide an unsettling influence, even the most benevolent of socialists were sufficiently convinced of their capability to distinguish genuine needs to be willing like Morelly to imprison 'as a mad dog and an enemy of mankind' anyone who would appropriate common goods beyond his needs (cited ibid., p. 78). How could this be so? In general the principle of equality was believed to dictate the nature of one's true needs, and once survival was taken care of an arithmetical division of what remained of the common product would ensure the satisfaction of any outstanding needs.

There were a few dissenters from the principle of strict equality. For instance, Weitling, to relieve possible boredom, provided for 'supplementary hours' in which the workers may earn non-essential goods. Besides the sciences, fairs and public amusements which the life of a simple community of goods would offer, provision was to be made for the gratification of those individual whims that it seems man cannot live without. Weitling's concessions express precisely the predicament of the socialists who tried to operate the principle of true and false needs. How was a state of human happiness compatible with the limitation of needs to those few necessary for subsistence? But once needs are expanded beyond this limit, where are objective criteria for the distinction between true and false needs to be found? In practice the distinction is arbitrary. Even socialists like Théodore Dézamy, a communist in the tradition of Enlightenment materialism, as Marx declared, who in the manner of Helvétius and d'Holbach took as his 'criterion' or 'rule of conduct . . . the science of the *human organism*, that is to say, the needs, the faculties and passions of man', nevertheless felt compelled to include among those needs on which human happiness and 'the free development of our being' depend, 'intellectual and moral' as well as physical and material needs (Bravo, 1970, Vol. 3, p. 155).

Jean-Jacques Pillot is another example of a socialist in the Babouvist and materialist tradition who, when it comes to a definition of true needs, also equivocates. Like so many of his forebears he refers to the creation of society as a transition from the state of nature undertaken expressly to guarantee men their 'true needs' on a reciprocal basis (ibid., Vol. 2, p. 247). But then he goes on to say that 'one has the right to satisfy one's true needs only when all possess the necessities of life', clearly indicating that 'true needs' are something over and above these basic physical needs. And he makes the classic equivocation: 'The useful and agreeable are distributed in the same proportions as the necessary; the superfluous is banished from every society founded on the basis of true equality' (p. 247).

He suggests that 'universal reason, composed of the greatest sum of individual reasons, emanating from healthy minds in full enjoyment of all their faculties', is capable of rising to meet any challenge such distinctions might occasion. 'Science is public opinion's sole guide and public opinion is sole sovereign', he proclaims (p. 247). It was precisely public opinion, and not any principle, which would settle the difference between the 'agreeable' and the 'superfluous' in the crucial distinction between true and false needs. With a confidence in the general will and the unanimity of the totality typical of most socialists since Rousseau, Pillot believed that in public opinion he had found a guardian of equality far more durable than any principle: 'Equality admits no dogma, mystical or religious, it neither promises nor does it accord any recompense other than what is in public estimation merited' (p. 248). Pillot advocated a law of equality '*réelle et positive*' and, as we have seen, decreed the distinction between true and false needs on no more substantial grounds than the general sanction of universal reason embodied in the general will.

Among the dissenters, Richard Lahautière argued against a *positive* law of strict equality in favour of the natural-law notion of an equality of rights:

> Man is born equal as man, not at all equal in strength and in needs, as Babeuf would ridiculously wish to say, but equal in rights. More precisely: all men have an equal right to live, to satisfy all the functions of the material and spiritual life and to satisfy all their needs. (ibid., Vol. 2, p. 167)

In his *Petit catéchisme de la réforme sociale*, of 1839, Lahautière asked, 'what are man's natural rights?' and catalogued them: the satisfaction of the necessities for existence, food, a roof, clothes, and so on (p. 170). He, too, believed that the fundamental article of the social contract was the assurance of these basic physical needs. He asked whether, once these natural needs have been taken care of, it would not be possible to distribute surplus goods according to some hierarchy, but then ruled out such a departure as destructive of the balance of equal rights and duties (p. 171). However, equality of rights under natural law did not mean a strict construction of equality; he insisted that it was a 'proportional' and not an 'absolute' equality of which he spoke: . . . the contribution of each ought to be measured according to his strength, and his share in the common fund pro-rated according to his needs' (p. 172). A principle rephrased in Marx's *Critique of the Gotha Programme*: 'From each according to his ability, to each according to his needs.'

Etienne Cabet, a major figure among the early socialists, subscribed also to the natural rights theory of equality. In the preface to his famous utopian novel *Voyage en Icarie* of 1842, he made the familiar socialist case:

> A society organized as a democracy on the basis of equality and fraternity must necessarily lead to the community of goods . . . [as a] general and mutual assurance against accidents and misfortunes, guaranteeing to each his nourishment, clothing, lodging, the ability to marry and raise a family on the only condition that he agree to reasonable work in return . . . Such a system is the only form of social organization which is able to realize Equality and Fraternity, prevent cupidity and ambition, suppress rivalries and hatred, destroy jealousies and antagonisms, render vice and crime almost impossible, assure peace and concord, and finally give happiness to a regenerated humanity. (ibid., Vol. 3, p. 75)

Cabet travels that well-worn socialist path from the community of goods to utopia, assuming man's basic rationality and benevolence, his willingness to merge his will spontaneously with that of the totality and to subordinate his needs to the interests of the group. He expects it to be possible to operate a system of distributive justice on the basis of natural law and the equality of rights. 'Have all people the same rights?', he asked:

> Yes because these rights pertain to the quality of being a man, and because all men are equally men. However, aren't men unequal in strength, for example? That is true, but strength is not a right . . . This equality, should it be perfect and *absolute* in such a way that each would have only the same quantity of food? No, equality is *relative to the needs of each individual*: he who has need of twice the amount of food to be satisfied has the right [to it]. (pp. 79–80)

This seems to suggest that no one can judge how much a man requires to satisfy his needs but himself. Under a system of equality proportional to need there would be no *objective* criteria to establish the limit to needs or, therefore, at what point they impinge on the interests of others. This is, of course, a major problem for those who try, in addition, to distinguish between true and false needs. Cabet does not in fact try to make this distinction and so does not involve himself in the contradiction that immediately arises between true and false needs, or natural and artificial needs, and the principle 'to each according to his needs'. He is, in this respect, unlike Weitling, Dézamy, Pillot, and even Marx. Nevertheless, by allowing superfluous needs to be satisfied once necessities have been taken care of, he enters dangerous ground of another kind. It is a fine line that he draws, since he still maintains that 'usurpation is theft' and that 'retention of the superfluous to the prejudice of other men lacking necessities' is a usurpation, and yet he expects disputes for which only subjective judgements and hearsay evidence can be supplied, to be resolved unanimously – or, indeed, never to arise.

Cabet is not persuaded that these problems are substantive. No, if 'a nation or a people forms a true society agreed on its common interest, *all the members are associated, brothers* . . . the nation is nothing but a family . . . a single moral person'. Despite appropriation according to need in practice, all goods are in principle held in common, forming 'social *capital*; the territory constitutes a *domain* exploited in *common* . . . each member having the duty to work the number of hours a day *equal to his ability* and the right to receive a share in all products *equal to his needs*' (p. 84). Once again, the famous formula adopted by Marx. But once the principle of equality failed to provide a basis for deciding true needs, by limiting them to those which all shared, the early socialists entered dangerous ground on which few dared to venture further. If, in fact, needs were not equal who could then decide what true needs were and whether what appeared to be fictitious or spurious needs were not, in fact, genuine needs for a given individual, for which he had a right to satisfaction?

Two major socialists who chronologically precede a number of those already discussed, are distinctive for the emphasis they place on the physiological and psychological differences between men, their *unequal* capacities, and the role of society in providing the greatest possible development of men's faculties rather than merely satisfying equal needs. These are Henri, Comte de Saint-Simon and Charles Fourier. By shifting the basis for distributive justice from the principle of natural equality, they felt no need to distinguish between true and false needs and therefore avoided the persistent socialist contradiction between this distinction, on the one hand, and advocacy of progress which would permit all needs to be satisfied, on the other. And apostles of progress they were.

Saint-Simon, influenced by the writings of Helvétius, Bentham, Condorcet, and so on, espoused Condorcet's principle of social harmony through progress, maintaining that society could be so organised that ignorance and misery would be mere accidents (Talmon, 1960, p. 68). He believed unquestioningly in the power of 'positive' science to solve social problems. Convinced that the route to progress lay with industry, he shifted his emphasis after 1813 from the life sciences, biology and physiology, to the industrialists and the science of production, claiming that 'the production of useful things' was 'the sole reasonable and positive goal that the political sciences could set themselves'.[8] He believed that competition had dissipated men's productive energies, but that production of useful things to satisfy genuine needs naturally constituted a common interest among them:

> It is an order of interests felt by all men, interests which pertain to the support of life and well-being. This order of interests is the only one on which all men understand one another and have need to be in agreement, the only one where they have to deliberate, to agree in common, the only one around which politics can be practised and which must be taken as the unique measure for the critique of all institutions and social things.[9]

Saint-Simon, like Adam Smith, Ricardo, The Ricardian socialists William Thompson, John Gray, Thomas Hodgskin and John Francis Bray, and Marx of course, developed needs as an economic category through the concept of use value. But, although insisting that the first moral duty of industrialists was 'to employ their energies to increase as rapidly as possible the social welfare of the poor',[10] Saint-Simon did not see the alleviation of basic needs as sufficient. His disciple Rouen, in the Saint-Simonian journal *Le Producteur*, expressed his mentor's view of the duty of the state towards the poor, 'to liberate moral man more and more from the influence of his purely physical needs'.[11]

Saint-Simon extended the criterion of utility to property, arguing that 'Property should be reconstituted and founded upon a basis which would render it more favourable to production'.[12] Property is for use and 'talent and possession should not be separated', nor should possession be settled for all time by laws of inheritance which will not permit property relationships to adjust to evolving systems of production. Consistent with the principle of allocation according to capacity for use, Saint-Simon argued that other goods should be distributed according to labour input and talent, endorsing the maxim of the liberal economists, 'to each according to his labour' rather than the socialist principle 'to each according to his need'. Saint-Simon's position on the relation of distribution to productivity emphasised the variability of men's capacities and drives as the appropriate basis for the division of labour and the distribution of goods it produced: 'Each person enjoys a measure of importance and benefits proportionate to his capacity and to his investment. This constitutes the highest degree of equality possible and desirable.'[13]

Marx, for one, did not agree and his attack on Kuhlman's principle of 'labour as the measure of need' could have been equally directed at Saint-Simon. Saint-Simon saw the problem of competition as the most serious objection to the principle of rewards according to talent and effort, but having seriously considered its effects he decided it was not harmful. While postulating aggression as a characteristic of the human species, he believed that if men turned their efforts from the exploitation of other men to the exploitation of nature, competition could be converted from a negative to a positive force. 'Up until now', he said, 'men have exercised, so to speak, on nature only purely individual and isolated efforts' which has meant competition, on the one hand, and waste on the other. These evils would disappear 'if men stopped managing one another and organized themselves to exercise their combined efforts on nature, and if nations followed the same system among themselves'.[14]

The writings of Saint-Simon are a curious mixture of elements with which we are already familiar: materialist psychology, faith in science and reason, which he inherited from Enlightenment forebears; principles of political economy; the socialist belief in labour as man's paramount right, duty and source of fulfilment − he went so far as to define the state as a company of workers − plus a theory of progress and confidence in an economy of abundance, which he took from the Idéologues. Many of these elements later found their way into the writings of Marx as well.

In many respects Fourier was very different from Saint-Simon and, indeed, won away from him some of his disciples. In his detestation of the bourgeoisie and the whole economic structure which permitted entrepreneurial skills to flourish there was none more vociferous, and this marked an important difference to begin with. Commerce, in Fourier's view, had bred evil problems and worse solutions, for having increased the gap between needs and their satisfactions, while purportedly narrowing it, commerce encouraged competition and oppression. He ceaselessly attacked the evils of 'civil society', the machinations of capital and the stock market, the squandering of natural resources incurred by the imperative to produce and exploit nature at whatever the cost. Here, too, he and Saint-Simon differed. But Fourier was no primitivist and he denigrated the Stoic ethic of self-denial as an instrument of repression, mocking the much-revered model of Sparta which Rousseau and many socialists commended. He attacked the virtue of poverty, on the one hand, and the evil of luxury, on the other. Poverty was worse than vice, he declared, but luxury, given the right social conditions, was the source of human fulfilment. In this he came closest to Marx, his man of rich needs and his concept of wealth, 'when its limited bourgeois form is stripped away' as 'the universality of individual needs, capacities, pleasures, and productive forces'.[15]

Like Marx, Fourier attacked the moralism of socialists who preceded him, who were concerned with how men ought to behave. He advocated scientific empiricism and hoped to discover what men really need, their basic drives and passions, in the true Enlightenment tradition. In his interest in the subjective forms of need or their psychological aspects, Fourier was very forward-looking. His doctrine of passionate attraction, his condemnation of the bourgeois family as the seat of sexual repression, the strait-jacketing of emotional creativity and sublimation in work, anticipated Freud. (Fourier was not, in principle, opposed to sublimation if it functioned as a stimulus to pleasure rather than simply as a constraint and here, of course, he was in agreement with Sade.)

Fourier's concern with the passions was also a backward-looking phenomenon, reflecting the eighteenth-century attempt to establish a materialist science of psychology as an extension of Newtonian laws of physical attraction and repulsion. His concept of the passions and ever-expanding needs as the motor of progress is closer to Rousseau, whom he detested along with the *philosophes*, than he would ever admit, and his critique of civil society owed a good deal to the famous Genevan. Fourier's system of social harmony was founded on the passions rather than the will, and here he differed from all those thinkers, including Freud, who believe the passions to be a source of conflict as much as harmony, anti-social in their effects. Fourier was explicitly anti-Stoic, an avowed hedonist or Epicurean, in the corrupted sence of that term. 'The learned world is wholly imbued with a doctrine termed MORALITY, which is a mortal enemy of passional attraction', he declared:

> Morality teaches man to be at war with himself, to resist his passions, to repress them, to believe that God was incapable of organizing our souls, our passions wisely; that he needed the teachings of Plato and Seneca in order to know how to distribute characteristics and instincts. Imbued with these prejudices regarding the impotence of God, the learned world was not qualified to estimate the natural impulses or passional attractions, which morality proscribes and relegates to the rank of vices.[16]

'My theory', he claimed, 'confines itself to *utilizing the passions now condemned, just as Nature has given them to us and without in anyway changing them.* That is the whole mystery, the whole secret of passional Attraction.'[17] 'Harmony, which will offer, particularly to the rich, a choice of pleasures every hour, nay, even every quarter of an hour, will prevent all excesses by the mere fact of the multiplicity of enjoyments; their frequent succession will be a guarantee of moderation and health . . .' (Fourier, 1971, pp. 65–6). The blame for excesses must be laid not

> . . . upon pleasures but upon the *rarity of pleasures*, which gives rise to excesses which seem to justify the moralists in condemning an epicurean way of life. Sanitary order, or equilibrium and moderation in the use of our senses, will spring then from the very abundance of pleasures which today are so pernicious on account of the excesses provoked by their rarity. (p. 66)

And in his views on the relation of sensuality to humanism, Fourier comes uncannily close to Marx's comments in the *Economic and Philosophic Manuscripts*, declaring:

> In the civilized order, where labour is repugnant, where people are too poor to participate in the consumption of choice foods, and where the epicure is not a cultivator, his epicurism lacks a *direct* bond with cultivation; it is nothing but sensuality, *simple* and ignoble, as is all else which does not attain to *composite* mechanism, or the influence of production and consumption acting upon the same individual. (Fourier, 1971, *Design for Utopia* . . ., p. 65)

Fourier constructed a philosophy of history which postulated sixteen stages between barbarism and the social harmony of the phalanstery. He drew up a typology of man's instinctual drives, which he identified as twelve in number belonging to three main branches: 'the luxury', 'the group' and 'the serial'. The first included the five senses and their corresponding appetites; the second − the group passions − comprised the desires for respect, for friendship, for love and for parenthood and came close to those passions which the eighteenth-century *philosophes* grouped under the desire for esteem, or ego-needs. The serial passions were concerned with another aspect of man's sociability, his instinct for organisation, the passion to make arrangements, the 'concordist' desire to conciliate, the discordant or cabalist passion, and the passion for variety of the changeling or the butterfly (Fourier, 1971, pp. 56–62; Manuel, 1965, pp. 220–6).

Considering that Fourier understood fairly well the conflictual and repressive aspects of civilisation, it is difficult to understand why he should have held out hopes for a regime of perfect harmony in the phalanstery, but he did so nevertheless. As a libertarian thinker, Fourier saw freedom in terms of the removal of constraint: it was inconceivable to him that self-directed behaviour could be contrary to self-interest or the dictates of the instincts. Like so many Enlightenment and socialist thinkers he carried over *laissez-faire* and utilitarian assumptions of a spontaneous balance produced by allowing natural forces free play. This was the basis of his 'natural harmony'. The slogan 'to each according to his needs', correspondingly, takes on a more libertarian sense with Fourier, insisting as he does on the free development of all erotic and pleasurable appetites. Under conditions of economic abundance the formula 'to each according to his needs' would raise no problems that could not be resolved by relatively simple administrative techniques.

But as Constantin Pecqueur, exceptional for his criticism of the principle 'to each according to his needs', pointed out, 'It is a formula which says absolutely nothing, for it presupposes man and all men to be perfect: it assumes that each follows his passion.'[18] This offends, in practice, against the fact of a more or less constant insufficiency of production, as well as against psychological facts which Fourier had pointed out. Where can a criterion of needs be found? It is found later: 'The formula which up to now was really utopian or illusory, a deception for the majority as long as one applied it to a society in which good and evil live side by side, would perhaps be able to become, if necessary, a practical truth . . .' As against such an optimistic prognostication, Pecqueur suggests that 'liberty seems here singularly compromised'.[19]

Pecqueuer had pointed to a real problem. The alternatives were, indeed, to assume a perfect world in which all needs would be satisfied as a possibility, as Fourier and the utopian socialists did; or to believe that through practice such theoretical problems could be transcended, as Marx did – under revolutionary practice the problem of needs would evaporate because of the identity of thought and reality. As Pecqueur noted, among the many difficulties with this latter notion is the fact that it goes against historical experience, psychology, the philosophical problem of the mind/body duality, and that it violates the concept of freedom as man's ability to go against the dictates of his instincts.

Although this is no place to go into it, there had all along been a number of theorists in the Enlightenment and early socialist period who held out an alternative to materialism and the doctrine of needs. Burlamaqui, Ferguson, Montesquieu, and others had maintained that man was capable of transcending his needs and instincts by exerting his will to endorse a moral principle. The most famous of these was, of course, Kant.

In his refutation of empiricism, utilitarianism and Humean scepticism, to which, in his view, empiricism ineluctably tended, Kant in the *Critique of Practical Reason* shows why it is that needs as natural inclinations and predispositions cannot constitute an *objective* criterion. 'All practical principles which presuppose an object . . . of the faculty of desire as the ground of determination of the will are empirical and can furnish no practical laws' (1954 edn, p. 107). This is precisely because desires or appetites, which have as their aim pleasure and the avoidance of pain, are fundamentally subjective and volatile. 'It is impossible to know *a priori* of any idea of an object whether it will be connected with *pleasure* or *pain* or be indifferent' (p. 108). It is a contingent and empirical question how people react, precisely because their judgements in such matters are subjective, and while Kant does not for one moment rule out the susceptibility of the individual to pleasure and pain as motivating principles, he shows conclusively that terms which have such motivations as their reference cannot at the same time constitute objective criteria.

Is it true that needs, like desires, have as their exclusive reference the pursuit of pleasure and avoidance of pain? Needs are not necessarily synonymous with desires although for those socialists who took seriously the environmentalist theory, as well as Fourier and Saint-Simon, they usually were. For those who subscribed to equality as a natural law principle and saw needs as those necessities of life common to all, it was not easy to arrive at agreement on what these were; and needs as a term is rarely understood in such a restricted sense. Kant is right, I think: the concepts of appetites, desires and needs do not furnish stable criteria for justice and the guidance of conduct more generally, as the various unsuccessful attempts by the early socialists to make them operative show. Kant argues against the satisfaction of needs and pleasure as man's goal from a consideration of what human nature is and how it is constituted:

In the physical constitution of an organized being, that is, a being suitably adapted to the purposes of life, we assume it as a fundamental principle that no organ of any purpose will be found but what is also the fittest and best adapted for that purpose. Now in a being which has reason and a will, if the proper object of nature were its *conservation*, its *welfare*, in a word, its *happiness*, then nature would have hit upon a very bad arrangement in selecting the reason of the creature to carry out this purpose. For all the actions which the creature has to perform with a view to this purpose, and the whole rule of its conduct, would be far more surely prescribed to it by instinct, and that end would have been attained thereby much more certainly than it ever can be by reason . . .

For as reason is not competent to guide the will with certainty with regard to its objects and the satisfaction of all our wants (which it to some extent even multiplies), this being an end to which an implanted instinct would have led with much greater certainty; and since, nevertheless, reason is imparted to us as a practical faculty, that is, as one which is to have influence on the *will*, therefore, admitting that nature generally in the distribution of her capacities has adapted the means to the end, its true destination must be to produce a *will*, not merely good as a *means* to something else, but *good in itself*, for which reason was absolutely necessary. This will then, though not indeed the sole and complete good, must be the supreme good and the condition of every other, even of the desire of happiness. (*Fundamental Principles of the Metaphysic of Morals*, 1949 edn, pp. 12–14).

NOTES

1   *De l'esprit* (1882), Vol. 1, pp. 117 and 369, quoted by Marx, *CW*, Vol. 4, p. 132.
2   *Système social* (1882), Vol. 1, p. 116, quoted by ibid., p. 133.
3   Quoted in M. Kaufman (1879), pp. 40–1.
4   Quoted from Seneca's 'Ninetieth letter', in Roche (1974), p. xi.
5   *Système de la nature* (1771), Vol. 1, pp. 245–6, quoted in Crocker (1959), p. 166n.
6   Reproduced in Lovejoy and Boas (1935), pp. 136–45.
7   See Bravo's excellent anthology of early socialist writings, *Les Socialistes avant Marx* (1970), Vol. 2, p. 74.
8   *Oeuvres complètes*, Vol. 18, pp. 186, 188, quoted by Leroy (1950), Vol. 2, p. 205.
9   ibid., p. 188, quoted in Leroy (1950), pp. 205–6.
10 *Le Nouveau Christianisme, Oeuvres complètes*, Vol. 23, p. 192, quoted by Leroy (1950), p. 219.
11 *Oeuvres complètes*, Vol. 3, p. 309, quoted by Leroy (1950), p. 219.
12 *Organisateur, Oeuvres complètes*, Vol. 20, p. 59, quoted by Talmon (1960), p. 63.
13 *Oeuvres complètes*, Vol. 20, quoted by Manuel (1965), p. 132.
14 Quoted by Leroy (1950), p. 207.
15 *Economic and Philosophic Manuscripts, CW*, Vol. 3, pp. 301 ff. and *Grundrisse* (1973*a* edn), p. 488.
16 *Le Nouveau Monde industriel et societaire* (1848), p. 125, trans. in Fourier (1971), p. 55.
17 *Theorie de l'unité universelle* (1838), Vol. 4, p. 157, trans. in Fourier (1971), p. 66.
18 Leroy (1950), p. 264, from Pecqueur, *Theorié nouvelle d'économie sociale et politique* (1842), pp. 584, 585.
19 Leroy (1950), quoting Pecqueur, op. cit., p. 587.

5

Civil Society as a 'System of Needs' in Hegel

Hegel, in the *Philosophy of Right*, develops a theory of needs which synthesises his own reflections on ontology and the significance of desire in the *Phenomenology* with certain themes of classical political economy, while referring back and forth to Rousseau, Locke (although not by name), the Hellenistic schools, Enlightenment materialism and moral sense theories on the question of needs, desires, the will, judgement, the expansion of needs, luxury and their relation to civil society and the state. One may safely say that these reflections of Hegel on the subject of needs contain the substance of most of what Marx has to say on the subject, even though, we may guess, he was not keen to admit this – in Marx's *Critique of Hegel's 'Philosophy of Right'* mention of Hegel's theory of need or his concept of a 'system of needs' is conspicuously absent.

It is to the *Phenomenology* and not the *Philosophy of Right* that Marx sees himself indebted and the short tribute he pays in the 1844 Manuscripts (*CW*, Vol. 3, pp. 332–3) to the Hegel of the *Phenomenology* is balanced by his curt dismissal in the essay 'On the Jewish question' (ibid., pp. 153–4) of Hegel's theory of the state. Marx expressed a wish to see the Hegel of the *Phenomenology* who had for so long been overshadowed by the Hegel of the *Logic* (ibid., p. 327) resuscitated even though, as most authors now agree, there is much of the *Logic* in Marx's works as well. As we shall see, the *Philosophy of Right*, which receives so little favourable acknowledgement, is the secret clue to the significance of the concept of needs in Marx, for it is this concept which takes account of the social and economic ramifications of wants and desires to which political economists made passing reference, but which Hegel most fully articulated. Hegel, it is, who explicates the implicit connection between the appetitive passions, which Adam Smith investigated in his *Theory of Moral Sentiments* (1812) and the 'wants of mankind' and 'necessaries and convenience of life' to which in the *Wealth of Nations* he frequently refers (1937 edn, pp. lvii, lviii, 22, 30, 33, 159, 163–4, 259, 433, 822, 824–5, 836, 839, 880).

There is a parallel to be drawn between the transition from the concept of desire to the concept of needs which Hegel makes, and the corresponding transition from an ontological conception of needs to a materialist one in Marx and later Jean-Paul Sartre. The significance of desire belongs to the realms of psychology and ontology, but needs and wants are concepts whose significance lies for Hegel, as for his successors, in the political and economic realms. 'Self-consciousness', Hegel claims in *The Phenomenology of Mind*, 'is the state of *Desire* in general', that 'first moment' in which 'self-consciousness occupies the position of consciousness and the whole expanse of the world of sense is conserved as its object' (1949, p. 220). Indicating the direction the transition will later take, Hegel remarks further on in the *Phenomenology*: 'The procuring and maintaining of power and wealth turn, in part merely on needs and wants, and are a matter that has to do with desire . . .' (p. 469).

It is through desire, Hegel argues, that consciousness becomes aware of itself, that the person as a unified will emerges from the collection of differentiated faculties that make up the individual, and that the autonomy of the ego is affirmed. For it is by virtue of the challenge of external nature and self-subsistent others as objects of desire that the self becomes aware of itself as self, '. . . self-consciousness is thus only assured of itself through sublating this other, which is presented to self-consciousness as an independent life; self-consciousness is *Desire*' (p. 225). It follows from this that it is the object for which the 'simple ego' feels a lack, which permits its very self-awareness. In other words, were man a wholly autonomous and self-contained creature, and not pricked into awareness by insufficiency, lack of food, lack of shelter, lack of security, and so on, his existence might well be one of vegetative somnambulance since the need to differentiate the self from the external world and from others would not exist:

> Desire and the certainty of its self obtained in the gratification of desire, are conditioned by the object; for the certainty exists through cancelling this other; in order that this cancelling may be effected, there must be this other. Self-consciousness is thus unable by its negative relation to the object to abolish it; because of that relation it rather produces it again, as well as the desire. The object desired is, in fact something other than self-consciousness, the essence of desire; and through this experience this truth has become realized. (p. 225)

It is in the logic of desire that an inanimate object as the object of desire will not produce ultimate self-affirmation: only a self-conscious other whose awareness and powers are equal to those of the one in question can bring this about. For one experiences his own powers against the resistance of the other, and sees his own natural powers reflected in the powers of the other: 'Self-consciousness attains its satisfaction only in another self-consciousness . . . The object of desire . . . is . . . independent, for it is the universal, ineradicable substance, the fluent, self-identical essential reality. When a self-consciousness is the object, the object is just as much ego as object' (pp. 226–7).

In the important chapter on lordship and bondage in the *Phenomenology* Hegel shows how, through work performed at the instigation of desire, a man in general, and the bondsman in particular, objectifies himself:

Desire has reserved to itself the pure negating of the object and thereby unalloyed feeling of self. This satisfaction, however, just for that reason is itself only a state of evanescence, for it lacks objectivity or subsistence. Labour, on the other hand, is desire restrained and checked, evanescence delayed and postponed; in other words, labour shapes and fashions the thing. The negative relation to the object passes into the *form* of the object, into something that is permanent and remains; because it is just for the labourer that the object has independence. This negative mediating agency, this activity giving shape and form, is at the same time the individual existence, the pure self-existence of that consciousness, which now in the work it does is externalized and passes into the condition of permanence. The consciousness that toils and serves accordingly attains by this means the direct apprehension of that independent being as its self. (p. 238)

Through 'shaping or forming the object . . . the bondsman becomes thereby aware of himself as factually and objectively self-existent' (pp. 238–9), an awareness that the master does not enjoy in the same way, for 'the master relates himself to the thing mediately through the bondsman' (p. 235). In other words, the master whose daily necessities of life are taken care of by his servant does not experience either the sense of power or the sense of finitude that comes from working the external world to satisfy one's needs. His domination of the servant, which at once guarantees his independence from material things, at the same time guarantees his dependence on his servant:

The master is the consciousness that exists *for itself* . . . a consciousness existing on its own account which is mediated with itself through an other consciousness, i.e., through an other whose very nature implies that it is bound up with an independent being or with thinghood in general. The master brings himself into relation to both these moments, to a thing as such, the object of desire, and to the consciousness whose essential character is thinghood . . . The master relates himself to the bondsman mediately through independent existence, for that is precisely what keeps the bondsman in thrall; it is his chain, from which he could not in the struggle get away, and for that reason he proved himself to be dependent, to have his independence in the shape of thinghood. The master, however, is the power controlling this state of existence . . . Since he is the power dominating existence, while this existence again is the power controlling the other [the bondsman], the master holds, *par consequence*, this other in subordination. In the same way the master relates himself to the thing mediately through the bondsman. The bondsman being a self-consciousness in the broad sense, also takes up a negative attitude to things and cancels them; but the thing is, at the same time, independent for him, and, in consequence, he cannot, with all his negating, get so far as to annihilate it outright and be done with it; that is to say, he merely works on it. To the master, on the other hand, by means of this mediating process, belongs the immediate relation, in the sense of the pure negation of it, in other words he gets the enjoyment. What mere desire did not attain, he now succeeds in attaining, viz., to have done with the thing, and find satisfaction in enjoyment. Desire alone did not get the length of this, because of the independence of the thing. The master, however, who

has interposed the bondsman between it and himself, thereby relates
himself merely to the dependence of the thing, and enjoys it without
qualification and without reserve. The aspect of its independence he
leaves to the bondsman, who labours upon it. (pp. 234–6)

The outcome is not what the master might wish:

> . . . for just where the master has effectively achieved lordship, he
> really finds that something has come about quite different from an
> independent consciousness. It is not an independent, but rather a
> dependent consciousness that he has achieved. He is thus not assured
> of self-existence as his truth . . . (pp. 236–7)

As we know, the allegory of lordship and bondage is a figure for Greek
culture at the time of Plato where, due to what were in Hegel's eyes
excessively puritanical fears about the corrupting influence of manual
labour and commerce with the world of things, the citizen was prevented
from taking care of his material needs which were in the hands of slaves.
Interestingly, Hegel argues against Plato that freedom comes not from
insulation from the world of material things, but rather from a triumph
of the will in which the attraction of wordly desires provides the ground
on which virtue excels. The slave has the prescience of freedom that the
master cannot have, since the slave at once knows the powers of man
over the world of nature and the dangers that lie therein. Stoicism and
Scepticism, which arose in reaction to the Platonic and Aristotelian
systems, are the first, if negative, expression of freedom as virtue in
relation to the material world:

> . . . just as Stoicism answers to the *notion* of independent conscious-
> ness, which appeared as a relation of lordship and bondage,
> Scepticism, on its side, corresponds to its *realization*, to the negative
> attitude toward otherness, to desire and labour. (p. 247)

Stoicism and Scepticism asserted the essential equality and brotherhood of man, the necessity of holding property in common and the right
of every man to appropriate for his use those goods to which his labour
has been applied for the satisfaction of his needs: as such they represent
the very affirmation of man's independence and his essential human
nature that the master-slave relation sanctioned by Plato and Aristotle
precluded. But due to a certain negativity, because the world of things is
still seen by the Hellenistic schools to represent evil and the world of
temptation which in the name of *ataraxia* must be vanquished (p. 248),
the outcome is '*Unhappy Consciousness*, the Alienated Soul which is the
consciousness of self as a divided nature . . .' (p. 251); 'consciousness of
life, of its existence and action [as] merely pain and sorrow over this
existence and activity', wherein 'consciousness finds only consciousness
of its opposite as its essence – and of its own nothingness' (p. 252).
   Hegel rejects the idealism of Stoicism and Scepticism, which see man
as soul locked in mortal combat with the needs and desires of the body,
although he praises their heroic concept of freedom. Epicureanism or
hedonism, as a response to Stoicism, no more realises the ontological

significance of desire and work for human objectification since it, like the paradigmatic master, concentrates on satisfaction and pleasure without in any way suffering the resistance or challenge of the material world:

> It plunges thus into life, and carries to its completion the pure individuality in which it appears. It does not so much make its own happiness as take it directly and enjoy it. The grey shades of science, laws and principles, which alone stand between it and its own reality, vanish like a lifeless mist that cannot contend against the living certainty of its reality. It takes to itself life much as a ripe fruit is plucked, which comes to meet the hand that takes it.
>
> Its action is only in one respect an act of Desire: it does not aim at abolishing the objective fact in its entirety, but only the form of its otherness or objectivity, which is an unreal appearance; for it holds this to be inherently and implicitly the same reality as its own self. The sphere in which desire and its object subsist independently and indifferent towards each other is that of living existence; the enjoyment of desire cancels this existence, so far as it belongs to the object of desire. (pp. 384–5)

Gratification as the way of vulgar hedonism reduces human life to natural life and natural life to fate. From it the notion of freedom is entirely absent.

The answer to the question of man's proper relation as subject to the external world as object of his desires is to be found, not in the *Phenomenology*, but in the *Philosophy of Right*, where 'need' becomes a crucial category. There Hegel uses the concept in two important contexts, first of all to characterise man as a natural creature, to define the realm of subjectivity constituted by needs, desires, passions and interests, over against which the objective world of mind or the idea is set. This is at the same time the realm of the particular over against which he sets the universality of man as appropriator and subject of his own destiny. Through the mediation of work, the realm of need becomes transformed by purpose to form the human world of society and history. Here we have a transition from the first level at which need is an important category − the level of the personal and the individual − to the second or social level, where he characterises the totality of private interests and personal motivations which constitute civil society as a 'system of needs'. In this way, Hegel synthesises his own conception of human nature with the observations of the political economists − Smith, Say and Ricardo whom he names specifically − on society as a balance of competing interests. Hegel reintroduces in his own characteristic way, and not without some revisions, the Platonic analogy between man as a creature whose particular needs and desires come under the architectonic control of will, and particular social needs and interest as they come under the control of state. In the first paragraph in the subsection on 'The system of needs', he sets out the general argument:

> Particularity is in the first instance characterized in general by its contrast with the universal principle of the will and thus is subjective need . . . This attains its objectivity, i.e., its satisfaction, by means of

(a) external things, which at this stage are likewise the property and product of the needs and wills of others, and (b) work and effort, the middle term between the subjective and objective. The aim here is the satisfaction of subjective particularity, but the universal asserts itself in the bearing which this satisfaction has on the needs of others and their free arbitrary wills. (*Philosophy of Right*, 1957, para. 189, p. 126)

In the Remark to this paragraph Hegel indicates the connection between his concept of needs and the view of the political economists for whom society is a totality of individuals pursuing their self-interest, defined in terms of particular needs, wants and satisfactions, to the mutual benefit of all:

> Political economy is the science which starts from this view of needs and labour but then has the task of explaining mass-relationships and mass-movements in their complexity and their qualitative and quantitative character. This is one of the sciences which have arisen out of the conditions of the modern world. Its development affords the interesting spectacle (as in Smith, Say, and Ricardo) of thought working upon the endless mass of details which confronts it at the outset and extracting therefrom the simple principles of the thing, the Understanding effective in the thing and directing it. (Remark to para. 189, pp. 126–7)

In an important Remark to paragraph 190, Hegel indicates the significance for his theory of 'needs' as a category. In the various subdivisions of his treatise certain defining concepts are introduced:

> In [abstract] right, what we had before us was the person; in the sphere of morality, the subject; in the family, the family-member; in civil society as a whole, the burgher or *bourgeois*. Here at the standpoint of needs . . . what we have before us is the composite idea which we call *man*. Thus this is the first time, and indeed properly the only time, to speak of *man* in this sense. (p. 127)[1]

What does it mean to speak of man as a creature characterised by needs? True to his general formula for organic development of all kinds as a process of actualising potentiality, movement from the implicit (*an sich, potentia, dynamis*) to the explicit (*für sich, actus, energeia*),[2] Hegel characterises man as pre-eminently a creature who expresses his nature through 'activity'. This quasi-Aristotelian concept he sums up as 'the fact that the subject puts himself into whatever he is to look upon and promote as his end. Men are willing to be *active* in the pursuit of what interests them or should interest them, as something which is their own' (para. 123, p. 83). Hegel already intimates the significance, on which we shall later comment, of property for this concept of personality and individual autonomy. The 'determinate content' of human activity, which constitutes 'the still abstract and formal freedom of subjectivity', is to be found 'in its natural subjective embodiment, i.e., in needs, inclinations, passions, opinions, fancies, etc. The satisfaction of these is welfare or happiness, both in general and in its particular species — the ends of the whole sphere of finitude' (para. 123, p. 83). And 'here', he says, 'when the subject is characterized by his self-difference and so counts as a particular', is where 'the natural will comes on the scene' (Remark to para. 123, p. 83).

'The will', he has already established, 'contains . . . the element of pure indeterminacy or that pure reflection of the ego into itself which involves the dissipation of every restriction and every content . . . immediately presented by nature, by needs, desires, and impulses . . .'; it is 'the unrestricted infinity of absolute abstraction or universality, the pure thought of oneself' (para. 5, p. 21). Hegel admits to being aware of how 'empirical psychology details and describes these impulses and inclinations, and the needs arising from them, as it finds them, or presumes it finds them, in experience' (Remark to para. 11, p. 25). But his purpose is to show 'the objective element in these impulses, both its true character stripped of the form of irrationality which it possesses as impulse and also . . . the manner in which at the same time it is shaped externally' (ibid., p. 26). The whole content of the psyche 'as we light upon it in its immediacy in the will, is there only as a medley and multiplicity of impulses, each of which is merely "my desire" but exists alongside other desires which are likewise all "mine", and each of which is at the same time something universal and indeterminate, aimed at all kinds of objects and satiable in all kinds of ways'. It is 'the will [which] gives . . . the form of individuality' to this mass of particulars (para. 12, p. 26).

Hegel, here more in the Stoic than the Platonic tradition, cautions against seeing the mind as a collection of different compartments, where 'thinking' is regarded 'as one special faculty, distinct from the will as another special faculty', and so on (Remark to para. 5, p. 21). Nevertheless, the faculty of will, of judgement or of deliberation, is what constitutes freedom for the individual. Freedom, far from being the 'ability to do what we please', an idea which reveals 'an utter immaturity of thought' (Remark to para. 15, p. 27), is rather the capability to bring reason to bear on a course of action and to choose in accordance with right reason. 'The idea which people most commonly have of freedom is that it is arbitrariness — the mean, chosen by abstract reflection, between the will wholly determined by natural impulses, and the will free absolutely' (ibid.). Hegel rejects this view common among Enlightenment materialists, just as he rejects the view of the moral sense theorists that man has 'by nature the impulse towards right . . . towards property and morality', a natural impulse to 'love between the sexes . . . to sociability, etc.' (Remark to para. 19, p. 29), in favour of a concept of the 'reflective will', which comes much closer to Locke, the Stoics and Epicureans. 'When the will is reflective', he says, 'it contains two elements.' The first is 'sense-consciousness', the *content* of the will, which 'takes the form of desire and impulse' and, just as in 'sensation in general denotes externality', or the orientation of the individual to the pressures of the world around him. The second element, a *quality* of the will, is the capacity for 'universality of thought' (Remark to para. 21, p. 29):

> When the will's potentialities have become fully explicit, then it has for its object the will itself as such, and so the will in its sheer universality — a universality which is what it is simply because it has absorbed in itself the immediacy of instinctive desire and the particularity which is produced by reflection and with which such desire *eo ipso* becomes imbued. But this process of absorption in or elevation to universality is what is called the activity of thought. The self-consciousness which purifies its object, content, and aim, and raises them to this universality effects this as thinking getting its own way in the will. Here is the point at which it becomes clear that it is only as thinking intelligence that the will is genuinely a will and free. (Remark to para. 21, pp. 29–30)

In sum, Hegel maintains, 'in having universality, or itself *qua* infinite form, for its object, content, and aim, the will is free not only *in* itself but *for* itself also; it is the Idea in its truth' (para. 21, p. 29).

It is in the faculty of the will that man as such is distinguished from the animals:

> An animal too has impulses, desires, inclinations, but it has no will and must obey its impulse if nothing external deters it. Man, however, the wholly undetermined, stands above his impulses and may make them his own, put them in himself as his own. An impulse is something natural, but to put it into my ego depends on my will which thus cannot fall back on the plea that the impulse has its basis in nature (Addition to para. 11, p. 229)

The secret of the will is freedom. One need hardly remark on the degree to which Hegel's concept of freedom approximates to that of Rousseau, the Stoics and Kant as an affirmation of man's ability to subjugate his needs, desires and interests to a moral principle:

> In this element of the will is rooted my ability to free myself from everything, abandon every aim, abstract from everything. Man alone can sacrifice everything, his life included; he can commit suicide. An animal cannot; it always remains merely negative, in an alien destiny to which it merely accustoms itself. Man is the pure thought of himself, and only in thinking is he this power to give himself universality, i.e., to extinguish all particularity, all determinacy. (Addition to para. 5, p. 227)

From Hegel's analysis of needs, desires and impulses as the subjective and appetitive content of human consciousness, and the motivation to activity which is guided and adjudicated by the will, other important considerations follow. One of these concerns the relation between basic human needs common to all men and the expanded or artificial needs which civilisation produces. Since Hegel puts priority on the capability of the will to subjugate desire in its deliberations, as we may expect, the more multifarious human needs, desires and impulses become, the greater the field in which the will has its play. Hegel categorically rejects the Rousseauean and Cynic views (both of which he specifically denounces, para. 194 Remark, and para. 195 Addition), which argue that human needs should be restricted to those natural needs for food, shelter, clothing, and so on, whch men share in common. Were this to be the case, the rich diversity of subjectivity which gives to the realm of the moral its very essence would be lost for a drab uniformity where men followed certain natural but crude instincts. Such a naturalism is inconsistent with morality as such, as well as being uncharacteristic of human nature and the multiplicity of desires, impulses and needs which give to society a rich range of personalities.

'Particularity by itself', Hegel concedes, 'is a measureless excess, and the forms of this excess are themselves measureless. By means of his ideas and reflections man expands his desires, which are not a closed circle like animal instinct, and carries them on to the false infinite' (Addition to para. 185, p. 267). While it is true that 'there are certain universal needs such as food, drink, clothing, etc.' (Addition to para. 189, p. 268), what distinguishes man is the ability to vary his needs at the dictates of imagination and will:

> An animal's needs and its ways and means of satisfying them are both alike restricted in scope. Though man is subject to this restriction too, yet at the same time he evinces his transcendence of it and his universality, first by the multiplication of needs and means of satisfying them, and secondly by the differentiation and division of concrete need into single parts and aspects which in turn become different needs, particularized and so more abstract. (para. 190, p. 127)

In the Addition to this paragraph Hegel amplifies these comments, restating the distinction between animal and human needs in terms of man's capability to transcend particularity and attain universality by virtue of his ability to subjugate some needs in favour of others:

> An animal is restricted to particularity. It has its instincts and means of satisfying them, means which are limited and which it cannot overstep. Some insects are parasitic on a certain kind of plant; some animals have a wider range and can live in different climates, but there is always a restriction preventing them from having the range open to man. (Addition to para. 190, p. 268)

We hear Marx's echo of this idea in his assertion in the 1844 Manuscripts that while 'an animal forms objects only in accordance with the standard and the need of the species to which it belongs . . . man knows how to produce in accordance with the standard of every species, and knows how to apply everywhere the inherent standard to the object' (*CW*, Vol. 3, p. 277).

Hegel continues:

> The need of shelter and clothing, the necessity of cooking his food to make it fit to eat and to overcome its natural rawness [and here we are reminded of Marx's comments in the *Grundrisse*, p. 92, on the difference between eating food raw or cooked] both mean that man has less comfort than an animal, and indeed, as mind, he ought to have less. Intelligence, with its grasp of distinctions, multiplies these

human needs, and since taste and utility become criteria of judgement, even the needs themselves are affected thereby. (Addition to para. 190, pp. 268–9 ff.)

Hegel is no critic of civilisation. The multiplication of needs which the competition for honour and status encourages as society becomes more tightly knit, far from depraving man – as Plato, Hellenistic primitivists and Rousseau all argued – in fact breaks the tyranny of need which characterises animals:

> Finally, it is no longer need but opinion which has to be satisfied, and it is just the educated man who analyses the concrete into its particulars. The very multiplication of needs involves a check on desire, because when many things are in use, the urge to obtain any one thing which might be needed is less strong, and this is a sign that want altogether is not so imperious. (Addition to para. 190, p. 269)

Once again an argument that Marx adopts with his claim that while 'an animal produces . . . only under the domination of immediate physical need . . . man produces even when he is free from physical need and only truly produces in freedom therefrom' (*CW*, Vol. 3, p. 276).

Hegel is much closer to Hobbes, Mandeville, Bayle, and those political economists who argued for the public utility of private vices than he is to Rousseau in his attitude to the refinement of needs under civilisation. He freely admits that the insatiability of needs opens the way for corruption as well as for virtue. But it is in the nature of things that morality pre-supposes the equal possibilities of good and evil. The prospect of greater comfort and satisfaction that an expansion of possible goods promises is, therefore, accompanied by a proportionate increase in the possibilities for discomfort and frustration, as well as creating the opportunity for others to profit from our passion for the improvement of our estate.

> What the English call 'comfort' [he says] is something inexhaustible and illimitable. [Others can discover to you that what you take to be] comfort at any stage is discomfort, and these discoveries never come to an end. Hence the need for greater comfort does not exactly arise within you directly: it is suggested to you by those who hope to make a profit from its creation. (Addition to para. 191, p. 269)

A sentiment which Marx expressed so graphically with his claim that 'every real and possible need is a weakness which will lead the fly to the gluepot', that 'every need is an opportunity to approach one's neighbour under the guise of utmost amiability and say to him: Dear friend, I give you what you need, but you know the [conditions] . . . you know the ink in which you sign yourself over to me: in providing for your pleasure, I fleece you' (*CW*, Vol. 3, p. 307).

Marx's view is rather more mordant than that of Hegel who sees nothing sinister in the desire for self-esteem or the price that one must pay for it in a willingness to promote the interests of others in order to secure one's own, to obey fashion and convention:

The fact that I must direct my conduct by reference to others introduces here the form of universality. It is from others that I acquire the means of satisfaction and I must accordingly accept their views. At the same time, however, I am compelled to produce means for the satisfaction of others. We play into each other's hands and so hang together. To this extent everything private becomes something social. In dress, fashions and hours of meals, there are certain conventions which we have to accept because in these things it is not worth the trouble to insist on displaying one's own discernment. The wisest thing here is to do as others do. (Addition to para. 192, p. 269)

Hegel sees positive advantages in the negative virtues of pride, self-interest, self-esteem and the desire for approbation just where Rousseau saw their greatest dangers: in the degree to which they tie the knots of society faster and faster. But Hegel has scant regard for this aspect of Rousseau's thought or for the whole tradition of primitivism from which it sprang:

> The idea has been advanced that in respect of his needs man lived in freedom in the so-called 'state of nature' when his needs were supposed to be confined to what are known as the simple necessities of nature, and when he required for their satisfaction only the means which the accidents of nature directly assured to him. This view takes no account of the moment of liberation intrinsic to work . . . And apart from this, it is false, because to be confined to mere physical needs as such and their direct satisfaction would simply be the condition in which the mental is plunged in the natural and so would be one of savagery and unfreedom, while freedom itself is to be found only in the reflection of mind into itself, in mind's distinction from nature, and in the reflex of mind in nature. (Remark to para. 194, p. 128)

The whole preoccupation with luxury and its condemnation is, Hegel argues, a very definite social product, an archaic reaction to the problems of modernity. 'When social conditions tend to multiply and subdivide needs, means and enjoyments indefinitely – a process which, like the distinction between natural and refined needs, has no qualitative limits – this is luxury' (para. 195, p. 128). It is true that this expansion and refinement of needs – luxury – has negative consequences: 'dependence and want increase *ad infinitum*, and the material to meet these is permanently barred to the needy man because it consists of external objects with the special character of being property, the embodiment of the free will of others, and hence from this point of view its recalcitrance is absolute' (ibid.).

Deplorable though the growth of inequality exacerbated by the institution of property may be, a return to the 'man of few needs' is no answer, 'want and destitution are measureless . . . and the discord of this situation can be brought to harmony only by the state which has powers over it' (Addition to para. 185, p. 267). The multiplication of needs does not change their character, and although the savage and the civilised man may need different things, they are still equally subject to the pressure of their needs.[3] As Marx commented, 'regression to the unnatural simplicity of the *poor* and crude man who has few needs and who has not only failed to go beyond private property, but has not yet even reached it', involves a misunderstanding of the role that civilisation has played in human freedom (*CW*, Vol. 3, p. 295). Hegel comments in these terms on the rigours of the Cynic regimen:

> The entire Cynical mode of life adopted by Diogenes was nothing more or less than a product of Athenian social life, and what determined it was the way of thinking against which his whole manner protested. Hence it was not independent of social conditions but simply their result; it was itself a rude product of luxury. When luxury is at its height, distress and depravity are equally extreme, and in such circumstances Cynicism is the outcome of opposition to refinement. (Addition to para. 124, p. 269)

The primitivists fail to understand the role that civilisation through the multiplication and refinement of needs plays in liberating man from mere animal existence. Refinement, which involves 'the means to particularized needs and all the various ways of satisfying these' being divided and multiplied, a 'multiplication [which] goes on *ad infinitum*', also requires 'a discrimination between these multiplied needs, and judgement on the suitability of means to their ends' (para. 191, p. 127). Deliberation on means and ends involves a recognition that 'needs and means, as things existent *realiter*, become something which has being for others by whose needs and work satisfaction for all alike is conditioned' (para. 192, p. 127). The universality of needs is 'a character of the reciprocal relation of individuals to one another'; it is 'the character to being recognized and is the moment which makes concrete, i.e., social, the isolated and abstract needs and their ways and means of satisfaction' (ibid.). Such is the nature of 'social needs' that they have the power of liberating man from the tyranny of nature and of instantiating his universality:

> This social moment thus becomes a particular end-determinant for means in themselves and their acquisition, as well as for the manner in which needs are satisfied. Further, it directly involves the demand for equality of satisfaction with others. The need for this equality and for emulation, which is the equalizing of oneself with others, as well as the other need also present here, the need of the particular to assert itself in some distinctive way, become themselves a fruitful source of the multiplication of needs and their expansion.
>   Since in social needs, as the conjunction of immediate or natural needs with mental needs arising from ideas, it is needs of the latter type which because of their universality make themselves preponderant, this social moment has in it the aspect of liberation, i.e., strict natural necessity of need is obscured and man is concerned with his own opinion, indeed with an opinion which is universal, and with a necessity of his own making alone, instead of with an external necessity, an inner contingency, and mere caprice. (para. 193 and para. 194, pp. 127–8)

Social needs are not, however, merely cerebral, nothing but the product of imagination, stimulated by the opinion of others and confirmed by their recognition. Reason, as the principle 'immanent in the restless system of human needs, which articulates it into an organic whole with different members' (Remark to para. 200, p. 130), is not confined to the realm of mind, but is actualised in the material world through the principles of 'property' and 'work'. 'The means of acquiring and preparing the particularized means appropriate to our similarly particularized needs is work', Hegel asserts (para. 196, p. 128). 'There is hardly any raw material which does not need to be worked on before use . . . It is by the sweat of his brow and the toil of his hands that man obtains the means to satisfy his needs' (Addition to para. 196, p. 269). And work entails 'property' or the right to appropriate from the external world those materials to which labour is applied in order to provide man with his subsistence.

The institution of property, as well as serving an immediate practical purpose, is a specific vehicle for man's transcendence of nature through culture, a tangible expression of human universality. Needs, as designating necessity and the physical constraints of human existence, justify possession 'power over a thing *ab extra*' (para. 45, p. 42). 'The particular aspect of the matter, the fact that I make something my own as a result of my natural need, impulse and caprice, is the particular interest satisfied by possession' (ibid.). But this power of the individual, as subject, over nature as object of his needs has a universal dimension as well, because 'I as free will am an object to myself in what I possess and thereby also for the first time am an actual will', and this aspect, Hegel says, is what 'constitutes the category of *property*, the true and right factor in possession' (ibid.).

> If emphasis is placed on my needs, then the possession of property appears as a means to their satisfaction, but the true position is that, from the standpoint of freedom, property is the first embodiment of freedom and so is in itself a substantive end. (Remark to para. 45, p. 42)

Without a single reference to Locke, Hegel replicates the Lockean argument to the effect that 'property is the *embodiment* of personality' (para. 51, p. 45):

> By being taken into possession, the thing acquires the predicate 'mine' and my will is related to it positively. Within this identity, the thing is equally established as something negative, and my will in this situation is a particular will, i.e., need, inclination, and so forth. (para. 59, p. 49)

It is the act of possession, as such, which affirms the true order of things in which man as the highest living creature subsumes and indeed, if necessary, destroys lower orders of organic nature, prey to his needs. 'My inward idea and will that something is to be mine is not enough to make it my property', he says, 'to secure this end occupancy is requisite. The embodiment which my willing thereby attains involves its recognizability by others' (para. 51, p. 45). In possession:

> . . . my need, as the particular aspect of a single will, is the positive element which finds satisfaction, and the thing, as something negative in itself, exists only for my need and is at its service — The use of the thing is my need being externally realized through the change, destruction, and consumption of the thing. The thing thereby stands revealed as naturally self-less and so fulfills its destiny. (para. 59, p. 49)

One can easily see in this statement of Hegel's a reaffirmation of the whole tradition which sees in progress and man's conquest of nature proof of latent human powers and their unfolding; an idea embraced by Marx, but specifically rejected by a new breed of Marxists concerned at the effects of this peculiar instrumentalism on the ecology of the environment and, therefore, on man himself. Of all nineteenth-century thinkers, John Stuart Mill and, perhaps, Freud were the only ones to consider seriously the as yet unseen ramifications of progress and to recommend a stationary state (see Mill [1909] 1976, bk. 4, ch. 6, pp. 746–51).[4] This was of no concern to Hegel who, like the classical political economists, their predecessors from the scholastics on, as well as Hobbes, Locke and their successors, justified property precisely on the basis of use:

> To use a thing by grasping it directly is in itself to take possession of a *single* thing here and now. But if my use of it is grounded on a persistent need, and if I make repeated use of a product which continually renews itself, restricting my use if necessary to safeguard that renewal, then these and other circumstances transform the direct single grasp of the thing into a mark, intended to signify that I am taking it into my possession in a universal way, and thereby taking possession of the elemental conditions or organic basis of such products, or of anything else that conditions them. (para. 60, p. 49)

Hegel presents a series of arguments on the ramifications of property and work which sets him absolutely against the tradition of the Stoics, Rousseau, the early socialists, primitivism in general, and even Plato in their condemnation of civilisation and its evils. Property, as Hegel sees it, represents the objectification of the individual will; it is by virtue of property as an externalisation of personality (terms that Marx was to use in a different context) that the individual will becomes visible and effective, the object of recognition of other wills similarly objectified. 'Existence as determinate being is in essence for another', Hegel says:

> One aspect of property is that it is an existent as an external thing, and in this respect property exists for other external things and is connected with their necessity and contingency. But it is also as an embodiment of the will, and from this point of view the 'other' for which it exists can only be the will of another person. This relation of will to will is the true and proper ground in which freedom is existent. (para. 71, p. 57)

The social contract as such is a contract between objectified wills who grant to one another mutual recognition; the institution of property is thus its presupposition (Remark to para. 71, p. 57).

Hegel is not afraid to admit that property exacerbates natural inequalities. But seen positively, this is a process by which differentiations of skill and resources contribute to the complexity and variety of civil society, as well as providing the basis for a division of labour and subsequent class structure. 'Men are made unequal by nature, where inequality is in its element', he insists, 'and in civil society the right of particularity is so far from annulling this natural inequality that it produces it out of mind and raises it to an inequality of skill and resources, and even to one of moral and intellectual attainment' (Remark to para. 200, p. 130). Anticipating the objections of socialist critics, Hegel adds: 'To oppose to this right a demand for equality is a folly of the Understanding which takes as real and rational its abstract equality and its "ought-to-be"' (ibid.).

Hegel has already argued, an argument that Rousseau to some extent foreshadowed, that it is the very multiplicity of needs which the progress of civilisation produces that permits the development of mind. 'The multiplicity of objects and situations which excite interest is the stage on which theoretical education develops' (para. 197, p. 129) under the pressure of a necessity to choose. 'This education consists in possessing not simply a multiplicity of ideas and facts, but also a flexibility and rapidity of mind, ability to pass from one idea to another, to grasp complex and general relations, and so on' – Rousseau's concept of the 'ability to compare'. Work similarly develops practical reason, 'adaptation of one's activity according not only to the nature of the material worked on, but also, and especially, to the pleasure of other workers' (ibid.). In other words, work has a socialising function in the humanisation of nature and the socialisation of men – not altogether a good thing according to Rousseau. Like Rousseau, however, Hegel argues that to treat the state of nature as a condition of natural virtue is to misunderstand the nature of the moral realm and the function of education and choice therein:

> The idea that the state of nature is one of innocence and that there is a simplicity of manners in uncivilized peoples, implies treating education as something purely external, the ally of corruption. Similarly, the feeling that needs, their satisfaction, the pleasures and comforts of private life, and so forth, are absolute ends, implies treating education as a mere means to these ends. Both these views display lack of acquaintance with the nature of mind and the end of reason. Mind attains its actuality only by creating a dualism within itself, by submitting itself to physical needs and the chain of these external necessities, and so imposing on itself this barrier and this finitude, and finally by maturing itself inwardly even when under this barrier until it overcomes it and attains its objective reality in the finite. The end of reason, therefore, is neither the manners of an unsophisticated state of nature, nor as particularity develops, the pleasure for pleasure's sake which education procures. On the contrary, its end is to banish natural simplicity, whether the passivity which is the absence of the self, or the crude type of knowing and willing, i.e., immediacy and singularity, in which mind is absorbed . . . The final purpose of education, therefore, is liberation and the struggle for a higher liberation still; education is the absolute

transition from an ethical substantiality which is immediate and natural to one which is intellectual and so both infinitely subjective and lofty enough to have attained universality of form. In the individual subject, this liberation is the hard struggle against pure subjectivity of demeanour, against the immediacy of desire, against the empty subjectivity of feeling and the caprice of inclination. The disfavour showered on education is due in part to its being this hard struggle; but it is through this educational struggle that the subjective will itself attains objectivity within, an objectivity in which alone it is for its part capable and worthy of being the actuality of the Idea. (Remark to para. 187, pp. 125–6)

The term for education, *Bildung*, which Hegel uses here, refers not, of course, to formal schooling, but rather to refinement, cultivation, or development, connotations of the Latin root *educere* which have been lost to some extent in our English derivative. Hegel is therefore arguing against the whole defence of the uncivilised (*ungebildeter*) state which Rousseau seemed to undertake. He may even have had in mind here, when he talks of the disfavour showered on education, Rousseau's first 'Discourse' where he criticised the arts and sciences as vehicles for the corruption of public manners.[5] Not all of Rousseau's criticisms were to this effect, however, and he reserved a place for genuine education as the route to virtue, a distinction which Hegel upholds in the Addition to para. 187 (p. 268), although in a different way. There he defines a genuinely educated man as one who has attained sociability, 'Who without the obtrusion of personal idiosyncracy can do what others do . . . while bastard originality adopts eccentricities which only enter the heads of the uneducated', a concept of education Rousseau would not have favoured.

In the same way, division of labour and co-operative labour, which Hegel saw following naturally from education and the specialisation of talents, were developments which Hegel praised but Rousseau condemned. Following Plato, who saw justice to be founded on the principle of each doing the job for which his aptitudes best fitted him, Hegel reaffirmed a tradition of seeing a division of labour as prerequisite to social justice against which Rousseau, Marx and a long line of thinkers critically reacted. 'The universal and objective element in work', Hegel argued, 'lies in the abstracting process which effects the subdivision of needs and means and thereby *eo ipso* subdivides production and brings about the division of labour' (para. 198, p. 129). Such a division of labour permits not only the diversification of production but a high level of specialisation which, coupled with technological development, may ultimately produce automation:

By this division, the work of the individual becomes less complex and consequently his skill at this section of the job increases, like his output. At the same time, this abstraction of one man's skill and means of production from another's completes and makes necessary everywhere the dependence of men on one another and their reciprocal relation in the satisfaction of their other needs. Further, the abstraction of one man's production from another's makes work more and more mechanical, until finally man is able to step aside and install machines in his place. (ibid.)

Property and the division of labour permit a progress in the differentiation and specialisation of human activity that puts men in a greater but beneficial dependence and, at the same time, socialises the environment through work:

> The means of acquiring and preparing the particularized means appropriate to our similarly particularized needs is work. Through work the raw material directly supplied by nature is specifically adapted to these numerous ends by all sorts of different processes. Now this formative change confers value on means and gives them their utility, and hence man in what he consumes is mainly concerned with the products of men. It is the products of human effort which man consumes. (para. 196, pp. 128–9)

Hegel argues with Rousseau, Adam Smith and the four stages theorists of social development that 'the real and original foundation of states has been rightly ascribed to the introduction of agriculture along with marriage, because the principle of agriculture brings with it the formation of the land and consequently exclusively private property . . . the tranquility of private rights and the assured satisfaction of [men's] needs', while marriage turns 'sexual love' into 'an enduring league' and 'needs expand into care for a family, and personal possessions into family goods' (Remark to para. 203, p. 131). So far has economic diversification progressed from these origins, however, that in contrast with the rural economy of subsistent households of former times, modern society represents a mass of reciprocally dependent individuals working for one another's subsistence — just Rousseau's objection to it:

> When men are thus dependent on one another and reciprocally related to one another in their work and the satisfaction of their needs, subjective self-seeking turns into a contribution to the satisfaction of the needs of everyone else. That is to say, by a dialectical advance, subjective self-seeking turns into the mediation of the particular through the universal, with the result that each man in earning, producing, and enjoying on his own account is *eo ipso* producing and earning for the enjoyment of everyone else. The compulsion which brings this about is rooted in the complex interdependence of each on all, and it now presents itself to each as the universal permanent capital . . . which gives each the opportunity, by the exercise of his education and skill, to draw a share from it and so be assured of his livelihood, while what he thus earns by means of his work maintains and increases the general capital. (para. 199, pp. 129–30)

The natural inequality in the distribution of talents in society, reinforced by the division of labour and an unequal distribution of capital, produces class divisions:

> The infinitely complex, criss-cross, movements of reciprocal production and exchange, and the equally infinite multiplicity of means therein employed, become crystalized, owing to the universality inherent in their content, and distinguished into general groups. As a result, the entire complex is built up into particular systems of needs,

means and types of work relative to these needs, modes of satisfaction and of theoretical and practical education, i.e., into systems, to
one or other of which individuals are assigned − in other words, into
class-divisions. (para. 201, pp. 130−1)

Hegel's theory of the modern state presupposes the plurality of
individual interests, the multiplicity of needs and means to their satisfaction, which the progress of civilisation built on property, class and the
division of labour have produced. It is against the reality of the diversity
and particularity, disorder and conflict of civil society, in which men are
busy about the pursuit of their private interests, that Hegel sees the
universality and order of the state emerging:

> Individuals in their capacity as burghers in this state are private
> persons whose end is their own interest. This end is *mediated* through
> the universal which thus *appears* as a *means* to its realization. Conse-
> quently, individuals can attain their ends only in so far as they them-
> selves determine their knowing, willing and acting in a universal way
> and make themselves links in this chain of social connexions. In these
> circumstances, the interest of the Idea − an interest of which these
> members of civil society are as such unconscious − lies in the process
> whereby their singularity and their natural condition are raised, as a
> result of the necessities imposed by nature as well as of arbitrary
> needs, to formal freedom and formal universality of knowing and
> willing . . . (para. 187, pp. 124−5)

It is this peculiar complexity and diversity of the modern state that arises
from an individualism sublated in the collectivity which is missing from
the concept of the *polis* in ancient philosophy. Social and economic
developments which, from the inception of Christianity and the growth
of Roman culture, were responsible for the diversification of social and
economic activity and religious beliefs, safeguarded in law and enshrined
in political institutions, have added a dimension to social life in the
sphere of civil society that Plato and the ancients, accustomed to the
unitary state, could not have envisioned:

> In his *Republic*, Plato displays the substance of ethical life in its ideal
> beauty and truth; but he could only cope with the principle of self-
> subsistent particularity, which in his day had forced its way into
> Greek ethical life, by setting up in opposition to it his purely sub-
> stantial state. He absolutely excluded it from his state, even in its
> very beginnings in private property . . . and the family, as well as in
> its more mature form as the subjective will, the choice of a social
> position, and so forth. It is this defect which is responsible both for
> the misunderstanding of the deep and substantial truth of Plato's
> state and also for the usual view of it as a dream of abstract thinking,
> as what is often called a 'mere ideal'. The principle of the self-
> subsistent inherently infinite personality of the individual, the
> principle of subjective freedom, is denied its right in the purely sub-
> stantial form which Plato gave to mind in its actuality. This principle
> dawned in an inward form in the Christian religion and in an external
> form . . . in the Roman world. It is historically subsequent to the
> Greek world, and the philosophic reflection which descends to its

depth is likewise subsequent to the substantial Idea of Greek philosophy. (Remark to para. 185, p. 124)

Hegel outdoes Plato in the parallel he draws between the architectonic function of the will in relation to needs — institutionalised through property — and the architectonic function of the state in relation to interests — institutionalised in the estates, corporations, police, and so on. In Plato's *Republic*, 'subjective particularity was not incorporated into the organization of society as a whole; it was not reconciled in the whole, and therefore — since as an essential moment it emerges there at any event — it shows itself there as something hostile, a corruption of the social order (Remark to para. 206, p. 133). The Greek states, like the Roman Republic, by not recognising the principle of 'subjective particularity', or the rights of the individual, were overthrown. 'But when subjective particularity is upheld by the objective order in conformity with it and is at the same time allowed its rights, then it becomes the animating principle of the entire civil society, of the development alike of mental activity, merit, and dignity . . . what is primarily meant by freedom in common parlance' (ibid.). In other words, the secret of the modern state, as a number of early commentators had observed, is to have the passions work for it and not against it. Property was an important instrument in the pacification of the passions and 'the general principle that underlies Plato's ideal state' and other utopian communist regimes 'violates the right of personality by forbidding the holding of private property' (Remark to para. 46, p. 42), which becomes a source of destruction from within.

Hegel's remonstrations against Plato and the repressiveness of the 'ideal state' built on the principles of community, equality and fraternity were aimed in part at Rousseau and the eighteenth-century socialists. As such, they pointed towards the future in a curious way, for left-Hegelians, among whom Marx is included, typically reacted against the benign interpretation that Hegel gave the division of labour, property and the class structure of the liberal state in favour of a form of socialism which reaffirmed community, equality and fraternity as governing values. Plato is in Hegel's eyes excused from a failure to understand the significance of property that only subsequent historical developments could have revealed. But a return to the unitary state and its repressive principles that socialists seem to want to undertake represents to him a violation of all that civilisation, in the name of freedom, has achieved:

> The idea of a pious or friendly and even compulsory brotherhood of men holding their goods in common and rejecting the principle of private property may readily present itself to the disposition which mistakes the true nature of the freedom of mind and right and fails to apprehend it in its determinate moments. (Remark to para. 46, pp. 42–3)

Hegel has harsh words for the 'moral or religious view' behind this idea: the sentiment of fraternity, which supports the concept of communism, mistakes the nature of friendship and trust; this Epicurus, when he forbade his friends 'to form such an association holding goods in common', clearly understood (ibid., p. 43). Hegel has equally harsh words for the sentiment of equality, for it represents an incorrect judgement on what constitute the foundations of the universal, as opposed to the particular, dimensions of social life. '"Equality" is the abstract identity of the Understanding; reflective thought and all kinds of intellectual mediocrity stumble on it at once when they are confronted by the relation of unity to a difference' (Remark to para. 49, p. 44). But equality will not provide this principle of unity because to speak of persons as equal is 'an empty tautology' since 'the person, as something abstract, has not yet been particularized or established as distinct in some specific way' (ibid.). Equality will not provide a substantive principle of justice to deal with individuals with particular needs because 'at this point, equality could only be the equality of abstract persons as such, and therefore the whole field of possession, this terrain of inequality, falls outside it' (ibid.).

> The demand sometimes made for an equal division of land, and other available resources too, is an intellectualism all the more empty and superficial in that at the heart of particular differences there lies not only the external contingency of nature but also the whole compass of mind, endlessly particularized and differentiated, and the rationality of mind developed into an organism.
> We may not speak of the injustice of nature in the unequal distri-bution of possessions and resources, since nature is not free and therefore is neither just nor unjust. That everyone ought to have sub-sistence enough for his needs is a moral wish and thus vaguely expressed is well enough meant, but like anything that is only well meant it lacks objectivity . . . (Remark to para. 49, p. 44)

Marx, who accepts much of what Hegel has to say on the ontological significance needs, while rejecting the general *laissez-faire* argument for a balance of interests that Hegel in his theory of civil society as a system of needs presents, goes along to a surprising degree with Hegel's critique of utopian socialism. That Marx followed Hegel in denigrating crude communism and the artificial levelling down which the holding of goods in common involves, we know. Such a society arises from generalised envy, he argued, a crude hostility to luxury from which its architects were formerly excluded (1844 Manuscripts, *CW*, Vol. 3, p. 295). In later works, Marx shows the same scepticism of the ideals of liberty and equality that he earlier showed for fraternity and community. In *The Holy Family* he accused Proudhon of failing to see that 'the idea of "equal possession" is a political-economic one and therefore still an *alienated* expression' (1956 edn, p. 60).[6] And in the *Grundrisse* he argued that 'equality and freedom . . . as developed in juridical, political, social relations', were 'merely the idealized expressions of this basis' (*Grundrisse*, 1973 edn, p. 245). In the *Critique of the Gotha Programme*, Marx argues that the right to equality presupposes inequality — 'this equal right . . . is therefore a right to inequality in its content, like every right' (cited by Heller, 1976, p. 123) — just as he earlier argued that the right to property presupposed the right to be dispossessed, the right of freedom of religion, the right to persecution, and so on ('On the Jewish

Question', *CW*, Vol. 3, pp. 162–8). Liberty, equality and fraternity are, like justice, bourgeois shibboleths to be transcended, not because as values they have been imperfectly realised but because of what they in essence are: abstractions which cannot take account of men's particularity or their peculiar needs. Marx maintains that to contribute to the community on the basis of one's ability, but receive from it on the basis of one's needs is a formula for justice superior to the principle of equality, which represents a bourgeois right to correct a bourgeois wrong – structured inequality:

> In a higher phase of communist society, after the enslaving sub-ordination of the individual to the division of labour, and therewith also the antithesis between mental and physical labour, has vanished; after labour has become not only a means of life but life's prime want; after the productive forces have also increased with the all-round development of the individual and all the springs of co-operative wealth flow more abundantly – only then can the narrow horizon of bourgeois right be crossed in its entirety and society inscribe on its banners: From each according to his ability to each according to his needs! (*Critique of the Gotha Programme, Marx/Engels Selected Works*, Vol. 3, 1966, p. 19)

Notes

1 This passage from Hegel is in fact reproduced by Marx in *The Holy Family* (*CW*, Vol. 4, p. 40) as an example of speculative philosophy which speaks of man but 'does not mean the *concrete* but the *abstract*, the *idea*, the *spirit*, etc.'

2 See translator's foreword, p. ix.

3 See translator's note to para. 195 and his reference to the *Encyclopedia*, para. 92, and Hegel's reference to the 'multiplication of needs never' lifting one 'out of the sphere of needs' (p. 355).

4 I owe this observation to William Leiss (1976), p. 104ff.

5 Hegel refers to Rousseau explicitly in the Remarks to para. 29 (p. 33), para. 258 (pp. 156–7), and the Addition to para. 153 (p. 261). And the translator, T. M. Knox, certainly sees Hegel's discussion of the distinction between uncivilised (*ungebildetem*) and civilised (*gebildetem*) need as referring to Rousseau's theory as well (see translator's notes to para. 195, Hegel, 1957, p. 355).

6 Cited by Heller (1976, p. 123), who discusses Marx's views on equality. (See *CW*, Vol. 4, p. 43 for a slightly different translation.)

6

Marx on Human and Inhuman Needs

Marx, at least twice, in the *Critique of the Gotha Programme* and *The German Ideology*, repeats the old socialist slogan 'to each according to his needs', interpreted as it usually was to mean that the goods of society should be distributed on the basis of genuine needs and not any other principle. When it came to deciding how genuine needs were to be identified most socialists of his time were happy to allow the principle of equality, taken in conjunction with the provision of basic necessities for survival for all, to decide the issue. In other words, genuine needs were by definition those equal needs for survival common to all and nothing more. Most socialists expected that under socialism production would be regulated by the provision of just-enough goods to satisfy these needs, so the problem of how to distribute a surplus did not arise.

But this common understanding of the slogan 'to each according to his needs' does not fit very well with other major aspects of Marx's thought. As we know, he advocated an economy of abundance and not one geared down to basic needs. In fact, he mocked the Babouvists and those primitivists who recommended 'the abstract negation of the entire world of culture and civilization, the regression to the *unnatural* simplicity of the *poor* and crude man who has few needs and who has not only failed to go beyond private property, but has not yet even reached it' (*CW*, Vol. 3, p. 295). The concept of needs is not for Marx, from what we know of his most characteristic use of it in the 1844 Manuscripts, a limiting concept at all. So far from being a primitivist, Marx is an advocate of both technological progress and man's increasing mastery over nature and his own destiny, and any increase in needs these involve. So he argued, for instance, that 'industry is . . . the *open* book of *man's essential powers*' (p. 302), and that socialism, which would be established only when the forces and relations of production had been developed to their highest point, would see a society based not on wealth and poverty but on 'the *rich human being* and the rich *human* need' (p. 304).

There certainly are passages in the 1844 Manuscripts, as Lucio Colletti (1972), Iring Fetscher (1962) and others have pointed out, that are highly reminiscent of the account of alienation due to property and artificial needs that Rousseau gives in the second 'Discourse'. Marx contrasts socialism geared to the satisfaction of 'human' needs, with capitalism which promotes 'inhuman' needs. Under socialism 'the *wealth* of human needs' signifies 'a new manifestation of the forces of *human* nature and a new enrichment of *human* nature' (*CW*, Vol. 3, p. 306).

> Under private property their significance is reversed: every person speculates on creating a *new* need in another, so as to drive him to fresh sacrifice, to place him in a new dependence and to seduce him into a new mode of *enjoyment* and therefore economic ruin. Each tries to establish over the other an *alien* power, so as thereby to find satisfaction of his own selfish need. The increase in the quantity of objects is therefore accompanied by an extension of the realm of alien powers to which man is subjected, and every new product represents a new *potentiality* of mutual swindling and mutual plundering . . . Subjectively, this appears partly in the fact that the extension of products and needs becomes a *contriving* and ever-*calculating* subservience to inhuman, sophisticated, unnatural and *imaginary* appetites. Private property does not know how to change crude need into *human* need. (pp. 306–7)

One cannot fail to notice the similarity with Rousseau's argument: advanced society creates needs of mutual dependence which are such that men cannot satisfy their personal needs without seeming to guarantee others the satisfaction of theirs; but this simply lays society open to massive dissembling that reduces them all to enemies. Marx, like Rousseau and a number of early socialists, believes that competition for the satisfaction of needs which society engenders is unnecessary and due only to the inequalities that it established. Society, through the institutions of property and money, creates artificial inequalities that are themselves the source of the greater powers of some over others and the gap between the inflated needs of the rich and the crude needs of the poor. Under alienated society:

> Every product is a bait with which to seduce away the other's very being, his money; every real and possible need is a weakness which will lead the fly to the glue-pot . . . every need is an opportunity to approach one's neighbour under the guise of utmost amiability and to say to him: Dear friend, I give you what you need, but you know the *conditio sine qua non*; you know the ink in which you sign yourself over to me; in providing for your pleasure, I fleece you. (p. 307)

All the institutions of bourgeois society contrive to maintain or increase the inequality of needs, because the expansion of capital, by means of a surplus accruing to some while others are exploited, depends on it. Thus, Marx argues, if 'industry speculates on the refinement of needs' for some, 'it speculates . . . just as much on their *crudeness*' for others, 'but on their artificially produced crudeness'; the irony of advanced society lies in 'civilization contained *within* the crude barbarism of need' (p. 311). On the subject of 'how the multiplication of needs and of the means [of their satisfaction] breeds the absence of needs and of means' (p. 308) under capitalism, Marx is at his most vociferous:

> . . . estrangement manifests itself in part in that the sophistication of needs and of the means [of their satisfaction] on the one side produces a bestial barbarisation, a complete, crude, abstract simplicity of need, on the other . . . Even the need for fresh air ceases to be a need for the worker. Man returns to a cave dwelling, which is now, however, contaminated with the pestilential breath of civilisation . . . Light, air, etc. − the simplest *animal* cleanliness − ceases to be a need for man. *Filth*, this stagnation and putrefaction of man − the *sewage* of civilisation (speaking quite literally) − comes to be the *element of life* for him. Utter *unnatural* depravation, putrefied nature, comes to be his *life-element*. None of his senses exist any longer, and [each has ceased to function] not only in its human fashion, but in an *inhuman* fashion, so that it does not exist even in an animal fashion . . . It is not only that man has no human needs − even his *animal* needs cease to exist. The Irishman no longer knows any need now but the need to *eat*, and indeed only the need to eat *potatoes* − and *scabby potatoes* at that . . . But in each of their industrial towns England and France have already a *little* Ireland. The savage and the animal have at least the need to hunt, to roam, etc. − the need of companionship. The simplification of the machine, of labour is used to make a worker out of the human being still in the making . . . (pp. 307−8)

Marx castigates a 'growth in the *cynicism* of political economy from Smith through Say to Ricardo, Mill, etc.' (p. 291). These political economists were well aware of the costs to the worker that the increase of capital levied, and yet they still dared claim for this economic system 'to have obtained political freedom for everybody; to have loosed the chains which fettered civil society; to have linked together different worlds; to have created trade promoting friendship between the peoples; to have created pure morality and a pleasant culture; to have given the people civilised needs in place of their crude wants, and the means of satisfying them' (p. 287). While this may be all true for the capitalist, civilisation is bought under this system only '(1) by reducing the worker's need to the barest and most miserable level of physical subsistence, and by reducing his activity to the most abstract mechanical movement; thus [the capitalist] says: Man has no other need either of activity or of enjoyment . . .' and '(2) by *counting* and the most *meagre* form of life (existence) as the standard − general because applicable to the mass of men' (p. 308). The political economist, who provides for the capitalist his 'scientific creed',

> . . . turns the worker into an insensible being lacking all needs, just as he changes his activity into a pure abstraction from all activity. To him, therefore, every *luxury* of the worker seems to be reprehensible, and everything that goes beyond the most abstract need − be it in the realm of passive enjoyment, or a manifestation of activity − seems to him a luxury. Political economy, this science of *wealth*, is therefore simultaneously the science of renunciation, of want, of *saving* − and it actually reaches the point where it *spares* man the *need* of either fresh *air* or physical *exercise*. This science of marvellous industry is simultaneously the science of *asceticism and* its true ideal is the *ascetic* but *extortionate* miser and the *ascetic* but

productive slave . . . Thus political economy – despite its worldly and voluptuous appearance – is a true moral science, the most moral of all the sciences. Self-renunciation, the renunciation of life and of all human needs, is its principal thesis. The less you eat, drink and buy books; the less you go to the theatre, the dance hall, the public house; the less you think, love, theorise, sing, paint, fence, etc., the more you *save* – the *greater* becomes your treasure which neither moths nor rust will devour – your *capital*. The less you *are*, the less you express your own life, the more you *have*, i.e., the greater is your *alienated* life, the greater is the store of your estranged being. Everything which the political economist takes from you in life and in humanity, he replaces for you in *money* and in *wealth*; and all the things you cannot do, your money can do. It can eat and drink, go to the dance hall and the theatre; it can travel, it can appropriate art, learning, the treasures of the past, political power – all this it *can* appropriate for you – it can buy all this: it is true *endowment*. Yet being all this, it *wants* to do nothing but create itself, buy itself; for everything else is after all its servant, and when I have the master I have the servant and do not need his servant. All passions and all activity must therefore be submerged in *avarice*. The worker may only have enough for him to want to live, and may only want to live in order to have that. (pp. 308–9)

Under these conditions money is needless to say the arbiter, 'the pimp', between the artificially inflated needs of the rich and the artificially diminished needs of the poor. Not only can money change needs into their opposite, but it can create needs where none existed before: 'If I have no money for travel I have no *need* – that is no real and realisable need – to travel' (p. 325), and vice versa. Lack of money has the power to deprive men of their capacities, transforming 'the *real essential powers of man and nature* into . . . merely abstract notions' (p. 325), just as having money can transform all incapacities into their opposite; so the ugly can procure beautiful women, the lame can furnish themselves with the means of locomotion, and so on.

Marx's invective against money, highly reminiscent though it is of Rousseau's argument that property reverses natural inequalities of strength and intelligence, is to a somewhat different effect. He does not condemn money as wealth, or even so much as the purveyor of false needs. It is money as 'the general distorting of *individualities*', the frustration of '*real essential powers* and *faculties*' (p. 325), 'the general *confounding* and *confusing* of all things – the world upside down – the confounding and confusing of all natural and human qualities' (p. 326), that he condemns. This is a judgement made once again with reference to his conception of the human essence and of the constitution of things in general. Money, because as a manifestation of alienation it contravenes the human essence, frustrating the unfolding of man's latent needs and powers, is an evil. But Marx, unlike Seneca, Rousseau, Babeuf, and the rest, does not argue that wealth and the fruits of civilisation are bad in themselves. Quite the contrary, he is scornful of the old prejudices against luxury, believing that culture improves on nature and he has nothing against wealth, seeing it, when its 'bourgeois form is stripped away', as 'the universality of needs, capacities, pleasures, productive forces . . . the full development of human misery over the forces of nature . . . the absolute working out of [man's] creative potentialities' (*Grundrisse*, 1973*a* edn, p. 488). Money is, in fact, the 'alienated *ability of mankind*', and private property the only medium that permits the 'ontological essence of human passion come into being, in its totality as well as in its humanity', as he had already claimed in the 1844 Manuscripts (*CW*, Vol. 3, pp. 322 and 325). This means that civilisation with all its trappings, far from being an unqualified evil, is actually responsible for the development of productive forces which want only the removal of certain fetters for man's powers to be realised fully.

It is a curiosity of Marx's theory of human nature that there is a close association between the concepts of needs and powers. This has to do with the belief in a reciprocal dependence between progress of knowledge, new needs and the availability of objects for their satisfaction that we have already noted in Rousseau as presuppositions for the development of man's latent potentialities. Marx's materialism, which is more thoroughgoing than that of Rousseau, makes this mutual dependence explicit in his theory of objectification. Needs, and the passions in general, Marx claimed, are 'not merely anthropological phenomena in the [narrower] sense, but truly *ontological* affirmations of being . . . and . . . they are only really affirmed because their *object* exists for them as a *sensual* object' (p. 322). Man's species-activity is such, Marx argues, that his capabilities exist *in potentia* as needs that require the material world as their field. Thus man's potential powers are characteristically expended in creating a world of objects. This is not only a precondition for man's self-realisation in a metaphysical sense, but it is also a precondition for survival. Man is a being whose nature it is to require objects outside himself in order to subsist: 'Man *lives* on nature . . . Nature is man's inorganic body . . . with which he must remain in continuous interchange if he is not to die' (p. 276). But this dependence of man on the objects of his needs is not confined to requisites for survival, it characterises all other aspects of the maintenance and development of the self. In this way Marx subsumes under the class of human sensuous needs, or those activities which presuppose a material object, not only the five senses, 'seeing, hearing, smelling, tasting, feeling', but even the peculiarly cognitive activities 'thinking, observing, experiencing, wanting, acting, loving', which he refers to as 'so-called practical senses' (pp. 299–300). The emergence of all these capabilities depends on a culture being able to provide appropriate objects for their exercise, so the emergence of a musical ear awaits the emergence of music, and so on. Subscribing to principles of sensationalist psychology, Marx argues after Feuerbach that since 'sense-perception must be the basis of all science', and since the scientific understanding of behaviour is one that 'proceeds from sense-perception in the twofold form of *sensuous* consciousness and *sensuous* need', the scientific understanding of society is one that sees that 'All history is the history of preparing and developing "*man*" to become the object of *sensuous* consciousness, and turning the requirements of "man as man" into his needs' (p. 303).

This is far from being a mechanistic materialism. Indeed, Marx differentiates man from other animals who also depend on nature for the object of their needs, and who also produce some of their means of subsistence (i.e. dwellings), on the grounds of freedom and consciousness: an animal 'produces only under the domination of immediate physical need, whilst man produces even when he is free from physical need and only truly produces in freedom therefrom' (p. 276). While the animal produces at the behest of instinct, as in the case of the bird building its nest, man can freely choose the goals for his production.

This view of objectification as the vehicle of human creativity accompanies an expressivist tendency in Marx that can be traced back to Hegel, for whom man's unfolding powers over nature, actualised as needs, are held to be manifestations of man's innate characterological traits, as we have seen. Far from being a deterministic mechanism in the form of instinctual urges as they are in animals, needs in man are expressive of his ability to transcend the limits of material existence and leave his own mark on the external world by shaping it in accordance with his elected ends. Marx in this way avoids in his conception of man's relation to the objects of his existence the mechanical determinism of eighteenth-century materialism and its man-machine theories of human nature. Needs are symptomatic not of the power of physical objects and processes over man so much as of his own powers over the physical world. The concept of 'needs' functions in Marx's philosophy much like the concept of 'desire' in Hegel's: to express an awareness of the limits and finitude of human existence that man as a creature reaching out for mastery of the given necessarily experiences. Desire, or need, is in this way expressive of a self-conscious subject who knows the area of his dependence on the material world and, therefore, understands the boundaries of freedom. This is why the slave is the paradigmatic figure for man's predicament in general: the pressing reality of slavery makes him that much more attentive to his own powers over nature and the possibility of freedom than the master who takes his independence for granted and forgets the degree of his dependence.

Desire and labour were the central categories of Hegel's account of the progress of consciousness in the *Phenomenology*. Man as a natural being is seen to be dependent on the material world for life support; but as an intelligent being, the individual ego experiences its autonomy by separating itself, as subject, from the external world, as object of its desires. The differentiation is *realised* in man's ability to *consume* the objects which satisfy his desires, demonstrating his superiority by obliterating them. To work on the external world in this way constitutes labour. Consciousness is the awareness of subject and object which this differentiation and its realisation through labour create; and self-consciousness requires, over and above this awareness, the confrontation of two consciousnesses, each of whom comes to conceptualise his ego by recognising himself in the other. Desire, as we have already seen, has an epistemological function beyond its role in the maintenance of life. The autonomy of the ego is measured against man's dependence on nature and other men through his needs; independence is seen to be a relative thing, owing its very existence to the awareness that need-dependence creates, while the progress of awareness has in these needs a material base.

It is not difficult to see how Marx's concept of needs derives from Hegel's concept of desire and the way in which desire and labour are sublated in the notions of freedom and history as the dialectical progress of consciousness — as we have seen, Hegel himself made the connection between 'desires', as they signify human objectification and motivations thereto, and needs as a defining category of the social and economic realms. It is not too much to claim, then, that the concept of needs has a primarily ontological function to perform in Marx's early writings, since Marx already suggested as much himself with frequent references to the Feuerbachian concept *Gattungswesen* or the 'human essence'. Needs represent basic human motivations and they represent the form in which man's relation to the world is actualised, but more than that they are tangible manifestations of an underlying human nature. So much is this so, that one is justified in asking whether, indeed, we are to understand Marx's concept of needs in a literal sense at all. In other words, Marx so characteristically refers to the whole range of human powers in the abstract as 'needs' that we are prompted to ask whether these have to be concretely expressed as needs to count as such or not. The free attribution of needs in the construction of theories of human nature that we have seen since Hegel, Marx and Freud, poses a general dilemma in that it now becomes open to anyone to attribute to man in general, and men in particular, needs irrespective of what they themselves feel they need. (This poses special problems in the case of Marx in that from *The German Ideology* on, when he develops more systematically his theory of historical materialism, needs have a special role to play as the motor of progress. Here it is inconceivable that the concept could refer to anything less than concrete or expressed needs.)

It is just this Hegelian legacy which came under attack by Max Stirner who criticised Feuerbach and those left-Hegelians who spoke always of 'man' and not of particular men. For all that Feuerbach had attempted to demystify the Hegelian eschatology, he had not succeeded in Stirner's view, for the very reason that he retained a notion of the human essence that it is the purpose of history to fulfil and could not, therefore, escape the realm of theology. 'To know and acknowledge essences alone and nothing but essences, that is religion; its realm is a realm of essences, spooks and ghosts', Stirner declared (1971, p. 56). And he held the peculiarly apocalyptic view of history which sees revolution as the means to man's diremption to be an extension of this ontological confusion. Man is not redeemed by history, revolution or anything else; he must take care of himself.

Somewhere between the 1844 Manuscripts and *The German Ideology*, Marx encountered Stirner's criticisms which impinged very directly on his theory although they were not addressed to it specifically.[1] His immediate reaction was to denounce Feuerbachian humanism in favour of a more tough-minded materialism. We find him constantly emphasising that his premises are 'not arbitrary ones, not dogmas, but real premises', that they take 'real individuals, their activity and the material conditions of their life', and that such premises can be 'verified in a purely empirical way' (*The German Ideology, CW*, Vol. 5, p. 31). Marx hoped in this way to turn against all the left-Hegelians, including

Feuerbach and even Stirner himself, the criticisms that Stirner had levelled by implication against him, and we find him declaring that all German philosophy from Strauss to Stirner is essentially theological (p. 29).

The substance of Marx's refutation of Stirner is to be found in a shift from the ontological conception of needs of the 1844 Manuscripts, to a thorough-going materialist psychology in *The German Ideology*. This psychology places new emphasis on needs as a motivational mechanism and serves two functions: first as an account of the psychological dynamics of social development; and second as a critique of capitalism in psychological terms. Marx begins with a three-phase account of the development of the forces and relations of production as a dialectic of needs; but his psychological critique takes the form of a distinction between 'fixed needs', those found in all social formations whose form merely changes, and artificial needs, those which are entirely the product of a specific mode of production.

Starting from the materialist premise that 'men must be in a position to live in order to "make history"' and that life involves first of all the satisfaction of material needs, 'eating . . . drinking, housing, clothing, and various other things' (pp. 41–2), Marx isolates three 'moments' or 'aspects' of the progress from primitive to civilised man: (1) primitive subsistence needs, whose satisfaction leads to (2) the production of new needs which in turn lead to (3) new social relations (*CW*, Vol. 5, pp. 41–3). It is important to notice that Marx sees these aspects as something more than historical stages in a descriptive anthropology – as with Rousseau they constitute analytic categories whose logic is proven by their extension in history. They are 'three moments which have existed simultaneously since the dawn of history and the first men and which still assert themselves in history today', and to emphasise this Marx adds a fourth which is not historical at all: the consideration of the production and reproduction of life as a double relationship, both natural and social.

Marx outlined three stages of consciousness which correspond to the three moments of material progress. The first was nature idolatry, 'consciousness of nature which first appears to men as a completely alien, all-powerful and unassailable force, with which men's relations are purely animal and by which they are overawed like beasts', accompanied by herd consciousness, where man 'is distinguished from sheep only by the fact that with him consciousness takes the place of instinct or that his instinct is a conscious one' (p. 44). The second stage of consciousness, where 'this sheep-like or tribal consciousness receives its further development and extension', comes with the expansion of productivity, 'the increase of needs, and, what is fundamental to both of these, the increase of population' (p. 44). With the division of material labour, for which Marx sees a basis in sex differences, comes a division between physical and mental labour, and this allows consciousness at the third stage to 'emancipate itself from the world altogether' and 'proceed to the formation of "pure" theory, theology, philosophy, morality, etc.' (p. 45). This is the age of ideology. The final phase of consciousness awaits social relations predicated on the full development of the forces of production, and will herald the age of science.

In the *Grundrisse* Marx considers the social and economic consequences of the expansion of needs as the motor of progress. Interestingly
enough, it is precisely in the context of his discussion of Adam Smith's
'invisible hand', or Hegel's 'cunning of reason', that he introduces the
subject. The truth that both these doctrines disclose is that each
individual by pursuing his private interests, or individual needs,
promotes the good of society as a whole. This is due, Marx claims,
neither to providence nor chance, but to the fact that private interests are
already socially determined. A given interest or need, although felt by the
individual to be his own, is nevertheless in 'its content as well as the form
of its realization . . . given by social conditions independent of all'
(*Grundrisse*, 1973a edn, p. 156). Historical progress is, therefore, in
terms of the unfolding of socially determined needs, because only they
provide the incentive necessary for the full development of productive
forces. And the 'cunning reason', or the hidden rationality of bourgeois
society, is seen to lie in the fact that despite all its exploitative effects
capitalism has a long-term civilising effect of which socially determined
needs are the bearer.[2]

On what basis is the extraction of surplus value and the accumulation
of wealth possible, he asks? On the basis of the increase and development
of productive forces, which requires, 'Firstly, quantitative expansion of
existing consumption; secondly: creation of new needs by propagating
existing ones in a wide circle; *thirdly*: production of *new* needs and
discovery and creation of new use values' (ibid., p. 408).

> Hence exploration of all of nature in order to discover new, useful
> qualities in things; universal exchange of the products of all alien
> climates and lands; new (artificial) preparations of natural objects,
> by which they are given new use values. The exploration of the earth
> in all directions, to discover new things of use as well as new useful
> qualities of the old; such as new qualities of them as raw materials
> etc.; the development, hence, of the natural sciences to their highest
> point; likewise the discovery, creation and satisfaction of new needs
> arising from society itself; the cultivation of all the qualities of the
> social human being, production of the same in a form as rich as
> possible in needs, because rich in qualities and relations –
> production of this being as the most total and universal possible
> social product, for, in order to take gratification in a many-sided
> way, he must be capable of many pleasures [*genussfähig*], hence
> cultured to a high degree – is likewise a condition of production
> founded on capital. This creation of new branches of production,
> i.e., of qualitatively new surplus time, is not merely the division of
> labour, but is rather the creation, separate from a given production,
> of labour with a new use value; the development of a constantly
> expanding and more comprehensive system of different kinds of
> labour, different kinds of production, to which a constantly expand-
> ing and constantly enriched system of needs corresponds.
>
> Thus, just as production founded on capital creates universal
> industriousness on one side – i.e. surplus labour, value-creating
> labour – so does it create on the other side a system of general
> exploitation of the natural and human qualities, a system of general
> utility, utilising science itself just as much as all the physical and

mental qualities, while there appears nothing *higher in itself*, nothing legitimate for itself, outside this circle of social production and exchange. Thus capital creates the bourgeois society, and the universal appropriation of nature as well as of the social bond itself by the members of society. Hence the great civilizing influence of capital; its production of a stage of society in comparison to which all earlier ones appear as mere local *developments* of humanity and *nature-idolatry*. For the first time, nature becomes purely an object for mankind, purely a matter of utility, ceases to be recognized as a power for itself; and the theoretical discovery of its autonomous laws appears merely as a ruse so as to subjugate it under human needs, whether as an object of consumption or as a means of production. In accord with this tendency, capital drives beyond national barriers and prejudices as much as beyond nature worship, as well as all traditional, confined, complacent, encrusted satisfactions of present needs, and reproductions of old ways of life. It is destructive towards all of this, and constantly revolutionizes it, tearing down all the barriers which hem in the development of the forces of production, the expansion of needs, the all-sided development of production and the exploitation and exchange of natural and mental forces. (pp. 409–10)

In other words, Marx generates his theory of the dynamics of culture as a tissue of structures and institutions which are built up around the creation and satisfaction of needs. One cannot but be struck by the similarities between Marx's account of the 'four moments' in the development of civilisation and the classic account of Seneca, Lucretius, Rousseau, and so on. There is, however, an important difference and this is in the much tighter relation that Marx draws between environmental factors and needs. The classic account had taken note that needs are such that the object must be within reasonable reach for one to conceive a need for it and thus the mutual dependence between the growth of knowledge, technical proficiency and new needs. Nevertheless, needs, although occasioned by, were not seen to be caused by environmental factors. From the Stoics and Epicureans to Rousseau, these philosophers, although sensitive to the material conditions of behaviour, nevertheless argued that the attraction of material goods, however great, could still be controlled through moral purpose. Their indictment of progress was made on the very assumption that men could still choose not to succumb to a life governed by the pursuit of an ever-wider range of material benefits. This marks the difference between Marx and his antecedents. Marx argues that those who attribute to moral purpose the capability of distinguishing between true and false needs simply fail to recognise the causal origins of needs in society:

> Whether a desire becomes fixed or not, i.e., whether it obtains exclusive [power over us] – which, however, does [not] exclude [further progress] – depends on whether material circumstances, 'bad' mundane conditions permit the normal satisfaction of this desire and, on the other hand, the development of a totality of desires. (*The German Ideology, CW*, Vol. 5, p. 225)

The communists, Marx argues, are the only ones who recognise this 'empirical connection' (p. 256n.). And,

> Since they attack the material basis on which the hitherto inevitable fixedness of desire and ideas depended, the communists are the only people through whose historical activity the liquefaction of fixed desires and ideas is in fact brought about and ceases to be an impotent moral injunction as it was up to now with all moralists 'down to' Stirner. (p. 255n.)

Marx's argument is not as clear-cut as it seems. It is not simply a matter of what needs become historically established or 'fixed' or not. 'A desire is already by its mere existence something "fixed"' and 'each need, which forms the basis of a "desire" is likewise something "fixed"' (p. 256n.). Thus Marx declares,

> . . . the communists have no intention of abolishing the fixedness of their desires and needs . . . they only strive to achieve an organization of production and intercourse which will make possible the normal satisfaction of all needs, i.e., a satisfaction which is limited only by the needs themselves. (p. 256n.)

Now it seems pretty clear that by 'needs themselves' Marx means genuine needs and he does draw a distinction between fixed and variable desires that comes close to the old distinction between natural and artificial needs, true and false needs. Fixed desires are those 'desires which exist under all relations, and only change their form and direction under different social relations'; variable needs are 'those originating solely in a particular society, under particular conditions of [production] and intercourse'. The communists will allow natural needs 'to develop normally', but artificial needs will be 'totally deprived of their conditions of existence' (p. 256n.).

Since socialism is a regime based on the satisfaction of genuine needs, Marx has to establish some criteria to differentiate needs other than simply what historical determination has produced. It seems, taking in conjunction his claim that communism will deprive artificial needs of the roots of their existence and his claim that communism will allow a satisfaction of all needs limited only by the needs themselves, that Marx does understand genuine needs in a special sense as those which are natural or universal as against those which are specific to a given culture. It seems to be the case that Marx is appealing against certain historical tendencies, at least certain forms of historically given needs, on the basis of his theory of human nature which, as we know from the 1844 Manuscripts, focuses on the ontological significance of needs.

The fact is, however, that in line with his rejection of Feuerbachian materialism and his insistence on 'empirical premises' in *The German Ideology*, Marx specifically rules out theoretical criteria to differentiate between needs: 'Which [of the desires] will be merely changed and [which eliminated] in a communist [society] can [only be determined in a practical] way, by [changing the real], actual ["desires" and not by making comparisons with earlier historical conditions]' (p. 256n.). This is a text with so many holes in it one would be loth to attach too much importance to it — indeed, much of the material on fixed and variable needs in relation to communist practice was crossed out in Marx's manuscript and has been relegated to footnotes in recent authoritative editions. But to the extent that these remarks are corroborated in other writings we can take serious note of them. One point that Marx is clearly making is that one cannot associate genuine needs with those which were to be found in a primitive society, since he explicitly rules out 'comparisons with earlier historical conditions' (p. 256n.) Like Rousseau, genuine needs for Marx, compared with the artificial needs of advanced society are not 'fixed' or 'natural' in the obvious sense. They are genuine not because they are in fact fixed, since all needs have that propensity, or because they are found in those cultures least altered by civilisation, but because they are constitutive of human nature as such. Marx reserves the term 'human' need for this special normative sense of the term in the same way that Rousseau uses the term 'natural' needs. But unlike Rousseau, whom he condemns in the *Grundrisse* as a 'Robinsonade' or primitivist, Marx never confuses those characteristics constitutive of human nature as such, with those which are to be found in nature.

In Marx we have a different difficulty and that is that while he retains the notion of a proper human nature, a human nature properly constituted, by which, for instance, the man of capitalism is judged, nevertheless at the same time this human nature is open to history to determine. Thus he claims that which needs will be changed and which needs will be eliminated by the communists will be decided in a practical way, and not on the basis of theoretical principles, in the same way that in the second of the *Theses on Feuerbach* he claims that the question of truth is not a theoretical but a practical question — man 'must prove the truth, i.e., the reality and power, the this-sidedness of his thinking in practice' (*CW*, Vol. 5, p. 6). Now, only if history itself conforms to rational laws uniform with those constitutive of the universe as a whole, can we accept the idea that we can leave it to history to decide which needs and which truth claims are genuine and which are not. This suggests a teleological, if not indeed, an eschatological, concept of history which sits badly with Marx's avowed secularism and his rejection of all theological positions.

It is fair to say, I think, that the suggestion of a distinction between true and false, natural and artificial needs, even in the early works never properly explicated, greatly recedes in the later works. Perhaps indeed, Marx's teleological conception of history militates against it. Despite the exploitation and alienation of capitalism, Marx, as we have noted, far from being a conventional critic of civilisation, subscribes to a general theory of progress. He therefore praises 'the great civilizing influence of capital'; its constant drive to create new use values and to search the earth for new commodities 'to which a constantly expanding and constantly enriched system of needs corresponds'; its capacity to subjugate all nature 'under human needs, whether as an object of consumption or as a means of production'; its ability to drive 'beyond national barriers and prejudices . . . as well as all traditional, confined, complacent, encrusted satisfactions of present needs . . . tearing down all the barriers which hem in the development of the forces of production, the expansion of needs, the all-sided development of production, and the exploitation and exchange of natural and mental forces' (*Grundrisse*, 1973*a* edn, pp. 409–10). Although in blacker moments Marx talks of the 'Juggernaut of capital' which drags not only the labourer but his wife and children beneath its wheels (*Capital* [n.d.], Vol. 1, p. 604), he still sees in the development of new needs an impetus to the all-round development of man which 'constitutes one of the civilizing aspects of capital' (ibid., pp. 457–60 and Vol. 3, p. 819).

Marx in the 1844 Manuscripts had criticised political economy for its inhumane perspective on the individual as nothing but a 'totality of needs' in which the pressing needs of the poor were not differentiated from the ephemeral needs of the rich. He was anxious, then, that his approach should not be equated with that of political economy and its indiscriminate treatment of needs as wants equally deserving of satisfaction. In his later more scientific writings, however, this is a distinction that Marx no longer tries to press. So by the time we come to *Capital* he is ready to argue that use value simply depends on something being wanted and that 'the nature of such wants, whether, for instance, they spring from the stomach or from fancy, makes no difference' (Vol. 1, p. 43). Marx is undoubtedly sufficiently aware that his concept of 'human' needs was a metaphysical and not a scientific concept. This does not mean that he abandons it altogether, however. In *Capital* Marx makes the general argument that, under the capitalist law of accumulation, production is geared to the self-expansion of capital rather than the satisfaction of needs, obviously referring to needs that are in some sense genuine in a way that run-of-the-mill wants are not. Only rarely does Marx in the later writings explicitly use the term 'needs' which is peppered through his early works; but in his criticism of the shoddy goods which capitalism produces because of its concentration on quantity and not quality, exchange and not use value, accumulation and not the satisfaction of needs; and his criticism of the drive to subdivide labour constantly into its simplest and most automatic tasks so that labour no longer satisfies 'one of life's prime wants'; we see the concept of needs resurfacing as a criterion.

It has recently been remarked that the attribution of 'human wants, needs and purposes' is one of the most characteristic ways in which people appeal to their own concept of human nature to make judgements and recommendations, and that even works that purport to be scientific and value-free frequently end by justifying themselves in this way (C. Taylor, 1969). This is, I think, true to say of Marx, for whom 'human needs' are an ultimate value criterion. This becomes explicit where he endorses the old socialist slogan '*to each according to his need*' in *The German Ideology* (*CW*, Vol. 5, p. 537) and the *Critique of the Gotha Programme* (*Selected Works*, Vol. 3, p. 19) where genuine needs are clearly implied. From the way in which Marx handles the distinction between essential and non-essential needs in *The German Ideology* in passages to which we have referred, we know that he cannot and is not prepared to argue a philosophical basis for such a distinction, but nor is he willing to argue that it is scientific. History will decide; for which needs would be changed and which eliminated can only be determined in a practical way. This does not prevent Marx from holding his own views on human nature to which he frequently refers by the attribution of genuine human needs. His list of genuine human needs is more or less co-extensive with his list of characteristically human powers and these range from the powers of the senses to the so-called 'mental senses', or man's spiritual powers. 'Each of man's *human* relations to the world, seeing, hearing, smelling, tasting, feeling, thinking, observing, experiencing, wanting, acting, loving', involve, as Marx declares an *'orientation to the object*, the appropriation of the object' (*CW*, Vol. 3, pp. 299–300), and for this reason they constitute a need, although not for this reason a human need, since animals also appropriate objects so as to consume them.

In the concept of need and the related concept of objectification we see Marx's attempt to define the bounds of freedom and necessity, to establish a materialism which encompasses without extinguishing the spiritual realm. This list of needs includes not only those which are shared with animals and represent the degree to which man is limited by his physical nature; it also includes the specifically human capabilities by which man distinguishes himself (thinking, observing, experiencing, wanting, acting, loving), and shows himself capable of transcending the material boundaries of his existence. But it is a question of whether it is efficacious to lump these together as needs which require the exertion of a subject on an object. Those critics who have accused Marx of collapsing Aristotle's three categories, theory, praxis and production, are perhaps right (Arendt, 1959; Lobkowicz, 1967). *Praxis*, as Aristotle conceived it, was synonymous with activity and covered acting, willing, loving, where the point is not to do something with the object, to alter it as one does in production. (That these verbs may all be used intransitively as well as transitively is significant, that is they are not nonsensical when used without an object.) The object on which to confer one's power of willing, loving, observing, and so on, is a matter of choice and not necessity, and so perhaps one can argue that Marx confuses their peculiar character by classing these powers along with physical powers which are primarily object-related. It is not in the object that I observe that my powers of observation display themselves, nor is it in the object of my love, or the content of my act of willing, that the significance of these powers is to be found. In this way, they differ from the power to create something or to work raw material into an object which is rightly classed as production by Aristotle and differentiated from praxis or activity in which, like Epictetus's ball game, the object, although the occasion for the exercise of our powers, is not the end for which these powers are exercised.

Marx's concept of objectification and his conception of human activity as primarily object-related has given rise to certain anomalies of wide-ranging significance in Marxist thought. It can be argued, I think, that the whole thrust of orthodox communism as it developed as a theory of economic determinism in ignorance of Marx's early writings, is in part due to a misreading of Marx's theory of the relation of subject and object and the power of commodities as objects over man. It is clear from the early writings, that Marx characterised man as a creature with almost unlimited powers to transcend given material conditions and to change the world in his own image. The distinction between man and other creatures is precisely in these terms. Far from being a need or instinct-governed creature, man is precisely differentiated from other animals by the fact that his productive activity is initiated by the will and that in its form and goal it represents choice and not instinctual or any other form of determinism.

The hallmark of the Marxian ontology, or concept of essence, is the notion of immanence derived from the Hegelian phenomenology: the belief that thought plays an active role in the reality that it comprehends, and that reason, as it were, both reflects and shapes the real world.[3] History is seen as the macrocosmic reflection of the unfolding of individual self-consciousness, not just figuratively but literally, because history emanates from the activity of individuals, and stages in the development of culture are seen to correspond to levels in the development of mind. The efficacy of self-consciousness in its most highly developed state, where the objective and subjective dimensions of *Geist* coincide, is ultimately proven in the ability of men to shape their environment to fit their understanding. And the necessity which underlies this movement is desire, or man's imperative to satisfy his needs. Reason and necessity come together, not only because reason explicates the implicit laws of reality, but also because mind has an ordering and causative power over reality. Transformation of the environment is, therefore, the ultimate test of man's integrity, both because it involves the materialisation of reason and because reason is at the same time the truth of reality. In such a world needs are easily seen as the practical expression of philosophical imperatives.

Marx's concept of the socialist revolution only extended the logic of Hegel's analysis of the processes of history already at work, which had so far produced the French Revolution. Hegel literally understood this exertion of the powers of mind on external reality as a social and political reordering. This was the significance to him of the French Revolution and his criticism of the English Reform Bill of 1832, for instance, singled out its failure to rationalise British institutions in a way that would both reflect the stamp of ordering mind and at the same time make them intelligible to citizens. His *Philosophy of Right*, consistent with this view, conceptualised politics as an integration of institutions, beliefs and customs in the rational form of the state. It is not difficult to see Marx's socialist revolution as a culmination of the Hegelian principle of social transformation as the test of rational necessity.

Marx always tried to avoid the problem of values, but by his use of the concept of needs to express conditions for the actualisation of the human essence he demonstrated that he could not. It was here, as he subsequently realised, that Max Stirner's criticisms of left-Hegelians, who spoke always of 'essential' man and never of particular men, touched Marx. Stirner argued that the concept of the human essence was still essentially a theological or metaphysical concept and that Feuerbach and those materialists who appealed to it fell into the very trap they were trying to avoid in their ruthless unmasking of all religious forms. Although Marx tries to correct this tendency with his insistence in *The German Ideology*, almost half of which is devoted to a refutation of Stirner, that his premises were empirical and not speculative, that he was speaking not of man, but of real men, he does not really drop the concept of human nature that he outlined in the early writings, or develop a less metaphysical alternative. Were it even true, as some have argued, that he relegates the individual to the dustbins of history from here on out, and speaks of structural determination by classes, and so on, this form of materialism would suffer from unavoidably metaphysical overtones too. Classes of individuals, like classes of things, for all their seeming reality, are analytical constructs, and cannot therefore be postulated as causes.[4] In this sense materialism cannot avoid its fate as a doctrine of essences, and the moment history is seen as the interplay of 'social forces', we are back in the world of 'essences, spooks and ghosts', and Platonic ideas and scholastic universals have been reintroduced in a more mundane form, just as Stirner maintained. The idea of collective determinism ignores the fact that individuals are the ultimate agents of social activity, and that 'social forces' only enter the aetiological chain through individuals. For reasons that we discuss, I do not believe that Marx ever succumbed to the principle of economic determination in the last instance, even though there is much in his work that points that way. But even if he had, he could not have avoided the problem of value, just as the Althusserians, despite their claims to a rigorous science, cannot avoid it (see Springborg, 1978).

The conflict in Marx between his normative concept of needs (necessary conditions for the actualisation of the human essence) and his descriptive use of the term 'needs' (open to history to determine, because the proliferation of tomorrow's needs, unforeseen today, constitutes the motor of progress), becomes very evident in *Wage Labour and Capital*, where Marx admits that needs are relative, determined by society. He points to the man who lives in a small house which 'as long as the surrounding houses are equally small . . . satisfies all social demands for a dwelling'. But, says Marx,

> let a palace arise beside the little house, and it shrinks from a little house to a hut. The little house shows now that its owner has only very slight or no demands to make; and however high it may shoot up in the course of civilization, if the neighbouring palace grows to an equal or even greater extent, the occupant of the relatively small house will feel more and more uncomfortable, dissatisfied and cramped within its four walls. (*Selected Works*, Vol. 1, p. 163)

Marx notes that the same logic applies in the case of the worker and the capitalist, and that as long as the capitalist's share of the wealth increases at a faster rate than that of the worker, as it is bound under his theory to do, the worker will suffer from relative deprivation; this despite the fact that his basic needs are met:

> Thus, although the enjoyments of the worker have risen, the social satisfactions that they give has fallen in comparison with the

increased enjoyments of the capitalist, which are inaccessible to the worker, in comparison with the state of development of society in general. Our desires and pleasures spring from society; we measure them, therefore, by society and not by the objects which serve for their satisfaction. Because they are of a social nature, they are of a relative nature. (p. 163)

Marx's admission that there is a psychological aspect to needs casts a shadow over the hope that socialism can be run on the basis of 'each according to his needs', since it seems that our needs will not run out until we stop making comparisons, or until we run out of objects to satisfy them − whichever comes first. This means that we shall see man in societies of the future exerting the same old constant pressure on his environment that he exerts in today's societies, with all the attendant conflicts. It also means that to specify the conditions for the satisfaction of the human essence in terms of needs leaves it open what form those needs will take − which makes it impossible to give those conditions any specificity. Is it ultimately left to history to decide whether or not something constitutes a need? And if so, what does this signify for Marx's distinction between 'human' and 'inhuman' needs?

Marx from 1845 on, it is true, talks considerably less about human nature and 'human' needs. Max Stirner in his harsh criticism of the Young Hegelians had convinced him of the incongruity of rejecting all theological assumptions while retaining a notion of the human essence. This does not mean, however, as some have assumed, that Marx in his scientific phase has succeeded in ridding himself of these metaphysical presuppositions. Nor does it mean that dialectical materialism is a theory of economic determinism in the last instance. We know from the concept of the fetishism of commodities in *Capital* that Marx is not arguing that the material artefacts that man creates in the process of objectification do necessarily exert an alien power over him, but only that he thinks they do and that by the self-fulfilling prophecy this can come to be the case. Although, as Marx notes, like Sartre after him, the commodities, social structures and institutions that man creates through the organisation of production and everyday life tend to take on a dynamic of their own, so that man becomes a victim of his own creations, it is only under alienation that this is necessarily the case. And even then this is not due to any inherent powers in the object but only to the social powers that man himself unwittingly confers on them. The thrust of Marx's various dissertations on the power of money, from the 1844 Manuscripts to the *Grundrisse* and *Capital* itself, are to the effect that this power is due not to money's intrinsic worth, but only to the social conventions by which money becomes a measure of wealth. The fetishising of commodities lies in the failure to see the fragility of their power and its social origins. Once men understand that they are in principle free to withdraw the power that they have invested in these material things, commodities, like money and authority structures, all of which rest on conventional agreement, will lose their alien character and the domination of material conditions will be broken.

Perhaps the very reason why Marx felt the gibes of Stirner so strongly was because he was not ultimately a determinist, and yet he realised the difficulties of self-liberation which Stirner pointed out. There is a strong Stoical element in Stirner's thought that is not absent in Marx: one of the assumptions that they hold in common is the notion of freedom of choice in the face of all odds. Freedom requires an indifference to material conditions, self-determination and liberation from fixed ideas. To Stirner this meant the ability to subjugate the appetites in true Stoic fashion, and then to extricate oneself from the tyranny of false opinion. So far there is no disagreement between Marx and Stirner, except that Stirner's conclusions are more orthodoxly Stoic than Marx's (Marx lumps him with the Stoics as a philosophical quietist in *The German Ideology*): he advocates freedom through self-discipline and a self-sufficiency that is impervious to all pretensions that some universal panacea can be offered to liberate man *en masse*. Man can expect 'no salvation from a change of *conditions*' he claimed (Stirner, 1971, p. 221), and any attempt to seek freedom through the transformation of society, as revolutionaries do, can only succeed in creating a new fetter, a new *idée fixe* (p. 115).

In providing a critique of the socialist programme of personal freedom through the transformation of society, Stirner shows that in fact the whole emphasis on liberation as the conquest of nature and society has only succeeded in creating a further obstacle to human freedom in culture itself. Unlike his Stoic forebears Stirner is no primitivist and he sees in the expansion of man's powers and the civilising effects of culture real benefits and the force of human aspirations at work. Culture has certainly made man powerful. Through the sciences and the arts it has given him control over nature, and more importantly it has enabled him to master his own nature, his appetites, pleasures and emotions. What remains beyond his control, however, is culture itself. The benefits of civilisation are real and the complacency of the primitive man who never felt his own limitations is only an illusion of freedom. Nevertheless, the unfreedom of the man who has created railways and yet feels weak because he cannot fly, as he puts it, is endemic, 'the freer I become, the more compulsion piles up before my eyes; and the more impotent I feel myself . . . and, if I have solved a problem whose obscurity disturbed my mind, at once there await me innumerable others, whose perplexities impede my progress, dim my free gaze, make the limits of my *freedom* painfully sensible to me' (p. 111). To change social conditions will not change all this. Liberation is a process with no end in sight, and every step forward involves new obstacles; it is in the nature of freedom to be a goal that is never attained. The conclusion is obvious: 'I say: Liberate yourself as far as you can, and you have done your part; for it is not given to everyone to break through all limits, or, more expressively: not to everyone is that a limit which is a limit for the rest' (p. 106).

Stirner's election of an individual moral solution to the problem of freedom was unacceptable to Marx for various reasons. As we have mentioned, Hegel's influence had left its mark on Marx in his conception of needs as the ontological expression of man's characteristic powers over a world of objects. The Hegelian philosophy of history which saw man's nature as unfolding in time, put an emphasis on the growth of these latent powers as new sciences and technologies provided objects for them. In a curious way, however, Marx shares with the Stoics a common view of the correct relation between man as subject and the objects of his existence — that they are for enjoyment and use and not to possess, nor should man be possessed by them — that puts him closer to Stirner than one might otherwise think. Marx shared with the Stoics the ideals of equality, the community of goods and the universal brotherhood of man — an ethic that rejected individual property and the appropriation of goods except on the principle of use. One can see in Marx's declamations against the passion for 'having', similarities with Epictetus's conception of man's correct attitude to material objects in the allegory of the ball-player, on which, however, Marx in his theory of activity and production does not quite follow through. The good ball-player, says Epictetus, lavishes his attention on the ball not because of any intrinsic merits in the object, but because it provides the opportunity for him to display his skill. In his 'struggle for possession' the ball-player does not really want to keep or own the ball, but only to establish mastery. Man's relation to the material world in this way constitutes the durable framework within which he plays out the characteristic traits of his nature: an ability to humanise the world by the exercise of moral purpose.

It is, of course, a moral purpose that Marx will not recognise as such, and yet if we think of the significance of the doctrine of the fetishism of commodities and the various forms in which he foreshadowed it, we can see that the whole point of Marx's insistence that men need not feel terrorised by the material artefacts that they themselves have created, and that they can destroy the alien power of commodities through correct understanding and the right disposition towards them, suggests a concept of moral purpose as it was traditionally understood. Epictetus's parable states very well a central Marxian theme:

> So ought we also to act, exhibiting the ball-player's carefulness about the game, but the same indifference about the object played with, as being a mere ball. For a man ought by all means to strive to show his skill in regard to some of the external materials, yet without making the material a part of himself, but merely lavishing his skill in regard to it, whatever it may be . . . It is, indeed, difficult to unite and combine these two things — the carefulness of the man who is devoted to material things and the steadfastness of the man who disregards them, but it is not impossible. (*Discourses*, ii. v. 1925 Loeb edn, Vol. 1, pp. 243, 239)

In this sense, Epictetus expresses the logic of Marx's position where, although sometimes drawing on the distinction between natural and artificial needs, Marx ultimately sees all needs as indifferent, the link with material existence that gives man the opportunity to develop his human potential. As we have seen, however, this was a logic to which Marx was not always faithful.

The difference between Marx, on the one hand, and Epictetus, Stirner and the Stoics, on the other, is that the latter conceived man's relation to material objects negatively, while Marx conceived it positively. On the whole the Stoics saw the use of material goods as an unavoidable necessity, their attraction posing a distraction from moral purpose. But

Marx saw the creation of a world of material objects as a positive expression of man's species-nature – and if these artefacts sometimes created an obstacle to man's further advancement, it was one the very overcoming of which increased his power. We have only to look at the opening lines of Epictetus's *Encheiridion* to see the difference:

> Some things are under our control, while others are not under our control. Under our control are conception, choice, desire, aversion, and in a word, everything that is our own doing; not under our control are our body, our property, reputation, office, and in a word, everything that is not our own doing. Furthermore, the things under our control are by nature free, unhindered, and unimpeded; while the things not under our control are weak, servile, subject to hindrance, and not our own. Remember, therefore, that if what is naturally slavish you think to be free, and what is not your own to be your own, you will be hampered, will grieve, will be in turmoil, and will blame both gods and men; while if you think only what is your own to be your own, and what is not your own to be, as it really is, not your own, then no one will ever be able to exert compulsion upon you, no one will hinder you, you will blame no one, will find fault with no one, will do absolutely nothing against your will, you will have no personal enemy, no one will harm you, for neither is there any harm can touch you. (1928 Loeb edn, Vol. 2, p. 483)

This is a concept of freedom that could hardly be more diametrically opposed to the Promethean view of Marx. Freedom, as he saw it, was precisely the ability to subject the material world to human needs, to exert an increasing power over nature. Not only did Marx not foresee the constant obstacles to its own end that such a process necessarily throws up, as Stirner had explained, but he holds that a transformation of society, or a widespread change in the relation of man to his external environment, is the only true criterion for freedom, which is not to be sought in the state of the perfect will, as Kant maintained, or any moral condition arrived at through introspection and understanding, as Hegel and the ancients had declared.

The belief that the transformation of society in accordance with his goals was the ultimate test of human freedom, related as it was to the Hegelian phenomenology, had deeper roots in a materialist tradition that long predates Marx himself and to which he made constant reference. This tradition, which runs from the Hellenistic philosophers, and Epicurus in particular, to Francis Bacon, culminating in the Enlightenment, focused on man's relation to nature and the function of science and technology in human betterment. One of its axioms was the belief that *theoria*, or science, was only valid in so far as it had a practical application to human welfare. The very distinction between theory and practice, which becomes so important in Marx's philosophy, had its origins in the Greek philosophy of nature; for *theory* is etymologically derived from the term for spectator and a theorist in antiquity was an observer of nature, where a practitioner was one who put this knowledge to work. Marx had written his doctoral dissertation on 'The Difference between the Democritean and Epicurean Philosophy of Nature' and the first major work that he planned on its completion was a comprehensive history of the Hellenistic schools, the Stoics, Epicureans and Sceptics. He was attracted to these philosophers as materialists who, following in the wake of the great idealistic systematisers, Plato and Aristotle, reopened the questions of man's relation to nature, the unity of theory and practice and the problem of freedom and necessity. Once the universal systems of Plato and Aristotle had been called into doubt, men were forced back to these elemental questions and the problem of reconciling materialism with the belief that human activity is efficacious in itself (*CW*, Vol. 1, p. 491).

Marx praises Epicurus over Democritus precisely because his 'atomic swerve' permits human intervention in a material world whose basic entities consist in 'atoms and the void'. It was, indeed, the classic Epicurean view to see man as a creature who, although belonging to a world governed by a chain of physical causes, could initiate action on his own behalf and eventually conquer the world through science. The Stoics were less positive than the Epicureans in their attitude to science and it was just one of the ramifications of their reaction to Platonic idealism to insist that the study of nature should not be seen as an end in itself but instrumental to ethics, undertaken to permit man to 'live according to nature'. This position was not merely pragmatic: it involved a philosophical denial of the efficacy of bifurcating theory and practice. 'The virtuous man is both theoretical and practical with respect to things to be done', Diogenes Laertius declared, summarising the Stoic position (VII. i. 126).[5] Cicero followed Chrysippus in asserting that 'man is born to contemplate and imitate the world; the prime purpose of *theoria* is to imitate nature, that is to lead a life in accordance with it' (*De natura deorum*, II. xiv)[6] Seneca attacked the artificiality of the Aristotelian tripartite division of life into the theoretical, the practical and the productive, maintaining that it was equally 'impossible to pursue pleasure or to act *sine contemplatione . . .* as it is impossible to contemplate *sine voluptate* and *sine actione*' (*De otio*, ch. xxxii).[7]

It is interesting to notice that the separation between theory and practice was forcefully re-established by the neo-Platonists from Plotinus on, and specifically included a denigration of practical-political life in response to the worldliness of the Epicureans, Stoics and Sceptics. But the Stoic position re-emerged with Francis Bacon (it is no accident that Marx eulogises him in *The Holy Family*) who saw 'fruits and works . . . as it were sponsors and sureties for the truth of philosophies' (*Novum Organum*, I. lxxiii)[8]; who emphasised the barrenness of a philosophy 'for which there cannot be adduced a single experiment which tends to relieve and benefit the condition of man'; but who believed that 'works themselves are of greater value as pledges of truth than as contributing to the comforts of life' (*Novum Organum*, I. lxxiii, cxxiv).[9] Bacon it was who went on to claim: 'Human knowledge and power coincide, for ignorance of the cause deprives one of the effect. Nature to be commanded must be obeyed; and that which in contemplation is as the cause, in operation is as the rule . . .' (ibid., I. iii).[10]

Marx's materialism has a much more ancient ancestry than many contemporary discussions of the subject would suggest. Materialism was far from being an invention of Feuerbach which Marx transformed by the addition of political economic principles. Marx saw Feuerbach's materialism as one-sided, contemplative, passive and falling short of its goal. In the *Theses on Feuerbach* Marx gives one of the most trenchant criticisms of hitherto existing materialism that extends arguments already implicit in his 'Introduction' to the *Contribution to the Critique of Hegel's 'Philosophy of Right'* concerning the relation of theory and practice. In a very classical way, Marx relates the passivity of Feuerbachian materialism to its contemplative nature which, he implies, reflects the artificial Kantian distinction between pure reason and practical reason, itself a product of man's alienated conditions. The premises of Feuerbach's materialism were arrived at theoretically by the passive and uninvolved onlooker. For this reason his materialism was mechanical, concerned with the interaction of physical and sensual forces and impervious to the influence of man as a human subject.

This 'passive' materialism had its counterpart in an 'active' idealism which concentrated all man's intellectual, cultural and spiritual forces in a realm of ideas that is divorced from the material world. Both materialism and idealism were, in Marx's view, equally abstract and superficial, containing contradictions which can only be resolved when they are collapsed in the unity of '"revolutionary" or practical-critical activity' (*CW*, Vol. 5, p. 6). Objectivity is not a theoretical but a practical question and contemplative theory misses its mark because it fails to see that truth concerns real processes and not their appearances in thought. 'Man must prove the truth, that is the reality and power, the this-sidedness of his thinking in practice.' Pure reason is merely scholastic in Marx's view, objectivity can only be proven by testing the power of ideas in practice – that is to say, man's capability to intervene in natural processes and to marshal natural and social forces.

It was perfectly consistent of Marx to argue that those socialists who believed in a new society through education on the basis of Lockean sensationalist psychology and the environmental argument, people like Robert Owen, represented further examples of passive materialism. These thinkers characterised man's behaviour as the merely instinctual responses to environmental stimuli, seeing him as the merely passive mediator of material change. Such a view was wrong, Marx held, because circumstances do not change themselves, men change them. Man is by no means a passive intermediary, and it is the purpose of human activity to work on the external world so as to change it: 'the coincidence of the changing of circumstances and of human activity can be conceived and rationally understood only as revolutionizing practice' (*Theses on Feuerbach*, *CW*, Vol. 5, p. 7).

Marx's exhortation to philosophers not only to understand but to change the world, in the last of the *Theses on Feuerbach* related to his earlier considerations of the relation between theory and practice in his 'Introduction' to the *Contribution to the Critique of Hegel's 'Philosophy of Right'*. There Marx had argued that 'revolutions require a material basis. Theory can be realized in a people only in so far as it is the realization of the needs of that people' (*CW*, Vol. 3, p. 183). Material force must be met by material force and theory could only become a material force if it 'gripped the masses'; its findings had to become 'radical needs'. To do so, of course, theory had to deal effectively with the concerns of the masses. 'Will the theoretical needs be immediately practical needs?' Marx asks himself (p. 183). How could one ensure that the theoretical needs of philosophy will translate into practical imperatives? Only by ensuring that the human predicament of the masses guides philosophy and that the movement for the emancipation of the masses is guided by truth. Thus theory and practice would be united. In fact, Marx maintained, conditions were already ripe for this translation of theoretical into practical needs. It was only a matter of publicity and increasing the pressure of real circumstances by adding to it conscious pressure: those 'petrified [social] relations must be forced to dance by singing their own tune to them'. In this way, an 'imperative need of the German nation' would be fulfilled and 'the needs of nations are the ultimate grounds of their satisfaction' (p. 178). What material conditions would produce radical needs? Only the 'formation of a class with radical chains' (p. 186), a unique class characterised by universal suffering and for which need is universal, both in the sense that it lacked the satisfaction of all human needs, and that it could only obtain this satisfaction by the dissolution and emancipation of all classes. Such a class was the proletariat and when it has fully emerged as a class and practical imperatives have been matched by material conditions, 'then the *day of the German resurrection* would be proclaimed and the Gallic cock would crow!' (p. 187)

Although the conclusions of philosophy to which Marx refers as 'theoretical needs' were specific proposals rising out of appropriate historical analysis, they were vouched for in terms of his concept of human nature and what this dictated for the society of the future. Once again we come up against the problem to which Marx's use of 'needs' both to characterise the attributes of human nature in general and to take account of concrete or historically expressed needs, gives rise.

There is a parallel to be drawn here between the assumption that an analytical construct like class can function as a link in a causal process, and Marx's assumption that theoretical needs can somehow become a material force. The full implications of the problems to which this latter assumption give rise are only seen when Wilhelm Reich, Erich Fromm and others, noting that Marx himself does not succeed and that ideology does not provide the material link it is purported to, try to convert ideology into a 'material force', by introducing mechanisms of psychic determinism from Freudian theory. The project, as we shall see, is no more successful, and Freudian drives remain as metaphysical constructs in physiological disguise. Marx's penchant for explaining man's function in terms of human needs shares in a confusion between needs as imputed attributes of human nature in general and concrete or expressed needs, that has become a feature of some forms of need theory ever since. Wherever there is a gap between the ideal picture of human nature and human reality, a need is inserted – hence needs for love, security, relatedness, creativity, and so on. There is nothing wrong with this way of talking about human nature as such as long as it is recognised for what it is, metaphorical.

In other words, the imputation of needs produces a theory of human nature at a metaphysical level that cannot at the same time do service as an account of the motivation of particular men. This is a mistake that can be seen whenever a move is made from theory of human nature in terms of imputed needs, to the analysis of the behaviour of individuals as need-based, on the assumption that imputed needs and expressed needs are the same thing, or indeed that a need can be imputed even when it is not felt. This becomes more dangerous when people get the idea of bringing people's concrete needs into line with needs imputed to them according to a theory of human nature. The theory of environmental conditioning from the early socialists to the Skinnerians has provided a basis for doing this. Marx, who commended the communists for seeing the solution to the problem of man in terms of a transformation of needs and of society at large, was himself not immune from making this link.

Notes

1   On the relation between Marx and Stirner see Nicholas Lobkowicz's very good article 'Karl Marx and Max Stirner' (1969).
2   The 'civilizing influence of capital' is a dominant theme of the *Grundrisse* (1973a edn), see pp. 325, 408–10, 488, 540–2.
3   See Kolakowski's brilliant essay on the Hegelian phenomenology, 'Anti-utopie utopique de Marx' (1974a), espec. pp. 11–12.
4   For this and other aspects of Marx's theory of needs not developed here, see Patricia Springborg, 'Karl Marx on Human Needs' (1977).
5   As quoted in Lobkowicz (1967), p. 51.
6   As cited by Lobkowicz (1967), p. 51.
7   As cited by Lobkowicz (1967), p. 51.
8   1889 edn, p. 265, as cited by Lobkowicz (1967), p. 89.
9   As cited by C. Taylor (1975), p. 8.
10 1889 edn, p. 192, cited by Lobkowicz (1967), p. 89.

7

Jean-Paul Sartre on Needs and Desires

The twentieth-century renaissance of the concept of needs requires some explanation. It cannot be accounted for wholly in terms of the rediscovery of the 1844 Manuscripts, although these were certainly an important source. One of the most significant factors was the need to explain the unexpected longevity of capitalism, a function to which the doctrine of true and false needs seemed admirably suited. According to Marxist theory modified in this direction, the predicted crises – economic depression and two world wars – had not brought capitalism's demise because the inculcation of false needs had created a new basis for its continued existence. But this important role does not in itself explain why the doctrine of needs was seaworthy. Were true and false needs a mere pragmatic device to make good a shortcoming of original Marxist theory, the concept would have lasted hardly a day in the heightened intellectual climate to which it was introduced.

One of the outstanding features of the concept of needs is its apparent ease in bridging the gap between subjectivity and objectivity. It claims to succeed in explaining how the dialectic of history unfolds behind the backs of its actors, yet with their complicity. Marxism, in postulating the *objective* determination of social structures, immediately raises the question: what motivations and beliefs, what *subjective* disposition does historical determinism presuppose of individual actors? As we know, the concept of false consciousness was utilised to explain how individuals were the unwitting victims of historical forces. But false consciousness as a theory lacked teeth until the articulation of the doctrine of true and false needs. Only with its advent was it possible to explain precisely how individuals could will what dominant forces required them to will against their own interests, or, in other words, could want what they did not need. Or so it was thought. Although this doctrine was, as we have seen, implicit in Marx's theory, its full elaboration awaited twentieth-century Marxists, Sartre, Marcuse, Fromm, and others.

But here again we have accounted for the doctrine's *raison d'être* negatively – in terms of what was lacking to original Marxist theory seen retrospectively. This once more casts the doctrine of needs in the role of a device, a *deus ex machina*. It does not explain the force of the doctrine or why its début was so long delayed.

In post-Marxian thought two tendencies, present and in conflict in

Marx's thought on needs, take separate directions. One is the ontological concept of needs where needs are conferred an existential status, most notably in the thought of Sartre, Fromm and Laing. The other is a naturalistic interpretation of needs which follows from an emphasis on the primacy of material conditions, typified by the thought of Marcuse and a number of neo-Freudian Marxists. One may even speculate that the development of existentialism, on the one hand, and Freudian thought, on the other, made possible the separation of these tendencies which are to be found together in Marx who was both an Hegelian and a materialist. (Of course, to isolate these two tendencies does not mean that they were not both to be found in the thought of some of these men. Fromm, for instance, holds both to the ontological concept of needs, in his notion of existential needs, and to the doctrine of true and false needs, which is essentially materialist. Sartre himself moved gradually away from existentialism to embrace dialectical materialism.)

In each of these two tendencies the concept of needs receives a much higher degree of elaboration than in the thought of Marx himself. In the case of existentialism, man's whole orientation to the world is seen precisely in terms of his needs and desires. This departure marks a major philosophical turning point. To begin with, the Cartesian problem of the duality of mind and body is declared resolved. Not only is the existence of the material world no longer in doubt, but man comes to know himself precisely because of the way the external world impinges on him. His needs and desires register an insufficiency and dependency which press him into activity for survival, forcing him both to know and to manage his environment. The need for shelter and sustenance are the most rudimentary level of man's dependence, but his posture at every level is seen as one of a creature reaching out for mastery of what is given, and of making the material world his own by socialising it.

Such a view emphasises man's openness and the degree to which his nature is self-created in the process of an environmental interchange: the exigencies of the natural world spur man to action, but in acting he both changes the natural world and forms himself. Seen this way every need and desire is expressive of man's essence, the proliferation of needs representing his expanding powers and awareness. The only natural limit to such a process is the eventual satisfaction of all needs and the capitulation of the material world to man's control. It is a small step from here to argue that once the problems of production have been conquered and the resistance of the external world no longer forces man to fight for his existence, those tensions which underlie the class struggle and capitalist domination and repression will be released and men will enjoy the simple exercise of their powers and the appropriate gratification of their needs. Such is thought to be the condition of socialism with its motto 'to each according to his needs'.

One can easily see the Hegelian roots of such a doctrine, even if the dénouement is in terms of utopian socialism. Hegel's *The Phenomenology of Mind*, or 'the science of the experience of consciousness', posed man's encounter with the world dramatically in terms of desire. It was Hegel who first drew the analogue between life and consciousness. The organism confronts inorganic nature as the object of its needs. It must explore and indeed consume its host in order to survive. This natural process, involving as it does a totalisation, the structuring of a situation which discloses the essence of each of its parts, was seen to provide a paradigm for consciousness. Man, too, is situated in dependency and as an organic being he, too, preys off his host. His interchange with nature constitutes a totalisation, or a structuring of events that is an analogue for his intellectual grasp on the world. Here, too, his knowledge of himself is only disclosed by conflict and desire for self-certainty through the conquest and nihilation of the other. In the case of man as consciousness, his host is not inorganic nature but another consciousness, capable of refracting his own powers as a mirror image.

Hegel it was, and not Marx, who first postulated self-knowledge through the activity of restructuring the external world and he first saw consciousness arising from man's situation as a being under threat who gripped the world first through his needs and then through his desire for autonomy. It is a curiosity of history that such a thinker should have been cast for so long in the role of a mere idealist. (Perhaps not so curious if one considers what Marx contributed to this myth.) This injustice was precisely what the Hegel-renaissance of the 1930s sought to mitigate. In their efforts to reinstate Hegel, the Hegel of the *Phenomenology* in particular, a group of famous French intellectuals, Alexandre Kojève, Jean Wahl and Jean Hyppolite, influenced a whole generation of French thinkers and may be credited with inspiring the existentialist movement. Kojève's lectures at the Ecole Practique des Hautes Etudes from 1933 to 1939 drew such pupils as Raymond Aron, Maurice Merleau-Ponty, Raymond Queneau, Jean Desanti, Jacques Lacan, and even Sartre was fabled to have enrolled (Poster, 1975, pp. 8–9).

The opening pages of Kojève's commentary on the famous chapter 4, section A of the *Phenomenology*, 'Autonomy and dependence of self-consciousness: mastery and slavery', immediately reveal 'desire' as the most significant category in explaining the phenomenon of consciousness. With an implied allusion to Descartes, Kojève points out that passive contemplation of the external world could never reveal to the subject his own identity: it is only by actively desiring material objects that man the historical subject can appropriate the world both in reality and in thought:

> Contemplation reveals the object, not the subject . . . The man who is 'absorbed' by the object that he is contemplating can be 'brought back to himself' only by a Desire; by the desire to eat, for example. The (conscious) Desire of a being is what constitutes that being as I and reveals it as such by moving it to say 'I . . .' Desire is what transforms Being, revealed to itself by itself in (true) knowledge, into an 'object' revealed to a 'subject' by a subject different from the object and 'opposed' to it. It is in and by − or better still, as − 'his' Desire that man is formed and is revealed − to himself and to others − as an I, as the I that is essentially different from, and radically opposed to, the non-I. The (human) I is the I of a Desire or of Desire. (Kojève, 1969, pp. 3–5)

The degree to which Sartrean themes are foreshadowed in Kojève's interpretation of the unfolding of the dialectic of master and slave is striking. The parallel between life and consciousness; the concept of man as a being whose essence is 'not to be what it is and to be what it is not'; desire as a challenge to man to transcend the material world; the human project as negating-negativity, are concepts already explicit in his commentary. One cannot fail to notice how perfectly Sartre's tragi-heroic conception of man's plight in *Being and Nothingness* captures the spirit of the *Phenomenology*. Once again the concept of desire is central, and if Sartre sees man's predicament as bleaker and more solitary than Hegel it is because he was unwilling to postulate an Hegelian God who would resolve the dilemmas of man's existence and redeem history by revealing a supersensible purpose. (The bleakness of man's prospects was, however, something with which Sartre was not content to live for long and the *Critique of Dialectical Reason* represents an attempt to reconstrue the world in the light of the truth of history and its immanent tendencies.)

The concept of needs in the work of Sartre itself provides a remarkable analogue for the history of that concept from Hegel's concept of desire to Marcuse's true and false needs. An understanding of the problems that guided Sartre's course provides some clue to the meaning and history of the doctrine of needs in general.

Before taking up this subject we must briefly consider the second and conflicting direction that the concept of needs takes. Opposed to the ontological understanding of needs, where desire expresses the very conditions of man's existence and the dynamic in terms of which he is able to transcend materiality, there is a naturalistic understanding of needs, the implications of which are quite contrary. This naturalistic interpretation became more dominant in Marx's thought with the refinement of his doctrine of materialism, so that vestiges of the onto-logical version only remain in the socialist dénouement. (As we have seen, there are reminders in the course of the *Grundrisse* and *Capital* that Marx's man is still conceived in terms of expanding needs and powers and the appropriate form of social organisation is still seen as one in which these will have full play – 'to each according to his needs'.) The naturalistic conception of needs was arrived at from different considera-tions. Here Marx was concerned with the preconditions for the develop-ment of the capitalist mode of production and the configuration of human motivations which makes it possible. In this respect, far from being a vehicle of transcendence revealing to man his essence, needs represent an inert structure of objective requirements interiorised in the individual. As the mere reflex of material conditions, 'needs' were seen to constitute a striking corollary of ideology or unreflected conscious-ness, epitomising the very antithesis of man's authentic existence.

We have already speculated that the full elaboration of the doctrine of true and false needs latent in Marx's thought awaited the emergence of its historical role in explaining the prolongation of capitalism. As for its theoretical basis, Freudian theory, which postulated the objective and structural determination of motivations, contributed in no small measure to the acceptance of the doctrine of true and false needs as an account of the structure of motivations presupposed by the continued existence of capitalism.

It is undoubtedly no accident, then, that those who subscribe to the doctrine of true and false needs are for the most part neo-Freudian. If Sartre, who has also come to subscribe to the doctrine seems to be an exception, that is due to an antinomy in his thought which parallels that in the thought of Marx. Sartre's ontological conception of needs focuses on man's predicament in the world, his existence under challenge, and yet by virtue of that very challenge — the lack which his needs represent — forced to transcend given conditions and humanise the material world by projecting on to it his own purpose. Desire, or need as a lack, signifies at the same time the permanent resistance of the world of things and its ultimate intractability. Only within certain limits is man able to control events and all the time he is forced to accept and even take responsibility for circumstances which turn out differently from what he intended. According to this view, needs and desires reflect the very essence of the individual, his values and the personality that he has created for himself.

One may speculate that it is this very indefiniteness and ambiguity, the paradox that man must always act as if he is free to determine events and willing to take responsibility for his actions in the complete absence of certainty that things will go the way he expected, that Sartre finds ultimately intolerable. He, like Marx, had an overriding concern to give an account of reality that was true not only from the perspective of the individual actor, from whom the future and the consequences of his actions are concealed, but which was also true retrospectively, from the standpoint of history. Sartre, like Marx and Hegel, wished to construct a single truth, a 'true interpretation of the total movement of ideas and events', a task which, as Aron points out, 'all authors since Hegel, both neo-Kantians and analysts' have declared to be impossible (1975, p. 87).

It is this search for the truth of the totality that leads Sartre to shift his focus from 'desire' in *Being and Nothingness*, to 'needs' in the *Critique of Dialectical Reason*, from freedom to necessity. Sartre believes that he has found in dialectical reason itself the medium through which the truth of the totality may be known — the 'totalization without a Totalizer'. Dialectical reason involves an ineluctable necessity through which we see consciousness structured. In this way we get the grim conclusion that consciousness or the for-itself, is absorbed by the in-itself, reality, because consciousness is the product of dialectical determination by the totality of the conditions of existence. In the *Critique of Dialectical Reason* we have the bleak picture of man as a creature trapped in the prefabricated world of the *practico-inert*. All the material constraints of existence plus the artifices and structures that man has historically created to deal with them draw the noose around freedom tighter and tighter. Man is no longer a creature whose nature it is to be what he is not and not to be what he is. On the contrary, all the forces of nature and history are seen to have conspired to make him what he is. And Sartre's best insights on the problem of freedom as negativity are lost.

In his transitional essay 'Materialism and revolution' we see them most clearly stated, but for the last time:

> No opposition really exists between these two necessities of action, namely that the agent be free and that the world in which he acts be determined. For these two things are not both necessary from the same point of view or in relation to the same realities.
>
> Freedom is a structure of human action and appears only in commitment; determinism is the law of the world. And the act only calls for partial linkages and local constants. Similarly it is not true that a free man cannot hope to be liberated. For he is not free and bound in respect to the same things. His freedom is like the illumination of the situation into which he is cast. But other people's freedoms can render his situation unbearable, drive him into rebellion or to death. (Sartre, 1955, pp. 228–9)

In some senses an ambivalence between freedom and determinism was inbuilt in the concept of desire. Desires may be seen as imperatives, they shift over easily into the realm of needs. Desire is held to express a real lack and not merely a passing whim; it reveals the fragility of human existence and the relation of man to the world as one of necessity. But this is not how Sartre saw desire primarily in *Being and Nothingness*, where the negativity of desire signified for him not necessity but the possibility of transcendence, and this distinguishes the concept radically from his concept of 'need' in the *Critique*. The lack does not appear in the world of necessity, where its expression would be pointless, but only in the human world, since the very concept presupposes an intuition of what is lacking. It is only on the basis of a projected synthesis that the lack reveals itself, just as, for instance, the crescent moon has significance conferred by an understanding of what it is for the moon to be full (Sartre, 1969, p. 87). Thus Sartre in *Being and Nothingness* rejected the idea of desire in any way signifying the necessity or determinism of the material world. He rejected its interpretation in terms either of a psychic state or a physiological force, since the correspondence of a specific object-lack such as thirst or hunger to biochemical processes can only be understood by already presupposing a general concept of desire as transcendence or the anticipation of completion (pp. 87–8). It is precisely because his being is experienced as incomplete that it is man's destiny freely to create the synthesis which 'the lack' represents. Although this destiny is played out in the world-in-itself, the material world of physical causality, it transcends that world. Although exposed to the exigencies of everyday life, the individual is only trapped by them if he seeks refuge as a thing in the world of things, and this constitutes Bad Faith (pt. 1, ch. 2, pp. 47–70).

But once the seemingly imperceptible shift is made from desire to needs in the *Critique*, the degree to which these needs are expressive of the desiring subject is forgotten and the aperception of freedom is lost. Needs then represent the dictates of necessity interiorised in the individual. As we shall see, however, the fragility of Sartre's earlier position was already intimated by certain problems that he posed in *Being and Nothingness*. Having distinguished between being-in-itself as what is the case, and being-for-itself as reality for consciousness, he in effect nullified the force of this distinction by insisting that the human project, or freedom, constitute *the truth* of existence. Sartre wants to bridge this ontologically irreducible gap between phenomena and noumena, reality and appearances, being-in-itself and being-for-itself. One of the great attractions of Marxism for him must surely have been its claim to be able to apprehend the truth of the totality. Nevertheless, in adopting this view, Sartre cannot avoid the charge made against Marxism, too, that in order to pronounce on the truth of history and existence, one must stand outside it — and how this can be done they cannot in turn explain. In order for Sartre to proclaim, as he does, that the project of being is *the truth* of human desires he must assume the stance of an omniscient observer. This prejudice in favour of an explanation which will account both for the specificity of desires and their meaning in relation to the totality is already evident in *Being and Nothingness*. It becomes the very project of the *Critique of Dialectical Reason* where Sartre sets out to present an account of those facets of human existence which constitute both the subjective and objective truth of history.

Already in *Being and Nothingness* Sartre's negative concept 'freedom' presented certain weaknesses. Because he has decided in advance that particular desires represent merely a concrete instantiation of the desire to be, this leaves little room for a positive concept of freedom. Desires, it would seem, cover all possible choices, and their truth is not freedom, but being. Thus Sartre takes his only option when he declares that 'Freedom . . . is strictly identified with nihilation' (p. 567). In other words, freedom is only distinguishable from being as a negation of being which, like bad faith, merely affirms being. Indeed, it is the very negation by which, and by it alone, being can be consciously affirmed. Here we have the situation where 'the lack' is freedom, and where being is 'the lack'. In this sense, Sartre's freedom becomes an empty formalism incapable of giving to choice the significance he otherwise attributes to it. The fundamental project of being, as the 'free realization of human truth' which illuminates man as a person, makes it impossible to make the distinction between good and evil that would make freedom significant. It is not surprising that Sartre should conclude that it is ultimately a matter of indifference whether a man is a leader of nations or a drunk (p. 627).

There is something quite arbitrary about Sartre's locating a totalisation in *being* as man's fundamental project. Why, since man's organic existence is uncontentious, should he reject a totalisation through *knowledge* for a totalisation of *being* as the most important aspect of human existence? As we shall see, this emphasis on organic life as a material synthesis or totalisation is related to Sartre's search for realism. As he once put it, his preoccupation was always

> . . . at bottom to provide a philosophical foundation for realism. Which in my opinion is possible today, and which I have tried to do all my life. In other words, how to give man both his autonomy and his reality among real objects, avoiding idealism without lapsing into a mechanistic materialism . . . — to validate the historical dialectic while rejecting a dialectic of nature, in the sense of a natural process which produces and resolves man into an ensemble of physical laws. ('The itinerary of a thought', in Sartre, 1974, pp. 36–7)

A search for realism explains Sartre's rejection of the ontological concept of desire for the materialist concept of need. Through needs, and particularly the elementary needs for food, drink, shelter, and so on, man can be seen as an organic creature who by working on the inorganic environment gives it meaning. What underlies this change of orientation is the search for a larger truth which will comprehend not only man's 'subjective' grasp on the world through knowledge, but the truth of history seen from an omniscient standpoint. Being, since it includes all of life, rational as well as sentient existence, is seen to comprehend both the subjective and objective dimensions of reality. Not only is it the truth of existence, but it is the instantiation of that truth in the lives of all particular individuals. Here we have once again the concept of 'immanence' which derives from the Hegelian phenomenology and which becomes so important an element in Sartre's theory of dialectical reason. It is interesting to recall that for Hegel himself in his early writings it was 'life' or 'being' and not 'mind' as such that was the animating principle of his philosophy.[1]

The *Critique of Dialectical Reason* represents an elaborate attempt to restructure the Marxist system by bringing it back to its Hegelian roots. The orthodox communist movement, as Sartre saw it, had reduced Marxism to a form of crude determinism which ruled out the reciprocity of freedom and necessity permitted by the Hegelian philosophy of history. From this point of view the shift from 'desire' to 'needs' is crucial, for while, like desire, needs imply transcendence and therefore freedom, they also suggest necessity. The interchange between man and nature which needs and their satisfactions involve, is seen to provide a paradigm for totalisation as a real process. The concept is thus a suitably dialectical one. Not only is the concept of needs an important link in establishing the reciprocity between the individual and history as a totality, comprehending as it does the sources both of man's dependence, through material necessity, and of his autonomy, as a self-conscious being who works his environment to realise his purpose. But the concept of history as a totality is equally crucial in establishing the objectivity of needs.

Yet the difficulty with the whole argument in favour of the truth of the totality is that it depends for its validity on two things: the first and most obvious being the theory which propounds it, since we have recourse to no other evidence than its own claims; the second being the very possibility of such a 'truth of history' being attainable at all, much less in advance of its own unfolding. How, in the absence of a Totaliser (the Hegelian God) can history be seen as an active totalising process? It is one thing to describe the configurations of history as a retrospective totality (and even this can only be true in a certain sense), but how, in the absence of Divine Revelation, can such a totality be delineated prospectively? Both Marx and Sartre adopt what has been described as the quintessentially Hegelian perspective on history: that history is process, moving towards a rational dénouement where all contradictions will be reconciled; that its truth can be arrived at prospectively by critical theory; that 'methodological reciprocity' and 'ontological identity' (Sartre, 1976, p. 70) are guaranteed by the theory itself (one of the marks of its superiority is the fact that it includes its own function in its explanation, that is to say, the *explanans* is contained in the *explanandum*); that theoretical 'regression' corresponds to an historical 'progression', because the logic of the theory is dialectical and the truth of the dialectic is historical – a view which commits the error of conflating history as the historical development of certain tendencies, with logic as the rational extension of ideas.

As long as a philosopher remains committed to the Hegelian totality of history, and the dialectic as its handmaiden, freedom and necessity are seen to be two sides of the same coin. Freedom is the spontaneous realisation of predetermined tendencies, and *praxis*, as the human form of the dialectic, where man as an active bearer of history completes its design, is the fullest expression of the reciprocity of freedom and necessity. These Hegelian assumptions are faithfully reproduced by Sartre.

At the heart of Sartre's enigmatic concept of the dialectic as a 'totalisation of concrete totalisations effected by a multiplicity of totalising individualities' (p. 37), lies a confusion between the 'constitution' of reality and its 'intelligibility'. This confusion exists, for instance, in his characterisation of *praxis* as, at once, a moment of the 'dialectic as the living logic of action' (p. 38) and as 'constituent Reason itself, operating within History seen as constituted Reason' (p. 96). Sartre assumes that because the dialectic is the law of history, and because men under given conditions make their own history, the 'truth' of history as an emanation of human activity is fully accessible to human understanding. The dialectic is simultaneously the constitutive principle of reality and the principle of rational intelligibility. If necessity takes the form of the resistance of others and the inert world of things, freedom is the project of transcendence to which necessity gives meaning. All of history can therefore be viewed under the aspects of both freedom and necessity.

It is rather curious that when Sartre comes to explain the reciprocity of freedom and necessity – or what it really means 'to *make* history on the basis of earlier conditions' (p. 97) – he should take language, by which men express themselves freely on the basis of a given, highly structured grammatical system, as a model. The choice of language as an example once again reveals his inclination to treat history as an objectively meaningful totality. He assumes *praxis* to be a free extemporisation on the basis of given historical conditions, in the same way that speech is a free variation of the linguistic system which is its vehicle. But this is already too cerebral a notion of history, assuming for man a far greater degree of control over natural and social forces than he exhibits. It is also indicative of Sartre's tendency (a hazard of Hegelian thought, indeed) to conflate logic and history: the belief that the logical extension of an idea can, through the dialectic, be identical with the unfolding of an historical process. These assumptions can only arise from conceiving man's world as primarily constituted by 'mind'. The dialectic is seen as the law of the material universe, but more importantly it is the 'living logic of human action' and the principle of intelligibility, according to this view.

The ubiquity of the dialectic, the susceptibility of history to totalisation and the conciliation of opposites, mean in fact that many of

Sartre's distinctions — the negation of the negation, the distinctions between *praxis* and the world of the *practico-inert* or the project of transcendence and the material conditions on which it is predicated, freedom and necessity — are all merely *formal* distinctions, as indeed he admits:

> My formalism, which is inspired by that of Marx, consists simply in recognising that men make History to precisely the extent that it makes them. This means that relations between men are always the dialectical consequence of *their activity* to precisely the extent that they arise as a transcendence of dominating and institutionalised human relations. Man exists for man in given circumstances and social conditions, so every human relation is historical. But historical relations are human in so far as they are *always* given as the immediate dialectical consequence of *praxis*, that is to say, of the plurality of *activities* within a single practical field. A good example is language. (pp. 97–8)

Sartre's formalism comes from the juxtaposition of the Hegelian thesis of history as reason to the Marxian antithesis that actions in the world are materially determined. He begins by postulating for man an unqualified freedom which cannot account for the unintended consequences of actions apart from man's project. Since the human realm is quintessentially free and rational, he has to invoke the concept of a zone in which necessity holds sway in order to explain systematically the fate of actions in the world. Had he initially taken account of these realities and realised that such an unrestricted freedom is not a necessary condition for individual autonomy at all, he might have seen that indeed both the hope and the tragedy of human existence lie in the fact of such a limited freedom and that even though our actions may have consequences which we never could have foreseen, we are nevertheless compelled to take moral decisions and even to take responsibility for those consequences.[2]

The concept of needs is only intelligible in the light of these two concepts that Sartre came to accept only gradually. The first being the notion that history as such exhibits rationality and that in its unfolding lies man's intellectual and social salvation; the second, that a zone of necessity illuminates man's freedom and is responsible for the contradictions which history must resolve. Needs are seen to provide the mechanism by which the individual is inducted into history: he internalises a desire for objects that he conceives as necessary to him, but whose subjective necessity is objectively determined by history itself (under the aspect of the development of the forces of production). Human need therefore bridges the gap between subjectivity and objectivity. Needs are seen to denote both the zone of necessity and man's transcendence of materiality: his response to needs creating, through *praxis*, a whole social super-structure that is expressive of his freedom.

As we might expect, given the crucial role of the concept of needs, it, too, exhibits two aspects, a material and a formal. In the first place need is the impetus to life of any organism. But need is also the ontological 'lack'. When Sartre begins his exposition in book I of the *Critique*, need is the first concept that he introduces. We know from what he later says that he intended 'to record, *in order*, the structures of dialectical intelligibility', first need, then scarcity, and so on (p. 121). We immediately see that 'need' here substitutes for 'desire' in *Being and Nothingness* — 'need . . . expresses itself as a *lack* within the organism'; a 'lack . . . defined in relation to a *totality . . . a lacuna . . . a negativity*' (p. 80).

But the choice of need rather than desire bespeaks a real change in orientation for a number of reasons. First of all because it includes the concept of necessity and because it already raises the spectre of the material world as 'the total field of possibilities of satisfaction'. Secondly, because it provides a paradigm for totalisation. The significance for Sartre of need is not that it reveals man as a human subject, but that in its inclination to satisfaction it consumes or transforms elements of the real world. In this way 'everything is to be explained through *need*', for 'need is the first totalising relation between the material being, man, and the material ensemble of which he is part' (p. 80).

This means that the difference between the man of need of the Hegelian analogue, in relation to the material environment, compared with other organisms in relation to the inorganic world as their host, is reduced almost to vanishing point. The significance of need — for instance, the need for food which Sartre takes as his example — is not that it reveals to man the material basis for consciousness, but that it creates an organic synthesis, a material unity, in which man is merely a part of the whole. In eating, the

> . . . need for food reproduces the elementary [alimentary?] processes of nutrition: chewing, salivation, stomach contractions, etc. Transcendence here takes the form of a simple unity of a totalising function working in a vacuum. Without a unity of basic behaviour within the whole, there would be no such thing as hunger; there would only be a scattering of disconnected, frantic actions. Need is a function which posits itself for itself and totalises itself as a function . . . This initial totalisation is *transcendent* to the extent that the being of the organism lies outside it, immediately or mediately, in inanimate being; need sets up the *initial contradiction* because the organism, in its being, depends directly (oxygen) or indirectly (food), on unorganised [inorganic?] being and because, conversely, the control of its reactions imposes a biological statute on the inorganic . . . As soon as need appears, surrounding matter is endowed with a passive unity, in that a developing totalisation is reflected in it as a totality: matter revealed as passive totality by an organic being seeking its being in it — this is Nature in its initial form. Already, it is in terms of the total field that need seeks possibilities of satisfaction in nature, and it is thus totalisation which will reveal in the passive totality its own material being as abundance or scarcity. (pp. 80–1)

While Sartre's description is strikingly similar to Marx's characterisation of man as a natural being whose objects of existence lie outside him as objects of his need, in the *Economic and Philosophic Manuscripts*, there is an important difference between them (*CW*, Vol. 3, p. 336). While for Marx, man is a natural being, he is also one who opposes himself to, and transcends nature through *praxis*. For Sartre, however, the transcendence which satisfaction of a need implies does not differentiate man as an animate being from other organisms. While for Marx it is only under alienation that 'life is reduced to the unnatural simplicity of need' (ibid., p. 316), that 'life itself appears only as a means to life' (p. 276), and that man's human needs are reduced to his animal functions; for Sartre, on the other hand, man's performance of his animal functions in the fulfilment of his natural needs is what constitutes *praxis* and transcendence first of all: 'In other words, *praxis* as the free development of the organism [totalises] the material environment in the form of a practical field' (*Critique*, 1976, p. 121). Thus, 'Organic functioning, need and *praxis* are strictly linked in a dialectical manner' (p. 82).

Sartre offers some refinement of this argument, but it only serves to emphasise an identity of structure between the natural and the human world. He arrives in this way by the concept of needs at a materialism that is much more relentless than that of Marx, arguing that the exigencies of the material world demand precisely that man make of his life a *means to life*:

> . . . if it is to find its being within Nature or to protect itself against destruction, the organic totality must transform itself into inert matter, for it is only as a mechanical system that it can modify the material environment. The man of need is an organic totality perpetually making itself into its own tool in the milieu of exteriority. (p. 82)

If the organism's need for its host still constitutes an analogue, it is not for man's relation to his material environment, which as we have seen is identical to that of the organism, but for totalisation itself, a totalisation which proceeds, moreover, in the Hegelian manner, via negation of the negation:

> . . . it is through need that the first negation of the negation and the first totalisation appear in matter. Need is a negation of the negation in so far as it expresses itself as a *lack* within the organism; and need is a positivity in so far as the organic totality tends to preserve itself *as such* through it.
> . . . need is a link of *univocal immanence* with surrounding materiality in so far as the organism *tries to sustain itself* with it; it is already totalising, and doubly so, for it is nothing other than the living totality, manifesting itself as a totality and revealing the material environment, to infinity, as the total field of possibilities of satisfaction. (p. 80)

Praxis is the carrying out of this negation. Because an 'organic totality' can only act on inert bodies 'through the medium of the inert body which it is and which it *makes itself*', the organic being makes of itself its own tool. But here *praxis* as the organic function by which a physical body maintains itself in space and time, seems far removed from the concept of *praxis* as the conscious activity of men. That is to say, *praxis* is constituted not by the individual goals or projects which men set themselves, which for Marx distinguish 'the worst architect from the best of bees' (*Capital* [n.d.], Vol. 1, p. 174), but by objectification, as the exteriorisation of man's 'immanent function' in activity.

The significance of *praxis*, therefore, is not for Sartre, as it is for Marx, that it represents first of all an essential reciprocity between men that supplies the meaning of all human artefacts. Sartre sees the most singificant aspect of normal human relations to be their instrumental quality: as 'a mediation of materiality'. By giving priority to man's elementary needs (eating, breathing, and so on), he is forced to consider man's relation, as an organic being, to nature, an inorganic totality, as one of necessity. A materialist 'objectivity' is introduced in the notion that man treats himself as a material force in order to appropriate the means for his survival. By a conflation of all man's relations to the world with these primary organic relations (via the concepts of lack, scarcity and an expanded concept of need), Sartre is able to extend this objectivity to all those inert structures human action throws up.

This is the whole significance of the world of the *practico-inert*. And its reality, because it is the outcome of processes which have priority over all others (the original totalisation of reality that is re-enacted by each individual as he pursues the satisfaction of his needs), is considered by Sartre to be pre-eminent. Objectivity in the human world comes in the form of inert objectifications. This is why he later gives the prefabricated objectivity of class a real status which is denied contingent and 'jelly-like' human relations themselves (1976, pp. 120 and 250–1). The inert residues of *praxis* have a greater reality than the actions which created or reactivate them, because they remain as material evidence long after the subjective and transitory activity that threw them up has disappeared. This is, of course, one of the curiosities of Sartre's position. The 'hell of the *practico-inert*', that prefabricated world of historical and social forms into which men are born, lies precisely in the fact that it defies their subjective understanding. In the light of the immanent totality which critical reason divulges, the subjective experience of life compartmentalised in differentiated structures is seen to be incomplete. Only in frightening moments of illumination does the individual see how his subjectivity deceives him, and that his *praxis* 'merely carries out a sentence which history has passed on him' (p. 247). This concept of the *practico-inert* as a world of passive structures which send forth edicts, internalised as imperatives in the subjective consciousness of individuals, is the basis for Sartre's theory of true and false needs in the *Critique*, as we shall later see.

If needs constitute for Sartre an account of human motivation, it is as an instinctual structure (in the Marcusean sense), rather than as a cognitive structure. This is related to the dual role of needs as a material and a formal principle. Needs are material because they are, after all, the first premise of material life; as Marx declared 'men must be in a position to live in order to be able to "make history"', and 'life involves before anything else eating and drinking, housing, clothing and various other things (*The German Ideology, CW*, Vol. 5, pp. 41–2). But needs also constitute a formal principle as the *a priori* of human action. They may be a socially determined *a priori* but for any man as an individual they are given, and for this reason they define the zone of necessity, over against the zone of freedom.

That this formal aspect of needs features large in Sartre's thinking is demonstrated over and over again by the way in which the concept is related to the concepts of *praxis*, scarcity and necessity. As he says, it is the function of *praxis*, 'as a perpetual reorganization of the field in the light of needs', to realise 'the practical unity of this objective multiplicity' (*Critique*, 1976, pp. 511–12). This is a formalism which harks back to Marx, who in the 'Introduction' to his *Contribution to the Critique of Hegel's 'Philosophy of Right'*, first made needs the formal link between theory and *praxis* and their totalisation in revolution. (The private needs of civil society should be reincorporated into the political realm as the basis of man's *species-life*, he insisted, so as to restore the natural unity between the private and the political, and to subject needs to public and objective scrutiny.) There are some important differences, however. Needs for Sartre are not so much the link between theory and *praxis* (as we have shown, Sartre's concept of needs is naturalistic, needs are instinctual and do not include self-awareness), but rather the formal principle of the zone of scarcity, and a principle to differentiate the realms of freedom and necessity.

Sartre's formalism is never more evident than in his concept of scarcity (*rareté*). Scarcity, necessity and the *practico-inert* all hang together. *Praxis* is conditioned by inertia; past practices become inert constraints on present activity orientated towards the future. Inertia is the law of the zone of necessity, and scarcity is, among other things, the subjective experience of the resistance of materiality and its intractability.

Sartre boldly attempts to make of scarcity both a necessary and a contingent condition: '*Scarcity* is a fundamental relation of *our* History and a contingent determination of our univocal relation to materiality' (p. 125). It is partly from a methodological consideration that he wishes to make it contingent, to avoid 'a conception of the world which the facts could neither confirm nor refute', the error of Marxists who base history 'on some essential necessity' (p. 126). As we shall see, however, the real reason why Sartre can claim for scarcity both contingency and necessity, is that he conflates in one term two heterogeneous concepts. One is scarcity as poverty, a contingent and finite state, identifiable by an inability to meet the basic physical needs for subsistence; the other is scarcity as the principle of negativity, where any insufficiency or lack, any need unfulfilled, is sufficient to designate its presence. In truth, a world of difference lies between the two. As poverty, or the 'fact that after thousands of years of History, three quarters of the world's population are undernourished' (p. 123), scarcity is undeniably a contingent condition since men have demonstrated their ability to reduce, if not to eliminate, it. But Sartre does not confine scarcity to the lack of basic necessities for existence. Scarcity is whatever resistance men feel from the forces of the material world, the weight of inertia as it bears down on them, their collective existence as 'threat', the 'negation of mankind', the very orientation of men under alienation.

Sartre unleashes a flood of definitions which only serve to confirm our suspicion that scarcity is the formal principle of the zone of necessity. Indeed, he first introduces the concept as the very principle governing the state of alienation: 'The origin of struggle always lies, in fact, in some concrete antagonism whose material condition is *scarcity* (*la rareté*), in a particular form' (p. 113). 'History' is, therefore, 'born and developed within the permanent framework of a field of tension produced by scarcity' (p. 125). Of all the collectivities and structures that man throws up in the process of history as byproducts of his attempt to neutralise nature, defend himself, and satisfy his needs, the most fundamental is the structure of scarcity itself, as 'the negative unity of the multiplicity of men' (p. 127). At one point scarcity is as specific as a 'quantitative state' (poverty and its limits), while at another it is as insubstantial as 'the lack' itself, expressing the finiteness of life, the fact that reality eludes men and that satisfaction eludes needs. This, of course, gives rise to intolerable contradictions, for scarcity as poverty, which is certainly a specific and contingent state, simply cannot be conflated with the indeterminate negativity of existence, the sense of lack and finitude which are endemic to the human condition.

The enlargement of the concept of scarcity to include the domination of materiality, or necessity, only succeeds in rendering both terms vapid. This is demonstrated by the indiscriminate use he makes of these concepts. For instance, Sartre points out in several places that one of the consequences of the productive activities undertaken to allay scarcity of the necessities of life, is, through transcending scarcity (poverty), to produce a scarcity of men in relation to resources (labour shortage) and '*a scarcity of consumers in relation to products*' (pp. 137–8). Our suspicions that Sartre is making the most of a word play are not set to rest by his assurances that 'transcending scarcity, not only as the threat of death, but also as immediate suffering, and as the primitive relation which *both* constitutes Nature through man *and* constitutes man through Nature' is man's 'fundamental project'. And that '*for precisely this reason* scarcity will, without ceasing to be the fundamental relation, come to qualify the group or the individual who struggles against it by *making themselves scarce so as to destroy it*' (p. 137).

What Sartre is trying, very unsuccessfully, to establish is that all forms of scarcity − scarcity as poverty, scarcity as the structure of negative reciprocity, scarcity as alienation, scarcity as class struggle, and scarcity as 'the lack' − are a subspecies of scarcity as the domination of man by materiality. But the very anomalies with which this attempt is fraught are evidence that it cannot be done. Nothing demonstrates this better than Sartre's description of scarcity in relation to class struggle, where scarcity turns out to be not poverty or exploitation but 'antagonistic activity by an Other' who, either by inertia or active resistance, adds to the impediments constituted by the resistance of matter which threaten to slow down production; an activity which 'in threatening to increase these impediments, appears as the *praxis* of an anti-human' (p. 739). Within this unlimited scope it turns out that scarcity, so far from being poverty or 'the stage at which famine and death threaten every individual', can actually be '*urgency*' or the possibility of a 'fabulously rich heir . . . not coming into his inheritance unless he reorganises his field of action as soon as possible' (p. 739).

The concept of necessity suffers corresponding anomalies. So at one point, for instance, necessity turns out to be among other things the fact that actions turn out differently from what one intended, and the hell of the *practico-inert* resides in the fact that things do not go according to plan (p. 223). Quite apart from the fact that things not going according to plan seems to be a consideration of an entirely different order from the fact of material necessity as the law of the physical world, the notion actually gives the lie to the concept of necessity it is supposed to illustrate. If man is governed by necessity then his intentions and any plan that he might have are irrelevant, as the theory of false consciousness in fact asserts. And yet Sartre insists that necessity 'must not be confused with constraint (subjection to an "exterior force") (pp. 222–3); nor is it a limit as such (the limitation of our options by others), but the much more intangible quality of 'Otherness' (p. 223).

Necessity is not, for all that, a social fact, but arises from the natural laws of inertia. Necessity is not so much the presence of others who can initiate action which affects me as I affect them, necessity is rather the fact that 'we are robbed of our action by worked matter' (p. 224). But then again, necessity is also the fact that men, each innocently working matter for his own ends, can jointly produce a result that none of them desired; as for instance in the deforestation of China which resulted from the clearing of the land undertaken by individual peasants (p. 225); or the inflation of the sixteenth century which resulted from the Spanish discovering and mining silver in the Americas (p. 224). These historical phenomena are seen to represent action undertaken by men making of themselves tools, and because action involves an interchange between man and the material world, they leave inert residues which react back on man.

It is here that we see most clearly the way in which Sartre, like Hegel, conflates objectification and alienation. If alienation is synonymous with objectification, or the fact that man through his *praxis* creates objects and structures over which he has little subsequent control, there is nothing to be done. The future for Sartre is even darker than it was for Hegel, for while in Hegel the relationship of man to the world of material objects 'is only provisionally one of necessity and therefore removable along with the alienation that it brings with it, in Sartre the relation to the object *qua* worked-upon material gathers into itself the characteristics of negativity and ineliminability which issue in the concept of permanent alienation' (Chiodi, 1976, p. 21).

Marx avoided this dilemma by insisting categorically that objectification and alienation were not synonymous. Objectification constitutes man's species-life: the creation of a social superstructure, initially a byproduct of the satisfaction of physical needs but ultimately surpassing that organic function in importance. Alienation is a specific aberration which actually contradicts the purposes of objectification as man's species-life. For alienation is production which far from being undertaken to satisfy the needs of the individual and express his humanity, is undertaken at the dictate of an alien power (the owner of the means of production), and involves the denial of all but the worker's minimum subsistence needs and of his human existence in a way that reduces him to a mere animal.

Sartre, because he substitutes an intangible scarcity for exploitation and the domination of materiality for alienation, ends up being unable to distinguish between alienation and objectification. When it comes to the issue he temporises: 'Should we go back to Hegel who sees alienation as a constant characteristic of all kinds of objectification?' he asks, and he answers 'Yes and no' (*Critique*, 1976, p. 227). But as we pointed out earlier, if Sartre were willing to concede from the outset that freedom is not incompatible with results turning out differently from what one expects, or the experience of otherness, he would not be forced to create a zone of necessity to counterpose it, nor to work out a *modus vivendi* such that freedom is merely the carrying out of a sentence imposed by history. Sartre's vacillation on the concepts of necessity and scarcity, whether to ascribe them to the human condition as such, or to a specific mode of production, produces a corresponding ambivalence on the question of objectification. Is it alienation or is it not? The answer is 'Yes and no'. Because he tries to subsume under scarcity both the domination of matter as a formal condition of existence and all the unpleasant features of alienation as a specific state, he is left with this impasse out of which no way can be found. Of all the concepts that Sartre might have chosen to designate alienation, scarcity seems to be the most unfortunate. Scarcity either as poverty, or as an intimation of the finiteness of life, the sense of incompleteness or discontent that men who live under the statute of materiality feel, is not peculiar to the capitalist mode of production. These limitations have been found in all historical epochs and are a perennial feature of the human condition.

If we consider scarcity in the broader sense in which Sartre uses it, as a sense of lack or a feeling of not being at home in the material world, which stands in relation to man as other, we find that many elements of Marxian and Sartrean thought actually rely on this being a constant feature of man's life as a conscious being. In what else does the openness of man's nature lie? If it were in man's nature to adapt himself perfectly to his environment like the animal and make his individual life indistinguishable from the life of the species, then it could not be said that man has the power to make of his life 'the object of his will and consciousness'; to determine his production autonomously by appropriating the standards of any and every species at will; to set himself such ends as the satisfaction of a metaphysical sense of beauty; and so on (*Economic and Philosophic Manuscripts, CW*, Vol. 3, pp. 276–77). It is only because human life is not governed by the satisfaction of needs in the same sense as the life of lower animals that plenitude does not produce automatic satisfaction, and that man suffers from a universal discontent which encourages him to experiment with physical and hedonistic, metaphysical and ascetic, spiritual, mystical, religious, or even sadistic and masochistic, in short every conceivable kind of self-definition of the purpose of life, as a panacea.

Almost all theories of culture, including the Marxist, which defines man as a creature 'who produces even when he is free from physical need and only truly produces in freedom therefrom', rely on this discontent to account for the gap between nature and culture. (Sartre himself admits that the struggle for life is more than the conflict of 'blind instincts', and by designating *praxis* as a *project* of transcendence, differentiates it from mere organic functioning.) Freud's *Civilization and Its Discontents* is, of all the studies of culture up to this point, the one which focuses most brilliantly on the sociological aspects of this disquiet. Not only do social structures arise to remedy scarcity which is materially aperceived, but man uses these structures to make of culture an end in itself, by bringing to bear socially induced pressures (repression), thereby encouraging a wider social and metaphysical sense of life as struggle and scarcity.

Sartre's early concept of desire, like Hegel's, made much of the analogue between life and consciousness in terms of struggle, the threat of death, autonomy through negation, the importance of recognition achieved through confrontation, and the attainment of self-certainty through the death of the other. The ontological significance of desire as the expression of man's project of being, turned on desire being analogous to, but distinct from, the physical needs of an organism. This significance was, of course, lost when Sartre in the *Critique* made of the relationship between the structures of life and of consciousness one of identity. This turns out to be no solution and to involve him in a vortex of vacillations. Having set himself the impossible task of unifying physical insuffiency and metaphysical discontent, Sartre can only accomplish it by making of necessity and its zone, the *practico-inert*, both a specific and contingent, general and relative, concept. The ambivalence which leads Sartre to temporise on the nature of necessity and scarcity, causes him no hesitation concerning the objectivity of needs, however, or the nature of false needs and the status of class as a collectivity under alienation.

As Sartre indicated already in *Search for a Method*, '*praxis* is inconceivable without *need, transcendence*, and the *project*' (1960, p. 171). These concepts between them account for the contradictions, and the underlying reciprocity, between the various realities of man's existence. Sartre notes:

> There is no question of denying the fundamental priority of need; on the contrary, we mention it last to indicate that it sums up in itself all the existential structures. In its full development, need is a transcendence and a negativity (negation of negation inasmuch as it is produced as a lack seeking to be denied), hence a *surpassing-toward* (a rudimentary project). (p. 171)

This conception of *praxis*, as that which gives rise to the contradiction between subjectivity and objectivity, the world of the *practico-inert* and its transcendence, follows, to a surprising degree, the arguments that Marx made in *The German Ideology*, to which Sartre makes explicit reference (*Critique*, 1976, pp. 232–5). Marx noted that the constitutive aspect of *praxis*, which as a mode of individual self-realisation at the same time forms a collective structure which acts as a limit on self-realisation, only presents itself to consciousness at certain historical junctures where the contradiction between the forces and relations of production bring it to light. Only from the perspective of communism can the impossibility 'that anything should exist independently of individuals, insofar as reality is nevertheless only a product of the preceding intercourse of individuals', be understood (*The German Ideology, CW*, Vol. 5, p. 81). Only communism, because it 'for the first time consciously treats all naturally evolved premises as the creations of hitherto existing men' and 'strips them of their natural character' (p. 81), is able to see that there is nothing accidental in this conflict which merely brings to light a permanent underlying reality: a tension between the objective existence of social structures and collectivities and the subjective world of the individual who imagines himself to be freely pursuing the satisfaction of his needs in accordance with his own goals.

Marx notes that the belief of the individual that he is free, and that such conditions of life that put limits on the pursuit of his interests seem only accidental, can only arise with the emergence of the bourgeoisie as a class, and its characteristic distinction between the public and private realms. Because class conditions seem to be the accidental product of natural competition and the struggle of individuals for survival:

> . . . in imagination, individuals seem freer under the dominance of the bourgeoisie than before, because their conditions of life seem accidental; in reality, of course, they are less free, because they are to a greater extent governed by material forces. (*CW*, Vol. 5, pp. 78–9)

This idea of a prefabricated objective existence which eludes man's subjective understanding very much appeals to Sartre. He follows Marx in employing it to account for class as an objective collectivity. In the interview published as 'The Itinerary of a Thought', he refers to the idea of history as class struggle involving a behind-the-scenes mechanism which is similar to Freud's notion of the 'unconscious' (to which he has now become reconciled):

> The thought of both Marx and Freud is a theory of conditioning in exteriority. When Marx says: 'It matters little what the bourgeoisie thinks it does, the important thing is what it does', one could replace the 'bourgeoisie' by 'a hysteric', and the formula would be one of Freud. (Sartre, 1974, p. 36)

This is a notion on which Sartre draws when he argues that even those aspects of life in which an individual seems to escape the dictates of class existence – the fantasies of the woman production worker in the Dop shampoo factory, for example – only serve to reinforce the imperious demand of the factory as a system of control, by lending to the imagination the illusion of freedom.

Sartre follows Marx in designating to needs a key role in mediating between the subjective existence of the individual and the requirements of the objective totality. It is precisely because man's human existence is dependent on first satisfying the needs of his natural existence that he can be conditioned in exteriority by structures which will only permit the satisfaction of these needs on certain conditions, or in a form that severely limits or totally denies his human existence. At its extreme, alienation is seen to involve the substitution of the dictates of the conditioning structure for the human needs of the individual. This is easily accomplished, since all needs, even the most basic needs for physical survival, take a social form. What determines that form – whether it is the welfare of the individuals or the interests of the conditioning structure – depends on the state of the social system as a whole: alienated or dealienated.

Under alienation an exception arises to Sartre's rule in *Being and Nothingness* against 'the *a priori* existence of essences' (*Critique*, 1976, p. 231), a violation of the principle that man is a being 'who is not what he is and who is what he is not'. For, under alienation, the existence and the essence of the oppressed are said to coincide: they are in their individual existence so totally conditioned to their objective class existence, through the manipulation of their needs, that no escape from this prefabricated destiny is said to be possible. Even the intimate refuge of 'privacy' betrays them and becomes simply 'a mode of subjective realisation of objectivity' (p. 233). For instance, the sexual fantasies of the Dop shampoo worker are said to induce a submissiveness to the mechanical rhythm of the production line that accommodates her more easily to the demands imposed on her externally, rather than providing, as she thinks, an escape from those demands. And her lapse into passivity and a trance-like state are seen to emphasise the degree to which she has been reduced to an automaton. (Marcuse also makes much in *One Dimensional Man* (1964, p. 27) of the case of the Dop shampoo woman, which Sartre took from an article by Claude Lanzmann in *Les Temps modernes*, and which Marcuse takes from Sartre.)

Lanzmann it was who suggested the coincidence of essence and existence through the manipulation of the needs of the oppressed:

> A working woman who earns 25,000 francs a month and contracts chronic eczema by handling Dop shampoo eight hours a day is wholly reduced to her work, her fatigue, her wages and the material impossibilities that these wages assign to her: the impossibility of eating properly, of buying shoes, of sending her child to the country, and of satisfying her most modest wishes. Oppression does not reach the oppressed in a particular sector of their life; it constitutes this life in its totality. They are not people plus needs: they are completely reducible to their needs. There is no distance between self and self, no essence is hidden within the bounds of interiority: the person exists outside, in his relation to the world, and visible to all; he coincides exactly with his objective reality.[3]

In this way the oppressed are reduced to the mere individuation of their class existence, and with their own complicity, since they are deceived into living out this 'prefabricated destiny as [*their*] *reality*' (ibid., p. 233). Not only are they 'completely reducible to their needs', as Lanzmann suggests but, as Sartre adds, they are conditioned into accepting the priority of the needs and national production requirements of such enterprises as Dop over their own needs. This, in turn, has the consequence that their individual existence is reduced to what Marx described as 'a bestial barbarisation, a complete, crude, abstract simplicity of need' (*CW*, Vol. 3, p. 307).

Perhaps the most sinister aspect of this inculcation of imperatives issued in exteriority which substitute for the personal needs of the individual, is the unwitting self-deception that it involves. In those very moments in which the oppressed person believes himself to be free (his imagination, his private life) he is most bound, '. . . all the actions he carries out *as an individual* merely reinforce and emphasize the objective being imposed on him' (*Critique*, 1975, p. 235). For instance:

> . . . when the woman in the Dop shampoo factory has an abortion in order to avoid having a child she would be unable to feed, she makes a free decision in order to escape a destiny that is made for her; but this decision is itself completely manipulated by the objective situation: she *realises* through herself what she *is already*; she carries out the sentence that has been passed on her, which deprives her of free motherhood. (p. 235)

It is not enough that 'the role and attitude imposed on [the Dop shampoo worker] by her work and consumption have never been the object of an *intention*', but have arisen from the exigencies of a mechanical process. What is worse is that '*at the same time*, this material apparatus in which everything is meticulously controlled as if by a sadistic will *is* the working woman herself' (pp. 232–3). No matter what she may decide to do, or how resolutely she tries to escape her destiny, she can do nothing which does not merely serve to carry out the sentence imposed on her.

In the same way, Sartre argues, the nineteenth-century worker

> in deciding his budget in accordance with the needs created in him by his work (by satisfying above all his hunger, to the detriment of clothes and lodging) . . . *made himself what he was*, that is to say, he practically and rationally determined the order of priority of his expenditure; he therefore decided in his free *praxis*, and through this very freedom he made himself what he was, what he is, and what he must be: a machine whose wages simply represent maintenance costs'. (p. 238)

False needs provide the device which permits history to be perpetrated behind the backs of individuals. It is not surprising that among Marxists who hope to marry Marx and Freud the doctrine of false needs should feature so large: it is precisely the same kind of *deus ex machina* which Sartre earlier rejected in Descartes's 'Great Clockmaker' and the Freudian concept of the 'Unconscious', but which he paradoxically later comes to embrace in the doctrine of false needs. It is difficult to overestimate what a *volte face* this involved from his position in *Being and Nothingness*, where he affirmed the ontological status of desire, no matter what its content, as expressive of man's essence.

On the other hand, the plausibility of the doctrine must not be under-estimated either. It does provide a neat solution to certain problems posed in the context of dialectical materialism. Since motivation is conceived in terms of needs: first the physical needs of the organism for survival, then the human needs of man as a social and not merely natural being; and since needs provide the impetus for the expansion of human productive forces and control over nature, the concept of false needs provides a plausible answer to the question of how such a supposedly well-integrated system could run amok. Marxism is a critique of civilisation which develops in a more thoroughgoing way the argument of its Enlightenment forebears that the dysfunctionality of social institutions for happiness arises from their capacity to become masters of those they were designed to serve – in this respect the Marxian critique of culture bears certain similarities to that of Freud. But if subsequent historical developments and sociological analysis have demonstrated anything, they have demonstrated that there is no reprieve from the repression which social institutions exert in order to perform their tasks. And that as more sophisticated social organisation and a more complex division of labour permit a greater surplus to accrue, the struggle among individuals for a share of that surplus, and the intensity of growing needs and frustrations, can only increase.

Sartre, like Marx, saw needs as the motor of progress. Needs were the key because they not only accounted for the form of individual motivation, but also for the form in which productive forces are developed and the relations of production that subsequently arise: 'The different forms of material life are, of course, in every case dependent on the needs which are already developed, and the production, as well as the satisfaction, of these needs is an historical process, which is not to be found in the case of a sheep or a dog' (*The German Ideology, CW*, Vol. 5, p. 82). It is easy to conclude that if by some dislocation the needs which feed this machine should be false, all aspects of life would reveal this inescapable falsity, precisely because the cultural system is conceived to begin with as an integrated structure.

Sartre's argument goes part of the way with Marx but takes a turn into a blind alley. In Marx's theory there is hope, albeit faint, that civilisation can be redeemed by a reassertion of true needs in the appropriate reorganisation of society under socialism, geared precisely to the fulfilment of authentic needs as the principle of distributive justice. In Sartre's theory, this hope is lost: false needs arise from the tyranny of social structures, the backlash of *praxis*, but this reflects not the anomaly on which Hegel, Marx and Freud remark: that institutionalised social relations may turn out to be a fetter; but rather the ineluctable tyranny of matter itself. (The spectre of Cartesian dualism looms up again.)

Yet Sartre does want to make of this domination of man by matter in the 'hell of the *practico-inert*' a *contingent* state. The tension of need permits man willingly to submit himself as mind to the tyranny of matter so long as scarcity reigns. *Praxis* as progress or the expansion of the productive forces depends on it:

> For organisms whose risks and practical movement, as well as their suffering reside in need, the driving-force is either danger, at every level of materiality (whether it be hunger, or the bankruptcy *whose meaning* is hunger, etc.), or transformations of instrumentality (the

exigencies and scarcity of the tool replacing the scarcity of the immediate object of need; or the modifications of the tool, seen in their ascending signification, as necessary modifications of the collective). In other words, without the original tension of need as a relation of interiority with Nature, there would be no change; and, conversely, there is no common *praxis* at any level whose regressive or descending signification is not directly or indirectly related to this original tension. (*Critique*, 1976, p. 349)

He does hold out the hope that socialism will see an end to the tension of need: the progressive unfolding of the world of the *practico-inert*, the domination of need and the reign of scarcity, will stop when man reappropriates his world under socialism.

Once again the illogicalities float to the surface. How can scarcity end when it constitutes not merely a shortage of goods to satisfy needs which themselves are without a limit, but every subsequent insufficiency of supply with respect to demand to which an attempt to overcome initial insufficiency for survival gives rise? Not only this, but Sartre also freely admits that scarcity, besides being a material shortfall, is an interiorised psychological attitude underlying every manifestation of competition and the human propensity to struggle and even the concept of evil itself. And if there could be no such thing as change without the tension of need under scarcity, on which Sartre is surely right, is socialism to be a condition of *stasis*, a passive heaven of tranquillity, and *praxis* to vanish from the earth? How can socialism put an end to human discontent, which is not only expressive of the essential openness of man's nature, to which he subscribes, but the occasion for man's perpetual redefinitions of his essence? And if there are such things as true needs, how do we know them, if, in the absence of an *a priori* human essence, every desire is expressive of the nature of human existence? How can any programme of social reform be undertaken on the basis of man's *real* needs when proof of his nature, which socialism is designed to realise, lies in the fact that unlike the animals he can redefine his needs in accordance with criteria that he consciously elects? Even if true needs were limited to needs for subsistence the case would be hard to make, since even subsistence needs take a human form (man does not graze in the fields, live under trees, or mate indiscriminately, ordinarily), so that the line between what is natural and what is cultural is hard to draw even there.

Notes

1 See the sections on 'Life' and 'The ego and desire' in *The Phenomenology of Mind* (1949, ch. 4), and the chapter on 'Life' in Hegel's *Science of Logic* (1969, Vol. 2, pt. 3, ch. 1).

2 Kolakowski, more than anyone has been responsible for pointing this out, as Pietro Chiodi (1976, p. 151) notes. See Kolakowski (1971*b*), pt. 2, espec. pp. 174–5.

3 *Les Temps modernes*, nos 112–13 (1955), p. 1,647. As cited by Sartre, *Critique*, (1976), p. 232.

8

Reich and Fromm on Needs and Social Character

Erich Fromm was one of those who undertook the project of supplementing Marxist theory with Freudian principles in order to explain how it is that individuals are inducted into the roles that the capitalist system structures for them. It is true, after all, that classical Marxism had paid little attention to the question of individual psychology. The discovery of Marx's early writings showed that he had a fairly well-developed theory of human nature, but one that lent itself to this level of explanation or an account of individual motivation as such. Freud, on the other hand, had produced a materialist and a causal theory according to which all cultural phenomena were related to specific needs in the individual. Wilhelm Reich was, it seems, the first to realise the mutual possibilities of a synthesis of Marxian and Freudian principles.[1] As he points out, Marx, for all that he was, from *The German Ideology* on, insistent that the principles on which materialism is based should be empirical ones, still had a very metaphysical concept of human nature. The view of man's characteristic attributes that Marx set out in the early writings was in terms of man's immanent power to break the hold of environmental conditions, and not an argument for bondage to the processes of material determinism. If, in the later writings, he refers to this image of man less, he still does not develop a theory of psychic conditioning.

It is true that what Marx has to say about needs as the motor of progress in *The German Ideology* could be interpreted this way, if one reads Marx back from twentieth-century writings that have made so much of the idea that society can control man through his needs. But in fact we know from *Capital* and the general thrust of Marx's later writings that he does not see man primarily as a need-governed creature, but as one with the unique capacity to take charge of his environment and change it. The whole doctrine of the fetishism of commodities would make no sense if its point were not to make it clear to man that it is in his power, as well as being his duty, to break the circle of domination that commodities represent.

The emphasis on man's rational and cognitive powers in Marx's early writings, which he never really abandoned, left some of his other concepts unexplained. For instance, it does not fit very well with his later argument about the class nature of existence. As early as *The Holy Family*, Marx had spoken of the proletariat executing the sentence that private property passed on it, as if indeed history takes place behind the backs of individuals (*CW*, Vol. 4, p. 36). We have to conclude from Marx's argument as a whole that this was a feature of alienation and the phenomenon of ideology, and not endemic to the human condition as such as, for instance, Hegel had argued with his idea of 'the cunning of reason'. Even so, it is a problem remaining to be explained why, if in fact man does have this innate capability to unmask all the illusions and frauds to which under alienation he is subjected, ideology seems to have a peculiar power over him. As Reich points out, ideology is seen to arise in the cultural superstructure as a ramification of certain processes in the economic structure. This is convincing enough from the point of view of Marx's economic theory, but wholly unconvincing in terms of his theory of man (Reich, 1975, pp. 50–1). It is not enough to assert, as Marx does, that ideology accompanies class existence as a prefabricated reality into which man is born. We have to know by what precise mechanisms this is achieved and why we would submit to them. Marx argues that under ideology classes achieve 'an independent existence as against the individuals, so that the latter find their conditions of life predetermined, and have their position in life, and hence their personal development, assigned to them by their class, thus becoming subsumed under it' (*CW*, Vol. 5, p. 77). He adds: 'We do not mean to be understood from this that, for example, the rentier, the capitalist, etc., cease to be persons; but their personality is conditioned and determined by quite definite class relations' (p. 78), without explaining in psychological terms how this is done.

In Marx's earlier writings, he had declared that theory to be a material force must grip the masses but, for all that, he never succeeded in explaining how ideology could become a material force, or how it could in fact become a mass psychology. This problem became the object of Wilhelm Reich's work, and the first chapter of *The Mass Psychology of Fascism*, written between 1930 and 1933, bears the title, 'Ideology as a material force'. Here he sets out the theoretical basis of his work which he had developed from *The Function of the Orgasm* of 1927, to *Dialectical Materialism and Psychoanalysis* of 1929 and *Character Analysis* of 1933.

Reich argues, in this chapter, that Freud took four important steps, crucial to an understanding of how, through ideology, alienation takes place. The first was the construction of a causal theory that allows that no psychic experiences are accidental; those that cannot be explained in terms of conscious processes, as for instance the meaning of dreams, are understood in terms of unconscious processes. The second significant step was locating the causal mechanism that underlay these processes: the libido, which operated off sexual energy. As Reich remarks, to locate the source of psychic processes in human sexuality offered the great theoretical advantage of showing that 'the biologic presuppositions [of material existence] and social conditions of life overlap in the mind' (1975, p. 60). Freud's third great discovery, according to Reich, was the function of the child–parent relation in repressing infantile sexuality through the Oedipus complex. And the fourth was in seeing that moral codes are 'derived from the educational measures used by the parents and parental surrogates in earliest childhood' and were not of divine origin (p. 61); and that the super-ego is formed out of the child–parent conflict where the unconscious takes over the task of sexual repression that the parents initiated.

In this way, Reich argues that Freudian psychology, and specifically the theory of sex-economy which holds that civilisation is built on sexual repression, allows an explanation of the structure and dynamics of ideology, a phenomenon that classical Marxism could explain only in terms of its historical origins. In general the thrust of Reich's argument is this, that sexual suppression by society at large and sexual repression in the individual produce 'conservatism, fear of freedom, in a word, reactionary thinking' (p. 65). It is through sexual repression and its agents, the patriarchal family, that men under alienation have been kept subdued, tied by fear to institutions of domination. Frustration of sexual needs, Reich argues, actually produces the opposite result of frustration of material needs. While the frustration of material needs leads to rebellion, the repression of sexual needs drives these needs down into the unconscious and the material needs with them, so that no traces remain in consciousness. The results are twofold: first of all man unconsciously seeks substitute gratifications, and artificial needs which actively support the authoritarian order take their place. In others words, since real needs cannot be satisfied, the energy that remains when they are sublimated can only be expended in socially approved forms − which in an authoritarian regime are pernicious and typically take the form of sadism and militarism. Secondly, we have the phenomenon of character structure which represents the material form of ideology and the link between sexual repression and the economic base, 'sexual inhibition changes the structure of economically suppressed man in such a way that he acts, feels, and thinks contrary to his own material interests' (p. 66). Curiously enough, as Reich hints, the very concepts from Marx's early writings such as 'needs of the masses' which he dropped as being too metaphysical to fit with his dialectical materialism, can   now be rehabilitated as materialist and scientific concepts, thanks to Freud (p. 49).

So powerful was this synthesis of Marx and Freud which Reich brought about considered to be, that a whole generation of neo-Marxists adopted it − largely without acknowledgement. Erich Fromm's *The Fear of Freedom* (1942) is clearly based on Reich's work, from which the very title is taken, as is his concept of social character. Reich's theory that, under the agency of the patriarchal family, society creates through sexual repression the kind of character structure suitable for its purposes is an idea that Eric Fromm never abandons, even though under the impact of the newly discovered early writings of Marx his thought dramatically changes direction. We can see in Marcuse's notion of 'repressive desublimation' Reich's idea that sexual repression leads to substitute gratifications which, although offering satisfaction, nevertheless, because the form they take is determined by the established order, only succeed in tying the subject more closely to it. Due to Reich and his followers, Marcuse, Fromm, and others, the concept of true and false needs became inextricably associated with the concepts of ideology, or false consciousness, and libidinal structure or the Freudian theory of the instincts.

Erich Fromm in his early essay 'The method and function of an analytic social psychology', first published in the German *Journal for Social Research* in 1932 (republished in English in Fromm, 1971) noticed immediately that this synthesis of Freudian theories of psychic determinism and Marxian economic determinism involved a conflict. These were, after all, rival causal theories which found the ultimate explanation of the dynamics of culture in the instincts in one case, and in economic conditions, in the other. One had to choose between them in deciding where the mechanisms of determinism actually lay. In order to decide, Fromm asked himself this question: which of the two, economic conditions or the instincts, is more the variable, the more flexible in the form that it takes? The answer, once the question was posed in this way, was obvious: given a specific mode of production, the forces and relations that make up the socio-economic system are relatively fixed, and adaptation and development are slow processes, which is precisely why lags, fetters, contradictions and crises are to be found. By contrast, the variation of forms by which the instincts, and particularly the libidinal instincts, can be satisfied is virtually without limit. It seems reasonable to conclude then, since economic conditions are the less flexible or modifiable, that 'in the interplay of interacting psychic drives and economic conditions, the latter have primacy' (1971, p. 147). (One might question the way in which the question is set up. A fairer comparison would have taken the structure of needs and motivations of individual character as given in the same way that the structure of economic forces and relations within a mode of production is assumed to be given. Then it would have been equally difficult to decide between them as ultimate structures of causation, but this Fromm does not do.)

To see the specific form that human nature takes under different historical epochs as a function of social modification to economic conditions offers a more convincing explanation of ideology, which Fromm believed Marx and Engels were too ready to see as an *'immediate* expression of economic interests'. 'They saw intellectual and psychic creations as "the material basis reflected in man's head"', without being able to explain *'how* the material basis was reflected in man's head' (p. 55). The great strength of an analytic social psychology lies primarily in its ability to show how ideology is materialised through the adaptation of libidinal structure. Instinctual drives are seen to account in general for the psychic energy on which the social and economic formation process is built. But the quality and distribution of the drives are, in turn, affected by the nature of the particular socio-economic structure and an individual's specific location in it. Under the pressure of necessity, and facilitated by the greater modifiability of libidinal than the ego instincts, a fair share of 'wishes, instinctual drives, interests and needs' of the individual end up, albeit unconsciously, in the service of the economic system as rationalisations for its own requirements, that is to say as ideology. *'Hence, psychoanalysis can show how the economic situation is transformed into ideology via man's drives'* (p. 155).

The concepts of sex-economy, character structure and false needs which Reich developed and Fromm and Marcuse elaborated, answered certain problems in Marxist theory, although not without creating others. Classical Marxism, like subsequent structuralist theories, characterised the capitalist mode of production as an integrated system. It then tended to explain the development of the structure in terms of changes in the internal relations of its components, ruling out quite explicitly an account that credited such movements to the machinations of individuals. Classes and structures were integral parts, but individuals were merely incumbents who took up and vacated the roles that the system created for them. How precisely individuals were inducted into these roles was never quite explained, beyond the fact that the concepts of ideology and the ruling ideas of the ruling classes postulated that they were. The innovations of Reich provided a tight theoretical answer to this problem. The suppression of infantile sexuality through the agency of the patriarchal family, which Freud had documented, represented a process by which a certain authority structure was introjected into the psyche of the child whose character was moulded by social pressures to fit the role he had to perform. Primary material and libidinal needs were repressed and driven down into the unconscious and, as a result, the individual became prey to artificial forms of gratification, false needs, that the system provided as a substitute.

Although the reasons that Reich gave for bringing this synthesis about were in terms of a more scientific and rigorous materialism, the result is a theory at a high level of abstraction. It is difficult for us to conceive such an entity as a disembodied character structure into which individuals are inducted. As a collection of traits or an ideal-type to which people more or less approximate, the notion becomes more acceptable, but the theory seems to demand something more tangible than that. Character structure, as that which converts ideology into a material force, must be some sort of real entity, and Reich and Fromm refer to it as if it is.

Nor is it easy to see how by such a happy coincidence the child-rearing habits of patriarchal families uniformly succeed in repressing the sex-instincts of their children in a way that serves the regime so perfectly, without foreknowledge or understanding. From what we know of child-rearing, it is a haphazard and differentiated affair which produces a fair range of character types, and a wide variation in conformity and non-conformity to approved norms. If the comparatively harsh sexual repression of the Freudian era was as uniform as we are led to believe, it is certainly not the case today.

Once again the false needs which provide substitute gratification for the repressed material and libidinal needs strike us as altogether too fortuitous. The concept is exceedingly abstract: their falseness seems to reside, as Marcuse explicitly states, in the fact that they serve the interests of the regime and not the individual. But if they are false in this sense, it is surely only in this sense since, as Fromm has already conceded, the form the instincts may take admits of an almost infinite variety, the modifiability of the instincts and the variety of forms they take being the very reason he gave for arguing economic determinism in the last instance. This does not, in point of fact, rule out forms of gratification that may be socially approved by, or even serve the interests of, the regime as being legitimate. It is assumed that since the regime is unjust and exploitative, needs that suit its requirements will not at the same time serve the best interests of the individual. But this is not necessarily the case − it would have to be established − any more than it is necessarily the case that people's instincts seek objects that serve their interests best. This, too, in an empirical theory has to be established.

In many respects the marriage of Marx and Freud was misconceived from the outset. Freud does not, in point of fact, provide a straightforward theory of psychic determinism that could be slotted into dialectical materialism to account for the motivations, disposition and characterological structure of individuals, determined as to their content by the instincts, as to their form by the way in which societal institutions come to bear on these. To the extent that he was interested in culture and the relation of the individual to society, Freud moved away from a strictly physiological explanation of behaviour, or an account of its determination in terms of exclusively internal processes. For one thing he sees human nature as composed of basically conflictual tendencies, the pleasure principle, which is egoistic and anti-social in its implications, and the reality principle, or the need for survival, which permits man to adjust his goals to the demands of the group. Not only do these conflictual tendencies give man a built-in need for society − much like Rousseau's principle of perfectibility − but they suggest an ambivalence in the determination of behaviour between internal (instinctual) and external (societal) causes. Man depends on others in order to satisfy his needs for pleasure (the libidinal instincts), and his needs for survival and self-maintenance (the ego-instincts) presuppose and regulate his social relations.

In his assumptions about human nature, Freud draws a picture of the psyche as a complex entity, the parts of which are in competition with one another, held together by some governing principles, that is reminiscent of Plato's tripartite division of the soul. Nor do the similarities stop there. Freud, like Plato and Hegel, sees society as the macrocosmic expression of microcosmic principles, the dynamics of culture representing the conflictual tendencies in the individual playing themselves out. Just as Rousseau, in the principle of perfectibility, laid the basis for society in human nature, so Freud lays it in the need to play out and reconcile incompatible instinctual tendencies, the libidinal and the ego-instincts, the pleasures and the reality principles, and later, sex and aggression. But, like his predecessors, Freud sees in society itself the source of independent conflicts, and modifications to the structure of needs and desires that lead human nature away from its original tendencies. In other words, as human nature plays itself out in the larger field of culture, society intervenes in its internal processes.

All this considered, what then could Freud have meant by attributing to human nature a drive structure in terms of which all cultural developments were causally explained? One thing is clear, and that is that he did not see human behaviour mechanically determined by such drives, if for no other reason than that the drives themselves were conflictual. In the psyche itself, the pleasure principle could not exert itself without coming into conflict with the reality principle, which is not an instinct at all, but represents reason as it is brought to bear to ensure that the instincts do not threaten the wider interests of the individual − survival. The force of Freud's concept of needs and drives is not to suggest that these are instincts which, as in animals, work automatically to permit the maintenance and adjustment of life to the exigencies of the environment. Far from producing the kind of ecological equilibrium that we ascribe to animal instincts, the instincts Freud ascribes to man − sex and aggression − have a disequilibrating effect. Adjustment to reality is not a function of the instincts at all, according to his theory, but of the higher cognitive faculties − reason − as it is brought to bear through the ego; and all psychic and instinctual behaviour involves a struggle between reason and the instincts, whose outcome cannot be declared in advance.

What we see in Freud is a translation of the old terms of analysis of the psyche: the passions, reason and the will, into a new scientific language: the id, the ego and the super-ego. Freud has essentially the same view of the passions (the id) as Plato and others who saw them as an instinctual and relentless force which sweeps over us, and which can only be brought under control by a well-disciplined will (the ego), reinforced by religious and societal sanctions (the super-ego). This tripartite model of the psyche does not allow for a theory of instinctual determinism, as such, to which a unitary theory of the personality is much better suited. As long as the psyche is seen as a complex of differentiated and competing parts, some of which operate unconsciously (the id and super-ego) then we can never know precisely what causal sequences account for particular behaviours. That there must be such sequences, even if they are at present unknowable, Freud remained confident, but we have no quibble with that. We have to assume that there are physiological mechanisms at work translating psychic events in order to be able to explain how these have physiological effects. To say that psychic events have physiological causes is perhaps even acceptable as long as that is understood to mean that physiological phenomena do not generate psychic phenomena but only parallel them. Freud misleads us on the nature of the instincts by describing their operations in hydraulic or homeostatic terms as exerting a pressure which destabilises the organism, which then seeks the restoration of equilibrium through release. This suggests, for instance, that the libido is some kind of force like electricity, that builds up a resistance that must in some way be released if destruction is not to result. But, in fact, the libidinal instincts are nothing as specific: since they are unconscious we can only postulate their existence without being able to isolate them. The libido is simply an economical way of referring to a complex of multifarious phenomena, different in form with every individual, which has in the past been referred to as the passions.

We can see the function of Freud's account of the psyche by asking ourselves what force he understands the concepts of ego, id and super-ego to have. Now it is inconceivable that he would be asking us to believe that the psyche is literally divided up into these compartments, any more than we can now take literally Plato's three divisions of the soul. Nor can Freud be claiming that there is a parallel tripartite physiological structure that corresponds to the id, ego and super-ego. For all that he never gave up hope of a physiological account of behaviour, Freud never suggested this. The distinctions between the functions of the id, ego and super-ego are not descriptive but analytic distinctions, employed to explain human behaviour by differentiating cognitive processes.

The analytic nature of Freud's concepts comes out in the two works, both unfinished, in which he tried to produce a comprehensive theory of the mind: the *Project for a Scientific Psychology* of 1895 and the *Outline of Psychoanalysis* written at the end of his life. The *Project* is oriented around the attempt to explain behaviour neurologically in terms of needs and responses, and it tends, as stimulus-response models since the man-machine theories characteristically have, to present the mind as an integrated structure in such a way that little account is taken of the substantive form of needs or instincts. As one critic notes, 'the tendency of the *Project* was to blind Freud to the significance of intentions, aims, motives, desires, in human nature – something which his clinical experience otherwise forced him to recognise – and to strengthen in him a conception of the mind as a machine subject to causal laws of the utmost simplicity' (Wollheim, 1971, pp. 62–3). In other words, the attempt by Freud to treat his analytic model of the psyche as a descriptive model produced incongruities in relation to his clinical observations that were intolerable. He never published or referred to the *Project* again.

What we can gather from all this is that Freud in speaking of human behaviour as need-governed or based on instincts or drives, does not understand this in a literal or straightforward sense. Not only is there a gap between the instincts as unconscious phenomena and concrete needs or desires, but it is not clear that the needs or drives that Freud hypothesises are necessarily materialised at all, because of the role of the ego in the complicated deliberative process which constitutes motivation. In this way Freud, like Locke, made provision for the intervention of judgement and the ability of man through reason to go against his instincts. Freud's account of behaviour in terms of needs and drives belongs for the most part in the realm of metapsychology as a model of the psyche that provides a reference point for his clinical observations. It is in this respect not so different from the theories of human nature in which human needs are attributed as manifestations of the human essence in the thinkers that we have considered so far.

One of the peculiarities of Fromm's theory is his attempt to maintain the Reichean idea of social character alongside the concept of the human essence of the early Marx. Elaborating on Reich's ideas, he develops a typology of character types specific to successive stages in the evolution of the capitalist mode of production, and the need structures that typify them, which he then evaluates with reference to a genuine human nature and genuine needs. In *Man for Himself*, Fromm classifies four non-productive character types, which are said to represent man's progressive alienation and degeneration in the direction of anality. They are (1) the 'receptive' character type, which is weak and susceptible to manipulation; (2) the 'exploitative' character typical of eighteenth-century pre-capitalist development; (3) the 'hoarding' character type characteristic of nineteenth-century non-progressive capitalism; and (4) the 'marketing' character, a product of twentieth-century capitalism where the individual must sell not only his labour-power but his whole personality. In his most recent book, *The Anatomy of Human Destructiveness* (1973) Fromm adds to these a fifth character type which represents a further pathological development: the necrophilous character type historically correlated with advanced capitalism and the rise of fascism.

One can see without too much difficulty in the first four of these 'non-productive' character types, counterparts to Freud's fixated personalities. Fromm's 'receptive' character type corresponds to Freud's oral-receptive; his 'exploitative', to Freud's oral-aggressive; the 'hoarding' to the Freudian anal-erotic; and the 'marketing' to the 'phallic' (Brown, 1964, pp. 162–3). It is difficult to be sure whether or not Fromm intends us to take his suggestion that the historical evolution of character types represents a degeneration in the direction of anality (Fromm, 1973, p. 349) this literally or not – the necrophilous character type certainly seems to be outside the Freudian series as the ultimate manifestation of sadism and libidinal perversion. If he does, then we should point out that Freud's deviant personalities were not correlated with historical epochs or modes of production, but quite simply attributed to fixation at a certain stage of early childhood development. Whether or not Freud succeeded in establishing that these fixated characters are the product of the specific causes he postulated, he at least arrived at them as constructs to explain behavioural problems that he came across in his clinical work; his character types were arrived at more or less inductively, on the basis of generalisation from specific cases. This puts them in quite a different category from Fromm's character types, which are not derived through the observation of and reflection on behaviour, but from the attempt to solve a problem in Marxist theory: how a social system ensures that individuals born into it have the motivations and predispositions it requires of them. (That individuals *do* have these required dispositions is already stipulated by the theory in the concept of ideology.) Fromm's social character types make no direct appeal to behavioural evidence; the criteria for their validity as constructs are not in terms of the explanation of actual empirically given behaviour, but rather in terms of their neatness as a theoretical solution to the problem posed.

In contrast to the five non-productive forms of social character, there is one 'productive' character type in Fromm's taxonomy, in terms of which the others are judged: the spontaneous and loving character, who shows 'care, responsibility, respect and knowledge' (*Man for Himself*, 1949, p. 98). This is clearly an a-historical character type and Fromm makes no claim that it ever was, or ever could be, the product of a socio-economic system, although there is the suggestion that man under socialism will come closer to it than most. It is an ideal, his concept of genuine human nature, in terms of which the historical forms of character type are to be judged. But here we see a profound anomaly, because if, in fact, social character is determined historically by the response of the family and socialising agencies to economic conditions and the way in which they determine the form that the instincts take, then one cannot hold up an ideal character type with any hope that it may be realised.

This is exactly the same kind of mixture of historical and value criteria that Fromm employs with respect to needs. In *The Sane Society* he declares that he has 'chosen the concept of *alienation* as the central point from which . . . to develop the analysis of the contemporary social character' (1955b, p. 110). Fromm's use of alienation and the 'productive' character type as bench-marks to evaluate other historical types represents his response to Marx's newly discovered early writings. In Fromm's 1932 essay on psychoanalysis and historical materialism, his argument is hardly distinguishable from that of Reich and he adheres strictly to the notion that character is historically determined by the interplay of psychic and economic forces. But under the impact of the 1844 Manuscripts Fromm credits man with the power to transcend material conditions and dealienate himself. He subscribes to the notion of the human essence of Marx's early writings whereby man 'experience[s] himself as the active bearer of his own powers and his own richness' (p. 124). He cites Marx on alienation and the dependence created by each man speculating on creating a new need in the other so as to prey off him, and concludes that 'our craving for consumption has lost all connection with the real needs of man' (p. 134). He uses the Reichian argument that consumerism represents substitute gratifications to stave off aggression once real needs are sublimated. The fact that the needs which capitalism promotes do not contribute to productiveness or real satisfaction accounts for their insatiability, Fromm argues. True needs are finite, but false needs are insatiable and this is what keeps the capitalist system going.

This argument has a certain arbitrariness. It suggests that Fromm is identifying true needs with basic physical needs for survival, which are finite because of the way they have been defined. He refers to the 'self-regulating mechanisms' which put a limit on physiological needs, contrasting these with such needs as 'ambition, lust for power, and so on, which are not rooted in physiological needs of the organism' and 'have no such self-regulating mechanisms' (p. 91n.) and are, for this reason, insatiable. But we know from his catalogue of existential needs that Fromm is not willing to restrict true needs to physiological needs, which provide no basis for his assessment of social character types. And he has already made a distinction between 'animal' needs and 'human' needs, derived again from the early Marx, which will not permit him to associate true needs with physiological needs.

What then are the existential needs by which the human essence is actualised and all forms of social character type are to be judged? In the definitive account that he gives of existential needs in *The Sane Society* (1955b, pp. 30–66), they fall under five headings. The first is the need for relatedness, that is to say, the need for social ties to replace instinctual bonds and for human relations that will be expressive of man's reason and his freedom. The second is the need for transcendence, or the need to create an existence in culture − for which the natural foundations are weak − as the rational, free creature that potentially man is. The third existential need is the need for rootedness or security, and the social and institutional structures which will provide a cultural palliative for his natural weakness. The fourth existential need is the need for a sense of identity, the need of the individual to feel himself 'as subject of his actions', and to extricate himself from the primary bonds of nature, family and clan, while at the same time preserving his sense of security. And the fifth is the need for 'a frame of orientation and devotion'. This is not, as it might at first appear, a need for a *Weltanschauung*, or secure world view in which the individual may locate himself, in the form of religion or myth. The need for a frame of orientation and devotion is in Fromm's view the need for reason itself, the need for 'objectivity', or 'the faculty to see the world, nature, other persons and oneself as they are, and not distorted by desires and fears' (p. 64).

The first and most obvious thing about these five existential needs is that it is very difficult to keep them distinct. The need for relatedness is hardly distinguishable from the need for rootedness; the need for transcendence may very well take the form of a frame of orientation and devotion; the need for identity is merely a qualification of the needs for relatedness and rootedness. And there are other ways that one could draw out the internal relations between these concepts as well. What they all add up to is the need for 'productive love', as he puts it, or relations which combine love, effectiveness and reason.

The second thing to be noticed about these existential needs is that they have almost nothing in common with the basic physiological needs to which he elsewhere refers as being man's fundamental needs. We can see how far Fromm has come from the Freudian theory of the instincts. Existential needs as he catalogues them are more or less the antithesis of instinctual needs, since they together constitute the imperative to man to transcend nature and the state of animal existence and realise his unique potentialities as a rational creature. Fromm argues variously that satisfaction of material needs still leaves 'the profound needs in man' unsatisfied (*The Sane Society*, 1955*b*, p. 11); that 'Man's instinctual drives are necessary but trivial' compared with 'man's passions that unify his energy in the search of their goal' (*The Anatomy of Human Destructiveness*, 1973, p. 266); and that: 'Even the most complete satisfaction of all his instinctive needs does not solve his *human* problem; his most intensive passions and needs are not those rooted in his body, but those rooted in the very peculiarity of his existence (*The Sane Society*, 1955*b*, p. 28). Fromm, like Marx, tends to confuse needs as conditions for the actualisation of the human essence, with needs as motivations. This is a mistake of some moment in a theory which purports to account for motivation deterministically in terms of the interplay of psychic and social factors. Admittedly, Fromm has abandoned strict determinism for a weaker form in his later writings, explicitly rejecting the Freudian theory of the instincts, but since he retains the concept of social character as a product of material conditions, he does not avoid the problem. If we look carefully at the catalogue of existential needs that he gives, we find that there is little or no point in calling them needs at all. What he is presenting is a set of cultural values or normative stipulations. If the requirements of relatedness, transcendence, rootedness, identity and a frame of orientation and devotion were really 'needs', man would show a greater propensity to satisfy them, if not indeed a compulsion, and they would not be problematic at all. Needs as motives, or expressed needs, are given, but if in the same breath the concept is expanded to cover solutions to 'existential dichotomies' and the ontological requirements for the realisation of 'the human essence', it becomes meaningless. The use of the term at this point is strictly rhetorical, and philosophers trade off the association of need with necessity to impress their readers that their normative recommendations are incontrovertible.[2]

Fromm has an added incentive to take this route because it seems to enable him to reconcile ethics to the principles of dialectical materialism. By exploiting the usual association of the term 'needs', Fromm feels free to argue that the 'higher' non-physiological requirements of a genuinely human existence represent potentialities in man's nature which are striving for fulfilment in the same way as physiological needs; and that unfavourable conditions alone determine the successful or unsuccessful attainment of this immanent goal. The principles of dialectical materialism are thus faithfully preserved, while what really constitutes an ethics is passed off as a set of indubitable facts. But there is a hidden cost to this strategy and that is that to call them needs is to obscure the peculiar character of values and to undermine the integrity of ethics, which Fromm is not otherwise anxious to do.

The plausibility of the argument rests in large part on the confusion between universality and necessity. Man's world-openness and the burden of creating his own mode of existence and goals are exigencies of the human condition that persist both across cultures and across time. The ontological needs which Fromm and Marx describe represent an attempt to account for these universal exigencies, and their analysis is indeed pitched at such a level of generality that there is almost no culture that cannot be seen to subscribe to them in some form or other. But what is at issue is not whether these conditions prevail, but whether or not they constitute needs, that is to say, whether they can be empirically (rather than philosophically) located, and whether they entail an innate urge for satisfaction (necessary if Fromm is to be consistent).

Since Fromm includes as manifestations of needs both success and failure at satisfying them, almost any form of behaviour is taken as evidence for their persistent force. For instance, he considers everything from sado-masochism and pathological narcissism to productive love as constituting proof of the need for relatedness (*The Sane Society*, 1955*b*, pp. 30–6). Similarly, for rootedness, the spectrum of possible manifestations ranges from fraternity to incest or, at another level, from patriarchy to matriarchy (pp. 38–60). The need for transcendence is said to be reflected in any passive or active behaviour which acknowledges that man is a creature 'thrown into this world without his knowledge, consent or will', and 'removed from it again without his consent or will', so it covers everything from creative love to necrophilic destructiveness (pp. 36–8). The need for identity may take the form of the herd mentality, that is to say, conformity (never mind that this seems to be its opposite), Cartesian cerebrality (where man's integrity is seen to reside exclusively in his capacity to think), or genuine individuality as Fromm conceives it (pp. 61–3); while the need for a frame of orientation and devotion is fulfilled by a range of solutions from the fetishism of primitive (and capitalist) societies, to the 'great religions' and the objectivity of pure reason (pp. 63–6).

What we see in Fromm's catalogue of existential needs is a set of pre-scriptions for resolving the universal problems of human existence. Because he is anxious to establish these prescriptions as having the force of necessity, he is willing to consider as evidence for them everything from their optimum expression to their complete perversion. But if, indeed, the need for transcendence, for example, can be fulfilled by anything from the highest art forms to the most base forms of destructiveness, it simply cannot be maintained that transcendence is a need as such. The range of acceptable forms of satisfaction that a need permits is strictly limited and does not include complete opposites. It is as absurd to say that the need for food can be met by food or hunger, as to say that the need for relatedness can be met by love or hatred, the need for transcendence by creativeness or destruction, the need for rootedness by incest or fraternity, and so on. Fromm is not even logically consistent, because the way he defines the respective existential needs entails that in the positive instances he cites the need is indeed met, but that in the negatives it is not. The fact that existential needs can exhibit such hetero-geneous manifestations reflects on their dubious legitimacy as needs in the first place. Not only do these so-called needs lack specificity to such an extent that there no prescribed form that their satisfaction must take, but it turns out that complete opposites will count as evidence for their existence.

Other factors argue against these exigencies of the human condition constituting needs in any literal sense. The careful observation of human behaviour does not disclose them, nor do people ordinarily profess to feel these metaphysical problems to be needs as such. It is a characteristic feature of the concept of needs that it gives rise to need claims of the form 'I need X'. Even if one were not willing to go so far as to maintain that it is a necessary condition for a need to be present, that the person said to be needing it should in fact feel a need for the object he is said to need, it is perfectly defensible to maintain that the need he is said to be needing should, in principle, be capable of being the object of a need claim of the sort 'I need X'. This condition is easily fulfilled in the case of physiological needs, but lacking in the case of the existential needs which Fromm catalogues. The claim 'I have a need for transcendence', or, 'I have a need for relatedness, rootedness, etc.', certainly sounds odd, and for good reason. No one can reasonably claim to have a 'need' for anything as abstract as this, since a need is something which has finite limits which can, in principle at least, be met, but these concepts have no recognisable limits.

Fromm's reply to our objection would probably be that it is not a fair test and that existential needs are not felt directly but are inferred from more specific need claims. But it is precisely this link that is so difficult to establish. For instance, someone who buys a new car every year when the old one would do is classically interpreted by Fromm, Marcuse, Vance Packard and others as manifesting a need for identity which takes this specific, and rather perverse, form. But creating an identity for himself is only one of the many possible motivations that might account for his profligacy, and it is inappropriate to term these 'needs'. It involves a regress that is both redundant and erroneous to reduce an express need for something specific to an inferred need for something more general. If, in fact, a man says he feels a need for a car, it is probably the car that he feels a need for and not a sense of identity. It is possible to argue that his express need for a car is *motivated* by his attempt to create an identity for himself, as long as motive is clearly distinguished from the need itself. The important thing is that there is no causal necessity such that we can infer that in each and every case in which someone desires a new car, a 'need for identity' can be inferred; and this is what these theorists by implication claim.

This raises the thorny question of 'unconscious needs'. The concept of the unconscious is fraught with difficulties and its common use to signify false consciousness is wholly illegitimate. It does seem, however, that in the sense in which Freud intended it, the concept is both viable and compatible with a rigorous understanding of the concept of needs. In point of fact there are no grounds in Freudian theory for maintaining that there is any such thing as an unconscious need, unless this term is used as shorthand to identify needs for which the motivations are unconscious. Freud conceived of the unconscious as the realm of the instincts, precisely characterised by the presence of needs or desires for which no rational basis can be given. It is not the needs themselves that are unconscious – they are indeed the symptoms of unconscious processes. So, for example, the Freudian would interpret the need of the man for a new car every year, not as a subterfuge or hidden 'need for identity', but as an irrational or trivial want, on the grounds either that its motives are unconscious (which would be difficult to believe in the case of an action as deliberate as buying a car), or that they are not the outcome of a process of rational deliberation. This sort of interpretation does not involve attributing hidden needs and it is always subject to empirical validation by interrogating the subject.

Perhaps it was this kind of distinction between needs and motivations that Fromm was groping for in his concept of existential needs, but as it stands he is not even consistently Freudian. The Freudian properly restricts the use of the term 'need' to cases in which a concrete need is felt and evaluates concrete needs not in terms of some 'higher' or existential needs, but in terms of the rationality of the motivations that underlie them. Not only does Fromm allow existential needs to take precedence over concrete needs but, since existential needs are pitched at such a level of abstraction that their fulfilment may take any conceivable form, they do not even permit the derivation of specific needs, as his theory requires.

What after all was the point of the Reichean synthesis of Marx and Freud that Fromm adopted, if not to provide a 'scientific' diagnosis of the ills of advanced capitalism? Adaptation of the instincts through the agency of social character was said to provide the mechanism, the concept of the human essence the standard by which pathology was judged. Fromm claims in *The Sane Society* to provide an analysis of the 'pathology of normalcy' and how it is that not only individuals, but a whole society can be neurotic, in the light of — and here he radically diverges from Freud — the positive alternative, a 'truly human' existence. He sees as the symptoms of this societal neurosis those contradictions and anomalies which arise from a failure to live up to the level of advancement that a culture permits. He notes the irony that a society that has fought for a hundred years to halve the length of the working day, now finds free time a burden, so that people end up 'killing time'. He considers it grotesque that in such a society a good crop can be considered an economic disaster and production curtailed to 'stabilize the market' (pp. 5–6). He cites figures on insanity, alcoholism, suicide, homicide and other destructive acts to argue that the incidence of individual pathology is now so high that normalcy is itself pathological. He notes in addition that just those countries which are 'the most democratic, peaceful and prosperous . . . show the most severe symptoms of mental disturbance' (p. 10).

These observations strongly favour Freud's thesis that peace and progress are bought at the cost of sublimation and repression, and that the more complex, highly integrated and disciplined a society is, the greater its potential for aggression. If culture is built on renunciation, the more exacting a society is, the more peaceableness, civility, co-operation and selflessness it demands, the more likely it is that under such pressure propensities for evil and destructiveness will take pathological forms. But this is not the conclusion that Fromm draws, and he attempts what Freud believed to be impossible, the provision of objective criteria by which normalcy can be judged. Freud had once raised the question of whether it might not be conceivable that 'many systems of civilization — or epochs of it — possibly even the whole of humanity — have become "neurotic" under the pressure of the civilizing trends?' But he hastened to add, 'we are dealing only with analogies', pointing out that the diagnosis of 'collective neuroses' is confronted with the special difficulty that normalcy is a culturally relative concept (*Civilization and Its Discontents*, cited by Fromm, 1955*b*, pp. 19–20).

This is where Fromm disagrees. Objective criteria for mental health are supplied, he believes, by 'the laws which govern mental and emotional functioning', knowledge of human nature in 'psychic' as well as 'anatomical and physiological terms' (p. 12). Behaviour which departs from the attained level of rationality which a culture affords is by definition pathological, he argues, and reasons for the pathology of advanced civilisation are not in terms of repressed aggression, but of false needs which divert man from his (socially) given potential:

> Any regression today from freedom into artificial rootedness in state or race is a sign of mental illness, since such regression does not correspond to the state of evolution already reached and results in unquestionably pathological phenomena. Regardless of whether we speak of 'mental health' or of the 'mature development' of the human race, the concept of mental health or of maturity is an objective one, arrived at by the examination of the 'human situation' and the human necessities and needs stemming from it. It follows . . . that mental health cannot be defined in terms of the 'adjustment' of

the individual to his society, but, on the contrary *that it must be
defined in terms of the adjustment of the society to the needs of man
.* . . (*The Sane Society*, 1955b, p. 72)

Fromm explicitly traces the genesis of his theory of true and false
needs to the distinction Marx made between fixed and variable needs in
The German Ideology. With this distinction, Fromm argues, Marx laid
the foundations for a dynamic social psychology. It is questionable,
however, whether Marx saw needs in this way (see Fromm, 1971, pp.
65ff.). When in *The German Ideology* he talks about 'needs', and in the
Grundrisse 'interests', it seems that he is referring simply to motivations
which are historically given, or contingent, and which account for
developments taking the direction that they do. But Fromm rejects needs
as a descriptive category or a synonym for the concept of interests.
'Needs', he says, 'like the striving for happiness, harmony, love and
freedom are inherent in [man's] nature. They are also dynamic factors in
the historical process which, if frustrated, tend to arouse psychic
reactions . . .' (*The Sane Society*, 1955b, p. 81). Criteria for needs refer
'not necessarily to what [man] *feels* to be his needs, because even the
most pathological aims can be felt subjectively as that which the person
wants most; but to what his needs are objectively, as they can be
ascertained by the study of man' (p. 20). In other words:

> Purely subjectively . . . false needs are experienced as being as urgent
> and real as . . . true needs, and from a purely subjective standpoint,
> there could not be a criterion for the distinction. (In modern
> terminology one might differentiate between neurotic and rational
> needs.) Often man is conscious only of his false needs and
> unconscious of his real ones. The task of the analyst of society is
> precisely to awaken man so that he can become aware of the illusory
> false needs and of the reality of his true needs. (*Marx's Concept of
> Man*, 1966b, pp. 62–3)

But the distinction between true and false needs is a value distinction
disguised as fact, and the concept of the human essence on which it turns
is un-Marxian in character. Fromm sees human nature as some kind of
real entity or state of correct functioning, more like Plato's soul or the
Aristotelian human essence as a set of innate potentialities actualised
through growth, than Marx's concept of man. Marx had officially
abandoned his notion of the human essence or species-being by the time
he wrote *The German Ideology*. But even if one holds that vestiges of it
still remained in his belief that, under socialism, existence and essence
would coincide and human potentiality would, in some sense, be fully
actualised, and that it is this idea that lay behind the distinction between
fixed and variable needs, one has to recognise that Marx's was, nevertheless, a genuine teleology. He saw the human essence as an immanent
striving for the fulfilment of physical, cognitive and spiritual powers that
was historically open, and not something fixed by the biological limits of
human nature. Fromm's claim that 'man has an immanent goal and that
man's biological constitution is the source of norms for living (*The
Anatomy of Human Destructiveness*, 1973, p. 259) would fall under the

kind of biologically based materialism that Marx specifically rejected in Robert Owen and other nineteenth-century successors to Locke. The ontological character of human needs represented to Marx man's capacity for transcendence and the degree to which human nature is self-created and neither biologically given nor immutable. Marx's 'existential needs' are not, like Fromm's, merely the instantiation in existence of a fixed human nature.

Fromm's 'vitalism' stems, I think, from a confusion of Marxian and Freudian principles. Freud had provided a theory of human nature in terms of innate drives or instincts and the way in which these worked themselves out in culture. Fromm ultimately rejects the Freudian theory of the instincts as doing insufficient justice to man's potentialities as a rational creature, and representing an image of man foisted off on to Freud by the bourgeois ideology of his age (*Man for Himself*, 1949, pp. 34–5). But what he substitutes is a concept of the human essence in Marxian terms which, at the same time, represents an innate set of potentialities unfolding rather like the Aristotelian acorn growing into an oak. After all, to be an adequate substitute for Freud's instinctual mechanisms, human nature has to be some kind of real entity capable of explaining behaviour in causal terms. Freud explained neurotic or pathological behaviour in terms of instinctual dysfunction. Fromm believes that the frustration of man's 'human' needs gives rise to pathologies that may be diagnosed in the same way. Moral goodness as the goal of the total personality is analogous to health as the state of correct functioning of the body and Fromm considers it 'truly astonishing that this view should be considered "idealistic" or "unscientific" by so many who would not dream of questioning the relation between constitution and norms in regard to physical development and health' (1973, p. 260). He claims that 'a judgment that a person is destructive, greedy, jealous, envious is not different from a physician's statement about a dysfunction of the heart or the lungs' (1949, p. 236). Man is like a seed, he says, if his nature is nurtured in the right conditions it will flourish and achieve its potential, as the seed becomes a tree, but if not it will become 'crippled' and 'stunted' – the very example that the Aristotelians always used.

It is ironic, as Schaar in his excellent critique of Fromm notes, that 'Fromm starts from essentialist principles and arrives (unknowingly) at positivist conclusions' (*Escape from Authority*, 1961, p. 69). Ethics, as the attempt to establish some universal principles to arbitrate real conflicts between the values and interests of individuals, is reduced to triviality by the notion of 'man's function', or 'inherent potentiality'. If, indeed, human nature were a state of 'normal' functioning, like health, and psychic pathologies, like disease, represented a failure to attain to it, morality is out the window. And yet this is certainly the implication of what Fromm says. 'Just as the infant is born with all human potentialities which are to develop under favourable social and cultural conditions', he maintains, 'so the human race, in the process of its history, develops into what it potentially is' (*The Sane Society*, 1955b, p. 14). Or even more explicitly: 'One could say that the human race, like the infant, starts out with a primitive orientation and we would call healthy all forms of human orientation which correspond to the adequate state of human evolution' (p. 71), a position hardly distinguishable from the social Darwinism of Herbert Spencer.

Because Fromm assumes human nature to be an aggregate of really existing characteristics, a set of propensities embedded in the physiological structure, in the way that the Freudian instincts were held to be, it can, he thinks, be arrived at inductively from the empirical study of man, like any other natural characteristics:

> . . . the real problem is to infer the *core* common to the whole human race from the innumerable *manifestations* of human nature, the normal as well as the pathological ones, as we can observe them in different individuals and cultures. The task is furthermore to recognize the laws inherent in human nature and the inherent goals for its development and unfolding. (p. 13)

It follows from his emphasis on pathology as the test of whether man's essence is actualised or not, that in cases where it is not this should be due to false needs which substitute for true or 'human' needs, and this is what Fromm argues. Alienation is defined by him in terms of needs, and the failure of capitalism to promote those needs which express man's latent powers. What he sets out to accomplish is a Marxist critique of civilisation and its discontents. As we shall see, however, this involves broadening the concept of alienation to Freudian dimensions which far exceed the explicit exploitation which Marx had in mind. At the same time it involves the 'objective' evaluation of needs which Freud would have deemed highly inappropriate.

Fromm's analysis of alienation seems to follow roughly Marx's guidelines in the *Economic and Philosophic Manuscripts* on the four important areas in which its manifestations are felt: estrangement from nature; self-estrangement; estrangement from species-nature; and estrangement from other men. But the emphasis is entirely different. Although Marx does focus in these early writings on species-being and man's estrangement from the authentic form of his existence, even here, I believe, it is a mistake to see the alienation he describes as a primary psychological or cognitive phenomenon. Alienation, as he saw it from the beginning, is caused by the exploitation of labour and the division of society into two classes, the propertied and the propertyless. Once these causes have been removed, the social and intellectual consequences – hostile social relations, the egotism of the isolated individual, false ideas and a culture which reifies individualism and false ideas – will disappear, perhaps not overnight, but they will disappear.

Alienation of man from his essence, although it may have been in the eyes of the Marx of 1844 the most significant aspect of alienated labour, is still a consequence and not the root of the phenomenon. This is an important distinction, and one on which many neo-Marxists have been misled, because only if the psychological manifestations of alienation are attributed to specific and eliminable causes, is Marx's optimism that alienation can be eradicated, warranted. It is no accident that these neo-Marxists interpret alienation as a pervasive and possibly permanent societal malaise which characterises advanced capitalism; for once the specificity of the original concept is lost, the whole thesis is deprived of its internal necessity and alienation becomes an intractable state. Significantly the labour theory of value, which is the real key to Marx's analysis of the causes of alienation, even in early writings where it can be seen in rudimentary form, is conspicuously absent in the analyses of Marcuse, Fromm and Sartre. It is, therefore, perfectly consistent for Fromm, like Marcuse, to claim that alienation is truer of white-collar technocrats, 'organization men' with 'synthetic needs', than blue-collar workers (*Marx's Concept of Man*, 1966b, pp. 56–7), although such a claim would be preposterous to Marx himself, for whom the labour theory of value, and not the doctrine of true and false needs, provides the criterion of alienation.

Fromm's theory of alienation turns, it seems, not on the exploitation of labour, but on false consciousness. The 'asocial and egotistical attitude . . . is the essence of alienation', he declares (*The Anatomy of Human Destructiveness*, 1973, p. 283). He takes each of the four manifestations of alienation that Marx describes not as effects but as integral features. So he ends up with an amorphous phenomenon to which he attributes a truly improbable collection of properties, as Schacht has very well demonstrated.[3] Man is alienated from nature, which means, on the one hand, that he lacks the 'capacity to relate himself fully . . . to nature' (1966b, p. 5), but also that he seeks to submerge himself in nature in 'automaton conformity', on the other. He is alienated from others, forced to 'find new ties with his fellow men which replaced the old ones, regulated by instincts' (*The Sane Society*, 1955b, p. 30), and yet once again the most severe symptom of his alienation is that he too easily seeks a 'unity and oneness' with his fellow man in mindless conformity (pp. 60–3) – not forgetting either that 'Love presupposes alienation', because 'in order to love, the "other" must become a stranger' (*Beyond the Chains of Illusion*, 1966a, p. 60). Self alienation is characterised sometimes as 'lack of a proper sense of self', 'by alienation is meant a mode of experience in which the person experiences himself as an alien' (1955b, p. 120); but other times as failing *to be* a genuine self: the self-alienated man, 'driven by forces which are separated from his self', so far from feeling the lack of self, is often 'under the illusion of doing what *he* wants' (p. 124). His relation to society is defective under alienation because of the 'asocial and egotistical attitude' that it breeds; and yet 'the alienated character of our time' is precisely characterised by the qualities of 'adjustment', 'outgoingness', 'co-operativeness' and 'tolerance' (pp. 152–63).

In addition to these major arguments, Fromm toys incidentally with the un-Marxian notion of objectification as alienation – that view of Hegel's which Marx rejected precisely because it implied that alienation is a universal and a permanent state. Fromm describes man's 'emergence from a state of oneness with the natural world to an awareness of himself as an entity separate from surrounding nature and men', as a 'process of individuation', on which man's essence as an autonomous creature depends (*Escape from Freedom*, 1947, pp. 39–40). But to our surprise, he suggests that 'to transcend nature, to be alienated from nature . . . finds man naked, ashamed'. Then in a very Sartrean vein, he declares that 'one of the outstanding manifestations of alienation' is the fact that 'our own actions are embodied in the laws which govern us, but these laws are above us, and we are their slaves' (*The Sane Society*, 1955*b*, p. 138). As if the processes of individuation, separation and objectification, which make the world of culture and its laws possible, were themselves the source of alienation.

The amorphousness and the incoherence of Fromm's theory of alienation can be put down to the fact that he rejects the specificity of either the Marxian or the Freudian explanations of the causality of alienation – strictly interpreted, they are, of course, mutually exclusive – yet retains their account of its attributes. Once he relegates to obscurity the labour theory of value, which makes of alienation a specific theory of economic exploitation, and rejects the theory of instinctual repression, whereby alienation is a function of neurosis, his description of the phenomenon in Freudian and Marxian terms is entirely arbitrary. Alienation is, in Fromm's theory, a valley of despair from which there is no exit.

Notes

1 Paul Robinson in his book on Reich, Roheim and Marcuse, *The Sexual Radicals* (1972) recognises Fromm's indebtedness to Reich. Martin Jay in his definitive history of the Frankfurt School, *The Dialectical Imagination* (1973) surprisingly does not.
2 See the excellent essay by Ross Fitzgerald, 'The ambiguity and rhetoric of "need"', in Fitzgerald (1977*b*), pp. 195–212.
3 Schacht (1971), ch. 4, from which many of the following examples are taken.

9
Marcuse on True and False Needs

The problem of needs was first posed by Marcuse in his early essays in the *Zeitschrift für Sozialforschung* not in terms of the relation between ideology and materialism, or the relation between individual motivation and societal forces, as it had been for Reich and Fromm, but in terms of the ancient philosophical paradoxes of freedom and necessity, reason and pleasure, essence and appearance, potentiality and actuality, ideology and truth.[1] It was relatively late in his development that Marcuse turned to Freud and, when he did, it was not to investigate the problem of individual psychology, the weak link of dialectical materialism, but to pursue his interest in these classical philosophical dichotomies. In Freud's metapsychology, reason and pleasure represent the antithesis in whose terms the conflicts of civilisation play themselves out. Hegel's claim that history 'is not the soil in which happiness grows. The periods of happiness in it are the blank pages . . .' (Hegel, 1975, p. 79) might well have been uttered by Freud, who maintained that 'Happiness is no cultural value' (quoted by Marcuse, 1969, p. 23).

This 'contraposition of happiness and reason goes all the way back to ancient philosophy', Marcuse maintains ('On hedonism', in 1972*b*, p. 161). He sees Western philosophy as having been characterised by a persistent dualism, the belief that the rational faculties can be exercised only if the appetites are subdued, man's capacity for objectivity, or reason, being juxtaposed to needs, desires and wants as manifestations of his lower faculties, his subjectivity. The antithesis of reason and pleasure is seen by Marcuse to lie at the heart of bourgeois idealism, which had its roots in the philosophy of Plato, Aristotle, the German Romantics and Hegel.

These philosophers, and the societies they represented, are said by Marcuse to have resolved these antitheses by some form of accommodation. Thus the classical Greeks reconciled themselves to the fact that freedom was parasitic on necessity and that the leisure of philosophers was supported by the labour of slaves, by ranking human activity in a hierarchy which elevated intellectual pursuits and deprecated the satisfaction of material needs. Bourgeois culture, as represented by the German Romantics, actualised the dichotomies in a different way: once slavery was abandoned and equality was officially admitted, no one was spared from the labour necessary to satisfy his needs. But this aspect of social life was relegated to the play of natural forces through the mechanism of the market economy, while the satisfaction of higher intellectual appetites was sought through participation in the spiritual values of one's national culture.[2] Marcuse recognises Hegel's contribution to this peculiar separation of the material and mental spheres, noting that although the identification of freedom and reason was the goal of idealism, fascism was its logical tendency.[3]

The thrust of Western European culture from the ancient philosophers through Christendom to the Enlightenment and the German Romantics, has been to convince man that there is a fundamental incompatibility between his essence and the facts of his existence, Marcuse argues.[4] In this way, people have been persuaded to give up the satisfaction of their needs and desires for the sake of higher cultural goals. A handful of hedonists, the Epicureans and their Enlightenment successors, have from time to time emerged to protest against this unnecessary self-sacrifice, but the mainstream of culture has ignored them.[5] On the whole this incompatibility was exaggerated, though, and idealism, as he sees it, represents a long historical tradition of oppression and sublimation that served the material interests of a few at enormous cost to the many.

Marcuse is a fundamental hedonist: it is not, he believes, that man is not really destined for happiness on this earth, but only that he is made to believe this is so, in order that he will accept the exploitation and hardship that the powerful make him suffer. Culture is built on repression, but it need not be. In the early history of western civilisation it is true, he argues, that a genuine scarcity meant that cultural development and progress could only be supported by an allocation of resources that deprived and oppressed those at the lower end of the social scale. Thus in Greek society the leisure of philosophers was supported by the labour of slaves, a division of mental and material labour that was justified by asceticism and the belief that the satisfaction of material needs was the necessary but servile basis for higher forms of existence. In this way, philosophy accommodated itself to an alienated reality:

> It was the ancient desideratum of hedonism to join in thought both happiness and truth. The problem was insoluble. For as long as an anarchic, unfree society determines the truth, the latter could manifest itself either in the particular interest of the isolated individual or in the necessities of the hypostatized general interest, the society. ('On hedonism', 1972*b*, p. 194)

But now, Marcuse believes, since scarcity is a problem that has become technologically obsolete, there can no longer be any justification whatever for denying people the satisfaction of their needs and desires in the name of higher cultural values, good of the soul, and so on. Marxism is seen to provide a reading of history that shows hedonism and truth to be ultimately reconcilable goals, the unification of essence and existence in the society of the future. In the 1844 Manuscripts, Marx had already declared communism to be

> the *genuine* resolution of the conflict between man and man − the true resolution of the strife between existence and essence, between

objectification and self-confirmation, between freedom and necessity, between the individual and the species. Communism is the riddle of history solved, and it knows itself to be this solution. (*CW*, Vol. 3, pp. 296–7)

It is on this historical reconciliation that Marcuse pins his hopes.

Hegel had already provided a clue to the Marxist resolution of these dichotomies, as Marcuse discovered (*Reason and Revolution*, 1960, espec. pp. 112–13, 234). Although tending to subsume all human motives and passions under the concept of mind, dealing with human psychology only in the context of the interplay of historical forces, Hegel at the same time gave some consideration to the role of human passions, needs and appetites in culture as the material basis of progress. In the *Lectures on the Philosophy of World History*, he sees them as the whole impetus to human action, and in the *Philosophy of Right* he attributes the stability and depth of public life to the variety and purposefulness of the private life of citizens organised around the satisfaction of their needs. This for Hegel constituted the subjective side of history or its soft underbelly. Subjectivity represented, on the one hand, the experience of consciousness by which the individual arrives at certainty and knowledge, as he argues in the *Phenomenology*. At the same time, on the larger historical canvas, subjectivity represents a material life based on individual needs, desires and appetites, which promote the work of reason by supporting the public life of culture in which ideas work themselves out. In the idea of the 'cunning of Reason' Hegel had laid the basis for dialectical materialism, where material needs become an important theoretical category to explain the unfolding of the historical process. Marx had realised this potential in Hegel's thought as early as his Introduction to the *Contribution to the Critique of Hegel's 'Philosophy of Right'*, where he introduces the concept of 'radical needs'.

All the same, Hegel's theory of needs was unacceptable, Marcuse argues, because it once again accommodates the ancient paradoxes of philosophy, gratification and truth, happiness and reason, to the status quo, that is to say, to a mode of production which is untrue to man's potentialities. Although gratification is not the full answer to the question of happiness, Marcuse believes that hedonism discloses a truth which idealism conceals: that material and sensual gratification can be compatible with social justice and happiness for all under the appropriate (socialist) form of economic organisation. According to Marcuse, the idealism of classical Western philosophy and the materialism of the liberal economic mode of production can be reconciled, but only under dialectical materialism, where the free development of human needs is compatible with the harmonious life of the community. The principle under which this true reconciliation falls is the old socialist one, which Marx repeated in the *Critique of the Gotha Programme*: 'From each according to his abilities to each according to his needs.' Rewards should be distributed not on a *quid pro quo* bais, but on an objective assessment of need.

In his essay 'On hedonism' of 1938, Marcuse repeats this slogan, commenting in terms which state one of the dominant theses of his work:

Here reappears the old hedonistic definition which seeks happiness in the comprehensive definition of needs and wants. The needs and wants to be gratified would become the regulating principle of the labour process. But the wants of liberated men and the enjoyment of their satisfaction will have a different form from wants and satisfaction in a state of unfreedom, even if they are physiologically the same. In a social organisation that opposes atomized individuals to one another in classes and leaves their particular freedom to the mechanism of an uncontrolled economic system, unfreedom is already operative in the needs and wants themselves; how much more so in enjoyment. (1972*b*, p. 182)

Happiness and social justice are not compatible, as it might at first appear, with any or all needs, but only with the true needs of man, as his essence discloses them:

> In view of the possibility of a happier real state of humanity the interest of the individual is no longer an ultimate datum. There are true and false interests even with regard to the individual. His factual, immediate interest is not in itself his true interest . . . Insofar as unfreedom is already present in wants and not just in their gratification, they must be the first to be liberated − not through an act of education or of the moral renewal of man but through an economic and political process encompassing the disposal over the means of production by the community, the reorientation of the productive process toward the needs and wants of the whole. When all present subjective and objective potentialities of development have been unbound, the needs and wants themselves will change. Those based on the social compulsion of repression, on injustice, and on filth and poverty would necessarily disappear. (pp. 192−3)

It is not as if restrictions on pleasure and gratification can be simply lifted to restore man to his essence. Under alienation his very needs themselves have become estranged. In *One Dimensional Man*, published almost thirty years later, Marcuse indicates what this means precisely:

> In the last analysis, the question of what are true and false needs must be answered by the individuals themselves, but only in the last analysis; that is, if and when they are free to give their own answer. As long as they are kept incapable of being autonomous, as long as they are indoctrinated and manipulated (down to their very instincts), their answer to this question cannot be taken as their own. (1964, p. 6)

When Marcuse undertakes his investigation of Freud in *Eros and Civilization*, it is not to fill out his account at this point at which it is weakest: the psychology of the individual and how he comes to have the peculiar configuration of motives, desires, interests and needs that he does. Marcuse is not sympathetic to the reading of Freud given by Reich and Fromm, which puts stress on the psychobiography of the individual, infantile sexuality and the role of parents and parental surrogates in libidinal repression. In fact, Marcuse believes that the family, far from being an agent of capitalism, was a buffer between the individual and the ideological apparatus of the state, which permitted a measure of individual autonomy. Thus Marcuse argues that under the authoritarian family, 'through the struggle with the father and mother as personal targets of love and aggression, the younger generation entered societal life with impulses, ideas, and needs which were largely *their own*' (*Eros and Civilization*, 1969, p. 87). In this way he emphasises the mythological and more fanciful aspects of Freud's theory – the Oedipal drama and the slaying of the primal father.

In his own way, as we have seen, Freud was interested in the eighteenth-century theme of the costs of civilisation on which Marxism, and Marcuse's version particularly, may be seen as an elaborate commentary. The progress of civilisation, as Freud sees it, depends on the postponement or sublimation of instinctual gratification, the subordination of the pleasure principle to the reality principle. The struggle for existence, characteristic of all natural life, is mitigated but not eliminated under the conditions of civilisation, due to the universal problem of scarcity. As we shall see, this central argument of Freud's is greatly modified by Marcuse, who believes that domination, scarcity and alienation are peculiar to the capitalist phase of history and represent the costs of capital accumulation rather than of civilisation in general. He makes a distinction between repression and surplus repression, between the reality principle and the performance principle, which represent the peculiar domination and controls which capitalism adds to 'the basic (phylogenetic) restriction of the interests which mark the development of man from the human animal to the *animal sapiens*' (ibid., p. 46).

Marcuse links repression to scarcity and the constraint of need. Repression, far from being the foundation of culture, a diversion of sexual energies for social purposes, as Freud saw it, is for Marcuse the effect of specific forms of domination which will be eradicated under socialism as the society of abundance: 'Non-repressive order is essentially an order of *abundance*: the necessary constraint is brought about by 'superfluity' rather than need. Only an order of abundance is compatible with freedom' (p. 156).

It is clear that freedom to Marcuse is synonymous with liberation, or the removal of the material and psychological constraints of culture itself. 'Man is free', he claims 'only where he is free from constraint, external and internal, physical and moral – when he is constrained neither by law nor by need' (p. 152). Such a liberation is possible, he believes, under socialism as a society governed by the maxim of gratification according to need:

> To the degree to which the struggle for existence becomes cooperation for the free development and fulfillment of individual needs, repressive reason gives way to a new *rationality of gratification* in which reason and happiness converge . . . Reasonable is what sustains the order of gratification. (p. 180)

This reconciliation of reason and pleasure contains its own laws: 'What distinguishes pleasure from the blind satisfaction of want is the instinct's refusal to exhaust itself in immediate satisfaction' (p. 182). In other words liberation would not be licence:

> No longer employed as instruments for retaining men in alienated performances, the barriers against absolute gratification would become elements of human freedom . . . Men would really exist as individuals, each shaping his own life; they would face each other with truly different needs, and truly different modes of satisfaction – with their own refusals and their own selections. The ascendency of the pleasure principle would thus engender antagonisms, pains and frustrations – individual conflicts in the striving for gratification. But these conflicts would themselves have libidinal value: they would be permeated with the rationality of gratification. This *sensuous* rationality contains its own moral laws. (pp. 182–3)

The logic of this rationality is once again the spontaneous absorption of the individual into the totality: 'Once privacy must no longer be maintained apart from and against the public existence, the liberty of the individual and that of the whole may perhaps be reconciled by a "general will" taking shape in institutions which are directed toward the individual needs' (p. 181).

But Marcuse's revisions produce a fundamental distortion of Freud's theory. A real understanding of Freud gives no room for hope that repression and conflict are eliminable, or that scarcity is a temporary state. Freud is neither an optimist nor a primitivist: culture had proceeded too far for man to be able to return to a more natural existence; and, anyway, the primitivists mistook for original human nature what was a happy coincidence of environmental conditions and primitive needs in those tropical island paradises which have survived alongside civilisation, he believed (*Civilization and Its Discontents* [1930] 1961, p. 87). Cultural progress is bought at the cost of repression, but this does not mean that its benefits do not outweigh its costs, or that human nature is not itself a source of conflict. The libidinal instincts were seen by Freud as a mixture of aggressive and pleasure-seeking traits far removed from the pacific and beneficent Eros which makes its appearance in Marcuse's theory.

Freud was a convinced Manichean – there is no way that the conflicting tendencies of human nature, the equal propensities for good and evil, can be eliminated. Although his characterisation of this dualism changed in the course of the development of his theory from the dichotomy of the conscious, primary and secondary processes, to the trichotomy of id, ego and super-ego, Freud always believed that a psychological theory must include dualistic elements if it seeks to understand the psyche in terms of inner conflicts. 'Our views have from the very first been *dualistic*', he declared, 'and today they are even more definitely dualistic than before – now that we describe the opposition as being, not between ego-instincts and sexual instincts but between life instincts and death instincts' (*Beyond the Pleasure Principle*).[6]

Freud's whole metapsychology was developed in terms of the incompatibles with which the individual is faced and the tensions that they create in the psyche (Wollheim, 1971, p. 175). And if culture permits the mitigation of these conflicts and their displacement into less harmful areas, their sublimation, or even repression, this does not mean that the source of conflict is itself eliminated. If that were so, culture would cease to be necessary. But, as we know, it is in Freud's view only the mediation of culture that holds in check destructive forces which, if combined with advanced technology, would be sufficient to blow the world apart.[7]

This idea that psychic conflict is innate underlies the various schematic descriptions of the psyche from the 'system *Ucs.*' of the *Project for a Scientific Psychology* of 1895, to the id, ego, super-ego trichotomy of *Beyond the Pleasure Principle, The Ego and the Id*, and the *New Introductory Lectures* of 1932. In the distinction between unconscious and conscious, primary and secondary processes, Freud gave an early indication of what he considered to be distinct psychic functions, summarised in the pleasure principle and the reality principle. The first, or primary process, concerns the stimulus that the individual receives from within, from the instincts and his unconscious orientation towards the satisfaction of pleasure and the avoidance of pain; the secondary process, by contrast, concerns the outward orientation of the individual, his perceptual and psychic response to the stimulus of the environment and the presence of others and the conscious strategies that he adopts to deal with threats from both within and without to his stability and autonomy.

The duality of these two sets of processes underlies, although is not necessarily identical with, Freud's other major dichotomies: the distinction between the ego-instincts and the libidinal instincts; between conscious and unconscious processes; the reality principle and the performance principle. Secondary processes represent the efforts of the ego to conquer the id and confront the unconscious libidinal instincts with reason. And as these two functions are transferred from the individual psyche to the battleground of culture, they are played out on a grand scale in the systems of substitution, sublimation and repression to which culture, in turn, gives rise. Culture is not, as the primitivists maintained, in radical opposition to nature, but a continuation of its processes by other means. Far from postulating a natural harmony which culture disturbs, Freud showed in the original conflict between the reality principle and the performance principle, a disequilibrium that culture to some extent mitigates.

The achievements of civilisation and the inherent tendencies of human nature which provide its dynamics can only be understood on the assumption that psychic conflict, of which aggressiveness is a major component, is innate. Only if the tension between the unconscious processes and the ego, as that which fights to bring them under conscious control, is understood, can the function of civilisation for the individual be grasped; for there were, as Freud saw it, no cultural developments that do not correspond to real needs in the individual – and this is true for religion and myths as well, all of which have a genuine function to perform (1930*a*, p. 94).

Freud's trichotomy of the id, ego, and super-ego, provides a framework of analysis that is congruent with the classical analysis of the personality in terms of reason, the passions and the will, even if, because of certain prejudices, Freud was not always keen to emphasise this point. While the super-ego corresponds to conscience, the ego corresponds to the rational faculty of judgement. The ego has both an epistemological and a practical function to perform. Oriented to the external world, it confronts the id, and by reality-testing progressively revises the subjective picture which the pleasure-seeking instincts paint. It is the ego which intervenes to bring the unconscious and compulsive behaviour of the id under conscious examination and to submit it to rational judgement: 'The ego controls the approaches to motivity under the id's orders; but between a need and an action it has interposed a postponement in the form of the activity of thought'. ('The dissection of the psychic personality', [1932] 1973, Vol. 2, p. 108).

While the id, the unconscious in the systematic sense (the 'system *Ucs.*'), struggles to gratify the instincts under the pleasure principle, the ego strives to extend its territory. Psychoanalysis has its own contribution to make:

> Its intention is, indeed, to strengthen the ego, to make it more independent of the super-ego, to widen its field of perception and enlarge its organization, so that it can appropriate fresh portions of the id. Where id was, there ego shall be. It is a work of culture − not unlike the draining of the Zuider Zee. (p. 108)

Marcuse is not willing to admit the fundamental conflict which Freud postulates between reason and the instincts. To the degree that he recognises psychic conflict at all he considers it a mere biological hazard common to all animate existence: fear of death and the attempt to preserve life. For this reason, he sees a certain level of repression to be natural, in contrast to surplus represssion which is socially induced. (The fact that he confuses repression, which is in Freud's theory an unconscious process, with oppression, which is overt, actually makes nonsense of the whole distinction, particularly as repression is not natural anyway, but runs counter to the instincts.) Consistent with his assumption of a natural social harmony, Marcuse sees all forms of conflict which do not emanate from the simple fear of death and attempts to stave it off, as part of a conspiracy by which bourgeois culture persuades its workers to postpone or sacrifice instinctual gratification in the interests of their continued aggrandisement. This necessitates a form of false-consciousness, which Marcuse's theory of ideology, with some borrowings from Freudian theory on the role of the unconscious and the super-ego, supplies.

Quite apart from the question of its truth or falsity, Marcuse's revisions made for a bad theory. It is indeed a theory without a centre, and in no way able to account for its own internal dynamics. As a result, the various aspects or stages which he traces have a completely arbitrary quality. For instance, he makes much of the correspondence between man's ontogenesis and phylogenesis, emphasising the trauma of the Oedipus complex in the individual, which harks back to the original historical slaying of the father by the primal horde. But without the notion of instinctual conflict, of which these events are in Freud a representation, they are of course quite arbitrary, manifestations of a cruel fate and blind chance over which man has no control. It is not surprising that they appear in Marcuse's theory as historical events of the same order as Eve's temptation in the Garden of Eden and fundamentalist accounts of the Fall: dreadful events, but they happened and ever since we have been repairing the damage.

All the negative aspects of culture in Marcuse's theory are similarly arbitrary: since man is, in his view, essentially good and his nature harmonious, all the evil in the world has been heaped on his head for nothing except the pleasure of some malevolent forces. Marcuse's naturalism is quite thoroughgoing, and no matter what aspect of civilisation one considers, it turns out that more was lost by it than was gained. Of course, since man's nature is seen to be essentially harmonious and an original symbiotic relation with nature afforded him the immediate satisfactions, plus the prospect of some improvements, that would keep him happy, there was, by definition, nothing to be gained from civilisation – and nothing to explain its existence adequately either! Even the work of Eros in creating greater libidinal entities, on which Marcuse lays considerable stress, lacks all drama since it is merely a restitution of what was unnecessarily lost: the original harmony of individual and community.

Liberation itself is also a form of restoration: Freud had once claimed that 'all thinking "is merely a detour from the memory of gratification" ', as Marcuse reminds us (*Eros and Civilization*, 1969, p. 42), and he advances the hypothesis one more step by claiming that liberation is 'a restoration of remembrance to its rights' (p. 185). 'Remembrance retrieves the *temps perdu*, which was the time of gratification and fulfilment', Marcuse declares, adding, 'without release of the repressed content of memory, without release of its liberating power, non-repressive sublimation is unimaginable' (p. 186). Marcuse's idea that the 'memory of gratification is at the origin of all thinking, and the impulse to recapture past gratification is the hidden driving power behind the process of thought' (p. 42) certainly reduces the achievements of civilisation and the progress of reason to complete insignificance (not to speak of the confusion it makes of the distinction between instinctual and cognitive processes).

Whatever truth there may be in Marcuse's analysis and the central distinction between repression (natural) and surplus-repression (societal), it is certainly not something that Freud himself overlooked. There does, indeed, seem to be considerable variation in the amount of domination and regimentation which societies impose, and in the severity of the repression and the degree of sublimation that they require members to enforce on themselves, as comparative anthropology can demonstrate. And this, according to Freud, is in direct proportion to the complexity of social organisation and the type of goals which society sets, as our own experience and knowledge of history can confirm. The high level of interpersonal tension and the ever-increasing rate of violent crime which seem to accompany the increasing rationalisation of society for production, and which Marcuse tries to account for with the notion of surplus repression, are unfortunately indicative of the costs of sublimation and repression that are necessarily paid, and do not single capitalism out as a peculiar case.

Marcuse modifies Freud's theory in such a way that passions, drives, instincts and the essentially unstable and irrational aspects of human behaviour, with which Freudian theory attempts to deal, are once again denied serious consideration. What for Freud is the price of civilisation, is for Marcuse senseless domination and, where for Freud sublimation was the only hope for civilisation and the aversion of destruction, for Marcuse sublimation is the very cause of destruction: the vengeance of Thanatos is in direct proportion to the frustration of Eros.

Marcuse recognises in passing the positive aspects of civilisation on Freud's account, but without successfully incorporating them into his theory. By considering capitalist society as an aberration and a special case in the history of civilisations, he denies the relevance of Freud's theory just where the latter felt it was most applicable. Marcuse concludes by drawing completely the opposite inferences from Freud concerning the effects of Western culture on the human personality: rather than civilising him, it has had the effect of further reducing him to an animal, for economic performance requires that man become a mere instrument of labour for which characteristically human capacities of enjoyment, pleasure, love, creativity, are superfluous and even counter-productive. These conclusions draw heavily on the French literature on labour and clearly flow from Marxist premises and not from a correction of Freud which takes psychology seriously in its own terms.

Marcuse's doctrine of true and false needs was foreshadowed as early as his essay 'On hedonism' of 1938, and in *Eros and Civilization* he gave it some Freudian trappings in the form of the distinction between the reality principle and the performance principle. By *One Dimensional Man* it has reached its full development as a theory of false consciousness in the concept of 'The conquest of the unhappy consciousness: repressive desublimation' (1964, ch. 3) – the idea that alienation and exploitation are only tolerable because guilt and discontent, the residues of unfulfilled needs, are siphoned off in the permissive gratification of the lower appetites. Marcuse, like Reich and Fromm, believes he has found in Freud a basis to explain the phenomenon of false consciousness, which posed such a problem in Marxist theory, in terms that are more concrete and specific than Marx's concept of ideology permitted. This project ignores the fact that the concept of false needs is a spurious concept for Freud who several times emphasises that it is incumbent on us to assume that societal processes, however bizarre, are nevertheless instigated by genuine human needs. For instance, the transition from the state of nature to society was motivated by a genuine need for security, and when speaking of the different religions, and the multiplicity of cultural values men have created, beauty, order, justice, hygiene, and so on, Freud is insistent that these, too, correspond to real needs:

> If we assume quite generally that the motive force of all human activities is a striving towards the two confluent goals of utility and a yield of pleasure, we must suppose that this is also true of the manifestations of civilization which we have been discussing here, although this is easily visible only in scientific and aesthetic activities. But it cannot be doubted that the other activities, too, correspond to strong needs in man – perhaps to needs which are only developed in

a minority. Nor must we allow ourselves to be misled by judgements of value concerning any particular religion, or philosophic system or ideal. Whether we think to find in them the highest achievements of the human spirit, or whether we deplore them as aberrations, we cannot but recognise that where they are present, and, in especial, where they are dominant, a high level of civilization is implied. (*Civilization and Its Discontents* [1930] 1961, p. 94)

There are no such things as false needs according to Freud, since needs belong to the id which does not set rational criteria for what it admits to experience. The only criterion that needs must meet is to be felt. The frame of reference in which the ego evaluates them is not that of truth or falsity, which could only be a question of whether or not they exist, but in terms of external criteria: their compatibility with goals of self-preservation and certain cultural values that it consciously elects.

In the distinction between the reality principle and the performance principle, made first in *Eros and Civilization*, Marcuse tries to make the case that under alienation the subjects of bourgeois culture are duped into taking for reality the interests of the capitalist system and its ruling class. In this way, they freely undertake to modify their libidinal instincts in accordance with the demands of the labour process:

> . . . the societal authority is absorbed into the 'conscience' and into the unconscious of the individual and works as his own desire, morality, and fulfillment. In the 'normal' development, the individual lives his repression 'freely' as his own life: he desires what he is supposed to desire; his gratifications are profitable to him and to others; he is reasonably and often even exuberantly happy. (*Eros and Civilization*, 1969, p. 51)

We see here the idea of which Sartre is to make much, that men freely carry out the sentence which history has imposed on them, an idea taken from Marx who spoke in *The Holy Family* of the proletariat executing the sentence private property had passed on it (*CW*, Vol. 4, p. 36). But we cannot sufficiently stress how at odds this concept is with Freud's own theory.

The concept of repressive desublimation commits the same mistake which Sartre and others have repeated, and which plays a crucial role in the theory of true and false needs, of identifying the Freudian notion of 'the unconscious' with the Marxian concept of 'false consciousness'. Marcuse, in claiming that 'the societal authority is absorbed into the "conscience" and into the unconscious of the individual and works as his own desire, morality and fulfillment' (p. 51), confuses two separate processes: the first is the function of the id, or the unconscious operations of the instincts; the second is the function of the super-ego by which the individual introjects certain social prohibitions and values. But these are not the same thing, nor could they logically be so: the conscience, or the super-ego, cannot be identical with that upon which it brings its influence to bear.

Nor is this a trivial point. Marcuse by conflating these two processes is able to assume that cultural values substitute for the instincts, from which they are, to the individual, indistinguishable. But Freud's point in the id, ego, super-ego classification is that instinctual strivings are never completely suppressed and that the relation between id and super-ego is not one of identity but one of conflict. The individual is never in any doubt about his instinctual needs – they after all are a compelling force – and it is a question of how strongly he feels the pressure of cultural norms through the super-ego, whether or not these succeed as impediments.

Wollheim points out that Freud developed the id, ego, super-ego classification precisely because of the inadequacy of the conscious/unconscious dichotomy to make this distinction. 'The attributes of being conscious', Freud wrote in 'The Unconscious', 'which is the only characteristic of psychical processes that is directly presented to us, is in no way suited to serve as a criterion for the differentiation of systems' (*Standard Edition*, Vol. 14, p. 192).[8] And he added, 'The more we seek to win our way to a metapsychologically real view of mental life, the more we must learn to emancipate ourselves from the importance of the symptom of 'being conscious' (ibid., p. 193).[9]

This is very important, since the force of neo-Freudian Marxism has to a considerable extent turned on the assumption that the unconscious serves as a vehicle for false consciousness, on which the doctrine of true and false needs in turn depends. It is believed that the introjection of norms is successful to the point where men are no longer capable of distinguishing between their own instinctual needs and the external requirements of the cultural system. It only requires a moment's thought to see, however, that if this were the case, psychoanalysis either as therapy or as metapsychology would be doomed. The viability of psychoanalysis depends on the patient being able to recognise, with the analyst's help, the source of his neuroses. The very phenomenon of neurosis is proof of the fact that the conflict between the demands of the instincts and the demands of society, represented by the super-ego, although displaced by repression, is never entirely eliminated. Indeed, the closer cultural values come to substituting for instinctual needs, the more severe the neurosis is likely to be. To the extent that unconscious processes do involve self-deception, or at least a willingness to go along with whatever forces most easily prevail, the contribution of psychoanalysis to culture depends on the truth of its assumption that a much greater self-awareness is possible than most people are ready to admit.

For this reason we ought to treat with caution the claims of those who attribute irrational behaviour to the working of the unconscious, postulating unconscious needs. The concept of the unconscious in fact puts a major stumbling block in the way of any theory of psychic determinism, suggesting as it does, causal mechanisms at work that can never be identified specifically. To presume that libidinal forces produce behaviours that strike us as irrational is at the same time to acknowledge that these forces are unknown because they are unconscious. This means that we must understand 'unconscious needs' as needs in a different sense from expressed needs and more in the nature of unexamined motives. That there is such a thing as 'the unconscious' seems highly unlikely: it is not Freud who talks this way but his successors. The unconscious for him simply differentiates that area of unreflected behaviour from the area of reflected or rational behaviour under the control of the ego. To assume that it constitutes some kind of real entity is a category mistake.

Nevertheless, it is not true to say that Freud's concept of the unconscious is merely descriptive: that is, merely a category to cover the gaps in consciousness. Freud's concept of the unconscious was dynamic, in other words, the events of unconscious behaviour are significant in the explanation of overt behaviour (Wollheim, 1971, pp. 161–3). By reading back from conscious behaviour presuppositions that could only be found in the unconscious, Freud postulated the contents of the unconscious: cognitive entities and ideas of certain sorts, perceptions that have not yet been verbalised. He attributed peculiar characteristics to its phenomena: the exemption of such ideas, beliefs and impulses from contradiction, and other constraints of external reality, so that they can, for instance, be timeless, disembodied, as in dreams, and so on. The unconscious is also said to contain phenomena that have been driven back into it by the ego through the mechanism of repression. Indeed, the unconscious came to denote such a heterogeneous field that Freud himself began to doubt the efficaciousness of the concept. It is certainly possible on Freud's theory for behaviour to be motivated by unconscious ideas or desires, but what this seems to mean is that it is motivated by irrational desires, a concept that presents no great difficulties.

It must be noted, however, that in some respects Freud himself laid the ground for the kind of oversimplification in which the neo-Freudian Marxists indulge: and that was in his underestimation of the validity of cultural values. Since he, too, saw culture as an integrated system, he was tempted to see cultural values solely in terms of their integrative function, without giving them credence in their own right. His position is a relativist one, and he assumes out of hand that ethical values are contrary to reason, the ultimate criterion. This prejudice stands in the way of a realistic account of the force of those demands that the super-ego makes. If, indeed, the commands of the super-ego are no more than a reification of parental authority and 'the distorted relics of infantile experience and environment', we are forced, in an attempt to account for the origins of conscience, into an infinite regress:

> . . . parental moral influence can have no deeper roots than the parent's own conscience, derived in turn from his parents before him; and the problem of the origin of values is shelved rather than solved by attributing the whole of one generation's morality to the conduct of their parents. (Stafford-Clark, 1967, pp. 168–9)

Such a precarious existence hardly fits with the durability of morality, for conventional morality may or may not be congruent with rational principles, depending on its specific content. It is this assumption of Freud's that morality is a form of self-deception, which makes it that much easier for those seeking a marriage between Marx and Freud to identify morality with ideology and to see the role of the super-ego as the introjection of false needs.

Marcuse's fully developed theory of true and false needs in *One Dimensional Man* is an elaborate development of the theme of 'repressive desublimation':

> We may distinguish both true and false needs. 'False' are those which are superimposed on the individual by particular social interests in his repression: the needs which perpetuate toil, aggressiveness, misery, and injustice. Their satisfaction might be most gratifying to the individual, but this happiness is not a condition which has to be maintained and protected if it serves to arrest the development of the ability (his own and others) to recognize the disease of the whole and grasp the chances of curing the disease. The result then is euphoria in unhappiness. Most of the prevailing needs to relax, to have fun, to behave and consume in accordance with the advertisements, to love and hate what others love and hate, belong to this category of false needs. (1969, pp. 4–5)

Although the theory of true and false needs is already well developed in *Eros and Civilization*, there is a missing ingredient which has yet to be supplied before it reaches final form in *One Dimensional Man*. That is the critique of mass society, undertaken by C. Wright Mills, Vance Packard, and others to whom Marcuse in *One Dimensional Man* acknowledges a debt.

It is worth retracing our steps somewhat to get some perspective on the significance of this addition. To begin with Marcuse was primarily interested, as his early essays indicate, in the role of culture as a substitute for the gratification of needs which the forces of production were not yet sufficiently developed to meet. In this way, without yet resorting to Freudian ideas, Marcuse was arguing that culture, through the ideology of idealism, involves a sublimation of needs, but one which was, nevertheless, justified by a genuine inability to satisfy true needs for technical reasons (scarcity).

Once culture is postulated as an integrated structure which represents an adaptation to, or compensation for, material needs, it may seem plausible to argue that cultural needs can actually displace genuine needs and ideology thereby complete its task with the willing help of the individuals themselves. But we have only to take the reduction one step further to see that this, in fact, tells us nothing. Because, if culture is a (rather complicated) intellectual response to material needs, and if needs are historically determined, then as long as needs are understood as something over and above the minimum physical needs for survival, genuine needs must be culturally determined, too, and there is, on this basis, no way to distinguish true from false needs. For if culture is conditioned by needs and needs are determined by culture, then we do not have an explanation of the genesis of culture (as a product of false needs), nor do we have an argument for the genesis of false needs (as a product of culture). And we are left with no satisfactory explanation of why the 'superfluous goods' of capitalism represent false needs at all.

It was at this point that a body of work that postdates the work of Marx and Freud, and to some extent draws on their ideas, fell into Marcuse's hands. This was the critique of mass society which focused on advertising and the media and their power to manipulate consumer preferences to keep the economic system functioning at optimum levels of production.

The critique of mass society was the work of sociologists, professional and amateur, among them Vance Packard, C. Wright Mills, William H. Whyte, Fred J. Cook, whom Marcuse names (*One Dimensional Man*, 1964, p. xvii). These writers were concerned specifically with the question of the impact of technology, scientific management and corporate structures on the mass public. They offered an account of the detailed mechanisms by which individual consumer preferences, political attitudes, and even social values are collectively determined. Once again the assumption of an integrated structure, comprising a mass of particulars (individuals), governed by certain mechanisms (needs), according to uniform principles (realisation of profit), was made.

But what Marcuse overlooks in this critique is that the success of capitalism is attributed by these sociologists not to the inculcation of false needs, but precisely to the fact that it appeals to genuine and deep-seated needs. There is no evidence to suggest that marketing experts were ever able to create artificial needs for products to solve the problems of overproduction and underconsumption, even though they set out explicitly to do so, in cases which Packard, for instance, carefully documents. Where advertising campaigns have succeeded most resoundingly they are said to have done so by appealing to well-established needs which were neither artificially created, nor even culture-specific. Needs such as the need for emotional security, which can take the form of keeping up with the Joneses; the need for self-esteem, where a reflection of one's personality and tastes is sought in consumer goods; the need for ego-gratification, which is more or less similar, and where consumer preferences also reflect the need for recognition and status; the needs for creativity, love, a sense of belonging; the need for power and a sense of immortality; all of which can be played out in the realm of consumption. (These being more or less the 'eight hidden needs' to which marketing theory is oriented, according to Vance Packard, 1957, ch. 7).

There is, in short, no suggestion in the arguments of these critics that capitalism depends on the creation of false needs, on the one hand, or false consciousness, on the other. The needs it appeals to are genuine enough, even if it manages to overdramatise and exploit them, and the consumer is never entirely duped by the game that advertising plays, as consumer resistance demonstrates. Where he goes along with it, he does so more or less willingly, because it suits him, because it is a matter of indifference to him in the long run, or even because he gets positive enjoyment out of the hopes that are raised, despite the shortfall between what he expects and what he gets. And, of course, not all advertising claims are false anyway. The hoaxters can only trade off the good faith of the consumer because a relatively high number of products turn out to be what they purport to be.

The evils of advertising and the media, as Packard documents them, are rather straightforward ones: cheating, pretending there is a difference between products which are in fact identical, unwarranted claims for products sanctioned by the aura of science, and so on. These evils do not testify to the stupidity of the mass public, so much as to the deviousness and unscrupulousness of the marketers, who violate the trust of consumers who themselves have neither the time nor the inclination to verify the claims for every product that is put before them. And whatever truth there may be in what Marcuse has to say about the degeneracy of capitalism is proof, on this evidence, not of 'false needs' but of the old human vices of acquisitiveness, love of luxury, venality and greed, and the fact that men pay for short-term pleasures by long-term moral corruption. That capitalism can be specifically indicted is due to the fact that affluence gives free reign to such vices.

In *Eros and Civilization*, Marcuse already indicated the conclusions that he draws from the literature on mass society:

> Most of the clichés with which sociology describes the process of dehumanization in present-day mass culture are correct; but they seem to be slanted in the wrong direction. What is retrogressive is not mechanization and standardization but their containment, not the universal coordination, but its concealment under spurious liberties, choices and individualities. The high standard of living in the domain of the great corporations is *restrictive* in a concrete sociological sense: the goods and services that the individuals buy control their needs and petrify their faculties. In exchange for the commodities that enrich their life, the individuals sell not only their labour but also their free time. The better living is offset by the all-pervasive control over living. People dwell in apartment concentrations – and have private automobiles with which they can no longer escape into a different world. They have huge refrigerators filled with frozen foods. They have dozens of newspapers and magazines that espouse the same ideals. They have innumerable choices, innumerable gadgets which are all of the same sort and keep them occupied and divert their attention from the real issue – which is the awareness that they could both work less and determine their own needs and satisfactions. (1969, p. 89)

This is once again the argument that capitalism has doubly deceived its subjects, not only by exploiting them as labourers, but also by manipulating them as consumers. In permitting them gratifications which seem to be freely chosen, the system both buys their support and ensures that their leisure as well as their labour is employed to serve its own ends. Not only this, but by channelling free time into cheap and sordid pleasures, capitalism has destroyed 'high culture' which once represented a protest against materialism and exploitation.

In terms of the pleasures by which capitalism seduces its subjects, Marcuse exaggerates. Although certainly the American consumer, whom he takes as his model, has an omnivorous appetitite for mass-produced commodities, one is struck immediately by the snobbishness of Marcuse's objections to mass culture. For he does not seriously argue against consumerism in terms of the social injustice it causes by the misuse of scarce resources (scarcity is to him, like Sartre, a figment of the bourgeois mind), or even in terms of the damage to the environment that must be plundered for raw products. His main arguments are in terms of aesthetics and the decline of culture: he deplores the fact that mass society has destroyed the truth of higher culture by converting it from a sublimated realm into a realm of consumption and he mourns the loss of alienated intellectuals that has accompanied this transition (*One Dimensional Man*, 1964, pp. 58–65).

Quite apart from the incongruity of the argument in the context of Marxist premises, if this is his concern, the problem is likely to correct itself under capitalism. For most of the consumer bad taste of which he complains, overflowing freezers, vulgar second cars, split-level homes, hi-fi sets, and the gadgets which enthrall people, are craved by the under-privileged rather than the bourgeoisie, who affect the 'low profile'. Practically speaking, the direction in which Marcuse hopes to see change occur – increased sensitivity and liberation from consumer fetishism – is more likely to be achieved by *embourgeoisement* than by levelling down and centralised control under socialism. Experience shows that there is no better palliative to escalating needs than a surfeit, and that once the *nouveaux riches* became accustomed to easily accessible luxuries they become more discriminating.

Marcuse's own theory supports in a strange way the phenomenon of which he complains. For Marxism encourages the development of pro-ductive forces to their highest point, 'exploration of all of nature in order to discover new useful qualities in things; universal exchange of the products of all alien climates and lands . . . the discovery, creation and satisfaction of new needs . . .' (*Grundrisse*, 1973*a* edn, pp. 409–10) as the basis from which a transition to socialism could be made. By holding out the promise that socialism would permit the free gratification of all needs, Marxism promotes the same pursuit of gratification that it condemns on other grounds.[10] It is probably no accident that consumerism in socialist and communist countries is rapidly approaching the levels of those which are overtly capitalist.

The principle on which Marxism staked its hopes was that the permissiveness for which gratification according to need opens the way, would be held in check by the rational restraints inbuilt in socialism as the form in which the human essence is properly realised. Critical theory was seen to vouch for this by showing the dialectical unfolding of reason in a progression of social forms of which socialism was the culmination.

These are Marcuse's assumption as well. That capitalism has not yet given way to socialism when all the conditions are ripe, requires an elaborate explanation of which the doctrine of true and false needs is the linchpin. He sees the major challenge to revolutionary consciousness to lie in the power of the capitalist state, which has at its disposal not only the instruments of overt coercion, such as the police and armed forces, but also the 'hidden persuaders', or the mass media. The state, by artificially inducing a sense of ever-present danger, sells its interests as those of reason, through the advertising media, 'the political needs of society become individual needs and aspirations' (*One Dimensional Man*, 1964, p. ix). The implantation of false needs is the most enduring form of war against liberation, and the result is the 'welfare/warfare state'. False needs are those 'superimposed on the individual by particular social interests in his repression' (p. 5) and the catalogue of false needs includes 'stupefying work', 'production and consumption of waste', 'modes of relaxation which soothe and prolong this stupefication', and so on (p. 7).

However, Marcuse takes care not to overemphasise the role of the media in all this, since as a mere instrumentality they are incapable of explaining false needs as a systemic effect. People are already pre-conditioned before the media reach them, he maintains; forces are already at work to 'flatten out' the contrast between the given and the possible, satisfied and unsatisfied needs. He wonders at the fact that people, far from feeling alienated in advanced capitalist society, actually 'recognize themselves in their commodities', and concludes that 'the rational character of this irrationality' can only be explained by the fact that 'social control is anchored in the new needs which it has produced' (p. 9). Marcuse appeals to Marx's arguments in the general introduction to the *Grundrisse*, where he argues that patterns of distribution and consumption are an efflux of the productive system, to show precisely how these false needs are 'introjected'. 'The productive apparatus and the services which it produces: then "sell" or impose the social system as a whole' (1973*a* edn, pp. 11–12). A modern form of bread and circuses which 'bind the consumers more or less pleasantly to the producers' through their commodities:

> In this society, the productive apparatus tends to become totalitarian to the extent to which it determines not only the socially needed occupations, skills, and attitudes, but also individual needs and aspirations. It also obliterates the opposition between private and public existence, between individual and social needs. (*One Dimensional Man*, 1964, p. xv)

Marcuse's appeal to pluralism in the old distinctions between the public and the private, the individual and society, is just another anomaly in his theory. He is not without his own justification, however: bourgeois rights and liberties were, at their inception, 'essentially *critical* ideas'; once they were institutionalised this critical function was lost (pp. 1–2). But this is pure idealism, for, to realise the distinction between the public and private spheres would require the institutionalisation of bourgeois liberties and rights which Marcuse hopes to see abolished under socialism. Does he imagine that the central administration of vital needs will better actualise these distinctions, or are they ultimately of merely instrumental value, to be transcended under socialism? It is hard to say.

It is worth noting the extent to which Marcuse's appeal for the restoration of pluralism or two-dimensional culture, is prejudiced by his materialist social theory. He is faithful to Marx in defining the criteria for the evaluation of historical projects as: (1) material feasibility, (2) the promotion of material well-being, and (3) the free development of human needs (pp. x–xi). But he continually erodes these premises by other aspects of his theory. For instance, Marcuse states that a social programme, to be valid, must be expressive of actual tendencies that reflect 'the real need of the underlying population' (p. xi), echoing Marx's famous claim that 'theory can be realized in a people only insofar as it is the realization of the needs of that people' (Introduction to *Critique of Hegel's 'Philosophy of Right'*, *CW*, Vol. 3, p. 183). Quite apart from the fact that he quickly sets about establishing that capitalism's tenacious hold is precisely due to the way that it has supplanted true needs with false ones, so that its subjects are no longer capable of perceiving their true needs, this insistence on the potential for materialisation as a criterion of authenticity runs against his contentions about the critical role of ideas.

Marcuse laid the basis for this notion of the critical function of ideas in his essay on 'The concept of essence', and, as he resorts to it often, it is important to see what it means. He said in that essay that it was a hallmark of idealist philosophy since Plato to be able to subsume all material objects, ranked in categories of genera and species, under universal concepts. Marcuse then concludes, idiosyncratically, that these concepts become the criteria 'by means of which the distance between existence and what it could be, its essence, is measured in each case':

> The Being of things is not exhausted in what they immediately are; they do not appear as they could be. The form of their immediate existence is imperfect when measured against their potentialities, which comprehension reveals as the image of their essence. ('The concept of essence', 1972*b*, pp. 45–6)

Marcuse draws the perverse conclusion that logical and epistemological functions are secondary to the 'critical' function of ideas, which is as good as turning philosophy over to the poets, if concepts are to be judged for their elasticity instead of their rigour. And besides, how can ideas maintain their critical function, their ability to transcend reality, if they are also to be judged by their potential for realisation? His theory of truth is quite incoherent. In some places truth is a prognostication of 'arrested possibilities' (*One Dimensional Man*, 1964, p. xi), in others it is synonymous with material realisation.

There is a genuine problem here which has been at the centre of the idealism/materialism debate since Plato, who first raised it when he attempted to have ideas function both as material cause and as logical criteria for the particulars which fell under them – a problem which Aristotle tried to elucidate with his concepts of potentiality and teleological determination. It is clear that Marcuse is very far from resolving these problems and, while officially espousing the principles of dialectical materialism, his whole critical theory continues to be based on idealist premises, evocative of the 'critical criticism' for which Marx pilloried Bauer and the Young Hegelians.

Not unrelated to this, and a further source of tension in Marcuse's work, is the attempt to reconcile materialism and humanism in the concept of *praxis*. If *praxis* means the realisation in practice of the image of man which philosophy has extracted as the human essence, it is undoubtedly a utopian concept. The actualisation of philosophical categories is likely to become their materialist reduction, which Marcuse virtually guarantees by the role he has the concept of needs play. By characterising all human activity as determined by needs, Marcuse undercuts the famous Marxian distinction between the architect and the bee and begins the chain of thought that reduces passions to drives, thoughts to motives, desires to needs and will to instinct.

This is not to say that a reconciliation of mind and body, the conceptual and the material, in a Marxian-type *praxis* is inconceivable and a number of cultures seem to have come closer to it than ours. But one cannot ask for this unity, on the one hand, and expect pluralism in philosophy, ethics, tastes, needs and everyday life to flourish, on the other, especially not if the unity of *praxis* is to be enshrined in a socialism which centrally administers all needs. The final demystification which Marxism tends to seek goes against the grain of Western European culture and its history of persistent dualism. Moreover, it would involve the abandonment of certain values which Marcuse, especially, would be unwilling to relinquish: humanism, liberty, and so on. Humanism, as Hegel and Marx were among the first to see, is an historical creation and, in the form we know it, culture-specific. Its creation had a good deal to do with an otherworldly religion, deprecation of the material, and certain freedoms which were won in the course of doctrinal struggles. It is questionable how mundane humanism can become.

Marcuse is forced to apocalyptic solutions by his persistent exaggerations. He too readily assumes that the masses are manageable and can be easily manipulated, and he goes far beyond Marx in his imputation of malice and conspiracy to societal institutions, showing himself to be insensitive to the peculiar understanding of social forms which the Marxian term 'superstructure' denotes: that the institutional, legal and cultural aspects of the mode of production are created as a by-product of the organisation of everyday life. Marcuse imputes to the informal structures of society the characteristics of formal organisations, such as factories, armies, and so on, attributing to them a far higher level of authority, legitimacy and control than they exhibit. One can understand that having lived through the horrors of Nazism he might be tempted to feel this way; but if classes really were as intractable as bureaucratic structures, and if General Motors really were to exercise the same control as the Hitlerjugend, we would expect them to manifest some of the same characteristics.

The owl of Minerva flies truly only at dusk. Whatever truth Marcuse's portrait of the one-dimensionality of American society in the cold war era and the monolith of American capitalism, might have had – wielding nuclear threats, stoking its fires on foreign wars, whipping its populace to ever-increasing production and consumption – it had lost by the time he wrote, when riots in the cities and on the campuses and vociferous political debate produced a fever of self-criticism and wide social cleavages. That is not to say that American imperialism is not real enough or, indeed, deplorable in its effects. But its irrationality and malignancy are hardly more impressive than that of the Ottoman Empire where the thrust of a dagger ritually decided the succession; or of the Byzantine, where the Great Basileus hovered in a basket suspended by chains, floating in a cloud of incense over his court; or of the Egyptian king who basked in a hammock over a lake of mercury so that he could see reflected the lights of his realm, and died of mercury poisoning.

These empires made of their citizens slaves and eunuchs, and not merely profligate consumers, to serve their ends. Great power leads to great excesses as Machiavelli told us and as we have had sufficient opportunity to experience in the twentieth century. Capitalism is not in this respect historically exceptional, nor does it require exceptional remedies, which threaten to kill rather than 'cure' the patient. (Marcuse, like Fromm, tends to talk in terms of capitalism as a 'disease'.)

One of the most remarkable aspects of Marcuse's theory is his increasing naturalism. In a series of essays written after the publication of *Eros and Civilization*, Marcuse admits a fundamental incompatibility between his theory and that of Freud.[11] His argument turns on a rejection of all claims that the individual may liberate himself through increasing rational control of the instincts. Freedom, he declares, is a bourgeois shibboleth that underestimates the degree to which social control is now anchored in the instinctual structure itself. Capitalism represents the 'repressive transformation of the instincts' which modifies 'the biological constitution of the organism'. In this way 'history rules even in the instinctual structure; culture becomes nature as soon as the individual learns to affirm and to reproduce the reality principle from within himself, through the instincts' ('Freedom and Freud's theory of the instincts', in Marcuse, 1970, p. 11).

Although employing Freudian terminology, this is an un-Freudian argument. To Freud the individual could never learn to affirm or reproduce anything in his instinctual structure because instinctual processes are unconscious. Freud never believed that the reality principle was reproduced *through the instincts* at all: the reality principle was set *over against the instincts* by the ego, in order to bring them under control.

Curiously enough, Marcuse, whose picture of man's destiny at this point seems unrelievedly dark, nevertheless clings to the hope that a restructuring of the instincts will provide a 'real weapon' for the establishment of utopia. In the first chapter of *An Essay on Liberation*, entitled 'A biological foundation for socialism', he outlines his solution in the new morality of the Great Refusal, presaged by hippies and draft card burners. 'Morality', he declares, 'is not necessarily and not primarily ideological' (1972*a*, p. 18). Morality, despite Marcuse's earlier dissertations on the subject, is not confined to the realm of ideas at all. 'Prior to all ethical behaviour in accordance with specific social standards, prior to all ideological expression, morality is a "disposition" of the organism.' It is a manifestation of Eros, 'rooted', that is to say, 'in the erotic drive to counter aggressiveness, to create and preserve "ever greater unities" of life' (p. 19). Morality is also instinctual, and Marcuse claims, not inconsistently, to have discovered a morality 'this side of all "values", an instinctual foundation for solidarity among human beings' (p. 19). If changes in morality, the precondition for political change, can '"sink down" into the "biological" dimension and modify organic behaviour' (p. 20), a solution can, Marcuse believes, be found to the dilemma of alienation through the introjection of false needs:

> Such a change would constitute the instinctual basis for freedom which the long history of class society has blocked. Freedom would

become the environment of an organism which is no longer capable of adapting to the competitive performances required for well-being under domination, no longer capable of tolerating the aggressiveness, brutality and ugliness of the established way of life. The rebellion would then have taken root in the very nature, the 'biology' of the individual; and on these new grounds, the rebels would redefine the objectives and strategy of the political struggle, in which alone the concrete goals of liberation can be determined. (p. 14)

If morality which is 'this side of all values' sounds a little strange to us, actually Marcuse was not the first to propound such a notion and, in the second chapter, entitled 'The new sensibility', it becomes apparent that his conception of morality comes very close to the moral sense theories of the eighteenth and nineteenth centuries (Hume, Hutcheson, Shaftesbury, and so on), as well as owing something to André Breton and the surrealists in the twentieth.

Like these forbears, he sees in morality an appeal to imagination and sensibility against 'the rationality of domination' (p. 37). Beauty, perhaps not surprisingly, is considered the supreme moral value, because beauty, as Nietzsche maintained, 'has the "biological value" of that which is "useful, beneficial, life enhancing"' (pp. 34–5). Indeed, Marcuse believes that beauty is what holds aggression in check; that as a manifestation of Eros, the sense of beauty is also instinctual; and that 'the primary distinction between beautiful and ugly, good and bad' is 'prior to all rationalization and ideology, a distinction made by the senses (productive in their receptivity), distinguishing that which violates sensibility from that which gratifies it' (p. 34). A fundamentally un-Marxian view, assuming as it does that values are biologically given and not socially created.

Nevertheless, Marcuse attributes to sensibility, and the 'political, instinctual and moral rebellion' it will produce, everything from 'the prohibition of transistor radios in public places' to 'control of the birthrate', in short, the solution of all urban and ecological problems (p. 35). Sensibility is the ethos of the 'new society' and the new man of socialism, and for a fleeting moment he sees in the hippies, mini-skirted students, rock'n'rollers, militants and guerrillas, both a protest against the 'mutilated experience . . . false consciousness . . . false needs . . . false values . . . false morality', which make liberation a '"vital" biological need' (pp. 56–7), and a prognostication of the utopia that lies in the future. Happiness in the individual awaits only the solidarity of the species for its realisation:

> The notion that happiness is an objective condition which demands more than subjective feelings has been effectively obscured; its validity depends on the real solidarity of the species 'man', which a society divided into antagonistic classes and nations cannot achieve. (p. 23)

Notes

1   'The struggle against liberalism in the totalitarian view of the state' (1934); 'The concept of essence' (1936); 'The affirmative character of culture' (1937); 'Philosophy

and critical theory' (1937); 'On hedonism' (1938); collected in Marcuse (1972*b*).
2 See especially, 'The affirmative character of culture' in Marcuse (1972*b*).
3 See 'The struggle against liberalism in the totalitarian view of the state', in Marcuse (1972*b*).
4 See 'The concept of essence', in Marcuse (1972*b*).
5 See 'The affirmative character of culture', in Marcuse (1972*b*), pp. 100–1.
6 Quoted in Wollheim (1971, p. 180).
7 See closing paragraph of *Civilization and Its Discontents* [1930] 1961, p. 145.
8 Cited in Wollheim, 1971, p. 174.
9 Cited in ibid., p. 174.
10 This is the argument made by William Leiss in *The Limits to Satisfaction: An Essay on the Problem of Needs and Commodities* (1976).
11 'Freedom and Freud's theory of the instincts' (1956); 'Progress and Freud's theory of the instincts' (1956); 'The obsolescence of the Freudian concept of man' (1963); collected in Marcuse (1970). See also Marcuse, *An Essay on Liberation* (1972*a*).

10

Farther Reaches of Need Theory

Abraham Maslow developed his hierarchy of needs alongside of, and with direct reference to, Erich Fromm's work on existential needs, and both thinkers are key figures in the school of 'humanistic psychology'. Maslow documents other sources for his theory as well: the functionalist tradition of Dewey and James; the holism of Wertheimer, who saw man as a creature who strives 'to see rather than be blind'; the concept of self-actualisation as developed by Kurt Goldstein; the homeostatic theory of Canon who, in his *Wisdom of the Body*, postulated an innate disposition of the organism to seek what it needs – for example, minerals, protein, vitamins, etc.; the work of Adler, Horney, etc., on self-esteem needs; Gestalt theory; and the dynamic psychology of Freud ('A theory of human motivation', 1943, p. 371). Maslow sees a common denominator in this diverse body of literature in the concept of self-actualisation, 'the tendency to growth or self-actualization, in one vague form or another, has been postulated by thinkers as diverse as Aristotle and Bergson, and by many other philosophers', he observes. 'Among psychiatrists, psychoanalysts, and psychologists it has been found necessary by Goldstein, Rank, Jung, Horney, Fromm, Rogers, May and Maslow' ('The instinctoid nature of basic needs', 1954*a*, p. 327). Maslow claims that he was also influenced by Hartmann's definition of the 'good' as 'the degree to which an object fulfils its definition or concept'. And it is probable that the basis for his theory of prepotency is to be found in Erich Fromm's argument that 'after [man] has satisfied his animal needs, he is driven by his human needs' (*The Sane Society*, 1955*b*, p. 28).

In Maslow's hands the concept of needs is used to fuse Freudian instinct-based theory with a proper appreciation of human behaviour as goal-oriented. Maslow, in his later work especially, believes that a teleological explanation of human behaviour is appropriate, that 'is' and 'ought' are in many respects inseparable, and that a theory of needs is capable of providing an integration of facts and values ('Fusions of facts and values', 1963, pp. 117–31). His taxonomy of needs moves progressively from physiological to cognitive needs, providing an account of the priority of needs and the logical order in which they are satisfied. 'Higher' cognitive and aesthetic needs are said to be activated only when prior or more prepotent needs have been satisfied. In terms of prepotency he ranks needs in the following hierarchy: (1) physiological needs for food, shelter, respiration, reproduction, and so on, (2) safety needs relating to survival and security; (3) affection or belongingness needs; (4) needs for approbation and self-esteem; (5) needs for self-actualisation and development. These needs are said to be both universal and instinctoid; however, as the theory stipulates, needs higher on the scale are dependent on lower needs being satisfied before they come into effect, so that not all of them are necessarily realised in any given individual or culture.

Maslow's seems to be a very clear theory and it has been quite influential in the social sciences. Christian Bay, among other leftist writers, has drawn on Maslow and Fromm in his critique of the liberal-democratic state, arguing that advanced capitalism leaves basic needs unsatisfied, and advocating an alternative politics geared precisely to need-satisfaction and the guarantee of basic human rights. Nevertheless, this whole orientation to needs, and Maslow's theory in particular, have a number of problematic aspects that warrant discussion: (1) his postulate that all needs, both the 'lower' or physiological needs and the 'higher', aesthetic or cognitive needs are universal or instinctoid and that they are necessarily ranked in the order that he gives; (2) his belief that man's nature, goals and values are biologically given; (3) his concept of self-actualisation; (4) his denial of any incompatibility between reason and the instincts on the basis that reason is itself instinctoid; (5) his belief in the fundamental harmony of the individual and society; (6) his retention of the concepts of pathology, neurosis and the notion of the 'sick' society, despite (4) and (5); (7) his concepts of 'neurotic', 'pathological' and 'artificial' needs; (8) his notion of human rights as prior to and preconditions for needs; (9) his criteria for the discovery and ranking of needs; and (10) his case for the 'fusion' of facts and values.

Maslow classes as 'basic' and instinctoid the full range of human needs, both needs man shares with animals and the higher cognitive or aesthetic needs, such as needs for information, understanding, beauty, symmetry, order, perfection, and so on ('The instinctoid nature of basic needs', 1954a, p. 341). In support of this contention he marshalls some anthropological evidence. He cites Margaret Mead's findings on the Balinese who, as adults, manifest no signs of the needs for love and affection, showing that these needs are nevertheless evident in Balinese children who 'cry and bitterly resent the lack of affection' (p. 332). Maslow concludes from this evidence that the 'loss of the affectionate impulse is an acquired loss', which supports his case for the universality of the need for love which is repressed at great cost.

In fact, Maslow's example seems to count against his general argument, for while it may prove that the need for love is universal, it suggests that the value attached to love differs from culture to culture. Thus love, which ranks as a higher need in Maslow's hierarchy, seems to rank low for the Balinese for whom it is apparently overridden by values which are given higher priority. The priority of needs is determined by values and 'lower' needs give way to 'higher' ones according to how a culture ranks its priorities. The great cultural differences in value priorities is itself evidence that the organism, as such, does not in fact 'dictate hierarchies of value' as one of its innate functions in the way that

Maslow suggests ('"Higher" and "lower" needs', 1948*a*, p. 433).

The foundation on which Maslow's theory rests is a concept of human nature as biologically given, in conjunction with the axiom that this human nature is fundamentally good. This constitutes the humanistic element in humanistic psychology.

> Instinct theory [he argues] accept[s] the fact that man [is] a self-mover . . . that his own nature supplie[s] him with a ready-made framework of ends, goals, or values; that most often, under good conditions, what he wants is what he needs (what is good for him) in order to avoid sickness; that all men form a single biological species . . . and that on the whole, organisms left to their own resources often display a kind of biological efficiency or 'wisdom' . . . ('The instinctoid nature of basic needs', 1954*a*, p. 328)

Maslow therefore argues that 'the gratification of basic needs leads to consequences that may be called variously "desirable", "good", "healthy", "self-actualizing"' (p. 342), maintaining that : 'It is the general clinical finding that the organism, when fed safety, love, and respect, "works" better, i.e., perceives more efficiently, uses intelligence more fully, thinks to correct conclusions more often, digests food more efficiently, is less subject to various diseases, etc.' (p. 343).

Maslow's concept of self-actualisation follows from, and is logically dependent on, his belief that human nature is innately given and good. It requires only an hospitable culture and appropriate child-rearing patterns to develop this human nature in accordance with its concept. Maslow sees a certain but limited role for nurture as opposed to nature, due to the fact that man's instincts, although given, compared with other animals are relatively weak. Here he introduces the idea of 'canalisation': the idea that appropriate objects for higher needs are not themselves instinctively sought and that the instincts must be channelled so that the individual learns 'which objects are proper satisfiers and which are not' (p. 339). This is said by Maslow to be an objective and not a relative question and it is precisely on this basis that he differentiates healthy from neurotic behaviour: the 'healthy gratification of love needs, understanding needs, and the like is by canalization, i.e., by some intrinsically proper gratification and not by arbitrary association. Where the latter do occur, we speak of neurosis and of neurotic needs, e.g., fetishism' (p. 339). That is to say, healthy behaviour is behaviour in which needs seek their true objects, neurotic behaviour is behaviour in which they seek false objects: 'The organism itself, out of its own nature, points to an intrinsic range of satisfiers for which no substitute is possible as is the case, for instance, with habitual needs, or even with many neurotic needs' (p. 343).

Maslow argues generally that 'instrumental behaviours (means) are far more relative to local cultural determinants than are basic needs (ends)' (p. 329). He thus rejects cultural relativism, maintaining that a society is 'sick' to the degree that it represses innate 'human urges' or needs, or channels them in the wrong direction. For this reason he indicts child-rearing patterns which repress the child's 'healthy animality' (p. 336), or which encourage the mistaken belief that there is a fundamental conflict between the individual and society. He advocates a 'discriminate permissiveness', admitting that 'some minimum of acculturation, i.e., "training", acquisition of culturally demanded habits, would still be necessary' under such a regime, 'although in an atmosphere of basic-need gratification such peripheral and artificial acquisitions should make no particular trouble' (p. 336).

Maslow rejects the old Freudian dichotomies between the reality principle and the pleasure principle, the individual and society. He refers to the 'vital and even tragic mistake' that 'has been made from time immemorial of dichotomizing instinctive impulses and rationality in the human being', declaring: 'It has rarely occurred to anyone that they might *both* be instinctoid in the human being, and more important, that their results or implied goals might be identical rather than antagonistic' (pp. 332–3).

In the same way, he argues that the hypothesised tension between the individual and society is false and has led to the characterisation of 'civilization and all its institutions, school, church, court, legislation, as bad-animality-restraining forces' (p. 335). This 'false theory of human nature' constitutes a 'mistake so crucial, so tragedy laden, that it may be likened in historical importance to such mistakes as the belief in the divine right of kings, in the exclusive validity of any one religion, in the denial of evolution, or in the belief that the earth is flat' (p. 335). Quite apart from whether or not these examples constitute 'mistakes', as Maslow suggests, the very fact that he postulates such wide-ranging historical aberrations, and that he retains the concepts of neurosis and pathology, casts doubt on his contentions that human values and goals are given as a function of the organism, that reason and the instincts are fundamentally compatible, and that no real tension exists between the individual and society. Nevertheless, he concludes that 'any belief that makes men mistrust themselves and each other unnecessarily and causes them to be unrealistically pessimistic about human possibilities must be held partly responsible for every war that has ever been waged, for every racial antagonism, and for every religious crusade'. 'Recognize instinctoid needs not to be "bad", but neutral or "good"', he admonishes, 'and a thousand pseudoproblems solve themselves and fade out of existence' (p. 335).

Maslow slips from the assertion that instinctoid needs are good and that neurosis and pathology are a function of acculturation to false objects, to the postulation of 'neurotic, habitual or addictive needs'. 'No permissiveness is implied', he declares, 'with respect to neurotic needs, habit needs, fixations, or any other non-instinctoid needs' (p. 336). He seems here to be suggesting that culture has the power to induce false or artificial needs over and above its power to provide false objects for needs. But he provides no theoretical foundation for such a contention, given that he maintains human aims, goals and values to be innately given. In addition, his argument that pathology and aggression result from the frustration or diversion of basic instinctual needs is cast into doubt by his insistence that the healthy person is one who, having been satisfied in his needs in the early years, subsequently develops 'exceptional power to withstand present or future thwarting of these needs' ('A theory of human motivation', 1943, p. 392). He concludes rather strangely that 'in actual fact, most members of our society who are normal, are partially satisfied in all their basic needs and partially unsatisfied in all their basic needs at the same time' (p. 388).

The criteria for pathology and neurosis are thus considerably less clear-cut than at first appears. This presents certain moral dilemmas in deciding whether a need is worthy of satisfaction or not. For instance, Maslow argues that the seriousness or triviality of a need depends on how it relates to basic goals:

> A desire for an ice cream cone might actually be an indirect expression of a desire for love. If it is, then this desire for the ice cream cones becomes [an] extremely important motivation. If however the ice cream is simply something to cool the mouth with, or a casual appetitive reaction, then the desire is relatively unimportant (p. 392)

He goes on to argue that 'thwarting of unimportant desires produces no psychopathological results: thwarting of a basically important need does produce such results' (p. 393). Given that he accepts the notion of unconscious motivation, what in fact a given behaviour represents in terms of real motives is very difficult to establish. And how does his earlier claim about the proper objects of such needs as love, and so on, come to bear at this point? Are we entitled to hold that the need for an ice-cream cone is not an appropriate expression of the need for love, or must we gratify this need in any of its diverse forms, as he seems to suggest? As we shall see these problems run up against his contention that the criteria for isolating and ranking needs are obvious and unambiguous.

A further contentious aspect of Maslow's theory lies in his notion of preconditions to needs. 'Such conditions as freedom to speak, freedom to do what one wishes so long as no harm is done to others, freedom to express one's self, justice, fairness, honesty, orderliness in the group are examples of such preconditions for basic need satisfactions' (p. 383). Failure to satisfy these preconditions severely prejudices the satisfaction of basic needs, Maslow argues. But once again, if human needs, values and goals are innately prescribed, this argument seems to put a heavy burden on culture for which the theory in general makes no room. This is further complicated by the fact that these so-called preconditions, a list of freedoms, actually constitute rights or values in themselves. And why, if needs for information, understanding, beauty, symmetry, order, perfection, and so on, are innately given, are not needs for freedom, justice, honesty, and so on? Maslow concludes rather arbitrarily that 'these conditions are not ends in themselves, but they are *almost* so since they are so closely related to the basic needs, which are apparently the only ends in themselves' (p. 383).

We have already suggested serious problems with regard to Maslow's criteria for establishing and ranking needs. In one of his earlier papers '"Higher" and "lower" needs' of 1948, Maslow argues (1948*a*, pp.

433–6) that the criteria for ranking needs are as follows: the 'higher' the need (1) the more human, (2) the later in ontogenetic development, (3) the later it emerges in the species (that is, phylogenetically the more recent), (4) the longer its gratification can be postponed, (5) the easier for it to disappear permanently, (6) the greater the satisfaction derived from it, (7) the greater the value placed on it in a society that offers both lower and higher needs. We may briefly say of these claims that (1) is a value judgement; (2), (3) and (6) while apparently definitional are in fact subject to empirical investigation; (4) runs counter to Maslow's claims that basic need-frustration produces pathologies and that those needs which can be frustrated without pathological effect are trivial; (5) suggests, if a need can disappear permanently, that it is not instinctoid; and (7) is tautological, disclosing the fact that 'higher' needs are decided by value priorities.

Maslow believes that if a real psychological and operational distinction could be shown to exist between lower and higher needs, the need-hierarchy would be both instinctually dictated and scientifically observable. He claims to have derived his findings from clinical observation. 'In this area [psychotherapy]', he argues, 'the logic of facts, however unclearly seen, has been unmistakable; inexorably, the therapist has been forced to differentiate more basic from less basic wishes (or needs, or impulses). It is just as simple as this; the frustration of some needs produces pathology, the frustration of other needs does not' ('The instinctoid nature of basic needs', 1954*a*, p. 327). As we have seen, it is not in fact quite so simple, even on Maslow's own terms.

Maslow's work, far from succeeding in fusing facts and values, as he claims, has produced confusion in this area. To begin with, if in fact human needs are instinctoid, they cannot be said to be either good or bad as such. Needs as an expression of requirements for the natural functioning of an organism in physiological and psychological terms can only be judged good by the introduction of a value premise to the effect that natural functioning constitutes excellence.[1] But disagreement on this normative premise is wide and different value premises lead to a different ranking of needs, as we suggested in the case of the Balinese and as we have had opportunity to observe in need theories already discussed.

Maslow's recognition that his is a teleological theory accounting for human motivation as a goal-oriented phenomenon is an important admission. As several philosophers have recently argued (Louch, 1966; Peters, 1960; C. Taylor, 1964), human behaviour is intentional behaviour and when we try to take account of it we do so in terms of the reasons for acting that may be presumed on the part of the actor. Our legal systems and their criteria for accountability and responsibility, ethical theory and the common assumptions of everyday life suggest that this is the appropriate way of judging human conduct. And yet the scientific study of human psychology from Enlightenment man-machine theories through to modern behavioural science has favoured an explanation of behaviour in terms of causes rather than intentions. One, but not the only, reason has been a tendency to argue from the model of animal behaviour as instinct-governed to human behaviour in the same terms — the study of animal behaviour permitted experimentation and therefore a firm empirical basis for research, while humane ethics rules out such techniques in the case of man.

But far more important than this pragmatic consideration was the theoretical rigour that a theory of the instincts permitted. As we have argued before, theorists of man and society have for a long time favoured structuralist explanations. Complex and mutually conditioned phenomena cannot convincingly be explained in terms of the simple mechanistic causality on which the classical science of Newtonian physics was based. And yet a causal theory has to have some underlying principles. The concept of the instincts allowed a theory that accounted for the uniformity of human behaviour, while admitting a wide range of variation, explained in terms of instinctual frustration, repression, sublimation, and so on. Thus an underlying causality was preserved, but one which did not rule out the influence of societal institutions and structures, values and beliefs: the libidinal instincts were seen to represent the internal direction of behaviour, but the forms of release they took represented the influence of the family, society at large and its norms, as they were brought to bear on the individual.

Humanistic psychology seeks to preserve the rigour of a theory of the instincts while going even further towards recognising the goal-oriented nature of man and society. By postulating a logical spectrum of activities ranging, at one end, from the most physiological to, at the other end, the most cognitive, it achieves a fair degree of plausibility in its attempt. From our own experience and from empirical research on the subject — the Minnesota deprivation studies, and so on — there is much to suggest that satisfaction of what Maslow terms basic biological needs, is indeed a precondition for a humane existence or the satisfaction of those 'higher' needs on his scale that we think of as peculiarly human. The problem is, however, that to consider these higher needs as 'instinctoid', rules out the distinctions between innate and learned behaviour, voluntary and involuntary behaviour that allow us to differentiate characteristically human behaviour as goal-oriented, as Maslow has already admitted it is. And it leads to further curious conclusions.

The model of the instincts on which he draws is the homeostatic or tension-reducing model: needs for hunger, sex, and so on, represent a progressive build-up of tension for which relief is sought; overall the state of homeostasis represents the mechanisms of the healthy body at work. In the same way, Maslow is suggesting that higher needs for affection, belongingness, self-esteem, self-actualisation or development, represent conditions that must be met for psychic and mental health. He argues in fact that 'a man who is thwarted in any of his basic needs may fairly be envisioned simply as sick or at least less than fully human' (*Motivation and Personality*, 1954).[2]

These are arguments with which we are familiar in Fromm, who talks of the 'sick' society and pathologies induced by the frustration of needs. Christian Bay also defines 'need' as referring to 'any behaviour tendency whose continued denial or frustration leads to pathological responses' (1968, p. 242). Their belief that the non-satisfaction of cognitive or aesthetic needs necessarily produces pathologies, makes it clear that these thinkers assume the classic old Freudian mechanisms at work: the instincts if frustrated in their original purpose must seek substitute outlets and, as such, may turn up in the disguise of opposites, so the need for creativity, if blocked, ends up taking the form of a need for destruction, the need for love takes sadistic or masochistic forms, and so on. This account of pathology in terms of instinctual energy diverted from its original source presupposes a concept of behaviour governed by innate urges which have their somatic source in the physiological structure, which was precisely what these theorists, with their taxonomy of lower and higher needs and their recognition of behaviour as goal-directed, sought to avoid. This is what comes from arguing by analogy. Even if, as Fromm, Maslow and Bay argue, in the case of higher needs, pathology is due less to the diversion of instinctual energy than to the frustration of man's proper goals, this argument involves them in assumptions about human nature and excellence as a state of perfect functioning that are untenable for other reasons.

These are problems that we mentioned in the case of Erich Fromm and his quasi-Aristoteliam concept of the human essence. On the question of human nature and what it constitutes we enter a highly contentious area. It seems, on the good scientific principle that when we have uniform phenomena we seek to explain them in terms of a common denominator, that the universal nature of human inclinations and propensities does support the concept of an underlying human nature. The question is what kind of an entity this represents. It is not necessarily the case that the common denominator to which we refer in explaining uniform phenomena is necessarily a real entity as such, a simple or discrete thing. This is the problem posed by the theory of universals, raised first by Plato. It is not necessarily the case that the existence of tables in all shapes and forms must be explained by reference to a blueprint or archetypal table which represents their essence; no more is this the case with man. This Aristotle saw. However, the explanation of uniform phenomena does suggest real underlying *generative mechanisms*, in whatever hidden and complex form, that are capable of producing these uniformities: otherwise we are left with uniformity as an accidental phenomenon, the outcome of coincidental occurrences, as Hume and the nominalists have suggested, and which by way of an explanation offers very little.

But while nominalism is not a satisfactory solution to this problem, realism is not an unproblematic alternative either. Explanations of the real basis for a universal human nature have ranged as widely as classical theories of the soul as a non-corporeal substance that men have in common, to the notion of characteristically human activities which give rise to a human world with uniform characteristics.[3] At the very least one can say that this is an area so problematic that no definite answer can be given. The arguments of Fromm, Maslow and Bay which refer to the well-functioning personality, psychic health and all-round human excellence as if this were a condition that is naturally given, beg the question. Their propensity to argue for wide-ranging pathologies as an effect of psychic dysfunction points to a hidden prejudice in favour of the kind of homeostatic model of man which Freud had developed in conjunction with his theory of the instincts, and which favours an account of behaviour as causally determined rather than intentional, the very conclusion they hoped to avoid.

These confusions are nowhere more evident than in the work of Christian Bay who, in his classic article 'Needs, wants and political legitimacy' uses a concept of human nature to invalidate contemporary political regimes, namely the liberal-democratic state, on the grounds that these regimes do not uphold the goals, purposes and needs of the model of man he describes. He states: 'We cannot get much further toward an adequate normative theory of government, as Hobbes taught us, without a model of man, or at least a conception of priorities among man's most pressing needs' (1968, p. 242). He summarises his attempt to develop such a concept of man in terms of three alternatives which are seen to converge: (1) 'an empirical approach toward identifying needs by way of observing the destructive consequences of their frustration', (2) 'Maslow's more speculative approach toward establishing a tentative hierarchy of needs as actual or potential universal characteristics of human nature', and (3) 'a functional theory of attitudes and beliefs as an approach to a model of human development towards political rationality and responsibility' (p. 242).

The very fact that Bay believes it is possible to substantiate Maslow's speculative approach by empirical research bespeaks the fact that he believes human nature to be given in the same way that the nature of the gases is given, for instance, so that all approaches to the study of human nature, as with other materially existing phenomena, will converge. Since he defines needs as 'any behaviour tendency whose continued denial or frustration leads to pathological responses' (p. 242), he believes that it is legitimate to infer that 'the most obviously and grossly pathological kinds of behaviour indicate that relatively crucial needs have been denied or frustrated' (p. 243), concluding that 'for all the difficulties that are involved in identifying even the crucial needs of this kind, it is not empirically an impossible task' (p. 244).

The categories of behaviour he lists as pathological are '(1) suicide or serious attempts at suicide; (2) psychosis; (3) severe neurosis; (4) severe addiction to alcohol or drugs' (pp. 243–4). He instances empirical work on suicide in Scandinavia, where it is argued that babies 'are born with essentially the same needs but that mothers are culturally predestined, in most cases, to give less than complete succour' (p. 244). (This is bad news, given that the Scandinavian countries have usually been regarded as among the better models of the welfare state and humanitarianism in general.) In the most severe cases of deprivation of this sort, suicide results, in milder cases the other kinds of pathologies he lists. As if, indeed, establishing these links between need-deprivation and pathology were not difficult enough, Bay hopes to expand the list of pathologies 'to include, for example, anal fixations' to cover the person who, although demonstrating none of the gross pathologies he mentions, is 'doomed by early deprivations to become', for instance, 'the perfect accountant but to be capable of nothing warm and impulsive and playful in his whole life' (p. 246). (Maslow, too, like Marcuse and Fromm, placed great emphasis on 'playfulness, fun, pleasant aimlessness, casual, random and unmotivated behaviour' [1948*b*, p. 413] as symptoms of tension-reduction in the person whose needs have been properly gratified.)

It is Bay's bland assumption that his concept of human nature is uncontentious, describing a really existing entity in the same way that our concepts of other materially existing phenomena do, that permits him to conclude that empirical evidence will provide the support necessary for the normative assumptions and the theory of political efficacy that he advances. It is on this very assumption that he tries to develop a need-based theory of rights, 'assuming that a psychologically prior need must legitimate a politically prior right' (1968, p. 248). Taking sanctity of life to be the fundamental right, on the grounds that survival is a precondition for the enjoyment of any further rights, Bay sees an analogy between the Maslovian prepotency of needs and a hierarchy of rights. He therefore matches Maslow's schedule of needs with a schedule of rights which are said to hold on the same logic. Bay's argument that needs legitimate rights, assumes that needs provide the empirical grounds for rights, as if Maslow's hierarchy of needs, which Bay admits is 'speculative', described a set of facts.

One of the curiosities of Bay's position is that he develops it consciously to counteract the tendencies of value-free behavioural science, 'the absence of a model of man and of a professional concern with human needs *and* values . . .' (p. 252). So behaviouralists prefer 'forms rather than substance . . . rule of law rather than justice, pluralism rather than human right, present institutions (i.e., procedures) rather than possibly more humane alternatives' (p. 253). Bay suggests that the downfall of liberal-democracy is simply its failure to face up squarely to 'the facts'. The 'uncritical acceptance of our allegedly democratic order does not jibe with what political scientists *know* about the power of elites, or the techniques of mass manipulation', he insists. As if indeed the question of what human needs, human nature and appropriate political goals constitute were relatively unproblematic questions.

Just as he is condemning the behaviouralists for their failure to take account of values and the goals of man, he lapses into man-machine language, making reference to people as machines needing damages repaired, therapy, and so on:

> Apart from expanding and improving counselling and treatment facilities, it is possible to seek to reduce appeals to paranoid emotions in foreign and domestic politics, to recognize and seek to restrict the influence of externalizing political irrationality, and to seek to repair damages in children by way of extensive, well-staffed, and well-financed pre-school facilities. (p. 256)

Among the now considerable body of social theorists who accept, either tacitly or explicitly, the doctrine of true and false needs and the concept of an authentic human nature, there is a wide range of diversity in the conclusions they draw. For instance, R. D. Laing, in his various studies of madness, in contradistinction to Fromm, Marcuse, Maslow and Bay, rejects the idea of insanity as an illness or pathology, seeing it to result from obstacles to self-actualisation in the form of family, class, stigma, and so on. Far from recommending the kind of policies and treatment that Maslow, Bay, and so on, advocate as a panacea, Laing sees the psychiatric profession and institutions for the insane bearing a good deal of responsibility for the phenomenon itself. Marginal people in class terms, or those who fail to subscribe to socially approved norms, are seen by Laing to be conveniently labelled schizophrenic or insane in order to preserve the cohesion of the dominant group.

Laing who, with his associate David Cooper, produced one of the first digests of Sartre's *Critique of Dialectical Reason* (Laing and Cooper, 1964) specifically draws on a number of Sartrean ideas, the notions of a 'true' or authentic self and of totalisation as a dynamic process, in order to reject the artificial and static totalities created by institutions, labels and other forms of social control. This appeal to the 'authentic self', as Juliet Mitchell in her analysis of Laing has shown (1975, p. 252), is not itself unproblematic. Like Sartre himself, Laing seems to lapse into an existentialist form of individualism, seeing men as atomised individuals, cast into a hostile world in which their relations with others are for the most part intangible and incompatible with true authenticity.

One finds similar assumptions in the numerous works of Ivan Illich. Under the pressure of institutions, educational, medical, political, and so on, the hostile cities and technological devices, man's true nature and his authentic self-awareness are seen to be distorted, modified and corrupted. Illich subscribes to a Rousseauean vision of man who has tempted the fates in the exercise of his latent powers and now suffers the consequences, 'he attempts to create the world in his image, to build a totally man-made environment, and then discovers that he can do so only on the condition of constantly remaking himself to fit it' (1971, p. 107). Illich, like Laing, involves himself in the Rousseauean paradox of postulating man as a sociable creature, yet seeing his true nature corrupted beyond redemption by the societies he creates. 'We now must face the fact that man himself is at stake', he concludes (p. 107). 'Even desires and fears are institutionally shaped' (p. 108). Agriculture and manufacturing, the medical and educational establishments 'create needs faster than they can create satisfaction, and in the process of trying to meet the needs they generate, they consume the Earth' (p. 110). 'When values have been institutionalized in planned and engineered processes, members of modern society believe that the good life consists in having institutions which define the values that both they and their society believe they need' (p. 113).

Illich, like William Leiss and a number of ecology-conscious thinkers, rejects the Promethean myth that inspired Marx with visions of a future society based on the fruits of technology and development: 'The hope has vanished that the problem of justly distributing goods can be side-tracked by creating an abundance of them. The cost of the minimum packages capable of satisfying modern tastes has skyrocketed, and what makes tastes modern is their obsolescence prior even to satisfaction' (p. 112).

The doctrine of true and false needs, the common underlying theme in these works, puts a heavy burden on the concept of needs and what attributing needs to people involves. As we have seen, the development of scientific need theories since Freud casts this question in a new light. Freud made claims from time to time to having uncovered the causality of human behaviour in his theory of the instincts. But because he conceived the human personality as a complex entity, each of its components, ego, id and super-ego governed by different principles; and because, as he admitted, society reacted back on the psyche; in any given instance of behaviour one could not say with certainty what its causes were. It is not as if Freud were arguing that there are the drives of Eros and the drives of Thanatos and all behaviour can be reduced to these. The Freudian theory of needs or drives was never as simple as its popularists have suggested. The complex processes of adjustment and adaptation which involve the ego in trying to maintain a balance between the demands of the external world and the internal demands of the psyche, do not permit a mechanical theory of behaviour. So, in fact, the practice of psychoanalysis aimed not at scientific explanations of the causality of behaviour, but at an interpretative reconstruction of the individual's psychobiography.

Psychoanalytic therapy involved certain admissions that Freud's metapsychology obscured. From *Civilization and Its Discontents, The Instincts and Their Vicissitudes, Beyond the Pleasure Principle*, and so on, one might be tempted to conclude that Freud had indeed discovered the secret of human motivation and had arrived at a critique of civilisation on the basis of this. If we ask, however, what the psycho-analyst as a practitioner does, and how he brings his science to bear in individual cases, we see a number of surprising things. To begin with, the practitioner enters into a dialogue with his patient in which they together reconstruct the problem and the history in which it is embedded. What the psychoanalyst seeks is therapy through understanding, a hermeneutic exercise. After all, nothing in the past can be corrected by rearranging events or by changing what has taken place. But what is important is that the patient should understand his own psychic processes and their circumstances so that he can come to terms with them.

Therapy puts a heavy emphasis, not on the causality of behaviour, since this is beyond the control of the individual to a certain extent, but on the ability of the individual to understand, adapt to, and monitor his own development and his relations to the external world. The very form that therapy takes: the patient telling the analyst, rather than the analyst telling the patient, leaves it more or less in the hands of the patient to uncover the secret of his own psychic processes, which the analyst helps to interpret with reference to metapsychological principles. The delicacy of the relationship between patient and analyst and the reluctance of the latter to impose his explanations on the patient, make it plain that this is no laboratory situation in which the expert feels free to hypothesise about the causes of the phenomenon under investigation independent of any consideration of the subject's own understanding of it. Unlike Skinnerian psychology and the various forms of behaviourism with which we are familiar, psychoananlysis is not concerned with scientific explanations as such: that is, explanations in terms of objective processes independent of the perceptions of the subject. The subject's role is all-important and the interpretative function of the analyst stands or falls on whether or not he succeeds in convincing the recipient that his explanation is plausible.

Freudian theory could never have engaged in postulating needs and drives in the behavioural manner, precisely because it never presumed to have a scientific knowledge of the causality of behaviour in any literal sense. So psychoanalysts did not explain neuroses in terms of needs for security, needs for status, needs for achievement, as such. They did not presume to know the causes of behaviour independent of the self-diagnosis of the patient, so they avoided such abstract and unprovable postulates. Instead they sought an explanation in terms of the ramifications of actual events, only rarely stepping outside the frame of reference that the patient himself supplied.

The scientific explanation of behaviour in terms of needs is more or less doomed to failure because it is not sensitive to these very factors. To attribute overt behaviours to hidden needs for security, relatedness, self-actualisation, or any of the many needs that have actually been postulated, presupposes that there is conclusive evidence to establish this link objectively. But, of course, there is not. The processes of human motivation are private, and to some degree unconscious, processes; the only person in a position to have any knowledge of how this behaviour relates to underlying principles is the subject himself, but according to the canons of scientific objectivity we cannot take his word for it.

Yet if it is left to independent and impartial observers to decide what our motivations are, we can see that there are no restrictions on what they might suggest. Henry Murray in his *Explorations in Personality* (1938, pp. 144–5)[4] listed twenty manifest and eight latent needs, and Luther Bernard in 1924, reviewing the various versions of theories of the instincts, found that a comprehensive list would include some 6,000 items. James Davies has claimed that 'knowledge of human motivation is not yet adequate to establish the psychological equivalent of a periodic table of elements' (1963, p. 7). But nor, we suggest, will it ever be, precisely because it can never get direct access to the causal links that it tries to locate. It is precisely because it has no way of establishing the accuracy of its postulates that we see such a proliferation of explanatory principles, none proven, none disproven, to the point where some theorists arrive at as many needs or instincts as there are behaviours – Bernard, it seems, even catalogued an 'instinct to avoid eating apples in one's own orchard' (cited by Renshon, 1977, p. 57).

Freud's own theory of the instincts and the principle of instinctual variation, adopted by Erich Fromm, for instance, makes the link between specific behaviours and the instincts peculiarly difficult to establish. The idea of instinctual variation takes account of the ability of the individual to adapt to the exigencies of his environment. In a situation in which the objects which are available for instinctual gratification are to a high degree circumscribed, the instincts are fairly inventive in the outlets they seek. The only real restriction on what might count as the object of a need is that the object be available and that it 'make satisfaction possible' (*Instincts and Their Vicissitudes* [1915] 1961, p. 122). This being the case, there are no logical or objective criteria to establish a link between needs and their objects, needs and particular behaviours. Since, as we have acknowledged, empirical access to this link is also closed off, we are forced to conclude that when in fact needs are imputed to people by way of an explanation of motivation, for example, when I say that X's desire for a new car every year represents nothing but his need for status, an interpretation of their (X's) behaviour is being offered and nothing more. This is not an explanation that can be made 'scientific'. It is interesting to speculate on human motivations and their source, but this is a subject on which our comments cannot be anything more than speculative, precisely because in any given case the evidence we would require to establish a causal link between the hypothesised need and the overt behaviour is unavailable due to the private, and to a certain degree unconscious, nature of these processes.

Notes

1 See Ross Fitzgerald's fine article on Maslow on this point, 'Abraham Maslow's hierarchy of needs – an exposition and evaluation' (1977*a*), p. 47.
2 Cited by Renshon (1977), p. 55.
3 See Julius Kovesi's fascinating account of the source of concepts in these terms, *Moral Notions* (1967).
4 Cited by Renshon (1977, pp. 56–7) from whom the subsequent examples are also taken.

11

Agnes Heller and Ivan Illich on the Structure of Needs

In the 1970s need theory has seen a further development in the work of three significant thinkers, all of whom qualify as critical theorists in a broad sense, but each of whom interprets the concept of needs as it has been developed by Marx and his successors in such a way as to redress some of the revisionist aspects, in particular, the doctrine of true and false needs. These are Ivan Illich, whose *Tools for Conviviality* (1973) and *Toward a History of Needs* (1978) are directly relevant; Agnes Heller, whose *The Theory of Need in Marx* appeared first in German in 1974 and in English in 1976; and William Leiss, author of *The Limits to Satisfaction: An Essay on the Problem of Needs and Commodities* (1976). All three thinkers see the problem of needs and commodities as the matrix of the capitalist system, challenging as a chimera the old assumption of political economy, that the market system can automatically diagnose and meet people's needs.[1] Nevertheless, of the three, only Ivan Illich retains the notion of true and false needs in any recognisable form which Heller and Leiss specifically renounce. (Heller argues that Marx did not subscribe to such a distinction, although he was the first to discover the concept of manipulated needs.) All three are concerned with the problems of modern society which have been the focus of critical thinkers since Marcuse: the unsatisfactoriness of a consumer-oriented society, its shortfall in terms of individual satisfaction, and its damaging social consequences. In each case, the analysis of the problem by the three thinkers is more or less Marxist. Agnes Heller proceeds by a very careful textual analysis of the concept of needs in Marx and her own conclusions on the problem are to some extent concealed in her reinterpretation, although at crucial points she differentiates her view from that of Marx. Ivan Illich, by contrast, tackles head on the problems of modern industrial society and, in particular, the ecological and cultural ramifications of a high technology and consumer-oriented economy. His work is Marxist to the extent that he employs Marxist evaluative categories: use value, self-fulfilment of the individual, self-realisation of the species, the role of community, and so on, although he by no means advocates classical Marxist solutions. The same may be said of Leiss's work. In all three thinkers, the notions of revolution, class, the privileged role of the proletariat, class consciousness, are significantly absent. In the case of Leiss, a veiled criticism of Marx is implied to the extent that Marx also advocated economic growth, the conquest of nature and an economy of abundance as prerequisites for a society of the future geared to the satisfaction of human needs. While Heller continues to subscribe to the notion of socialism as an economy of abundance, but true wealth as free time, Leiss and Illich, preoccupied with the energy crisis and the environmental aftermath of postwar profligate consumption, reject the model of socialism as a 'saturation' economy (Heller's term for Marx's model) favouring economic contraction rather than economic growth and discrediting the whole notion of need-satisfaction as a duty-worthy social goal.

The energy crisis has forced on us a recognition that we could easily have reached independently, that consumerism is not only costly but guarantees no long-term satisfaction. Leiss and Illich, writing in the aftermath of the 1973 oil price rise, have a perspective on this problem as already dramatically registered in historical events that earlier writers could not have had. There is a special urgency in their exploration of the problem and of possible solutions. While the circumstances are now such that a more concrete analysis of the structure and dynamics of the imperilled consumer-oriented society seems imperative, the analyses of Illich and Leiss are not exempt from certain weaknesses of earlier critical thinkers: overly abstract and metaphysical categories, utopian assumptions (despite explicit attempts to avoid these pitfalls, especially by Leiss), and a failure to give due weight to the nature of the political.

A certain utopianism is freely admitted by Heller, who draws on Ernst Bloch's distinction between 'fertile' and 'infertile' utopias (1976, p. 130) to justify optimism for a solution along Marxist lines to the problem of commodity fetishism. This utopianism lies chiefly in the hope for a transition to socialism via the emergence of 'radical needs' and optimism that participatory social forms can be evolved out of the class-bound individualism of capitalism. On the whole, however, Heller, too, tries to minimise the utopian and apocalyptic elements of the Marxist theory of needs. To begin with, while declaring the concept of needs to be the central but hidden category in Marx's thought (p. 27), she rules out a doctrine of true and false needs in Marx precisely on the grounds that the true/false distinction presupposes an omniscient point of view, or the qualifications of some vanguard to decide what people should or should not need, which Marx would not sanction (p. 68). Heller denies that any objective criterion can be found to ground the distinction between normal and artificial needs for the same reason: '"normal" needs are those which individuals deem to be such' (p. 51). She notes, however, that there is some ambiguity in Marx's use of the term 'normal needs' which is sometimes equivalent to 'human needs', an outright value category (p. 48).

It is true, of course, as we have tried to argue, that Marx uses the criterion of 'human' needs as a bench-mark to measure the 'alienated needs' of capitalist society, but as we have also argued, this is not to be confused with the revisionist doctrine of true and false needs. Marx's argument is that under commodity production, where the market alone decides which needs will be satisfied and in what form, it is no accident that it is those needs which valorise capital (p. 51), and which by their very nature are not therefore the 'human' needs of the individual, whose satisfaction is made possible. This is a comment on the market mechanism and in whose interest it operates and not an argument for the inauthenticity of needs. Marx, unlike Marcuse, etc., does not argue that alienated men no longer have human needs, but rather than men are alienated because their human needs are denied satisfaction. It is not a question of false needs but of an imperious market system. In any given historical formation, the system of economic production and distribution is at the same time a system for the production and reproduction of needs, as Marx pointed out in the general introduction to the *Grundrisse*. We judge such a system as humane or inhumane according to the interests it serves — whether they are the interests of all citizens, of a powerful few, or of no one and serve only to perpetuate an ossified system itself. This form of judgement on a given system of needs accords much better with Marx's sociological understanding of such phenomena than the doctrine of true and false needs ever could.

It is not the natural/artificial and true/false dichotomy which is crucial in Marx, Heller argues, but the distinction between natural and socially produced needs of his mature works, where natural and physically necessary needs are counterposed to social needs (pp. 28–9). And even the category of 'natural' needs is gradually denaturalised as Marx moves increasingly to the view that all needs admit of a social or cultural element in the historical evolution of their form. So the concept of natural needs survives not as 'a group of needs but [as] a limit concept: a limit (different for different societies) beyond which human life is no longer reproducible as such' (p. 32).

Heller's interpretation of 'social needs' as the critically important concept in Marx is not without its difficulties. She argues forcibly that Marx understood needs, not in isolation from their historical or cultural context, but as an empirical phenomenon, developed in a specific cultural milieu in which tradition, morality and custom play a decisive role. Precisely because a given system of needs is culture-specific it is not efficacious to judge it by the standards that some other unique cultural system may produce. 'The structure of needs is an organic structure inherent in the total social formation', Heller argues (p. 96), and social needs represent the unique configuration of needs that people in a given social system do have.

> We are dealing here with an objective category [Heller insists], a given human being, belonging to a given class, at a given period of time, is born into a system and hierarchy of needs which, although it is determined by the objects of his needs and by the customs and morality of preceding generations, is nevertheless constantly changing; he will internalize this, even though in an individual manner (to a greater or lesser extent in different societies). (p. 71)

While pointing out that for Marx the content of 'social needs' 'corresponds essentially to the empirical and sociological content of *necessary* needs' and 'that this is an average; more precisely it is the average of individual needs (historically developed, handed down by custom and containing moral aspects)', she nevertheless adds that 'this is in no way, however, an autonomous structure, "suspended above" the members of a class or of a society. The need of the individual is what he knows and feels to be his need — he has no other needs' (p. 71).

So far the argument is unproblematic. Marx was asserting what sociologists and economists since him have affirmed: that although wants have an historical and moral element, at any point the necessary elements can be practically known. In other words, Marx in *Capital* (n.d., Vol. 1, p. 168) where he defines necessary needs, makes it plain that he meant by 'subsistence needs' not those which he considered morally defensible, but those which in fact prevailed. Discussing the determination of the value of labour power in terms of the costs of its reproduction, Marx noted that subsistence, both in terms of 'natural wants' and 'necessary wants', is a culturally relative phenomenon. While '[the labourer's] means of subsistence must . . . be sufficient to maintain him in his normal state as a labouring individual':

> His natural wants, such as food, clothing, fuel, and housing, vary according to the climatic and other physical conditions of his country. On the other hand, the number and extent of his so-called necessary wants, as also the modes of satisfying them, are themselves the product of historical development, and depend therefore to a great extent on the conditions under which, and consequently on the habits and degree of comfort in which, the class of free labourers has been formed. In contradistinction therefore to the case of other commodities, there enters into the determination of the value of labour-power a historical and moral element. Nevertheless, in a given country, at a given period, the average quantity of the means of subsistence for the labourer is practically known. (ibid. p. 168)[1]

On the basis of this piece of textual evidence primarily, Heller reconstructs the concept of a system of needs in Marx in such a way as explicitly to exclude the concept of false needs and also the concept of 'unrecognised needs', which she says Marx developed the category of 'radical needs' to circumvent (Heller, 1976, p. 69). (Once again, the concept of 'unrecognised needs', like that of 'false needs', plays into the hands of a vanguard whose business it is then to reveal to the masses their genuine needs (p. 68).) In addition, Heller interprets the central meaning of 'social need' as an empirical, non-value category to account for the given needs of individuals in a peculiar social system, so as explicitly to rule out any identification of needs with 'interests', a concept which she insists that Marx eschews along with the more specific notion of 'class interest', an innovation which she attributes to Engels. Heller by implication rules out the more conspiratorial notion of a system of needs as a prefabricated reality into which the individual is inducted in class society which we found in Reich, Fromm and Sartre, and which seems to have some support in certain passages of *The German Ideology* (see Chapter 8, pp. 141–2 above).

Heller's interpretation of the central sense of 'needs' in Marx as a sociological concept summed up in the phrase a 'system of needs' seems to accord with the spirit of his argument. From the early writings on, as I have already argued, the concept of need recedes as a value category and few references are made to the term as such. Marx's assertion in *Capital* that use values are determined by needs as they are to be found empirically, regardless of 'the nature of such wants, whether, for instance, they spring from the stomach or from fancy' (Vol. 1, p. 43) suggests that he wished to make no distinction between genuine and artificial needs. From what we know of Marx's analysis of such concepts as justice we conclude that he construed their content empirically and not metaphysically: that is, justice corresponds to the norms according to which market-dominated society is regulated, and not to some overriding value. It would be consistent for him to construe needs in a similar fashion.

It should be noted, however, that if the concept of social needs is, indeed, a central but hidden category in Marx's mature works, it is well hidden. Heller's reconstruction of the notion of a system of needs may be consistent with Marx's theory as a whole, but this is not to say that it is to be found there. In a very well-documented textual study Heller presents little evidence to suggest that Marx actually formulated the concept of social needs or a 'system of needs' as such. It seems to me that Marx may have wanted to avoid the term 'system of needs' to explain an economic system and its internal dynamics if for no better reason than that Hegel used it, just as he seemed to want to avoid any suggestion that an economic system could be explained in terms of needs and wants because of the significance of these concepts in classical political economy and utilitarianism.[2] It is true, as we have noted, that in *The German Ideology* Marx does briefly outline the dynamics of a socio-cultural system in terms of needs and their expansion, with some reference to forms of consciousness accompanying the expansion of needs (CW Vol. 5, pp. 41–3), but the concept still lacks the overall centrality that Heller suggests. What Marx has to say on the subject adds little to Hegel's own detailed examination of the concept in the *Philosophy of Right*, as I have tried to show (see above, Chapter 5). There Hegel appeals to the concept of needs to describe human finitude, the realm of necessity, the domain of subjectivity and particularity which man shares with animals to the extent that he has common basic needs, but from which he departs due to the variety and range that rich and constantly expanding needs manifest. It is the very capability of man to multiply his needs at will through the imagination which permits him to assert his universality in choice and, as subject, to master the external world as object of his needs. Similarly, civil society as a 'system of needs' exhibits the rich, even wasteful and corrupt proliferation of private interests, needs and wants, which invites the creation of the state as a synthesising structure to control and sublate the subjectivity and particularity of economic life (*Philosophy of Right*, 1957, paras 5, 12, 45, 49, 59, 182–200, 230, 237 plus relevant Remarks and Additions).

For various reasons, Marx was not keen to make these kinds of argument or even to use language that might suggest them. It is interesting that it is in the *Grundrisse*, a preliminary study that was not intended for publication, of all the later works, that Marx once again freely employs Hegelian terminology and ideas and that he has, after the 1844 Manuscripts, most to say about 'needs'. At least one of the reasons why the concept of needs appears less and less would seem to be the very incompatibility between an empirical or sociological understanding of needs and needs as a metaphysical or value category. There is no doubt that, had he wished, Marx could have tried to make the concept of use value, which *is* an important category in his late work, more objective by reference to a theory of genuine or true needs. Utility is only a value if the end for which a thing is useful is in itself good. The concept of needs could provide this reference point: for instance, cooking utensils have use value or utility: that it is a genuine utility is due to the fact that we need to eat and cooked food is more palatable, one could argue.[3] Interestingly enough, Marx not only does not try to objectivise the concept of use value by the use of need as an objective criterion — he says needs are indistinguishable from wants in determining use value — but as his interpretation of needs becomes increasingly sociological, so the concept of use value becomes a correspondingly sociological category.

However, to relinquish all value elements of the concept of needs and understand the notion in a strictly descriptive and empirical sense would pose problems for his theory elsewhere. If, indeed, needs are an historically given, organically integrated aspect of the social totality, and if they are nothing more than that, that is, no longer a criterion for the just society as Marx's earlier antithesis between human and inhuman needs suggested, why would people be better off to exchange one set of needs for another?

Agnes Heller poses this problem which is a serious one given her insistence that 'Marx's analysis of the society of associated producers is philosophically founded upon the concept of the *system of needs*' (1976, p. 96):

> From the philosophical point of view, individual concrete needs cannot be analysed in isolation, since neither isolated needs nor isolated types of need exist. Every society has its own characteristic system of needs, which is therefore in no way valid for judging the system of needs of another society . . . Production, the relations of production, social relations and systems of needs are, as we know, different aspects of a single formation, in which each is the precondition of the other. The structure of needs is an organic structure inherent in the total social formation. The structure of needs in capitalist society belongs therefore exclusively to *capitalist* society. It cannot be used to judge any other society in general and least of all that of 'the associated producers' . . . But if a system of needs is specific to a given social formation, how can the subjective forces arise which are to overturn this given society? (pp. 96–7)

In answer to this question Heller gives a classic Marxist formula: 'Every (civilised) society is a *class* society founded upon the division of labour, in which there is also a "division" in the system of needs. The exploited classes generally ask for no more than a better satisfaction of the needs assigned to them' (p. 97). In seeking better to fulfil the needs which the system has created for them, the disadvantaged must destroy those barriers that stand between them and the privileged, thereby creating a new system of needs for themselves and, in the event, overturning the given social system.

But, as Agnes Heller points out, whatever new system of needs may emerge from such a revolution does not completely transcend the bounds of the previous system: it is once again historically given, emerging from an attempt to realise more fully values that were embedded in the old society. There is no unique moral value to be attached to this historical imperative, any more than there would have been in the foundation of the original system of needs from which it broke. If the dynamics of history are such that one social formation, to which a system of needs belongs as an organic feature, follows another in this way, there is no reason to ascribe a higher value to each successive stage in this evolutionary process or to its corresponding system of needs, any more than there is reason to value the moth more highly than the worm which finally broke the bounds of the chrysalis.

It is here with the concept of 'radical needs' that an historical exception is made and that the apocalyptic and utopian element of Marxist thought becomes most pronounced. The needs of the slave to be free, which brought down ancient society, the needs of the bourgeois to take political power, were needs which 'transcend the present' but which do not 'transcend the system of needs as a whole but only the "division" of it' (p. 97); the needs of the proletariat which usher in the society of 'the associated producers' are 'radical needs', qualitatively different. Such is the nemesis of capitalism that out of its degradation is said to emerge a system of needs which not only represents an attempt to redress the historical grievances of specific men, but which corresponds to the needs of man as species as such. For this reason, Heller maintains, the society of '"the associated producers", since the latter is the opposite not only of capitalist society but of every civilised society that has existed to date . . . is the first non-alienated society, the "realm of freedom"' (p. 97).

Heller brings together Marx's early concept of 'radical needs' (to be found in the 'Introduction' to his *Critique of Hegel's 'Philosophy of Right'*) and his later more sociological concept of needs (to be found in *The German Ideology* and *Grundrisse* principally) in a synthesis which dramatises the inherent contradictions which these two conceptions create in Marx's writings. Historical change proceeds by changing needs, according to the first argument, 'revolutions require a passive base', a new conception of society will be actualised only to the extent that it corresponds to the needs of society (CW, Vol. 3, p. 183). Radical change presupposes radical needs, change from the root, corresponding to needs which relate to man's most fundamental being (p. 182). As 'a class with radical chains' (p. 186), the working class is a class with radical needs: its needs are necessarily radical because as a class outside civil society, 'a sphere of society having universal character because of its universal suffering', a class 'claiming no particular right' but having 'unqualified wrong . . . perpetuated on it', the working class to free itself must free humanity as a whole (p. 186).

At this point, Agnes Heller makes an important modification to Marx's argument, one which she maintains, however, is consistent with Marx's own later view. 'If indeed it is right to say', and in her opinion it is, 'that the working class can free itself only by freeing humanity too, it does not follow from this however that in terms of historical reality the working class actually wishes to free itself and that its needs are in fact radical needs' (Heller, 1976, p. 89). Heller notes that Marx foresaw the tendency of the working class to be reduced to the pursuit of 'paltry particular needs and interests' (p. 89) which came into conflict with its historical role as the bearer of radical needs, and that in the later writings it is not the proletariat specifically but capitalist society in general which 'gives rise to radical needs, thus producing its own gravediggers'; needs which are therefore 'an organic constituent part of the "social body" of capitalism' (p. 90) rather than an emanation from the most excluded class.

But this proviso of Heller's, that despite the logic of radical needs the working class does not always live up to its historically assigned task, does not, it seems to me, resolve what is a fundamental problem in the theory. Why precisely would the working class be able to escape the constraints of historical existence and free humanity rather than struggling for the satisfaction of needs which the expectations of the capitalist system as a whole encouraged? Marx's argument concerning radical needs in the 'Introduction' to the *Critique of Hegel's 'Philosophy of Right'* contains a quite obvious logical flaw which is not surprising in a piece which is so strongly rhetorical. If we accept his first premise that a revolution is successful only to the degree that its goals correspond to the needs (the real sociological or empirically given needs) of people, then we are bound to accept whatever outcome we find as being, in fact, that which these genuine empirical needs have produced. If, indeed, the working class and the trade union movement as a whole have been reduced to the 'struggle for wages' (p. 66), which Heller condemns, then we see that the needs of workers accord with the general rule – they are a reflection of the exploited redressing their grievances against the privileged – and that they are not an historical exception at all. And why should they be? There is nothing in Marx's analysis, or Heller's interpretation of it, to suggest that he could give a sociological basis for this historical exception which the proletariat is said to represent.

This is, in fact, precisely the point at which Marx's utopian and metaphysical conception of human needs comes into conflict with his sociological conception of needs. If social change follows the redefinition of historically given and empirically located needs, then historical change will follow whither these needs lead. There is no way such needs can at some juncture be transformed into needs of a totally different order. However much we may be tempted to judge a given system of needs by a ranking which can be better defended morally with respect to human goals and purposes, we cannot decree that at some point in the future such a prescriptive schedule of needs will coincide with the needs that people have as we may describe them. This is something that a succession of Marxists, and particularly those for whom needs is a central category (Marcuse, Reich, Fromm, and so on), have tried nevertheless to do. The basis for such a decree is metaphysical. So deeply is the image of man to which this hope corresponds embedded in Marxist thought that historical evidence is not proof against it. Although from all the evidence the case of the proletariat seems to fit the general rule of historical change as Marx describes it, and Heller after him, the world historical role of the proletariat as an historical exception is still anticipated.

How, indeed, this can come to be is explained by Heller in terms of radical needs as a 'collective' or Fichtean 'ought'. Recognising that 'Marx always attributes positive values to communism . . . which he characterised, subjectively, by 'Ought': communism *should* be realised' (p. 74), Heller argues that at the same time Marx from the very beginning 'is also forced to surmount this Ought (the subjectivity of Ought) theoretically' (p. 74). This he does in two ways, either by the Fichtean conception of 'ought' as the radical needs of the collectivity (the proletariat), or by the Hegelian conception of an immanent law of history of which the proletariat is the bearer. These two conceptions, the first according to which the needs of the proletariat spontaneously coincide with the needs of humanity, and the second, according to which they do so by historical design, are not necessarily differentiated by Marx. Heller finds the notion of a social formation at whose centre lies 'the structure of need' (p. 76) a convincing sociological translation of these metaphysical conceptions of the immanence of socialism:

> Every social formation is a total whole, a unity of structures coherently linked to each other and constructed interdependently. There is no causal link between these structures (no one of them is the 'cause' or the 'consequence' of another); they are only able to function as parts of an interdependent arrangement . . .
>
> Now from our point of view, why is the conception of the social totality (the 'formation') important? It is because this conception makes it possible to locate the foundations of the collective Ought in Being. For the present, let us briefly say that one of the essential interdependent structures of capitalism as 'formation' is the structure of need. To be able to function in the form characteristic of Marx's epoch, to be able to subsist as 'social formation', capitalism had to have, within its structure of need, certain needs that were not satisfiable internally. According to Marx, radical needs are *inherent* aspects of the capitalist structure of need: without them, as we have said, capitalism cannot function, so it creates them afresh every day. 'Radical needs' cannot be 'eliminated' from capitalism because they are necessary to its functioning. They are not the 'embryos' of a future formation, but 'members' of the capitalist formation: it is not the *Being* of radical needs that transcends capitalism but their *satisfaction*. Those individuals for whom the 'radical needs' already arise in capitalism are the bearers of the 'collective Ought'. (pp. 76–7)

Quite apart from the fact that this is a reconstruction of the concept of a 'structure of needs' which has scant support in the texts – Heller gives only one example of Marx's use of the term 'system of needs' and we have found one other[4] – it approaches the problem from the wrong end.

What we want to know is not how satisfactorily these metaphysical postulates can be grounded sociologically, but rather why we should be obliged to do so. The ultimate and underlying explanation lies, I think, in Marx's assumption, shared by Heller, that the coincidence of 'is' and 'ought' in the actualisation of objective values would constitute a restoration of the proper order of things and not a radical departure in history. In specific terms, the explanation lies in an understanding of what 'commodity fetishism' involves: because social power has been fetished in the 'things' which capital produces, because commodity production appears as the law '"fixed by Nature for every state of society"' (p. 81), the coincidence of 'is' and 'ought' and the actualisation of the human essence in a society of the future are wrongly seen to be utopian concepts, the argument goes. But the evils and degradation which commodity fetishism engenders under capitalism are more correctly read as proof that this social formation, far from corresponding to the natural condition of mankind, constitutes an historic aberration which actually contains laws for its own dissolution: dealienation and the transition of socialism are inevitable. That they are inevitable does not mean, however, that the system is self-correcting or that by the internal operation of its laws alone the 'overcoming of fetishism' (p. 81) can be brought about: 'Although it has economic aspects, the transition *cannot* be a purely economic process, but must be a total social revolution and is only conceivable as such' (ibid.).

Heller gives an excellent account of how the labour theory of value relates to the fetishism of commodities and why it is that under socialism socially necessary labour time will no longer be a measure of wealth. This is a frequently misunderstood aspect of Marx's theory and one that has had ironic political implications in the East bloc, where an attempt has been made to use socially necessary labour time to price commodities. Heller shows quite clearly from passages in the *Grundrisse* and *Theories of Surplus Value* that the labour theory of value should be seen as a strictly descriptive account of how wealth is derived in the capitalist system specifically and in no way carries Marx's commendation that this is how wealth ought to be measured. In the *Grundrisse* he made this clear: 'As soon as labour in the direct form has ceased to be the great well-spring of wealth, labour time ceases and must cease to be its measure, and hence exchange value must cease to be the measure of use value' (p. 705, cited Heller, 1976, p. 104). Under socialism, the argument goes, not only will free time rather than labour time be the measure of wealth but, as a consequence of the reorganisation of production to meet the needs of individuals rather than the expansion of capital, such an economic system will be capable of reconciling priorities of economic development and individual self-fulfilment.

From her analyses of these texts taken in conjunction with Marx's tentative outline of the various stages of socialism in the *Critique of the Gotha Programme*, we understand much better Marx's view on how bourgeois values and economic achievements could be both transcended and preserved in socialism as the society of abundance; why it is, for instance, that in the first and still fetished stage of communism distribution will still be on the basis of labour input according to a strict equality, and why in the final stage of socialism men will put bourgeois principles of labour time behind them for a social justice based on distribution according to need.

The sticking points of the theory still remain, however. In the first place, socialism as a 'subjective ought' is not successfully transformed by Marx into an objective ought, for all the depth of his sociological analysis of the systemic features of capitalism as a social formation and just because of them. The more elaborate his sociological account of the internal dynamics of capitalism becomes, as it does progressively in the mature works, the less reason we see to introduce notions of historical design. If anything, Heller exacerbates this problem by the centrality which she ascribes to Marx's earlier notion of need as a value concept and 'radical needs', alongside the later conception of the social formation, to which needs belong as an integral, but necessarily empirical, aspect. Heller's attempt to maintain a balance of early and later elements in her synthesis is due to a commitment to a vision of socialism to which it seems Marx refers less and less in his late works. This is the view of communism as the realisation of the human essence and the resolution of the antitheses between essence and existence, objectification and self-affirmation, necessity and freedom, individual and species. This conception of communism, summed up in the left Hegelian phrase that communism equals 'the negation of the negation', is surely the most religious of Marx's depictions, and the one which he would be least likely to air in later works (although this does not mean that he abandoned it entirely).

Heller gives a Marxist humanist account of communism as the resolution of these Fichtean antinomies. Why it is that radical needs will produce a society off the scale of all previous human endeavour and one which will lay to rest conflicts of human existence that have been hitherto considered endemic, is in part explained by historical design, with reference to Marx's peculiar notion of 'the cunning of reason' or how history operates behind the backs of individuals. The idea of progress is a hidden assumption in this theory which is integrally related to the notion of a society of abundance as well. The human essence is such, the theory goes, that the conquest of nature and the triumphs of technology will permit the progressive unfolding of latent human powers. Under capitalism, however, the individual contributes to, but does not participate in, the general raising of human prospects which the expanding economic system permits. Capitalism has a civilising role for the species, but not for the individual, for whom alienation is the everyday reality. One of the corollaries of commodity fetishism is that men do not understand this and assume the hardships of existence that they suffer, like the other historical constraints of the system, to be universal and timeless features of the human condition. Not so, argues Marx, and Heller as well, who shows how it is that 'the specific antinomies of capitalism . . . those between *freedom and necessity, necessity and chance, teleology and causality*', and consequently the special antinomy of 'social wealth and social impoverishment', in fact 'derive from commodity production' (p. 81) as an historically specific mode of production. Marx turns Fichte on his head, just as he turned

Hegel, Heller argues: the antinomies of freedom and necessity, subject and object, individual and species, and so on, 'are not antinomies in thought but in Being. Nor are they simply antinomies in social Being but rather in commodity-producing society, and in capitalism in particular' (p. 85).

We see that all of these antinomies turn, in fact, on the same axis: the fetishistic nature of social relations under capital, where the 'real' causality, 'the quasi-natural necessity of the economy . . . asserts itself behind the backs of the "free" actions of individual human beings' (p. 82). Capital requires that men break the bonds of traditional society in order to submit themselves to the tyranny of wage labour, and this represents the antinomy of freedom and necessity (pp. 81–2). Men thus 'emancipated' are treated as ' "accidental individuals" ', no longer born into 'any "natural division of labour" . . . their destiny is not predetermined from birth' (p. 82); and yet, despite the apparently accidental nature of the social division of labour to which men under capital submit themselves, it works with the same iron necessity to ' "allocate" their needs, which are no longer determined by their personality but by their position in the social division of labour' (pp. 82–3). This represents the second antinomy, that between chance and necessity.

The third secret of commodity production is the antithesis it create between individual and species: 'In capitalist society, *the individual teleology* can never become *the social teleology*' (p. 83). This is what it means to say that necessity 'asserts itself behind the backs of individuals' and that what appears to be the product of chance, is due in fact to the necessary operation of immanent laws. In an interesting comment Heller notes that the antinomy between causality and teleology, an understanding of the reason why the actions of individuals do not achieve the goals they intend but another goal, was a discovery unique to Marx which both Hegel and Engels overlooked. Hegel and Engels mistook for ' "the general dialectical character" of the historical process' (p. 83) what is rather a peculiarity of capitalist society: the fact that individuals initiate a train of action that produces consequences which work against them. Heller gives as an example of the operation of this principle, that the laws which govern the totality are more than a sum of the intentions of the individuals which comprise it, the law of the falling rate of profit: 'No individual capitalist aims at lowering the average rate of profit. But in order to further his actual aim (to make a profit and to survive under conditions of competition), he must keep increasing his fixed capital and thus constantly submit to the process that causally leads to the continuous lowering of the average rate of profit' (p. 83). Much of Jean-Paul Sartre's *Critique of Dialectical Reason* is a disquisition on the asymmetry of individual intentions and social causality. The deforestation of China is one of the extended examples he gives of an undesirable outcome of innocent intentions. But, unlike Heller and Marx, Sartre does not consider the fate of human actions to turn out other than we have intended as peculiar to capitalism but, in the tradition of Hegel, he sees the 'tyranny of the practico-inert' to be endemic to human kind, the curse of history from which we suffer.

The final and quintessential secret of commodity production is said to be the dichotomy it creates between appearance and reality, by which it disguises its operations. Heller restates Marx's view that under socialism the general paradox of appearance and reality will be resolved and that philosophy and the social sciences, which have their foundations in the attempt to explain this dichotomy, will therefore be deprived of their reason for existence: 'In fact there will no longer be any fetishism; in society essence and appearance will overlap. And so social science, which owes its existence to the contradiction between essence and appearance, will in effect be superfluous under communism . . .' (p. 128).

Why should we dwell at such length on the utopian concept of communism as the 'negation of the negation', 'the riddle of history solved', and how does it relate to the problem of needs?

One of the striking insights which Heller's reconstruction (and I have suggested it is in some ways an 'overbuilt' reconstruction) of Marx's theory of needs suggests, is the degree to which this is an elaborate variation on Enlightenment theories of progress based on economic growth. Heller is aware of this: at certain points she refers to Enlightenment elements in Marx's thought, his utopianism, and dissociates herself from some of his more extreme conclusions, although not from the general argument. For instance, while maintaining that she cannot imagine a society which did not produce a conflict of desire and needs, Heller also quite explicitly subscribes to the view that the 'Fichtean antinomies' are peculiar to commodity-producing society and that a future society of associated producers founded on a system of radical needs will remove the fetters that estrange the needs of individuals from the needs of the species. Poverty and wealth are seen by Heller as but a further ramification of the antagonisms which capitalism engenders and under future socialism, where these conflicts are transcended, a rational allocation of social production to meet social needs can be arrived at, which will give to all maximum free time, the true social wealth.

It is interesting that when Heller reflects on the reconciliation of the antinomy between freedom and necessity under socialism she sees two factors crucial to success. The first is that the economy should already be one of economic surplus, the second that a general industriousness should be internalised by individuals, so that the 'need to work' has become a social need, or taken-for-granted item in the empirically given system of needs on which socialism is based.

Heller is insistent that the society of associated producers is founded on economic growth: 'The society of the future is also a society of material wealth, which continues to grow. This idea is encountered in virtually all of Marx's works' (p. 101). And again: 'The idea of unlimited progress in material production is a clear characteristic of Marx's thought' (p. 101). The basis of economic growth under the society of associated producers is technological progress: an 'extraordinary growth in the proportion of fixed capital . . . to levels that are impossible under capitalism is the guarantee that material production will require ever less living labour. This is the only way to reduce labour time uninterruptedly whilst maintaining a constant increase in production' (p. 101).

Because production will be geared to social needs and not the accumulation of capital, the twin goals of the fulfilment of a rich variety of human needs and an increase in free time are said to be reconcilable. Heller notes that there is some ambiguity in Marx's writings on the *rate* of increase of production under the society of associated producers: if the development of the forces of production and the increase of fixed capital cease 'the rate of material production in the society of associated producers would have to be more rapid, at least in comparison with the situation in latter-day capitalism' (p. 102). Alternatively, if 'material consumer goods (those which serve immediate consumption) would play an increasingly limited role in the structure of needs of individuals' by being limited by other, non-material needs, there would be a 'fall-off in the rate of increase of production, at least after a certain level of wealth is attained' (p. 102).

Whatever the case, however, Marx assumes a 'saturation model', Heller argues, (p. 102), that is, a high technology economy, geared to the point at which all those needs which correspond to the actualisation of man's immanent powers are capable of being met. In the absence of a market and the necessity to price goods 'it becomes . . . absurd to see labour as the source of (material) wealth, or to apply the criterion of labour time to (material) wealth' (p. 102). Besides, automation and the rise in the proportion of fixed to variable capital reduce the labour input in the production of material goods. While, under capitalism, this produces the undesirable effect of a decline in the rate of profit, under the systems of associated producers which has abandoned the profit motive, this permits a greater measure of free time, which itself becomes the measure of wealth. As Marx argued in the *Grundrisse* (1973a edn, p. 705), an argument which Heller cites (p. 103):

> Labour no longer appears so much to be included within the production process; rather, the human being comes to relate more as watchman and regulator to the production process itself . . . In this transformation, it is neither the direct human labour he himself performs, nor the time during which he works, but rather the appropriation of his own general productive power, his under-standing of nature and his mastery over it by virtue of his presence as a social body − it is, in a word, the development of the social individual which appears as the great foundation stone of production and of wealth . . .

Heller follows Marx closely in her assumption that under the society of associated producers abundance will be compatible with the unrestricted satisfaction of needs, a satisfaction unregulated apart from the limits which the individuals' own priorities set. That advanced technology will continue to produce a high level of material goods is because, in the second phase of communism, labour becomes a 'vital need' and not just a 'social duty' (p. 110) as it is under capitalism, and people will be willing to provide the labour input that it takes. That an unlimited expansion of needs will not perpetuate the struggle for a share of the surplus that seems to have been a corollary of economic growth at all times, is due to the fact that 'the wage struggle' which characterises capitalism is said to give way to 'The struggle for free time' which 'transcends particular interests and contains in principle "that which conforms to the needs of the species"' (p. 91)

Here looms the spectre of the 'new-fangled man of socialism', who is no longer characterised by any of the baser or more acquisitive appetites we associate with men under capitalism, whose needs and desires are not in conflict with the interests of others and who is motivated to work, not by profit, but for the good of the totality. His, indeed, is 'the shape of the shrewd spirit' of history, 'as much the invention of modern time as machinery itself', as Marx was prophetically to remark in his 'Speech at the anniversary of the people's paper of 1856' (Marx, 1973*b*, Vol. 2, pp. 299–300).

It is not difficult to argue that the belief of Marx and his followers that the benefits of capitalism as the producer of affluence justify 'exploration of all of nature in order to discover new, useful qualities of things; universal exchange of the products of all alien climates and lands; new (artificial) preparation of natural objects, by which they are given new use values' (*Grundrisse*, 1973*a* edn, p. 409), the breaking down of all barriers to its continued expansion and the conquest of uncivilised nations in the name of capital and its civilising role, has in some way contributed to the very evils of alienation, exploitation, pauperisation, brutalisation, the destruction of culture, and so on, that Marx decried. Ivan Illich and William Leiss are rather singular in being able to see this, at least to the extent that they recognise that socialist countries built on the Marxist/Leninist model are just as committed to raising rates of productivity, providing higher levels of consumer durables, and so on, and using this capability to entrench their power, as capitalist countries.

The hedonist appeal of Marxism and the vision of self-fulfilment through the gratification of needs – and an increasingly intense gratification of an ever richer and wider range of needs – must serve to encourage man's view of nature and other men as potential instruments to his own satisfaction, for all that Marx ruled out using men as means rather than ends, as Heller rightly points out. There is a rather peculiar tendency in Marx to condone rationalistic individualism in so far as he sees traditional social forms and organisations as barriers to self-fulfilment to be smashed. The hope that history will take care of the side-effects of hedonism, and that progress in self-actualisation and a closing gap between the potentiality of the species and what it has become will lead to the development of newer and more authentic social forms, is of course a corollary of Marx's utopianism.

It is not surprising that Marxian optimism has in this century characterised the politics of affluence, accompanying a rising tide of economic aspirations, first in the period of reconstruction following the Great Depression, and secondly following the economic reconstruction after the Second World War. So intimately are its assumptions bound up with economic progress that in a period of sustained economic recession and declining rates of productivity, the very prospect of an economy of abundance based on a stable and possibly constantly reducing labour input seems fatuous. The energy crisis and the delayed repercussions of decades of technological tinkering on the environment and ecosystem have alerted us to the possibility that we may have to resign ourselves to a considerably reduced standard of living in terms of the level of goods and services to which we have become accustomed in order to survive as a species.

It is this negative approach to needs, and a condemnation of the whole orientation of post-industrial society to seek satisfaction through the production of a high level of material goods, which characterises the work of Ivan Illich and William Leiss. In a series of books beginning with the *Tools for Conviviality* of 1973, up to and including *Toward a History of Needs* of 1978, Illich has developed a searing critique of modern industrial society, its corrupting effect on human nature, the destruction of nature and other cultures that it has wrought. As a cornerstone of his critique, Illich has reanimated Rousseau's distinction between natural and artificial needs. By natural needs, he understands those culturally produced use values that correspond to our essential functions, survival and a measure of self-fulfilment; by artificial needs, the acceptance of the professionally engineered commodities which the system produces.

Like Rousseau, Illich is concerned with the psychological and political dependence in which the average citizen is placed by a culture in which needs have this artificial form. He deplores 'the peculiarly modern inability to use personal endowments, communal life, and environmental resources in an autonomous way', which 'infects every aspect of life where a professionally engineered commodity has succeeded in replacing a culturally shaped use-value'. (*Toward a History of Needs*, 1978, p. viii). The theme which he claims unifies all his work is to be found in the concept of 'industrialized impotence', a form of poverty unique to advanced industrial society:

> Where this kind of poverty reigns, life without addictive access to commodities is rendered either impossible or criminal. Making do without consumption becomes impossible, not just for the average consumer but even for the poor. All forms of welfare, from affirmative action to environmental action, are of no help. (p. viii)

It is clear that Illich is not referring to poverty in the usual sense and he clearly distinguishes the peculiarly corrupting influence of civilisation on the individual from its other systemic consequences: the growing gap between rich and poor in industrialised countries through the unequal distribution of the costs of advanced capital on the population. This modern experience of poverty in the form of industrialised impotence refers not to an insufficiency for subsistence, starvation, malnutrition, but rather to a spiritual impoverishment brought about by a surfeit of material goods: 'I am poor, for instance, when the use-value of my feet is lost because I live in Los Angeles or work on the thirty-fifth floor' (p. viii). 'The means for the satisfaction of needs have been radically altered' (p. 13), through technology and the welfare state, so that satisfaction of needs is no longer a personal, self-created satisfaction (p. 31). It is this, he maintains, which constitutes loss of freedom, the freedom of self-expression.

There are some comparisons between Illich's wholesale attack on technology and modernisation as the processes by which autonomy is undermined and Marcuse's concept of alienation as a restructuring of the personality that reduces autonomy and the ability to seek self-fulfilment through the employment of inner resources. This critique has its origins in Rousseau's indictment of modern society, the pressures and counter-pressures to emulate others and seek their acceptance, that an underlying economic dependence on co-operative labour and mass production for the essentials of life is said to encourage. But Illich, unlike Marcuse and even Leiss to a certain extent, is not attributing the attraction of false goods to subterranean psychic processes, but to political and economic phenomena with which we are familiar: the reign of special interests, privileged groups of experts who maintain a clientage on the basis of education, persuasion and even coercive power: 'Professional power is a specialized form of the privilege to prescribe what is right for others and what they therefore need' (p. 24).

Illich campaigns against big government, the presumption of experts whose power lies in their capability to diagnose new needs and then try to meet them:

> The new specialists, who are usually servicers of human needs that their speciality has defined, tend to wear the mask of love and to provide some form of care. They are more deeply entrenched than a Byzantine bureaucracy, more international than a world church, more stable than any labor union, endowed with wider competencies than any shaman, and equipped with a tighter hold over those they claim than any mafia. (p. 23)

Illich accurately describes a new political and cultural phenomenon: 'Educators and doctors and social workers today — as did priests and lawyers formerly — gain legal power to create the need that . . . they alone will be allowed to serve. They turn the modern state into a holding corporation of enterprises that facilitate the operation of their self-certified competencies' (p. 23). By recognising the relation between needs and commodities as a function of political power, and not some mysterious capability of capitalism to introject false needs into the psyche as Marcuse suggests, Illich takes a long step towards diagnosing the problem. Power is, however, an historical and cultural phenomenon to a considerable extent intractable to philosophy. Aristotle was one of the first to admit in his concept of 'appropriateness' and the doctrine of the mean that certain conditions must be accepted on choice, and that historical contingencies, the distribution of economic and political power, are just such conditions.

Illich, like Heller, shows a very good understanding of the organic integration of a system of needs in the political, cultural and economic institutions of a social totality. He notes that the very phenomenon of

> professional power could, of course, come into existence only in societies where elite membership itself is legitimated, if not acquired, by professional status: a society where governing elites are attributed a unique kind of objectivity in defining the moral status of a lack . . .

> Professional autonomy and license in defining the needs of society are [he declares] the logical forms that oligarchy takes in a political culture that has replaced the means test by knowledge-stock certificates issued by schools. (p. 25)

The use of classic political terms such as 'governing elite' and 'oligarchy', puts the phenomena exactly where they belong, in the realm of the political. 'In any area where a human need can be imagined, these new disabling professions claim that they are the exclusive wardens of the public good' (p. 27): once again the familiar phenomenon of 'special interests' and how they operate.

Illich does talk about specialists who 'implant and cultivate . . . ever newer strains of hybridized needs' (p. 30), and needs being 'created by the advertising slogan' (p. 31), but we can interpret this form of language as shorthand for the rather elaborate social processes by which specialists or companies first see a possible place in the market for a new product, create it and then try to educate the public to want it, processes which Illich elsewhere describes. As such, the concept of artificially created needs has none of the sinister overtones that we find in Reich, Fromm and Marcuse, who see this taking place through hidden and fetishistic processes, whether in the form of ideology, the unconscious, or both. Illich speaks of the good citizen as one 'who imputes standardized needs to himself with such conviction that he drowns out any desire for alternatives, much less for the renunciation of needs' (p. 21), and yet he notes: 'The prevailing addiction to imputable needs on the part of the rich, and the paralyzing fascination with needs on the part of the poor, would indeed be irreversible if people actually fitted the calculus of needs' (pp. 34–5). But they do not, and the frustration that people feel with the high level of state interference, the high levels of personal dependence and other unintended consequences of a high technology society are a constant reminder to them of the price they pay for reliance on the satisfaction of their needs in this form. In other words, false needs are not embedded in the psyche to the point where individuals are no longer capable of moral judgement, as Marcuse argued. On the contrary, people are all too well aware of the gap between the promised satisfactions of consumerism and a genuine satisfaction or peace of mind.

There are, however, elements of incongruity in Illich's diagnosis and remedy. It seems to me that he attributes to people expectations of levels of satisfaction and self-fulfilment through the gratification of needs that would flow from his and Marxist principles rather than from a just appraisal of people's actual attitudes: he puts an undue emphasis on need-satisfaction as the medium of human self-actualisation, and he presupposes these needs in some pure form. For instance, he speaks of people having 'recently lost the confidence to shape their own desires' (p. 16); the 'world-wide discrimination against the autodidact' having 'vitiated many people's confidence to shape their own goals and needs' (p. 16); of 'needs and wants' having 'acquired a character for which there is no historical precedent . . . for the first time, needs have become almost exclusively coterminous with commodities' (p. 13). This is due to no historical accident he suggests:

> . . . the rapid turnover of products renders wants shallow and plastic. Paradoxically, then, high aggregate consumption resulting from engineered needs fosters growing consumer indifference to specific, potentially felt wants. Increasingly, needs are created by the advertising slogan and by purchases made by order from the registrar, beautician, gynecologist, and dozens of other prescribing diagnosticians. The need to be formally taught how to need, be this by advertising, prescription, or guided discussion in the collective or in the commune, appears in any culture where decisions and actions are no longer the result of personal experience in satisfaction, and the adaptive consumer cannot but substitute learned for felt needs. As people become apt pupils in learning how to need, the ability to shape wants from experienced satisfaction becomes a rare competence of the rich or the seriously undersupplied. (pp. 30–1)

But, as Marx pointed out, needs are always experienced in a specific social form in which people learn to expect them: 'Hunger is hunger, but the hunger gratified by cooked meat eaten with a knife and fork is different hunger from that which bolts down raw meat with the aid of hand, nail and tooth' (*Grundrisse*, 1973*a* edn, p. 92). If men in advanced industrial society are habituated to needs which are satisfied in the form of commodities, this does not make them categorically different from men who expect to find the various elements of the objects of their needs around them in raw form on which they have to work to supply themselves with food, shelter, clothing, and so on. In each case, they accept that their needs will be satisfied in a prescribed form to which they have become accustomed, the determination of which is due to available resources, social practices, attitudes and various other cultural and historical factors. The social form of needs is thus taken-for-granted or given, as Heller in her use of the concept 'system of needs' as a sociological concept also suggests.

This is why it is curious that Illich should appeal against the given complex of needs, social institutions and practices, political and economic forms, in favour of a community governed by 'use values', which would suddenly abandon all these strange and irrational practices in favour of a form of social organisation and individual self-maintenance that better accords with the nature of man. In this sense, Illich does subscribe to the notion of there being a true or authentic form of needs. For instance, in his essay 'Outwitting developed nations', Illich gives a definition of 'what we can call in the language of both Marx and Freud *Verdinglichung*, or reification. By reification I mean the hardening of the perception of real needs into the demand for mass-manufactured products' (Leiss, 1976, p. 60). And he gives an example: 'I mean the translation of thirst into the need for a Coke.' This kind of 'reification', he believes, 'occurs in the manipulation of primary human needs by vast bureaucratic organizations which have succeeded in dominating the imagination of potential consumers' (p. 60).

Illich is, in essence, appealing against a sociological and historical process that has already taken place: 'In less than a hundred years industrial society had molded patent solutions to basic human needs and converted us to the belief that man's needs were shaped by the Creator as demands for the products we have invented' (p. 56). In this appraisal Illich demonstrates Marxist perspective on the interplay of needs and commodities. Marx delineated a brilliant anthropological account of the commodity and its significance in society, but concluded by seeing this careful tissue of symbols and artefacts as a gigantic and fetishistic hoax perpetrated on mankind. Illich follows him. But in so far as capitalism exists, it does not exist exactly as Marx showed it. *Capital* provides a schematic interpretation of the significance of the commodity and how social structures and institutions have developed in such a way as mutually to participate in this structure of meanings. But capitalism as a system is an ideal type to which the real thing only roughly approximates. Besides exhibiting features of this structure, those societies which are designated as capitalist are a haphazard conglomerate of different entities, some of which are a product of historical accident, others of human design, but all of which are integrated more highly in thought than in reality. That they are integrated at all is due to the fact that human beings bring to them a more or less unified structure of expectations and handle them in various customary and prescribed ways. Marx showed very clearly, particularly with his analyses on the 'money form', how the human mediation of material objects confers on them a symbolic power that allows them to perform important functions. This is true of all social and cultural artefacts and institutions which are similarly bearers of certain powers imputed to them, and from which it is very difficult to retrieve this power once it has been conferred.

Illich, like Marx himself and most radical thinkers,[5] underestimates the degree to which capitalism as a social and historical complex is intractable to social engineering, partly because they confuse the phenomenon with its ideal type: those systemic relations by which it is identified, for example, the commodity form. This confusion is of crucial importance, for it is only on the assumption of a highly integrated system that a radical solution is possible: attack the root and the whole structure collapses. In reality, social change is not like this: in order to effect a qualitative change every assumption concerning each one of the crucial operations involved in the social process must be altered in the minds of each one of the participants. This is why revolutions which have produced a political *fait accompli* must set about quickly to re-educate the people in order for this change to have social substance. Only in the rare cases of a revolutionary war that precedes the capture of power does a revolutionary regime find its subjects prepared in attitudes and aspirations for the new order into which they are being inducted.

Illich's alternative to the consumer society lies in 'the politics of conviviality'. He says in *Toward a History of Needs*:

I use this term in the technical sense I gave to it in *Tools for Conviviality*: to designate the struggle for an equitable distribution of the liberty to generate use-values and for the instrumentation of this liberty through the assignment of an absolute priority to the production of those industrial and professional commodities that confer on the least advantaged the greatest power to generate values in use (1978, pp. xii–xiii)

Illich deplores the destruction of traditional infrastructures for coping, 'this replacement of convivial means by manipulative industrial ware is truly universal and is relentlessly making the New York teacher, the Chinese commune member, the Bantu schoolboy, and the Brazilian sergeant alike' (p. 3). Illich notes with regret that every year for about two decades now, fifty languages have died, 'half of those still spoken in 1950 survive only as subjects for doctoral theses. And what distinct languages do remain to witness the incomparably different ways of seeing, using, and enjoying the world now sound more and more alike' (pp. 7–8).

Illich understands the mechanisms of the domination of culture. As we have noted before, he understands the political nature of this domination and the agencies through which it is perpetuated: the professions, the bureaucracy, the foreign aid administrators, the Peace Corps, and so on. He understands, as well, the economic relations which underlie political domination: the monopoly of energy supplies and raw materials, 'only a ceiling on energy can lead to social relations that are characterized by high levels of equity' (p. 112). He argues that excessive energy consumption becomes physically and psychically enslaving due to the social control, technocracy and waste it creates. For instance, for the privilege of travelling at a speed equivalent to that provided by a phalanx of horses, modern citizens resign themselves to spending hours each day sitting in traffic jams.

By a great insight in the concept of 'nemesis', Illich also understands the mental set which has produced these dubious developments in our system of needs: the infatuation with progress. In his excellent essay 'Tantalizing needs' (1978, pp. 93–109), Illich defines Nemesis as the fate of those who have 'fallen prey to envy of the gods' (p. 98). In a curious challenge to Marx for whom Prometheus was 'the most eminent saint and martyr in the philosophical calendar' ('Introduction to his doctoral dissertation', CW, Vol. 1, p. 31), Illich declares: 'Prometheus was not Everyman, but a deviant. Driven by *pleonexia*, or radical greed, he transgressed the boundaries of the human condition. In *hubris*, or measureless presumption, he brought fire from heaven, and thereby brought Nemesis on himself' (1978, p. 98). Illich acknowledges quite explicitly, as Leiss does, that 'most man-made misery is now the by-product of enterprises originally designed to protect the common man in his struggle with the inclemency of the environment and against wanton injustice inflicted by the elite' (p. 98). In other words, the peculiarly modern evils of civilization are 'the side effects of strategies for progress', an 'immortal reminder' to Prometheus of 'inescapable cosmic retaliation' (p. 98).

With brilliant insight Illich sees that *techné*, or the ability to know one's environment and how to handle it, much revered by the Greeks as a sign of practical wisdom, changed its meaning dramatically as it became technique or technology: 'Common to all previous ethics was the idea that the range of human action was narrowly circumscribed. *Techné* was a measured tribute to necessity and not the road to mankind's chosen action' (p. 98). But mankind's modern inability to envisage his relation to nature in other than manipulative and rapacious terms is, according to

Illich, 'an integral part of the curse from which he suffers':

> The contemporary crisis of industrial society cannot be understood without distinguishing between intentionally exploitative aggression of one class against another and the inevitable doom implicit in any disproportionate attempt to transform the human condition. Our predicament cannot be understood without distinguishing between man-made violence and the destructive envy of the cosmos; between the servitude of man to man and the enslavement of man to his gods, which are, of course, his tools. Nemesis cannot be reduced to a problem within the competence of engineers or political managers. (p. 99)

Illich distinguishes between intentional evil and evil as an unintended side-effect of action, but this is a distinction which the use of human needs as a moral criterion tends to obscure. Can the environmental problems which arise from the well-meant pursuit of needs be classified as crimes in the usual moral sense? To some extent the evils of exploitation and waste are skewed once again by Illich's rationalistic perspective. To members of traditional cultures who suppose a much more limited role for human intervention in social and historical processes and a much greater degree of acceptance of the given than radical thinkers, such phenomena are not necessarily seen as crimes to be punished but, rather, the will of God, the typical behaviour of the powerful, fate, and so on.

The capacity to undertake a searching self-criticism of one's culture, already evident in the social thought of the Greeks, has since Marx been increasingly put to use to purify society by undoing historical evils. But what is done cannot be undone. This belief that it is the function of social criticism to change history, rather than to understand and come to terms with it, is shared by Illich despite his own reservations on the limits of human competence and the way in which men are punished for overstepping them. Once again, such a project errs, contributing to the very evils of which it complains, by presupposing for man powers that he does not have: righting the wrongs of history, knowing the consequences of his actions in advance, and so on.

The banners of social justice are inscribed with the concepts 'equality', 'use value', 'need', but these are rationalistic criteria, the implementation of which contributes to the very flattening out of culture, levelling of experience, dulling of satisfaction of which Illich complains. Modernisation and progress have always proceeded under the aegis of the virtues of equality and utility, fraternity and social justice, which is why their access has been so easy to 'primitive' or under-developed peoples. No one is incapable of rising to the challenge of such sincere and alluring aspirations. But as Marx and Weber have made clear, the realisation of their rational appeal depends on breaking down affective relationships, old social bonds based on the affinal criteria of blood and kinship relations, attachment to region and tribe. Along with these historic ties, sentiments for nature, reverence for sacred objects, myths and mysteries, arcane languages and practices, all pass away.

The pointlessness of this destruction is clear to us when we reflect that the new cultural edifice of the welfare/warfare state no more corresponds to an immanent human nature than the slave societies of ancient times, although for most of us it is more comfortable to live in. The wheel has come full circle and writers such as Illich and Leiss more or less realise, without however admitting it, that the appeal to a community based on 'the autonomous creation of use-values' (Illich, 1976, p. 4) perpetuates the fallacy of a rational social reordering by which the myth of progress has been sustained.

NOTES

1 See introduction by Coates and Bodington to Heller, 1976, p. 11.
2 Marx first introduced the concept of needs in the 1844 Manuscripts by way of an attack on Adam Smith and the political economists who argued for a balance of wants and interests, to show how capital profits from poverty rather than being an equalising force (*CW*, Vol. 3, pp. 250ff.).
3 Hegel (*Philosophy of Right*, para. 63, p. 51) did so objectivise the concept of use value: 'A thing in use is a single thing determined quantitatively and qualitatively and related to a specific need. But its specific utility, being quantitatively determinate, is at the same time comparable with [the specific utility of] other things of like utility. Similarly, the specific need which it satisfies is at the same time need in general and thus is comparable on its particular side with other needs, while the thing in virtue of the same considerations is comparable with things meeting other needs. This, the thing's universality, whose simple determinate character arises from the particularity of the thing, so that it is *eo ipso* abstracted from the thing's specific quality, is the thing's *value*, wherein its genuine substantiality becomes determinate and an object of consciousness. As full owner of the thing, I am *eo ipso* owner of its value as well as of its use.'
4 Heller (1976, p. 96), cites an early remark from *The Poverty of Philosophy* (1970, p. 45): 'Is the entire *system of needs* founded on estimation or on the whole organization of production? Most often, needs arise directly, from *production* or from a *state of affairs* based on production'. See also the *Grundrisse* (1973a, edn, p. 409) where Marx uses the phrase 'a constantly expanding and constantly enriched system of needs'.
5 I mean by 'radical' those thinkers who believe that drastic political action is a corollary of their theoretical principles, and not merely that they are 'left-wing'.

12

William Leiss on the Problem of Needs and Commodities

With William Leiss's *The Limits to Satisfaction: An Essay on the Problem of Needs and Commodities*, we have perhaps the most penetrating and sophisticated of recent critiques of civilisation. His analysis owes as much to Weber as to Marx as a sustained exploration of modernity and its peculiar rationality, the rationality of utility, efficiency, need gratification, economic and affectional ties, source of liberation from those historical accidents of class, region, race, religion, sex, ethnicity and nationality, which represent barriers to the self-actualisation of man as species. 'Modern society represents the first large-scale attempt to found stability and authority not upon the earlier patterns of inherited privilege or traditional associations', Leiss argues, 'but rather directly on the achievements of economic production and the satisfaction of needs' (1976, p. 4). It is taken as axiomatic in this system that intermediate social bonds that stand between the individual and the totality, as represented by the traditional institutions and associations of pre-modern society: family, estate, church, guild, and corporation, merely frustrate a natural identity between 'the self-interest of the individual, intent upon maximizing the satisfaction of his needs' and 'the interest of society as a whole, which is to maximize total productive output' (p. 4). Economic expansion had its own justifications, as Albert Hirschman (1976) has convincingly argued: the production of useful things and the channelling off of aggressive instincts into the economic sphere seemed to promise the removal of these irrationalities from the political arena.

A number of early socialists made the same arguments which Hirschman has so well documented for the Enlightenment period, as we have already noted, Saint-Simon perhaps most explicitly: '. . . if men stopped managing one another and organized themselves to exercise their combined efforts on nature' competition could be turned from a baneful to a beneficent force (see above p. 68). Time and again we find the theme which Saint-Simon most volubly articulates that the production of useful things constitutes 'an order of interests felt by all men, interests which pertain to the support of life and well-being', an 'order of interests [which] is the only one on which all men understand one another and have need to be in agreement, the only one where they have to deliberate, to agree in common, the only one around which politics can be practised and which must be taken as the unique measure for the critique of all institutions and social things' (*Oeuvres complètes*, Vol. 18, p. 188; see above, p. 67).

Production geared to needs was advocated by Babeuf as the only way '*to bring our fate under control* . . . to make the lot of every member of society independent of accidental circumstances' (Babeuf, 1967 edn, p. 57, see above, p. 61–2). Owen echoed the appeal to production on the basis of need:

> For men of experience know, that all the materials to over-supply the inhabitants of the world now and for ever, with all that is necessary for their happiness, superabound, and that there is also far more power in the labour and skill of man, were they wisely directed, than is necessary to work up these materials into the most valuable products, and that all contests for their use and enjoyment will be unnecessary. (*The Book of the New Moral World*, 1836, p. 96; see above, p. 58)

A paean to progress which was even more lyrically sung by Morelly:

> As light sheds its rays equally upon all, so let happiness be equably diffused over all . . . Let myriads of active hands heap up in thy common treasure-house the fruits of abundance and the uncounted products of universal industry, adding, without ceasing, more than ever the needs of nature shall be able to exhaust (*Basiliade*, see above, p. 56).

The 'technological fix', or the propensity to turn 'political and ideological problems into technological ones' (Leiss, 1976, p. 42), which Leiss dates from Francis Bacon and his justification of the conquest of nature through science to relieve 'the inconveniences of man's estate' (p. 37), was advocated not only by *laissez-faire* utilitarians, but also by utopian socialists. Leiss does not argue this but it is an extension of his argument that is easy to document. Nor does he argue that Marx, too, advocated progress and technological development in so far as he insisted on the beneficial nature of progress, the expansion of the forces of production to their highest point, the many-sided production of useful things and the all-round development of man as preconditions to the society of abundance where the administration of men would be replaced by the administration of things (Saint-Simon's old phrase). But this, too, is easy to document.

One of the attractions of technological development from the point of view of the early socialists was the way round problems of natural inequality that it seemed to promise. Because there will always be a certain imbalance that those who are overendowed with brains and initiative can turn to their advantage, a constantly expanding plenum of goods allows society to keep the underendowed from being haplessly exploited. Of course, there were two schools of thought on the subject of equality, as we have noted, and those fundamentalists who held out for strict equality objected to economic development in all its forms and insisted on frugality and a general levelling down, which Marx, Fourier and the progressive, or 'scientific', socialists deplored.

Marx, as we have already argued, was uncannily attuned to the 'progressive' elements in bourgeois thought. He singled out for praise the sensationalist psychology of Locke, the materialism of Hobbes, Gassendi, Le Roy and Cabanis, and the radical environmentalist arguments of Condillac, Helvétius, La Mettrie and d'Holbach as harbingers of socialism. Nor did he reject out of hand the concept of a natural coincidence of self-interest and the benefit of society, Adam Smith's 'invisible hand', which we find rehabilitated in Marx in the concept of socially determined needs. And here I disagree to some extent with Agnes Heller who argues that Marx rejected 'interest' as a category of analysis. In keeping with his method of handling bourgeois categories explicitly outlined in the *Economic and Philosophic Manuscripts* (*CW*, Vol. 3, pp. 270–1), Marx retained the concept of interest, as he did the concept of needs, while trying to show how these seemingly accidental or arbitrary social phenomena, which the empiricists and political economists took at face value, were the product of deeper underlying laws which, in the labour theory of value, he expounds.

In the passages in *The Holy Family*, where Marx documents the roots of socialism in the progressive elements of bourgeois thought we have enumerated, a great number of the quotations are on the very subject of a natural coincidence of the self-interest of the individual and the wider interests of society. He quotes Helvétius's complaints about legislators who focus on the moral qualities of good and evil and fail to understand the scientific basis of human nature: that men are governed by their interests and that society represents a natural coincidence of the interests of the individual and the community. Consequently, Helvétius argues, these same legislators create the very evils of which they are complaining by placing 'the particular interest in opposition to the general interest' (*CW*, Vol. 4, p. 132, see p. 55 above). D'Holbach is also quoted to the effect that 'any morality which separates *our interests from those of our associates*, is false, senseless, unnatural' (ibid., p. 133, see p. 55 above), and Marx cites 'the apologia of vices by Mandeville', a defence of the long-term benefits of self-interest whatever its apparent short-term evils, as 'typical of the socialist tendencies of materialism' (ibid., p. 131, see p. 55 above). The utilitarian principle of 'correctly understood interest' as 'the principle of all morality' is not abandoned by Marx but sublated.

In the *Grundrisse* Marx subjects the general principle of classical political economy, that society is a balance of interests regulated by the market, to detailed criticism in all its aspects: the relation between 'production [and] consumption . . . demand and supply, of objects and needs, of socially created and natural needs' (*Grundrisse*, 1973*a* edn, p. 93). We see both how talk about interests becomes readily translated into talk about needs, and how Marx retains these concepts but in a different relation. The balance of interests theory is spelled out in terms of the reciprocity of needs. Marx restates the axioms of classical political economy in his general introduction:

No production without a need. But consumption reproduces the need . . . Production not only supplies a material for the need, but it also supplies a need for the material . . . Production thus creates the

> consumer . . . The need which consumption feels for the object is created by the perception of it . . . Consumption likewise produces the producer's inclination by beckoning to him as an aim-determining need . . . Production creates the material, as external object, for consumption; consumption creates the need, as internal object, as aim, for production. Without production no consumption; without consumption no production. [This identity] figures in economics in many different forms. (pp. 92–3)

Marx spells out in the course of the *Grundrisse* just how precisely this self-regulating mechanism, the market, which achieves a balance of the interests of individual and totality, works and how specifically this balance or unity is achieved on the basis of fundamental differences. With fine irony Marx echoes the high-sounding phrases of Bastiat, a 'socialist' exponent of the argument for a natural reciprocity of needs and interests, who closely replicates Hegel's arguments on the subject, and whom Marx takes to task for failing to progress 'beyond the classical economists of the English school' (p. 243):

> If individual A had the same need as individual B, and if both had realized their labour in the same object, then no relation whatever would be present between them; considering only their production they would not be different individuals at all. Both have the need to breathe; for both the air exists as atmosphere; this brings them into no social contact; as breathing individuals they relate to one another only as natural bodies, not as persons. Only the differences between their needs and between their production gives rise to exchange and to their social equation in exchange; these natural differences are therefore the precondition of their social equality in the act of exchange, and of this relation in general, in which they relate to one another as productive. Regarded from the standpoint of the natural difference between them, individual A exists as the owner of the use value for B, and B as owner of a use value for A. In this respect, their natural difference once again puts them reciprocally into the relation of equality. In this respect, however, they are not indifferent to one another, but integrate with one another, have need of one another, so that individual B, as objectified in the commodity, is in need of individual A, and vice versa; so that they stand not only in an equal, but also a social, relation to one another. This is not all. The fact that this need on the part of one can be satisfied by the product of the other, and vice versa, and that the one is capable of producing the object of the need of the other, and that each confronts the other as owner of the object of the other's need, this proves that each of them reaches beyond his own particular need, etc., as a *human being*, and that they relate to one another as human beings; that their common species—being is acknowledged by all. (pp. 242–3)

Marx attacks the naïveté of those like Bastiat who believe that the market and the reciprocity of the exchange relation are capable of producing a natural social harmony. This is a myth which 'the economists express . . . as follows':

> Each pursues his private interest and only his private interest; and thereby serves the private interests of all, the general interest, without

willing or knowing it. The real point is not that each individual's pursuit of his private interest promotes the totality of private interests, the general interest. One could just as well deduce from this abstract phrase that each individual reciprocally blocks the assertion of the others' interests, so that, instead of a general affirmation, this war of all against all produces a general negation. The point is rather that private interest is itself already a socially determined interest, which can be achieved only within the conditions laid down by society and with the means provided by society; hence it is bound to the reproduction of these conditions and means. It is the interest of private persons; but its content, as well as the form and means of its realization, is given by social conditions independent of all. (p. 156)

The hidden secret of competing private interests, which Hobbes and Adam Smith projected back into the state of nature and which it is the function of society to reconcile, is to be found by analysis of the very social conditions under which these private interests are constantly reproduced: the division of labour and commodity production under the regime of exchange value. 'The individual carries his social power, as well as his bond with society, in his pocket', Marx ironically concludes (p. 157).

Note, however, that to have found the secret of what was previously considered to be a *natural* balance of interests in society does not mean that Marx abandons the category of interest as such, or even any of the claims of the political economists that equality and freedom are presuppositions of the market system that it constantly reproduces. Marx shows operations of the market to be the product of certain economic laws to which stipulations about the disposition of persons, that is, free and equal, as components of the system are integrally related. The common interest which the capitalist, market-based, economy achieves is, however, not a common interest which self-motivated individuals have as their goal. It is a system, Marx argues, in which harmony is produced out of, and despite, hostile competition 'in which each is at the same time means and end' (p. 244), where 'the common interest which appears as the motive of the act as a whole is recognised as a fact by both sides; but as such . . . is not the motive, but rather proceeds, as it were, behind the back of these self-reflected particular interests, behind the back of one individual's interest in opposition to that of the other' (p. 244). Marx concludes wryly that 'in this last respect, the individual can at most have the consoling awareness that the satisfaction of his antithetical individual interest is precisely the realization of the suspended antithesis, of the social, general interest' (p. 244). The general interest is nothing more than the aggregate of private self-seeking interests. Through exchange men come to recognise each other as free and equal self-seeking individuals 'so that both know that the common interest exists only in the duality, many-sidedness, and autonomous development of the exchanges between self-seeking interests' (pp. 244–5).

This is not to say that there is no general interest, 'the general interest is precisely the generality of self-seeking interests' (p. 245). Marx shows that precisely 'the reciprocal and all-sided dependence of individuals who are indifferent to one another forms their social connection' and that 'this social bond is expressed in *exchange value*' (pp. 156–7). What classical political economists and utilitarians presupposed in the motives of autonomous individuals is, in truth, a function of the laws of social production and reproduction. Once again, Marx claims to have succeeded in demonstrating the material substratum of an otherwise arbitrary and abstract postulate of bourgeois social theory in the concept of the general interest.

Nor does Marx wish to deny that freedom and equality as presuppositions of exchange are not a genuine freedom or a genuine equality:

> . . . when the economic form, exchange, posits the all-sided equality of its subjects, then the content, the individual as well as the objective material which drives towards the exchange, is *freedom*. Equality and freedom are thus not only respected in exchange based on exchange values but, also, the exchange of exchange values is the productive, real basis of all *equality* and *freedom*. As pure ideas they are merely the idealized expressions of this basis: as developed in juridical, political, social relations, they are merely this basis to a higher power. (p. 245)

Not only does Marx argue that the structure of capital does produce a balance of interests (despite certain centrifugal elements), although this is far from being a 'natural' balance, but he argues for an ultimate system in which all irreconcilable conflicts between the individual and the public interest will be removed – for which the artificial social harmony of capital, produced by a dependence on things, is a preparation:

> Relations of personal dependence (entirely spontaneous at the outset) are the first social forms, in which human productive capacity develops only to a slight extent and at isolated points. Personal independence founded on *objective [sachlicher]* dependence is the second form, in which a system of general social metabolism, of universal relations, of all-round needs and universal capacities is formed for the first time. Free individuality, based on the universal development of individuals and on their subordination of their communal, social productivity as their social wealth, is the third state. The second stage creates the conditions for the third (p. 158)

One cannot underestimate the degree to which the expansion of needs under capitalism, brought about precisely by the hostility of 'free competition' and the necessity for one partner in the exchange to realise the needs of the other in order to achieve his own – what in Marx's early writings he saw as the 'mutual swindling and mutual plundering' whereby 'each tries to establish over the other an alien power, so as thereby to find satisfaction of his own selfish need' (*CW*, Vol. 3, p. 306) – represents the preparation for socialism:

> The great historic quality of capital is to *create . . . surplus labour*, surplus labour from the standpoint of mere use value, mere subsistence; and its historic destiny is fulfilled as soon as, on the one side, there has been such a development of needs that surplus labour above and beyond necessity has itself become a general need arising

out of individual needs themselves – and, on the other side, when the severe discipline of capital, acting on successive generations, has developed general industriousness as the general property of the new species . . . Capital's ceaseless striving towards the general form of wealth drives labour beyond the limits of its natural neediness [*Naturbedürftigkeit*],[1] and thus creates the material elements for the development of the rich individuality which is as all-sided in its production as in its consumption, and whose labour also therefore appears no longer as labour, but as the full development of activity itself, in which natural necessity in its direct form has disappeared; because a historically created need has taken the place of the natural one. (*Grundrisse*, 1973*a* edn, p. 325)

In other words, the whole propensity to see 'the primary social bond' in the identity of interests of the individual 'intent upon maximising his needs', and society as a whole, intent on maximising 'total productive output' (Leiss, 1976, p. 4), which Leiss attacks as the matrix of capitalism, and which Marx specifically isolated as such, is a feature of capitalism to which Marxism stands in an ambivalent relation. In the long term, Marx argues, under the future society of associated producers, the primary social bond will represent the rational coincidence of the self-interest of the individual, intent on the satisfaction of his needs, with the interest of society as a whole, but the form in which the satisfaction of needs is sought will be different: it will no longer be needs in the form of commodities, and correspondingly, it will no longer be a coincidence of interests which focuses exclusively on productive output. Nevertheless, Marx suggests, it is this misdirection of effort into the economic sphere to the detriment of other aspects of social and cultural life that inadvertently prepares the way for a mode of production that corresponds to the true identity of interests of individual and species; a society of the future predicated on progress and material abundance, which only such a colossal investment of effort in the economic sphere to conquer nature and wrest from her her fruits could have produced.

The extent to which this presupposition of bourgeois society is first extrapolated by Marx and then retained is not, however, something to which Leiss addresses himself. His focus is on the shortcomings of the need-oriented consumer society itself. He argues not only that rising consumption and the satisfaction of insatiable and rapidly multiplying needs is an impossible goal in terms of available energy, but also that even were it politically and economically feasible, the high consumption life-style cannot, in fact, achieve what it promises – satisfaction:

. . . we must face the real possibility that, even if this bounty were forthcoming, and even if it were distributed with some fairness, the meaning of what we call the satisfaction of needs will become increasingly ambiguous as the hapless consumer pursues the will-o'-the wisp of gratification through the jungle of commodities. There is no apparent end to the escalation of demand and no assurance that a sense of contentment or well-being will be found in the higher reaches of material abundance. The society which promotes the ideal of the high-consumption lifestyle seems to lack any reliable measure of the improvements in the quality of life that we should expect to result from its expanding productive capacity. The personal objectives sought in the frenetic activity of the market place are more and more obscure. (pp. 6–7)

Leiss decries the 'colossal auto-experiment by individuals, based on a naïve faith in the power of science to counteract any deleterious side-effects by means of further innovations and new products' (p. 17), implying that commodity society as such, and its very complacency in the face of a constant proliferation of needs, rests on the unproven and probably mistaken assumption of social harmony and all-round human benefit through the pursuit of self-interest. Capitalism is a society in which happiness is seen to lie in the individual's '"matching" his needs to the opportunities that are available for satisfying them' (p. 14). This concept of happiness puts a premium on the individual's ability to judge successfully the suitability of products to meet his needs, and it is precisely this judgement which under commodity production is vitiated, according to Leiss, due to four factors.

In the first place, the increasing complexity in the composition and presentation of goods puts them out of range of ordinary craft knowledge or common-sense judgements, so that the man in the street cannot, in fact, make a rational judgement between competing commercial products. Secondly, and related to this, the irresponsibility and deception of manufacturers is such that the consumer may actually judge in favour of products which will cause him 'physical and psychological damage' (p. 14). Thirdly, these problems are exacerbated by scarcity of time to research or deliberate decisions concerning competing commodities in proportion, as more decisions between an ever-wider range of products have to be made. And fourthly, this deterioration in the quality of decisions is compounded by 'the confused objectives of the person's wants themselves' (p. 14). One 'outstanding effect of the high-consumption lifestyle', Leiss argues, 'is to induce individuals to become more and more indifferent to each of their specific wants in proportion to the increasing amount of time and resources expended on the total activity of consumption' (p. 16). Here he echoes Marx's criticism in the 1844 Manuscripts of Hegel and the utilitarians who conceived of society as a system of needs in which all wants were equally deserving of satisfaction and no attempt was made to distinguish between human and inhuman needs; where, correspondingly, as 'industry speculates, on the requirement of needs' for some, 'it speculates however, just as much on their *crudeness*' for others, 'but on their artificially produced crudeness' whereby civilisation coexists with and is contained within 'the crude barbarism of need' (*CW*, Vol. 3, p. 311).

New commodities, which today appear steadily and in great numbers, simultaneously promise the satisfaction of wants and promote a feeling of dissatisfaction with regard to the previously existing array. The dizzy pirouette of wants and commodities presents to the individual an ever-changing ensemble of satisfactions and dissatisfactions in terms of which there is no resolution, but only

a continuous movement from a less extensive to a more extensive
participation in market activity. (Leiss, 1976, p. 27)

Leiss seems to echo the old Stoic protestation that happiness does not
come from seeking it; that the prospect of greater satisfactions which the
enjoyment of material goods holds out promises an equal increase in
dissatisfaction; and that a more tranquil existence will accrue to those
who can reduce their needs as far as possible. Leiss's analysis is not so
straightforward, however, and he develops his critique of the consumer-
oriented society more along the lines of Marxist critical theory, although
with important reservations. In other words, Leiss relates the problem of
needs and commodities to systemic features of the capitalist mode of
production and its imperative to valorise capital whatever the cost to its
victims.

He addresses himself to the expansion of consumption since the
Second World War, which he attributes to intensified advertising, the
expansion of credit, an increase in the number and complexity of goods,
and propagation of the myth that personal well-being is related to a high
level of consumption (p. 87). The fetishism of consumer society, as he
sees it, lies in the contrast between the promise and the reality. In fact,
the intensive market-oriented setting has produced a 'fragmentation and
"destabilization" of the categories of needing' along with the afore-
mentioned difficulties of '"matching" the quality of needs with the
characteristics of goods . . . growing indifference to the qualities of needs
and wants . . . and increasing environmental risk for individuals and for
society as a whole' (p. 88).

The underlying processes of commodity fetishism by which a
phenomenon can be represented as the exact opposite of what it is, that
is, by which consumerism can be seen as a route to individual satisfaction
rather than to the self-expansion of the economic system, involve the
reproduction of the individual as the subject of needs which the system
imputes to him. 'Of course the socialization process in every society
teaches individuals how to shape their desires and behaviour into the
"holistic" orientation that constitutes one's personality, into an
integrated perspective for interpreting one's needs', Leiss observes (p.
19). 'What is unique to the high-intensity market setting is the necessity
for being able to identify states of feeling systematically with appropriate
types of commodities', that is, the types of commodity that capitalism
wants him to identify with his well-being for its own ends. What then
happens, according to Leiss, is this:

> The vast number and variety of material objects enjoins the person
> to break down states of feeling into progressively smaller
> components and instructs him in the delicate art of recombining the
> pieces fittingly. The 'wholeness', the integration of the components
> tends to become a property of the commodities themselves: one who
> drapes the latest sartorial splendour over a properly deodorized
> frame, and then treats his locks with an old-fashioned pomade rather
> than the newest lacquer spray, will quickly learn what it really means
> to be an inattentive consumer. The point of all this is quite simple:
> the fragmentation of needs requires on the individual's part a

steadily more intensive effort to hold together his identity and
personal integrity. In concrete terms this amounts to spending more
and more time in consumption activities. (p. 19)

Deep-seated human needs for personal identity, self-esteem and the
esteem of others are manipulated by the media, instruments by which
individuals in the 'high intensity market setting' are acculturated to the
needs of the system as such. The average US citizen has by the age of 20
seen 350,000 television commercials (p. 82) and by this exposure 'learn[s]
how to want' (p. 19). The irony of commodity fetishism is that needs for
self-esteem and the esteem of others are not, in fact, satisfied by this
elaborate artifice which leads not to the integrity and consolidation of
the personality but to its fragmentation, a fragmentation proportional
to the fragmentation of needs themselves:

> No single person can possibly perform all the experiments on his
> desires that a complex market demands; . . . each aspect of a
> person's needs tends to be broken down into progressively smaller
> component parts, and therefore . . . it becomes increasingly difficult
> for the person to integrate the components into a coherent ensemble
> of needs and a coherent personality structure. For the sake of
> argument, let us assume that everyone has a need for self-respect and
> respect from others. In responding to this need individuals cultivate
> certain internal dispositions or personality traits and also adjust their
> external appearance in accordance with changing social norms.
> Today the need for an acceptable appearance is fragmented in
> association with the proliferation of products designed to satisfy it.
> Individuals treat their own bodies as objects made up of component
> units, each having its own demands. Hair, face, mouth, eyes, hands,
> axillae, neck, crotch, legs, and feet all require the application of
> specific and distinct chemical mixtures, which together will make
> one's body pleasing to others and therefore a means of winning
> favour. Each of these specific needs in turn can run through
> potentially infinite permutations in relation to the technological
> sleight-of-hand embodied in commodities . . . This fragmentation of
> needs is just another name for the fragmentation of personality . . .
> (p. 18)

The destabilising effect of the high-intensity market setting on the
personality of the individual and its inevitable failure to fulfil promises
of satisfaction through commodity consumption are said to be due to
two factors precisely. First of all, the propensity of the system to
acculturate individuals to needs in a form that serves its interests; and
secondly to a high level of confusion in the identification of needs and
wants and the products which are said to match them. Leiss takes over
from Kelvin Lancaster (1971) the argument that so complex have most
commodities become, and so sophisticated the level of scientific
knowledge required by the consumer to judge between them, that
rational evaluation is no longer possible. People are no longer buying
goods as such, but rather collections of characteristics, and not even
collections of real characteristics at that, but a complex of 'imputed

objective' characteristics: 'Rather than saying that people have an interest in food items *per se*, for example, we should say that they seek a bundle of characteristics such as nutritive content, convenience of preparation, packaging of portions, appearance and texture, and so forth' (Leiss, 1976, p. 80). According to Lancaster, people 'order their preferences directly in relation to collections of characteristics and indirectly in relation to the goods that possess those characteristics' (Leiss, 1976, p. 80). Conversely, the '"producer is ultimately selling characteristics collections rather than goods"' (p. 80).

Leiss compares the situation with that 'of a shopper in a more limited market economy' (pp. 26–7). He takes the example of an advertisement in an eighteenth-century newspaper to the effect that a ship has come in with 'tar, nails, tea, cloth', and so on, which are now available for sale. 'The qualities of such things are quite apparent and could be assessed at that time by the average individual's craft knowledge' (p. 27). Leiss is careful to make it clear that he does not mean to infer by this contrast that tar, nails, cloth, and so on, as more primitive and simple goods correspond better to real needs, a distinction which he explicitly dismisses as metaphysical. What he wants to argue is merely that 'the link between needs and commodities in this [premodern] setting is relatively simple' (p. 27) compared with the high-intensity market setting, that is, it is not fetishistic, people are getting what they think they are getting. Leiss is careful to point out that, 'considered as a whole, the symbolic mediations that shape the expression of human needs are no more complex in industrial market societies than they are in other patterns of need-satisfaction' (p. 84). He puts considerable distance between himself, Marcuse, Fromm and those advocates of the true/false needs distinction who see the problem of needs and commodities as one of human deviance. 'My objective has been to understand the high-intensity market setting not as an especially pathological phase in contrast to other phases', Leiss insists, 'but as one of the many possible responses to the inherent ambiguity of human needing' (p. 85). And again: 'In opposition to other commentators I have argued that the individual's dilemma consists not in falling victim to false or artificial wants, but in determining the suitability of produced objects for the requirements of needs' (p. 85).

Leiss rejects the dichotomies of true/false, natural/artificial needs for very similar reasons to those presented here. First of all, they ignore the mix of natural and cultural factors involved in any system of needs due precisely to man's peculiar capacity to socialise his environment and to seek his needs in a form that reflects his values, goals and purposes and not merely his physiological requirements. Secondly, and not unrelated to this, the contrast between true and false, natural and artificial needs, represents the attempt to measure 'concrete socio-economic reality wherein particular needs are formulated and wherein all attempts at individual satisfaction occur' (p. 9) by 'very abstract principles' for which a false objectivity is claimed. Arguing from the necessity of certain physiological requirements for survival, proponents of the true/false needs distinction claim for needs an objectivity that is contrasted with the subjectivity of 'wants' or 'desires' (p. 61). But, Leiss argues:

> . . . the real problems about the satisfaction of human needs arise
> only when we abandon the abstract categories of food, clothing, and
> shelter, and the similarly abstract characterizations of sociability
> needs (security, self-esteem, and so forth). All the most interesting
> and important issues arise when we study how the objective
> necessities of human existence are filtered through the symbolic
> processes of culture and of individual perceptions. In short, all the
> most important issues arise just in that nebulous zone where the so-
> called objective and subjective dimensions meet. (p. 62)

Thirdly, Leiss argues, the objective needs/subjective wants, true/false
needs, or natural/artificial needs distinctions all tend to presuppose the
primitive existence of basic needs in a more or less pure form, before men
were subject to the corrupting influences of market-induced affluence.
This assumption Leiss categorically rejects:

> Human development is not a progression from relative simplicity to
> relative complexity in the articulation of needs. Anthropological
> researches demonstrate that an incredible degree of complexity in the
> expression of needs has existed in so-called primitive cultures, and we
> may safely infer that this is the outcome of a process that reaches
> back into the evolutionary origins of our species. The available
> evidence shows clearly that there is no aspect of our physiological
> requirements (the famous basic needs for food, shelter, and so forth)
> that has not always been firmly embedded in a rich tapestry of
> symbolic mediations. Likewise, what are called the higher needs −
> love, esteem, the pursuit of knowledge and spiritual perfection −
> also arise within a holistic interpretation of needs and are not
> separated from the material aspects of existence. (p. 65)

The very assumptions (1) that the distinction between objective needs
and subjective wants is philosophically valid and (2) that it is
anthropologically well grounded in the history of the species encourage a
levelling down, a false equality, policies to legislate the form that needs
may legitimately take and the tendency to treat needs as a quantitative
problem − all of which Marx complained of as tendencies in early
socialist thought which accepted the true/false needs distinction. Leiss is
in agreement. 'It is trivial', he says, 'to calculate the need for food in
terms of minimum nutritional requirements, for example. The real issues
are: What kinds of foods? In what forms? With what *qualities*? And how
does the perceived need for certain kinds of food stand in relation to
other perceived needs?' (p. 62).

> If we attempt to answer these questions, the distinction between
> needs as objective requirements and wants as subjective states of
> feeling breaks down. It is important to understand this point because
> what is at stake is not only a theoretical or conceptual approach, but
> also practical issues of social policy. What is detrimental about the
> attempted demarcation between needs and wants is that it
> encourages us to regard the sphere of needs largely as a quantitative
> problem: each person needs a certain amount of nutrients, shelter,
> space, and social services. The practical outcome of this statement of
> basic needs is reflected in some of the social policies of the existing

welfare state: bulk foodstuffs for the poor, the drab uniformity of public housing projects, and the stereotyped responses of bureaucracies. The qualitative aspects of needs are suppressed in these policies, just as the qualitative aspects of needs are suppressed for society's more fortunate members in the quantitative expansion of the realm of commodities. (pp. 62–3)

Interestingly enough, Leiss recognises that even the omnivorous appetite of the conspicuous consumer does not represent a pathological departure. Conspicuous consumption represents an attempt at self-actualisation and not its opposite, Leiss argues against Maslow, Fromm and others (p. 57). Their fundamentalist interpretation of needs in terms of the true/false distinction makes it impossible to distinguish man as a creature with an almost infinite capacity to vary his needs from animals, for whom adaptation to environmental conditions is instinctual and whose needs and their satisfaction do not represent the rich interplay of nature and culture, the capacity for self-creation on the basis of certain fairly elastic physiological requirements, and the interpretation of mundane considerations of everyday life – survival and comfort – in the light of projected values, goals and purposes for the species.

On the same grounds, Leiss rejects in critical Marxism an undue emphasis on the distinction between use value and exchange value, and here he departs from Marx and even Illich in his judgement of the appropriate criteria for needs. He cautions against drawing 'too sharp a distinction between production for use and for exchange. In both cases the appropriation of nature is mediated through complex cultural forms; in other words, there is in both a dynamic interaction between the material and symbolic correlates of human needing' (p. 67). Leiss rejects the fundamentalist distinction between use value and exchange value in Marx because it down-plays the symbolic and cultural elements of all social interchange in favour of the natural or physical elements. Use values, composed of matter (*Naturstoff*) and human labour are seen by Marx as the '"material depositories of exchange value"' (p. 77), Leiss notes, an interpretation that even Adam Smith who used use value and utility interchangeably would not have supported, and which Jevons and the school of marginal utility rejected with their recognition that '"utility, though a quality of things, is *no inherent quality*. It is better described as *a circumstance of things* arising from their relation to man's requirements"' (Jevons, 1970, p. 105, cited Leiss, 1976, p. 78).

Leiss presents a considerable amount of anthropological evidence to show that other than the subsistence economy of the nomadic hunter and gatherer, where survival defined the satisfaction of needs and economic conditions of scarcity kept their interpretation at floor level, no other phase of economic development was characterised by production exclusively for use. The shift by the political economists away from a fundamentalist interpretation of use value and exchange value corresponded, he argues, to an increasing awareness of the symbolic and cultural aspects of needing under all social conditions. The positive aspects of exchange value as a social bond which permits the development of '"a system of general social metabolism, of universal relations, of all-round needs and universal capacities . . . free individuality, based on the universal development of individuals . . .'' is, of course, recognised by Marx in the *Grundrisse* (1973*a* edn, p. 158). Leiss argues that social reality forced on Marx a recognition that the connection between use value and need is ambiguous in his admission that ' ''the production in enormous mass quantities which is posited with machinery destroys every connection with the direct need of the producer, and hence with direct use value . . .'' ' (*Grundrisse*, 1973*a* edn, p. 694; Leiss, 1976, pp. 77–8). A formulation which, Leiss argues, corresponds more closely to the interpretation of the interaction between needs and commodities which he offers, that 'generalized exchange and industrial production' do not create 'the duality of natural and symbolic correlates in human needing' explained in the use value, exchange value distinction, 'rather, they open the way toward its most radical and problematic expression' (p. 78).

Here Leiss's argument takes a strange turn. His book contains in an even more dramatic manner than the work of Marx, Marcuse, Fromm, Reich, Sartre, Heller or Illich, the deep tensions of critical theory which, on the one hand, manages to achieve a detached sociological or anthropological perspective on capitalism as a unique and multifaceted system with its own logic and laws of determination but, on the other, aspires to intervene in these processes to reform them. I am not suggesting that an understanding of historical process, social institutions and structures does, in fact, rule out the necessity to make choices about the future or aspirations to improve those institutions and structures. My quibble is rather with the way in which these two considerations have been made incompatible within the frame of reference of the analysis. For Leiss, like his forebears in the tradition of critical Marxism, sees capitalism as a system of needs to be the outcome of certain economic and social processes at work behind the backs of its actors. To the extent that individuals in such a system are seen as victims of subterranean and mysterious processes, it is utopian to imagine that a rational social reordering is possible at all. The theory of ideology in all its forms is counterproductive to the ends it seeks. If, in fact, false or even 'splintered needs', the fetishism of commodities, archaic social forms such as family, caste, clan, guild, church, and so on, stand between man and his species-life as a rational, self-conscious and masterful creature, then he is caught in the terrible dilemma of having to smash everything that he has created in the battle to subdue nature by culture in order to achieve his goal. Family, tribe, class, beliefs, attitudes and values, social institutions and structures, church, state and nation all have to go. In addition, he must struggle to divest himself of those mysterious processes of which he is only half conscious and which operate against him in all the ways that beliefs, attitudes and values come to bear on him to shape him into a specific cultural mould.

The dilemma may be summed up as the product of an overly rational construction of human nature, on the one hand, which is contrasted with a judgement on modern industrial society and its tendencies as overly irrational, on the other. Willingness to recognise a continuity in the mix of individual intentions, unintended consequences, the interaction of individuals and collectivities, accidental and systemic features in historical processes since the inception of social life, rules out such dark pessimism about present societies, cultures and their familiar forms and artefacts, at the same time obviating any necessity to see the future in terms of unknown and unthinkable contours. Even capitalism, for all its waste and destructiveness is not, as I have argued, entirely off the scale of human irrationality and evil. The problem with the radical protest is that it assumes that it is.

Leiss began his book with an interesting observation:

> Civilizations have a propensity for enshrining their predominant social concerns in massive physical structures, the relative dimensions of which provide a clue to the differential urgency of the things most ardently desired. Pyramids and palaces, cathedrals and castles have thus given way to the severe glass-and-steel towers that form the horizons of cities and assert the predominance of economic affairs in everyday life. (p. 3)

The pyramids of Egypt, the monuments of other cultures and their surviving artefacts, all testify to an allocation of resources disproportional to the real (minimum) needs of the average citizen and extravagant even by modern standards. We have whipped ourselves into a frenzy by the pursuit of our essentially unrealisable modern goals of liberty, equality and fraternity, and a condemnation of whatever in their name we have achieved. It is this fundamentalism: a refusal to have a liberty which is not true liberation, an equality that is not strict equality, fraternity which is not enshrined in community, needs which are not *genuine* needs, which runs like a red streak through the work of radical thinkers in the wake of the French Revolution which, for all that it achieved nothing but the restoration of reaction, or the reaction of restoration, seemed to raise men's hopes about the future of society to impossible limits.

The antinomy between the conception of society as a system of needs and the concept of 'radical needs', which is recurrent in radical thought, is a peculiar corollary of the dilemmas of modern fundamentalism. The tension is exacerbated by attributing given institutions and structures to the behind-the-scenes operation of mysterious and subterranean economic, social or psychological laws. A failure to recognise in the evils of modern society very familiar political phenomena – the rule of special interests, expropriation of the weak by the powerful, competition between rival sources of authority, the emergence of new centres of power with new resources to dispense, the rise of new constituencies and the decline of old parties – increases the feeling that current problems are entirely beyond the scope of ordinary people to deal with. Such mystifications as 'false needs slipping into the unconscious'; the belief that we are over-determined by ideology to the point where we can no longer discriminate between good and evil; the notion that happiness is really a symptom of its opposite: repressive desublimation; exaggerated accounts of the degree to which we are controlled by hostile social forces (corporations, government agencies, and so on), all play into the hands of those who promise to rid us of all the irrationalities of the human condition in one apocalyptic sweep and would probably, like the regime of Pol Pot, have to send us back to the Stone Age to do it.

It is all the more peculiar that in Illich and Leiss the curious mix of utopianism and social realism we have noted should be accompanied by profound unease at the dangers of rationalism and its enlistment to pacify men into accepting an essentially irrational social system. Let me not make the mistake of implying that the empirical social sciences, behavioural orthodoxy, or any of the standard opponents of critical theory have a much better grasp of the problem. The safe havens of data banks and numerology have produced no better analysis of the phenomena of modern society, if they have succeeded in producing analysis at all. Their mystifications also seem calculated to further obscure the problem, although, like the mystifications of critical theory, they were certainly not intended to. It seems that the banality of an analysis of the problems of modern society in conventional terms that presuppose the coexistence of good and evil, actions for which we are responsible and conditions beyond our control, is something we cannot face. Rather than recognise new forms of greed, imperialism, exploitation and waste which coexist with the old virtues in many forms and a fair range of modern benefits, we prefer to think that we have fallen into the grip of new cosmic forces and that our fate is out of our hands. But science fiction is a diversion that we would do well to recognise as such.

In William Leiss's book these tensions live on, for all that this is perhaps the most sophisticated work in the modern critical genre and for all that this is precisely an analysis of the unintended consequences of the rationalism of modernity and its high-sounding promise of limitless satisfaction or gratification through the satisfaction of needs. Leiss's work, like that of Illich's, is in one of its aspects an exploration of the nemesis induced by the phenomenon of progress. 'What is chiefly lacking in our current understanding of needs', Leiss observes, 'is a general framework for evaluating the damages that individuals inflict upon themselves, upon the bonds of social interaction, and upon the world of non-human nature in a society intent upon maximizing the production of commodities for the satisfaction of needs' (p. 7). His essay 'seeks to outline one possible design for that framework'.

Leiss disavows the use of the concept of needs as a bench-mark to evaluate modern society which we find in the major critical Marxist thinkers who employ the concept, Marcuse, Fromm, Sartre, Maslow and Illich. He attempts to show 'the inadequacy of dealing with the character of human needs without explicit reference to the actual, everyday modes of satisfying needs in particular social systems' (p. 8). His is a defence of the sociological understanding of needs found first in those classical political economists and Hegel who viewed society for purposes of analysis as a *system* of needs. As Agnes Heller has shown, one can construe Marx's own analysis of the capitalist mode of production in these terms although, for reasons that I have given, I think that Marx chose not to do so. At least he down-played this element in his thought because of a perpetual ambivalence between the conception of society as a structured totality with its own internal dynamics into which men are inducted through socially given needs, and a theory of revolution in which the proletariat is the bearer of radical needs calling for a transformation of the prevailing social order. It is not an impossible theoretical task to maintain the concept of needs in both these functions simultaneously, but it seems quite arbitrary to do so.

The arguments for the proletariat as a class with radical needs are pitched at a high level of abstraction. In fact the only arguments we find to support the notion explicitly in Marx are to be found in a highly rhetorical piece which specialises in word play: 'radical' as from root; the root of man being man; radical needs consequently being the needs of humanity, or the need to restore man to his essence; the proletariat as a class with radical chains therefore being a class with radical needs, having the need to liberate the whole of humanity in order to liberate itself. As Marx was aware, however, it is not so clear that theoretical imperatives of this sort translate into practice — and this is due to their conflict with sociological realities. He argued, in fact, that in order for a theory to be actualised by the masses it must correspond to their *needs*. The prospects of a revolution therefore rise or fall according to whether or not the proletariat is, in fact, the bearer of radical needs. The more highly integrated capitalism as a system of needs seems to be, the smaller the prospects for 'radical needs' as a viable concept.

William Leiss rejects a '"positive theory of needs"' which would measure historically given needs by an abstract standard, in favour of a '"negative theory of needs"' which 'does not attempt to specify what are or should be the genuine or appropriate desires of individuals in the particular historical circumstances of the moment' (p. 101), but whose 'basic objective is to show why the expression of needs becomes increasingly incoherent in a high-intensity market setting and how individuals become unable to understand the objectives of their wants' (p. 101). This is an approach, Leiss argues, which 'certainly does not presume that any other form of social practice (past or present) provides a model for the expression and satisfaction of human needs that is superior in every respect and is applicable to every situation' (p. 101); and which 'refrains from defining the categories that might be appropriate to a coherent network of needs', which 'only the individuals and groups who discover for themselves the inadequacy of the existing system can provide' (p. 102). An argument very similar to Heller's (1976, p. 96).

All this notwithstanding, Leiss's analysis does hold in reserve conceptions of appropriate human needs. 'This negative theory of needs is not entirely agnostic', he admits, 'for while one must not presume to define the needs which would emerge in an alternative setting, one can postulate the necessary conditions for the emergency of alternatives' (p. 102). These conditions are two: 'the institutional reorganizations required to bring about a conserver society', and 'the practical understanding of human needs in relation to the needs of other living entities in the biosphere — indeed, in relation to non-human nature as a whole' (p. 102).

Leaving aside the question whether predicating needs of 'other living entities' is the same thing as having needs as a human being, and I agree with White (1974) that it is not, it is clear from the whole thrust of his book that Leiss is recommending one system of needs be replaced by another with concomitant wide-reaching political changes. (The 'conserver society' (Leiss, 1976, ch. 9) will be one in which needs are formed and adjudicated in a communal and participatory way to take account of the welfare of both human and non-human nature.) Of course, to understand any given society as a system of needs does not entail accepting or approving that system of needs or refraining from recommending alternatives. There would be no difficulty here were it not for the problem that Leiss, in the critical tradition, attributes to needs under capital a peculiarly fetishistic power, due to subterranean processes – ideology, the 'splintering' of needs – and certain 'pathologies' beyond the reach of the individual. He rejects the notion that 'the individual's dilemma consists . . . in falling victim to false or artificial wants' (p. 85), or 'modern consumer behaviour' revealing a 'pathological state of desire[1], but he judges in favour of it revealing a 'pathological state of *the objectification of desire*' (p. 85). In other words, it is not pathological to desire happiness, but it is pathological to believe that this desire can be met by the ephemeral commodity, nothing but a collection of characteristics engineered to manipulate the sensations of the consumer. 'The lowliest of things from soap-flakes to shoe polish carry with them images of spontaneous delight and happiness' (p. 85), and there is nothing wrong with wanting happiness were it not for the fact that 'the very rational producers who incur considerable costs in designing and transmitting those images do not do so for entirely whimsical reasons' (p. 85).

Leiss is perfectly well aware that the 'friendly critic' might see an inconsistency between this judgement and his argument concerning the symbolic aspects of needs (p. 85), but he maintains that this inconsistency is more apparent than real. This is because his attempt 'to establish the thesis that, under the conditions of generalized market exchange and industrialization, many commodities become increasingly ambiguous entities, i.e., unstable and temporary collections of relational characteristics' is based not on some abstract normative judgement but on 'the negative aspects of the market economy in which we live' (p. 86). Leiss catalogues the negative aspects of early industrial society: 'a market economy . . . created by the ruthless disruption of traditional ways of treating nature and human labour' (p. 86); where 'the market place became for the first time the basic arbiter of human destiny and of the human relationship to non-human nature" (p. 86); 'ownership and control of the production process' being 'vested in the hands of a dominant class whose power is based on transmitting the inherited inequalities of income and wealth' (p. 87); and where 'submission to hierarchical authority, exploitation, and alienated labour continue to be fundamental realities of the experience of work' (p. 87).

These negative characteristics correspond to the criticisms Marx made of capitalism with his theory of alienation and its scientific formulation in the labour theory of value. But when Leiss comes to catalogue the specific evils of modern industrial society, it is not straightforward exploitation, domination or pauperisation that he isolates, but rather, like Marcuse, the 'psychological' and ecological 'damage' inflicted by the necessity of inculcating a need for the surfeit of commodities that capitalism produces, that is:

> (1) a fragmentation and 'destabilization' of the categories of needing: (2) the difficulty of 'matching' the qualities of needs with the characteristics of goods; (3) a growing indifference to the qualities of needs or wants; and (4) an increasing environmental risk for individuals and for society as a whole. (p. 88)

Of these 'four most important . . . negative aspects of intensified commodity circulation', Marx seems not to have cared about (4), and (1) through (3) were problems he could not have foreseen arising: they are quite discontinuous with the negative characteristics of market-dominated society in its early stages, which Leiss also outlined.

There is clearly confusion in Leiss's mind about what the criteria by which he assails the high-intensity market setting and the system of needs it produces constitute. Concepts of 'the fragmentation and destabilization of needs' are nothing if not abstract evaluative concepts. His wish to defend his critique of modern industrial society *empirically*, by cataloguing 'the negative aspects of the market economy in which we live' was bound to fail for good philosophical reasons: judgements or recommendations are never derived strictly from the facts, but from suppressed normative principles or judgements. But in Leiss's case the so-called 'facts' are much more difficult to relate to empirical referents than those of Marx. We have rule-of-thumb criteria to identify exploitation, oppression, and pauperisation, but none to identify the 'fragmentation' or 'destabilisation' of needs. There is something perfectly unconvincing about the whole description of the destabilisation and fragmentation of needs that Leiss gives:

> When the characteristics of goods change quickly and continuously . . . the categories of needing through which individuals relate to these goods are in a state of permanent fluidity. When goods become rapidly changing collections of characteristics, the individual's judgements about the suitability of particular objects for particular needs are destabilized. Characteristics are distributed across previously distinct categories of needs, experiences, and objects. For example, the taste of menthol in a cigarette is said to be 'like' the advent of springtime and the purchase of a certain type of automobile 'like' gaining a new personality. Thus the expression of need itself is progressively fragmented into smaller and smaller bits, which are then recombined in response to market cues into patterns that are temporary, fluid, and unstable. Previous categories of need dissolve, and the resulting fragments are subjected to regular reshuffling into new patterns. The constant redivision and recombination of need-fragments renders it increasingly difficult, if not impossible, for individuals to develop a coherent set of objectives for their needs and thus to make judgements about the suitability of particular goods for them. Under these circumstances the sense of

satisfaction and well-being becomes steadily more ambiguous and confused. (pp. 88–9)

The use of atomic or molecular terminology – 'the expression of need' fragmenting 'into smaller and smaller bits', the fragments 'being recombined in response to market cues', or 'reshuffled into new patterns', the 'constant redivision and recombination of need-fragments' – suggests an underlying physiological process which takes place below the level of human psychic awareness.[2] The suggestion is, indeed, that the human psyche is fully determined by these ineluctable process at work in the unconscious or physiological realms. The examples Leiss gives of confusions to which these processes give rise in the mind of individuals are greatly overstated. He speaks of people confusing the taste of menthol in a cigarette for the advent of springtime, or identifying the purchase of a new type of automobile with gaining a new personality. This is what might happen if people took leave of their senses altogether and if, indeed, they were entirely in the grip of subterranean processes of the type Leiss describes. As it is, his use of the term 'like' is a giveaway: to think that menthol is 'like' the advent of springtime, or getting a new car 'like' getting a new personality, means simply that one thing evokes images of another, and people have been choosing on the basis of the association of aesthetic images from time immemorial. When people have more things to choose from and more images to live up to, as Thorstein Veblen and other acute observers of the phenomenon of affluence have noted, they tend to get more confused and more harassed and frustrated than those who have fewer choices, and of whom less is expected in the refinement of their tastes.

Leiss attributes to the advertisers far greater success in their strategies than is warranted by the facts. 'Messages about things transmitted in advertising link goods with certain images of well-being which serve as the background texture for the stimulation of desire', he says (p. 89). Advertisers, it is true, try to do this but that they succeed is not a foregone conclusion. Vance Packard in *The Hidden Persuaders* (1957), his very well-documented study of the advertising industry and its strategies to snare the consumer, gives numerous examples of advertising campaigns that failed just because they miscalculated the shrewdness of the consumer. For instance, the Schlitz campaign to enlist the tuxedo and opera set into drinking a champagne-like beer not only failed to capture the ladies in the long white gloves that it portrayed, but lost significant numbers of its ordinary hard-hat constituency who did not want to be associated with beer drinkers who put on airs.

'The advertisement's composition connects background imagery with products which have not the slightest intrinsic relationship to it', Leiss argues, such as 'the automobile or cigarette package displayed against a stunning picture of unspoiled wilderness, or the liquor bottle set in a farmhouse full of hand-crafted furniture' (1976, p. 89), a judgement on intrinsic relationships that seems to conflict with his earlier statements on the important role of symbols in the constitution of needs. 'Clearly', he infers, 'the attempt is being made to transfer the positive feelings evoked by the background imagery to the product which is so arbitrarily associated with it' (p. 89). But why should he assume that this incongruity, the irony that 'the expansion of the industrialized market economy is in fact the main reason why those settings depicted in the background texture of advertisements have largely disappeared from the everyday life-experiences of most individuals' (p. 89) is lost on consumers. Vance Packard gives hilarious examples of incongruities that the consumer saw but Madison Avenue overlooked: for instance, the gin company that tried to promote its bottles as future lampstands, overlooking the consideration that gin drinkers do not usually want to be surrounded by evidence of their weakness, and even less if it comes in a form reminiscent of some handcrafted artefact of former times!

Leiss's crucial assertion that 'the consumption ethic promoted today depends for its success on the destabilization of the categories of needing' (p. 89) attributes to the consumer society success at dominating its subjects through the manipulation of psychic processes that we criticised in Marcuse. This is an empirical question and Marcuse and Leiss assume what they are required to prove. That such processes of manipulation both could and do take place in the terms in which they are described is highly questionable. 'Repressive desublimation' is a phenomenon that, if it occurs, is indistinguishable to the ordinary observer from its opposite, happiness, since the symptoms of both are identical and it requires an omniscient point of view to decide whether this is a legitimate happiness or not. That 'repressive desublimation' does take place, Marcuse does not try to establish by (appropriate) empirical means, assuming as he does that to stipulate it as a systemic feature of the welfare/warfare state is sufficient. In the same way, Leiss's characterisation of needs 'progressively fragmented into smaller and smaller bits, which are then recombined in response to market cues into patterns that are temporary, fluid, and unstable' (p. 88) under the pressures of the high-intensity market and the 'rapidly changing characteristics of goods', is unconvincing as an account of what could be going on, and far from being established as an account of what *does* go on in consumer society. What would the fragmented expression of a need look like? A need could only be fragmented if it were already something very general and abstract, but as Leiss is careful to argue, needs are specific things and they take a specific and historically determined form in any given social setting. And how could it benefit the producer to destabilise people's needs in this way, since it would then make it impossible for him to calculate the consumer preferences of his clients?

It is both misleading and counterproductive to attribute the problems of consumer society, its malaise and dissatisfactions, to such arcane subterranean processes without exploring the possibility that such phenomena can be explained in terms of familiar processes to which we have some access. One can argue that advertising campaigns and the media generally have an educative function which influences choice by acquainting the consumer with carefully selected facts, without resorting to the notion that this involves implanting artificial needs in the psyche, or 'fragmenting' given needs. Theories of psychological conditioning tend to convince their subjects that they are passive instruments in the hands of others, and this is the last thing that those who wish to reform the system from the grass roots should be doing.

This is not in itself an argument against such theories, but Occam's razor is: there is a point at which the explanation outdoes the phenomenon it is trying to explain. The arguments for the fetishism of commodities to which Marcuse and Leiss resort are unnecessarily elaborate, besides putting the phenomenon they purport to explain off the scale of previous human experience and putting a solution out of all human reach. In addition, and by a supreme irony, their interpretation violates the very strictures of Marx's own theory of the fetishism of commodities, by attributing to things (commodities) *per se*, powers that people have in fact conferred on them. Commodities do not in fact have the power to dominate people, fragment their needs, destabilise them, and so on, they only think they have, and Marx's whole analysis was aimed at showing that the mysteriousness of the commodity, a 'social hieroglyphic' whose secret we must try to decipher (*Capital*, n.d., Vol. 1, p. 79) is due to a 'definite social relation between men', assuming 'the fantastic form of a relation between things' (p. 77). Social forms do not 'stalk about with a label' describing what they are (p. 79) and Marx hopes to 'dissipate the mist' through which commodities appear to us, not ascribing them to yet more mysterious and arcane processes, but rather by showing them to be the product of typical political and social phenomena: domination by a ruling group with a monopoly of material and intellectual resources, a hierarchical organisation of society in favour of this group, control of man-power, access to facilities, and so on. It was very far from Marx's intention to show that these commodities were in essence mysterious things, that they did in fact have a power over people deeply rooted in unconscious psychic processes and, to that extent, difficult (if not impossible) to dislodge, or that they were in any way outside the range of ordinary human experience.

William Leiss several times acknowledges that the symbolic aspects of commodity exchange are not qualitatively different from symbolic aspects of social interchange in any given culture. And yet he gives a description of various aspects of our culture whose bizarreness seems to reside in these symbolic mediations. For instance, he discusses the 'illusions' associated with the phenomenon of tourism and camping whereby, with the agency of the packaged tour and the chain hotel, the natural habitat of the tourist is nicely preserved alongside a carefully sanitised encounter with the new environment:

> Activities such as tourism and camping betray a profound confusion within the wants and objectives of individuals. Experience is filtered through a many-layered veil of commodities – the physical accoutrements of travel, mass-produced momentoes, planned menus, and interpretive portfolios indicating what should be seen – which refine the richness and diversity of both the natural environment and human culture into standardized states of feeling. In effect the material objects simulate experience. Filtered through layers of commodities, the natural and human environment is progressively simplified, more smoothly ordered; the abrasive particles which might disrupt the flow of everyday normal experience

— which might stir modes of feeling not dependent upon the acquisition of things — are trapped and removed. (p. 22)

Such an interpretation of 'tourism' and 'camping' belies the understanding Leiss has already shown for anthropological phenomena. For the presentation and interpretation of artefacts in a culture and, in particular, the accommodation of experiences of a foreign culture, always involve a symbolic exercise of this kind. Only the assumption that reality is transparent and that we should have unmedicated access to it allows us to see such a process as improper. Against his own strictures, Leiss interprets the fetishism of commodities to lie in their symbolic aspects. This is once again to succumb to the fundamentalism of modernity: an attack on all those mediations which might intervene between the function of an action and its expression. We witness this fundamentalism in more and more aspects of life, where the attempt is made to flatten out distinctions of all kinds that give rise to role differentiations which seem to violate our concepts of freedom, equality, appropriateness, and so on.

The concept of needs, as I have tried to show, has long been enlisted in this battle. If it can be shown that people have a few common and equal needs, then an unlimited range of human activities (such as 'camping', 'tourism', etc.) can be ruled out as superfluous, trivial, non-functional, 'fetishised', 'luxuries', and so on. This crude fundamentalism is, however, a trap that Marx and more humanistic critics of civilisation tried to avoid, not always with success. Hegel was perhaps its best critic: '"Equality"', he argued, 'is the abstract identity of the Understanding; reflective thought and all kinds of intellectual mediocrity stumble on it at once when they are confronted by the relation of unity to a difference' (*Philosophy of Right*, 1957, para. 49, p. 44). The problem is, however, that people wish to impose this abstract standard (because 'equality could only be the equality of abstract persons as such') in the realm of the particular and the concrete *par excellence*, that is, that of needs and the means to their satisfaction:

> The demand sometimes made for an equal division of land, and other available resources too, is an intellectualism all the more empty and superficial in that at the heart of particular differences there lies not only the external contingency of nature but also the whole compass of the mind, endlessly particularized and differentiated, and the rationality of mind developed into an organism.
>
> We may not speak of the injustice of nature in the unequal distribution of possessions and resources, since nature is not free and therefore is neither just nor unjust. That everyone ought to have subsistence enough for his needs is a moral wish and thus vaguely expressed is well enough meant, but like anything that is only well meant it lacks objectivity. (ibid., para. 49, p. 44)

The aspiration to a world in which needs and their satisfactions are equal for all, a world in which differentiations of sex, age, race, religion and tongue have all been transcended, arises out of well-intentioned sentiments, but it promises the spectre of hellish uniformity and inhuman drabness that may well be part of the world that we are creating, without guaranteeing that endemic human problems of hunger, exploitation, persecution and evil will thereby be resolved.

NOTES

1 For some reason Nicolaus translates *Naturbedürftigkeit* as natural paltriness although *Bedürftigkeit* as derived from *bedurfen*, to need, is usually translated as 'want, need, necessity'. I have amended the translation accordingly.

2 Marx, too, on occasion, used this kind of molecular language. For instance, in his 1843 *Defence of the Moselle Correspondent*, he criticised the tendency of social analysts to see social processes as the outcome of the intentions of individuals and to overlook the 'objective nature of relationships'. Objective relationships determine the actions of individual persons in such a way that a social observer may predict the outcome with the same certainty that a chemist determines under which circumstances some chemicals will form a compound. In the preface to the first German edition of *Capital*, Marx compares the study of economics to microscopic anatomy. In both, he says, 'the body, as an organic whole, is more easy to study than are the cells of that body. In the analysis of economic forms, moreover, neither microscopes nor chemical reagents are of use. The force of abstraction must replace both. But in bourgeois society the commodity-form of the product of labour − or the value-form of the commodity − is the economic cell-form. To the superficial observer, the analysis of these forms seems to turn on minutiae. It does in fact deal with minutiae, but they are of the same order as those dealt with in microscopic anatomy' (*Capital*, n.d., Vol. 1, p. 19)

Conclusion

It is a peculiar outcome of the marriage of materialism and dialectics that in spite of Marx, and to some extent because of him, the belief that human needs, drives and motives can be scientifically established was never lost. In this way, Marxism has contributed to the positivist account of human nature, just as William Leiss has demonstrated that the materialist orientation to nature − that it should be conquered if not plundered to facilitate production and economic growth − was not effectively countered, and was to some extent promoted, in Marxist thought.

What makes the concept of need a suitable candidate to explain behaviour scientifically? With the rejection of the traditional metaphysical systems, attention was once again focused on the basic philosophical questions for which the universal metaphysical systems of the past had provided their own answers. Are human needs their own grounds for satisfaction? What is man's function? What sanctions culture to demand, as it does, the renunciation of self-interest and unrestricted gratification of the appetites in the interests of society as a whole? Is man properly a natural creature, or should his nature be left to culture to determine?

The fundamental question on which these turn concerns the relationship between nature and culture. On the one hand, man is a natural creature, with appetites and physiological needs for food, respiration, reproduction, shelter, and so on like other animals. On the other, he is relatively instinct-free, able to modify his behaviour by conscious design and, within certain limits, freely to elect the principles by which to govern his behaviour. This ability to create for his life a meaning through the election of some options and the rejection of others, involves certain costs in terms of his natural propensies. To begin with, goal-orientated behaviour requires the postponement and even the renunciation of immediate gratifications. And while shared goals may be a source of social solidarity, conflict over goals is equally a source of dissension.

The further we have removed ourselves from nature via culture − and few would deny that the advance of civilisation has taken man further away from his natural origins − the more urgent the question whether the costs have been worth it seems to be. For this reason, perhaps, the doctrine of needs and its hidden prejudice in favour of natural man and the free gratification of his appetites has won greater support each time it has re-emerged. Once credence in an all-encompassing metaphysical system was lost and the direction that culture has taken was seen to be more or less arbitrary, the question concerning its costs seemed more and more urgent. Add to this the fact that more recent sceptics have discredited not only the metaphysical systems of the past, but the very propensity of man for abstract thought and the creation of values as ends. With orthodox Marxism and the theory of the social determination of knowledge, or the belief that abstract ideas are produced at the behest of the ruling class to legitimise their operations, we have a theory which challenges the whole philosophical tradition of antiquity and the quest for criteria for truth and falsity, good and evil, in whose name most of these renunciations have been made.

Those who believe that civilisation has strayed from the path of nature, and paid for it by the evils that we witness − corruption, anomie, dissension, destruction of the environment, war, misery, waste, and so on − have turned back to hedonism and the advocacy of simple pleasure as man's goal. Few commentators on human behaviour have not observed man's natural propensity to seek pleasure and avoid pain, although, as we have seen, to consider this propensity to be man's proper goal, involves taking a further and unwarranted step.

In almost all forms of utilitarianism, both the Epicurean and Enlightenment versions of it, the concept of needs lurked. Bentham's assumption that all pleasures are qualitatively alike and differ only in quantity, had its corollary in the old hedonist conclusion that all needs are equally deserving of satisfaction. Because pursuit of pleasure and avoidance of pain were seen to be men's primary motivations, optimisation of pleasure and minimisation of pain were considered to be the highest good for man. In this way, as we can see, utilitarian theory embraced naturalism, assuming that the transition from facts to values is imperceptible.

There had been attempts to modify this basic utilitarian position as early as Epicurus, who tried to inject a little objectivity into crude hedonism, which considered all desires equal, by ranking them in three classes: the first natural and necessary; the second natural but not necessary; and the third neither natural nor necessary. But here already − and this characterised both Epicurean and Stoic thought − a criterion for objectivity was found in the appeal to 'nature', and true and false needs were distinguished in terms of man's *natural* desires, as opposed to those which were artificial or culturally generated. The Stoic ideal of the 'man of few needs', or the notion that virtue required reducing one's needs, and hence one's susceptibility to corruption, to an absolute physical minimum, combined the valorisation of nature and the Socratic ideal of self-sufficiency, thus seeing in tranquillity or *ataraxia* the ultimate virtuous state.

As we have seen, the peculiar concept of nature to which the Stoics and Epicureans subscribed in the ideal of the life 'according to nature' made the distinction between natural and artificial needs a value distinction and not a matter of empirical inquiry. Natural needs were not those of man as a creature whose nature is empirically given, but rather those of man as a creature who through the exercise of reason and will was able to bring his character into accord with the laws of nature. Thus, for instance, the Epicurean Lucretius and Rousseau, who owes much to the Hellenistic schools, associated the golden age of mankind not with 'natural man' in a descriptive sense, or man in the state of nature, for whom there was, like the animals, an equilibrium between needs and their means of satisfaction, but rather with the early social development of the community of households. At this point in man's history the stimulus of new needs and progress in knowledge capable of providing a technology to satisfy them, had already prompted a development of man's cognitive powers far beyond those of 'natural' man. And yet social pressures were insufficient to cause the proliferation of needs which would ultimately corrupt him. But as we have seen, there was a primitivist tendency in the thought of these critics of civilisation that inclined them to confuse the distinction between a descriptive and a normative concept of nature that they had already made, and to associate the proper condition of human nature and human needs with the natural condition of man and his natural needs.

Enlightenment adherents to the doctrine of natural and artificial needs, and the early socialists in particular, for reasons that we have discussed, exacerbated this tendency. Lockean sensationalist psychology and its extension in theories of environmental conditioning in the work of Condillac, La Mettrie, Helvétius, d'Holbach and others, encouraged these Enlightenment and early socialist thinkers to see the distinction between natural and artificial needs as an empirical or scientific distinction and to undertake the scientific study of human nature to discover what precisely the basic motivations of man were, the role that needs played and whether or not the problems of social conflict and individual instability could be linked to the creation of artificial needs. Epicurean theory had already tended in such a scientific direction with its foundation in atomistic materialism. Although it can be shown that this was not the central thrust of either Stoic or Epicurean theory in its heyday, this turned out to be its Enlightenment legacy.

Plato, in his analysis of needs and pleasures in the *Philebus*, was the first to apply the criterion of truth and falsehood to desires and pleasures, declaring that pleasure has a cognitive function and that pleasures can be 'mistaken' just as opinions can be false. Pleasure was not to be valued as an end in itself, but as a symptom of happiness or the correct functioning of the total personality – good men have true pleasures, bad men false pleasures; a view with which Aristotle more or less concurred in the *Ethics*.

The Stoics, on the basis of their unitary theory of the personality, were able to give this principle the strongest possible weight. It has become customary to think of the personality in Platonic or Freudian terms as a complex and compartmentalised entity of which the parts are in competition, held in check only by some governing principle (reason or the ego). According to this conception desires or instincts (the libido) are a particularly unruly element, natural impulses that would carry the person away if the checks of reason and the will are insufficiently developed. The Stoics did not think in these terms at all: to them the personality was an organic unity. Far from sharply distinguishing between sensation and judgement (as Locke and most theorists of sensationalist psychology have since), they argued that all sensation involves some degree of assent, or judgement, and that the wise man has therefore a control over his needs and desires such that he simply does not feel the same needs and desires as the corrupt man. Rousseau, as I have tried to show, drew a similar conclusion, despite his willingness to go along with the principles of sensationalist psychology to a certain point.

In the long path from Stoic and Epicurean versions of the doctrine of natural and artificial needs, through the Enlightenment and early socialist variants, to the doctrine of true and false needs of Marcuse, Fromm, Sartre and a host of lesser-known leftist thinkers (Maslow, Bay, Illich, Laing, and so on) we still find certain clear lines of development. For instance, the major transition from the doctrine of natural and artificial needs, as an ethical doctrine, to the doctrine of true and false needs, as a scientific doctrine, had its roots in the materialism and sensationalist psychology of the Epicureans of whom Locke is a direct successor, whether knowingly or not. In fact, the majority of thinkers with whom we deal were well aware of the ancient sources of their theories, to which from time to time they made explicit reference. Epicurean materialism was, significantly, the subject of Marx's doctoral dissertation; the early socialists invoked their Enlightenment predecessors; Marcuse and Fromm documented their sources in classical hedonism; and the new critics of advanced industrial society cite Marx and Freud.

The relationship of the twentieth-century doctrine of true and false needs to Marxism is not unambiguous. Although these theorists think of themselves as Marxists, the doctrine of needs in some sense constitutes a *deus ex machina* to explain a failure in the original theory to foresee the longevity and tenacity of the capitalist system. When contradictions between the forces and relations of production, as well as the world-historical role of the proletariat, failed to bring capitalism to its knees, twentieth-century Marxists looked to something other than the labour theory of value to explain its foundations. Although this strictly economic theory seems to account for the generation of wealth by the extraction of surplus value through the exploitation of labour, it cannot explain how this exploitative system is tolerated when all objective conditions for its destruction are seen to be already present; how it is that alienation is not felt and that, indeed, workers, through the process of embourgeoisement, seem ever more effectively tied to their masters and the system that holds them in thrall.

The doctrine of true and false needs provided a very neat solution to this problem. Its heuristic suitability was suggested by a happy conjunction of Freudian and Marxian theory. Freud it was who raised the Enlightenment critique of civilisation to its highest point. From Lucretius's *De Rerum Natura*, to Rousseau's second 'Discourse' and Diderot's *Supplement to Bougainville's Voyage*, there had been a long and largely Stoic tradition of criticism of the evils of civilisation which focused on natural and artificial needs. The concept of needs found its way through this literature into early socialist thought, in the works of Meslier, Morelly, Mably, Babeuf, Buonarroti, Fourier, Saint-Simon, Cabet, Dézamy, Comte, Owen, Godwin and Weitling, among others, as a criterion of social justice. Could it be said, they asked, that the desires of the rich for luxuries were worthy of satisfaction, when for so many basic subsistence needs went unmet? Civilisation was seen to ride on the backs of the masses who could not enjoy its fruits and, in true Stoic fashion, the Enlightenment and early socialist writers saw its apparent benefits as symptomatic of a deeper corruption. So they cherished the ideal of natural man, the man of few needs, even the primitive, in whom none of the artificial vices of civilisation − competition, greed, envy, egotism, discontent − were said to be present.

This Enlightenment tradition found its way into certain aspects of Marx's thought as well − his theory of alienation, his belief in the ultimate harmony of individual and community, man's innate goodness and the possibility of his redemption under socialism. Freud, while he certainly shares none of the naïveté of his Enlightenment forebears, believing that the instincts themselves show an equal propensity for vice as for virtue and that conflict is more natural than harmony, nevertheless carries over the conviction that civilisation can only be built on the basis of renunciation and repression. It is not economic so much as psychic repression that he considers, and his conclusions are diametrically opposed to the primitivists: civilisation is man's only hope, culture transcends nature in which his asocial instincts may be sublimated, and the improvement of society rests on bringing the irrational power of the instincts under increasing rational control.

Twentieth-century neo-Marxists, trying to explain capitalism's unexpected longevity, saw a possible vehicle in the Freudian theory of the instincts. From the pages of Marx a rudimentary theory of needs as the basis of human motivation could already be gleaned. (Marx, too, had been a successor to the materialist psychologists, Helvétius, d'Holbach, Diderot, La Mettrie and the *homme-machine* theorists, who preceded Freud and tried to explain human behaviour in terms of the push and pull of pleasure and pain.) He had shifted from a more or less ontological conception of needs in the *Economic and Philosophic Manuscripts*, where needs were seen as the manifestation of man's immanent potentialities and the medium of their actualisation, to a materialist concept of needs in *The German Ideology*, where constantly expanding needs were seen as the motor of dialectical materialism and the impetus to the full development of the forces of production.

Despite its obvious possibilities, however, Marx's theory of needs fell far short of the later doctrine in its fully elaborated form in the works of Marcuse, Fromm, Sartre, and so on. To begin with, his theory of alienation was primarily an economic and not a psychological theory. Alienation was, from the beginning, 'alienated *labour*', and whatever feelings of discontent might be experienced were explained technically by the labour theory of value. In neo-Marxist theory, however, the doctrine of true and false needs not only complements, but more or less supersedes, the labour theory of value as the primary explanatory principle. What they see as requiring to be explained is not so much the generation of a surplus − capitalism has unequivocally demonstrated that it can do that − but how it is that constantly expanding production continues to find a market for its commodities in consumers who, in their dual role as workers and consumers, do not seem to resent a double exploitation − not only do they labour to produce this mountain of commodities, but they must also endeavour to consume them as capitalism requires. (This problem did not really arise for Marx who expected capitalism's demise under the tensions of overproduction and underconsumption.)

The neo-Marxists found an answer by conflating the Marxian notion of false-consciousness with the Freudian concept of the unconscious in their own version of the doctrine of true and false needs. Men are primarily motivated by their needs, as Marx and Freud suggested: first of all by the necessity to survive, which means satisfaction of the basic physiological needs; and then certain psychic needs — love, security, self-esteem, and so on. While the physiological needs are relatively fixed, the psychic needs are to a considerable degree modifiable, and it is here that the economic system is seen to exert its influence. Capitalism is able to reproduce itself by regenerating in its subjects a constant and expanding desire for its products, which are in turn geared to the promotion of certain psychic needs which feed off this calculated stimulation. The unconscious is, in this way, penetrated by the socio-economic structure itself, so that the libidinal instincts — the desire for love, self-esteem, security, sexual gratification, and so on — are placed at its service.

Due to these factors, alienation is experienced not as a sense of injustice at the exploitation of labour, but as a more generalised psychic malaise in which, although a wide and ever-increasing range of satisfactions is offered, a deep discontent persists. This malaise is explained not, as Freud would have it, as evidence of the psychic repression on which culture is necessarily based, but as the repressed awareness of the evils of capitalism — a repression that is willingly exchanged for the greater gratifications that the capitalist system offers.

There are many things wrong with the doctrine of true and false needs — as we have tried to indicate — the most important being that the criteria that it sets up cannot be met. To begin with, needs as a principle of motivation cannot simultaneously function as an ethical category: needs may be ethically significant, but they may also be ethically indifferent, depending on the moral context in which they are considered (the interests of the individual in relation to the rights of others). Capitalism, therefore, does not *eo ipso* produce false needs more than any other system. Admittedly the twentieth-century problems of exploitation, imperialism, conspicuous consumption, deprivation and waste, are grave ethical and political problems, but they do not admit of easy solution in the doctrine of true and false needs and the pious hope that under socialism all false needs will be eliminated. Indeed, the doctrine denies the ethical character of these problems and puts their appropriate solution further out of reach, by insisting that false needs are embedded in the unconscious, possibly even the instinctual structure itself, and are therefore beyond the rational scrutiny and control, or responsibility, of the individual. In addition, the doctrine has inherent contradictions producing anomalies in the context of original Marxian and Freudian thought which are not so easily married — the conflation of the Freudian 'unconscious' with the Marxian doctrine of false consciousness produces just such incongruities.

Then there is the hidden antinomy in neo-Marxist, as in early socialist and Marx's own thought, between the doctrine of true and false needs and the belief that under socialism all needs will be satisfied, summed up in the old socialist slogan 'to each according to his needs'; a slogan which assumes that needs are insatiable, expanding with every increase in the capacity to meet them, as the doctrine of true and false needs in fact suggests. The belief that a social system can be created in which all needs are good and worthy of satisfaction is utopian; moreover, to base social justice on need-satisfaction in this way, is once again to embrace naturalism. While the criteria for physiological needs are relatively straightforward — survival has an obvious threshold — such needs as the needs for security, love, self-esteem, may take any conceivable form, and no one but the individual concerned is in a position to say whether in a given case something satisfies a need or not. Objective needs, as such, cannot be located and the problem is not that of engineering a social system in which false needs will be eliminated, but of finding social mechanisms to mediate between the conflicting needs which necessarily arise.

The Marxian doctrine of true and false needs has had its spin-off in the social sciences and it is fashionable to talk of 'education according to need', welfare programmes tailored to needs, and so on. While it is, of course, appropriate to gear such programmes to the need-claims which people in fact make — their wants, as the utilitarians would have it — there is a tendency for theorists and administrators, feeling support in this now considerable body of need theory, to set themselves up as judges of what people really need. In command economies, for instance, this has become doctrinal orthodoxy and one could hardly begin to catalogue the anomalies and the injustices to which it has given rise. In the welfare states in which we live, powerful and unwieldy bureaucratic machines justify their existence on the grounds that they can assess and meet the needs of the masses expertly.

Appendix:
'Needs' as a Concept

The concept of needs is an old idea that has received a rather surprising revitalisation in the twentieth century. How do we account for the impetus to revitalise this concept and what are the advantages and shortcomings of the concept for the purposes that it is being used? This is not a concept that springs to mind as one of the perennial philosophical problems: no particular problem is framed by the concept of need as it stands. The very word suggests that its content is unproblematic — that what is 'needed' is necessary and therefore incontestable. From another point of view, too, needs are unproblematic: that is they are spontaneous, natural, universal, the demands of nature prior to and a precondition of all other moral or cultural requirements, which are predicated first of all on the fact of existence, or the need to survive. So we speak of the basic needs for respiration, food, warmth, shelter and reproduction as universal requirements of animate existence. Allowing, of course, for a certain elasticity in the tolerance of members of different species, in the case of animals, and different cultures, in the case of man, which the natural laws of differentiation and adaptation permit, it is fair to say that the satisfaction of these needs is incontestable, or that no one can sensibly deny it. Once again we do not seem to be dealing with a concept that raises philosophical problems.

When we reflect, however, that man as a creature distinguishes himself from other animate existence in peculiar ways, we may be tempted to account for his peculiar characteristics with reference to needs. If we think of man's peculiar species-nature as in some sense open, that is to say as a set of potentialities or inclinations rather than as an immutable essence, then the concept of needs seems peculiarly serviceable to describe these traits. First of all 'needs' suggest a striving or motivation towards something, so that the concept lends itself to being understood as a teleological or goal-oriented requirement. So from Aristotle to Hegel and the existentialists, a long line of philosophers has put emphasis on the concept of desire as being in some way symptomatic of the human condition. Man is a creature naturally insufficient, he desires objects from the external world in order to maintain and complete his existence. Desire therefore indicates the role that his own efforts to fulfil himself play in the formation and development of his identity. Desire, or need in a certain sense, is therefore expressive of man's freedom, the degree to which his nature is self-oriented in response to the insufficiency that his needs impress on him.

The concept of needs can be used to argue a quite different case, however. If one wants to argue a stronger connection between human nature and needs and to suggest that man's species characteristics are somehow innate, or embedded in his biological structure, the concept lends itself to this interpretation too, suggesting as it does physical requirements or necessities. So, for instance, a bevy of behavioural psychologists have argued that human nature can be explained on the stimulus-response model and that needs therefore constitute the stimulus, efforts to satisfy them the response. This is a rather old idea, too, and Sigmund Freud was by no means the first to argue that man is primarily motivated by the desire to pursue pleasure and avoid pain. As we shall see, this idea which has come to be associated with utilitarianism can be found as far back as the Epicureans of the fourth to the third century BC. What is most notable about it for our present purposes is the fact that the idea of freedom is entirely missing from this account of human nature, where the concept of needs is employed to advance the theory that human behaviour is fully determined.

To take a different tack again: if human nature is conceived as being different from that of other animals precisely because man's goal is open and the good for man is not biologically defined or prescribed by instinct, then it is tempting to use the term needs here with reference to the requirements of the 'good life', and the development of those spiritual and cognitive propensities that single man out as one whose perfectibility is his peculiar distinction. Here, of course, the term 'needs' would be used to differentiate the non-physical, the moral and cultural requirements, of a certain mode of self-realisation, over against the innate, spontaneous impulses which are common to all animals and which might be called needs in a different sense. Talk of the non-physical, the moral and spiritual propensities of man which lie beyond the exigencies of his strictly material existence, in terms of needs is rather more recent. In some senses it could be traced back to Hegel, but it is more accurate to date the concept to Marx and the modifications he made to the Hegelian concept of desire. Marx it was who first used the term 'needs' to refer to the whole range of peculiarly human powers and potentialities: capacities for thinking, acting, willing, loving, enjoying, suffering, as needs. In this way the entire contents of the Aristotelian idea of 'activity' or *praxis* became subsumed under the concept of needs, on the argument that in order to actualise his nature, man needed to act out or realise these potentialities. This is, of course, quite a different sense of need from the stimulus-response model, and is once again expressive of the idea of freedom, man's participation in his own self-creation within certain limits that the exigencies of his physical nature describe. From Marx to Erich Fromm and Abraham Maslow, needs have been used to describe the whole hierarchy of human motivations and aspirations, from those which are materially based, to those which express man's ability to transcend material conditions in the exercise of his wider spiritual and cognitive powers.

We can already see that the very lack of specificity of the term 'needs' permits it great flexibility in widely different theories of human nature; and our first impression that it is a concept that makes an obvious appeal to common sense, needs to be revised. If we turn to its use in common language this lack of specificity is already striking. As Paul Taylor in his attempt to classify need statements points out: the concept may be used in at least four categorically different senses (Taylor, 1959, pp. 107–10).

(1)   To indicate something needed to satisfy a rule or law; e.g. 'I need a sticker to park here.'

(2)   To indicate means to an end (either specified or implied); e.g. 'I need a watch (in order to tell the time)'; 'He needs a doctor (in order to get well).'

(3)   To describe motivations, conscious or unconscious, in the sense of wants, drives, desires, and so on. So we speak of people having a need for achievement, the need to atone for guilt, needs for status, security, etc. Needs in this sense constitute conative dispositions.

(4)   To make recommendations or normative evaluations. These are sometimes difficult to distinguish from (3) which are intended as strictly descriptive statements. So, for instance, it is asserted that men have needs for affection, identity, self-esteem, the esteem of others, etc. But what is meant by such claims when they fall into this category is that men have these needs, whether or not they actually feel them, or whether or not they in fact count them as needs. This category also covers those more obvious kinds of recommendations such as 'what this country needs is good fighting men', or 'people need freedom', etc.

The point of Taylor's classification was to show (a) that while some need statements are straightforward factual assertions, as in the case of 1, 2 and 3, the term has a normative use (4) which is often not recognised as such; and (b) that, furthermore, the factual claims in 1, 2, and 3 do not entail recommendations of type 4. In other words, to show (1) that a certain prerequisite is legally required, (2) that something is a necessary means to an end, or (3) that people have conscious or unconscious drives for or dispositions towards something, does not entail that these pre-dispositions, drives or inclinations should be satisfied. The assumption that a need once empirically established should be satisfied is due to a confusion between the factual nature of these claims and the normative character of the type of claims that fall under 4. This confusion, Taylor believes, involves the naturalistic fallacy.

Not surprisingly, Taylor has been seriously challenged for the sharp distinction he draws between the factual and normative aspects of the term 'needs', and in particular for his claim that 'even if it can empirically be shown that man has certain basic needs in senses 2 and 3, it is neither self-contradictory nor logically odd to refrain from recommending that such needs be satisfied' (p. 111). What human beings can be said to need on factual grounds, may not be desirable on moral grounds, Taylor maintains. On the whole, Taylor's classification as such has not been disputed but only these inferences he draws from it. The various parties to the debate have tended to divide into two camps, the descriptivists, who challenge the sharp distinction between fact and value to which Taylor subscribes, and who deny that assertions of type 4 are 'purely normative'; and the prescriptivists who uphold the fact-value distinction.

Kai Nielsen, in several articles (1963, 1969, 1977) has addressed himself explicitly to Taylor's argument that the question whether needs should be satisfied or not is a separate question from the question whether such needs exist. 'While Taylor is indeed right in saying that even if we establish that man has certain basic needs it is still not self-contradictory to refrain from recommending that they be satisfied, he is mistaken in his denial that it would be logically odd to so refrain from recommending them', Nielsen maintains ('On human needs and moral appraisals', 1963, p. 170). Nielsen focuses on Taylor's claim that the relationship between human needs and the good for man is not a logical one, believing that to maintain, as Taylor does, that the relationship is merely contingent is misleading. He believes that Taylor is suggesting that 'human needs are irrelevant to moral appraisal' (p. 178) and that Taylor 'has obscured how great the "importance" of discoveries about "fundamental human needs" would be to sound moral appraisals, if only such discoveries could be genuine discoveries, free from conceptual confusion and well-confirmed' (p. 178). But since Nielsen agrees with Taylor that the relation between needs, as they may be empirically established, and the stipulation that such needs should be satisfied is not one of logical entailment, he can hardly attack him for suggesting that it is a contingent relationship. To say that this relationship is contingent is not to say that it is arbitrary: if in fact human nature is of such a sort that certain fundamental human needs can be established then, since they are being empirically established, the fact that human betterment requires they be satisfied must be a contingent fact. There is after all no logical reason why human nature takes the form it does, and so there can be no logical relation between the form human needs take and human welfare.

The way that Nielsen sets out his case against Taylor is not very convincing. He argues from the premise that 'to honestly assert "People have many needs but *none* of them should be satisfied"' (which does not accurately represent Taylor's position anyway) 'is logically odd' ('Morality and needs', 1969, p. 196) to the conclusion that 'Generally to say "*x* is needed" or "*x* is a need" or "*s* needs *x*" is also to make a claim that there is a good reason for doing or having what is needed' (p. 197). Or, as he put it succinctly in 'On human needs and moral appraisals', 'If someone needs something there is a standing presumption that he ought to have it' (1963, p. 182). This inference is a result of faulty reasoning. To infer from the falseness of the claim that 'all human needs should be frustrated' ('Morality and needs', 1969, p. 198), the conclusion that human needs ought, all things being equal, to be met, is a syllogism with an undistributed middle. Less formally, if the original statement is false, it is not a sufficient ground to deduce its contrary as being true.

Other inferences of Nielsen's are similarly false. For instance, in the claim just cited that 'to say "*x* is needed" or "*x* is a need" or "*s* needs *x*" is also to make a claim that there is a good reason for doing or having what is needed' (p. 197) is inaccurate. It is a reason, but whether it is 'good' or not is precisely in question. And yet Nielsen is willing to state categorically: 'thus for a large and familiar class of cases, the connection between "*x* needs *y*" and "*x* ought to have *y*" is non-contingent and *x*'s needing *y* is *eo ipso* a good reason for claiming that *y* ought to be' (p. 195). This means (1) that Nielsen cannot hold that people can be mistaken about their needs; it also means (2) that human nature must be such that people only come to *need* what is logically required of them in order for human nature to be fulfilled (the Pelegian heresy in a very fancy form). Nielsen in fact argues definitionally that there cannot be destructive or harmful needs (p. 199) which would take care of (2) were it not for the contentiousness of the claim that the nature of man can be established as fact, and of his assumption in advance that needs are such that they cannot contravene its requirements.

This is the sort of naturalism against which Paul Taylor protests, but it is an explicit feature of Nielsen's position. He claims:

> In spelling out why something is right – and that question is, as I said, always *logically appropriate* – we would at least if pressed end up talking about *natural features* of the situation in question. When pressed to justify why certain properties are right-making properties rather than others, we would eventually end up referring to certain pervasive human needs and interests. Without such a reference our moral talk would be groundless and finally . . . unintelligible. ('Morality and needs', 1969, p. 204, my italics)

The contentiousness of this claim resides in Nielsen's insistence that 'natural features' constitute the grounds for moral judgement and his failure to specify what kind of 'logic' is involved. The logic of morality is not the same as logic *tout court*; it differs from mathematical logic, the logic of science, the logic of language, etc.

Nielsen's final position is somewhat modified. He concludes the article by arguing that human needs are 'in some important senses' like memories:

> We can challenge the correctness of any given memory belief, but in doing this we must assume that most memories are reliable. It makes no sense to ask if memory beliefs are *generally* reliable. Similarly, though any given need (unless it is described as 'a destructive need', 'a sadistic need', and the like) has a *prima facie* claim to be satisfied, it may turn out that it ought not to be satisfied due to some other overriding considerations (the harm its satisfaction would do to others, etc., etc.). But to say that generally human needs ought *not* to be satisfied makes no sense at all, if we try to take it as a *moral* claim. (p. 205)

But needs are not like memories and need claims are not generally reliable in the same way that memories may be said to be, just because need claims are heterogeneous and not all of them are factual claims. Only type 3 in Taylor's classification, as conative dispositions, are needs similar to memories in their reliability as representative of internal psychic processes; and as Taylor has demonstrated, we cannot generalise from needs in this sense to the general status of needs as being of a factual nature.

That Nielsen is able to argue the logic of needs in this way follows less from the nature of needs or a careful analysis of them than from his unstated philosophical axioms: that human nature is such that needs are a true manifestation of it; and that this can be known. There is a central ambivalence in Nielsen's analysis of needs and that is that he grants

Taylor's position concerning normative uses of the word 'need' as in claims about needs for affection, security, etc. of type 4, denying that 'what an individual will take to be good (in the widest sense of "good") can be *derived* from statements assertive of "the needs of man", where this expression is taken non-normatively' ('On human needs and moral appraisals', 1963, pp. 178–9); he 'agree[s] with Taylor that it is impossible to make such a derivation' (p. 179). And yet, he declares that 'in the name of clarity we must counterbalance against this the fact that given what morality is, a knowledge of what needs we humans have (most particularly in [Taylor's] sense three [i.e. conative dispositions]) is an important element in increasing our understanding of moral good and evil' (p. 179). He grants that even where certain conative dispositions are empirically established, e.g. 'Hitler's need to find a scapegoat' ('Morality and needs', 1969, p. 190), that 'Children have a need for love and affection' ('On human needs and moral appraisals', 1963, p. 175), that 'Men need Women', or that 'Adults as well as children need to be loved' ('Morality and needs', 1969, p. 190), where there are overriding considerations in the light of which the worthiness of these needs are established, there is, from the moral point of view, a standing presumption that these needs ought to be satisfied, while holding at the same time that moral criteria supply independent criteria for deciding the worthiness of such needs. This considerably weakens his claim that 'if something is a human need then it has a *prima facie* right to be realized' (ibid., p. 201).

The contentiousness of his claim rests on the qualifications 'human' need and '*prima facie*' right. The claim that needs ought on moral grounds ordinarily to be satisfied is seriously undermined if indeed the *prima facie* nature of this right is subject to independent moral considerations. Nielsen's reference to needs as conative dispositions as 'human' needs which have a *prima facie* right to be satisfied raises serious problems too. He presumes our judgements on human needs like our memories, to be generally reliable, while admitting 'I readily acknowledge that it is perfectly sensible to claim that *some* needs ought to be overridden or that *some* needs ought not to be satisfied' (p. 198). But this suggests that to judge some needs as undeserving of satisfaction is like judging some memories as unreliable, a judgement based on fact. He goes on to say 'For a given need we can always ask, "He needs it but should he have it?", but if we are reasoning morally we cannot ask "Should any human needs be satisfied?"' (p. 198) on the assumption that morality will usually condone the satisfaction of needs as its natural reference point, which the question 'Should any human needs be satisfied?' can only cast into doubt in a nonsensical way. He notes in addition that the postulation of general needs is usually platitudinous or involves psychological generalisation (p. 191). But are the 'human' needs to which he refers merely an aggregate of facts about individual conative dispositions, or are they postulates of universal *a priori* needs?

It is highly questionable whether the facts about human needs, drives and wants constitute the natural basis of morality as he suggests. He notes that certain ascetic moralities of Christian, Muslim, Hindu and Buddhist origin explicitly sanction the non-fulfilment of 'mundane human needs' (i.e. conative dispositions) in favour of 'deeper *needs*' (p. 196). 'If such beliefs are held', he admits 'there would quite naturally be a question about whether man's basic (mundane) needs ought to be satisfied; but it is crucial to realize', he insists, 'that the reason for *not* satisfying them is that by denying them, or inhibiting them, one could satisfy what is believed to be a still deeper need' (p. 197). This suggests that there can be genuine but conflicting needs, and thus radically undermines his persistent claim that the relationship between morality and the satisfaction of needs is a non-contingent one. It is not as if Nielsen is setting up criteria to distinguish between authentic and inauthentic needs, stipulating a non-contingent relation between the former and morality, or as if he is sanctioning one form of morality over another. Nielsen is prepared to consider the case of the relativist that:

> The linguistic regularities I have uncovered, it might well be argued, show little more than that we live in a society which just happens to have adopted a moral code which dictates that most needs ought to be satisfied. Our tribe has, as one of its leading and fundamental moral principles, the principle that most needs ought to be satisfied. But we could perfectly well understand an alternative *morality* which rejected this principle and did not assume that the satisfaction of human needs was, generally speaking, a good thing. *We* might well believe that such a morality would be unrealistic, absurdly false, and totally inhumane. But − and this is the significant thing − we would still recognize it to be (in a descriptive sense) a morality, and if people were actually to adopt such a code of conduct we would without any difficulty recognize it to be a moral code. (p. 201)

But, as I have tried to make it clear, if the relationship between the satisfaction of needs and morality holds only for *some* needs and *some* moralities it is not a non-contingent relation as such. This means that Nielsen's claim that morality appeals to human needs as its natural foundation can only be accepted in a highly qualified sense: morality does not appeal to a uniform set of needs as its foundation, nor are the needs it appeals to necessarily 'natural', either in the sense of basic physiological needs or given conative dispositions.

Having conceded a great deal to the relativists, he goes on to argue, 'Even if it is the case that what I have said holds only for all extant moralities', which on his own admission it does not, 'or even if it only holds for Western morality, it is important to see that it does hold for that − that given extant moral codes, or given our moral code, if something is a human need, then it has a *prima facie* right to be realized' (p. 201). He raises the obvious objection: 'why', if there are many different moral codes, 'adopt our *conventional* moral point of view . . .?' (p. 201). He replies:

> There would be a considerable force to this objection if there were any adequate reason for believing that opting for what is misleadingly called the 'conventional moral point of view' is without a sound rational point. But rational beings will want to have their basic needs satisfied and their interests respected. Given the fact that

human beings tend, broadly speaking, to be roughly equal in strength and intelligence, it is plain enough that to insure as well as they can that their needs and interests will be safeguarded, they need some social device which will fairly and equitably adjudicate their conflicting interests. Such an adjudication is a central function of morality and that any culture will have some stabilized ways of doing this is a perfectly natural and reasonable thing to expect. Without it rational living would be impossible. That human beings generally have a stake in such a point of view is perfectly understandable. No arbitrary decision of principle is involved here. (p. 202)

This, it seems to me, explicates the logic of politics rather than of morality as such. If it is not arbitrary to take as one's grounds for claiming a non-contingent relation between the satisfaction of needs and the content of morality, an assessment of what human beings broadly speaking tend to seek, it is not uncontentious either. This, as we shall see, is a question on which theories of morality are essentially divided, the naturalists or descriptivists claiming that it is appropriate, the neo-Kantians or prescriptivists that it is inappropriate. What is important to note is that this decision is itself a value decision and not one dictated by logic as such. The weakness of the naturalist or descriptivist position is to suggest that the contrary is true; that is the force that the claim that the relation between satisfaction of needs and morality is non-contingent may be said to have. Although not willing to claim that this relationship is logical, on the one hand, or a matter of fact, on the other, by maintaining that it is non-contingent they seem to be suggesting that it is a bit of both.

White (1974) in his careful analysis of needs and wants, although defending need claims as factual claims and even defending their general reliability, construes their logic quite differently because he takes as the grounds for his argument the logic of language. Setting out, as he does, explicitly to analyse 'a few of the logical characteristics of the notion of *need*' (p. 159), White sees the centrality of the concept to lie in its instrumental sense, or Taylor's category 1. Need claims take two characteristic forms, he maintains, the verb form '"A needs *to V*"' (as in 'A needs to work'), and the noun form '"A needs *X*"' (p. 159). He argues that need statements are always incomplete, implying a need for something in order to achieve a certain end. This instrumental or elliptical quality is obvious in the verb form, but concealed in the noun form of need statements. Partly for this reason, he says, philosophers have tended to conclude that need claims are normative in status, whereas he maintains they are factual claims about the necessary conditions to bring about a desired end. Need statements do not require the evaluation of ends in order to be true; the assessment of ends, he concludes, is a separate question. This means that he rules out the use of needs which Taylor listed under category 4 as goods in themselves — for instance, the needs for affection, identity, self-esteem, freedom, etc., where these claims are not merely descriptions of what people seek but recommendations. Because, as White argues, 'to have a need implies to need, whereas to need does not necessarily imply to have a need' (p. 160), the noun form of need statements is seen as logically derivative from the verb form, the instrumental or 'in order to' nature of the concept, so clearly evident in the verb form, being taken as central.

White argues that the logic of need statements is that they express a relationship of necessity. However, not all relationships of necessity can be expressed in terms of needs. 'Must', he argues, is the term more broadly used to handle necessity and 'need' indicates necessity only in the sense of 'in order to'. Thus, he notes, the claim 'I must have dropped my glove somewhere' cannot be rephrased 'I need to have dropped it somewhere' (p. 163). To say '"If a gas is touched by a spark it must explode" is different from saying "If a gas is to explode, it must be touched by a spark"; only the latter signifies a need' (p. 163), and so on.

White recognises that the logic in terms of which one can be said to need something is specific to a given context. In other words, it is not a general and ineluctable necessity that is being postulated but only a necessity in terms of specific means for specific ends:

> . . . a failure to notice the elliptical nature of statements about what A needs leads to arguments at cross purposes, for it can easily be the case that although legally A needs *to V*, he does not physically or morally need to, or, although he needs *to V* in order to *F* he does not need *to V* in order to *G*. When, therefore, someone disputes that A needs *to V*, he may be disputing this either because he does not think that given the circumstances and the end-state it follows that *to V* is something the absence of which would be the lack of something necessary or because he wants the question whether A needs *to V* considered in relation to a different end. My daughter's claim that she needs another pair of shoes is made in the light of her wish to keep up with the latest fashions; while my insistence that she does not need them appeals to the ordinary requirements of daily use. There is no non-relative answer to the question 'Does she need them?', though one may legitimately suppose that the need *to V* in order to *F* is more important than the need *to V* in order to *G* because to *F* is more important than to *G*. (p. 162)

White goes on to argue that 'this relative nature of a need is, however, misinterpreted in the current philosophical view that "the term 'need' is mainly normative"'. In this way, he dissociates himself from the prescriptivists, Benn and Peters, Komisar, Dearden and others that he cites (p. 179n). 'Whether A needs *to V* or not depends solely on whether or not *V*ing is in the circumstances the only way to reach the end-state, and whether there is such an end-state' he argues (p. 162).

> If I am going abroad, I need a passport; if the ball-bearing is to last a year, it needs oil; if you are no longer Dean, you don't need those files. It is just as much a question of fact whether there is such an end-state as whether such an alternative is necessary to reach it. The question whether there should or need be such an end-state is a different question and quite independent of the logic of *need*'. (p. 162)

By appealing to 'the logic of *need*' to insist that evaluation of the end-state is independent of the evaluation of the means to attain it, however,

White seems to be denying the relativity of the concept that he has already established. It is, I think, quite arbitrary to insist that all uses of the noun form of needs are elliptical and that the proper use of the term is confined to the meaning 'in order to', which the verb form openly expresses. Not only can one legally, morally, physically, need *to V*, all of which express means to ends dictated by different criteria, legal, moral, physical, etc., but one can also talk of having legal, moral, physical needs, without intending the claim to be elliptical in any sense. It is common to use the term needs with reference to goals. In the same way that one can say 'She needs food and warmth', one can say 'this car needs a new set of tyres', and claims are made that one needs security, affection, self-esteem, and so on. These are not elliptical statements in the sense that one can only complete their meaning by asking 'what for?' As Nielsen points out, it is decidedly odd to ask someone, 'Why do you need rest and relaxation?' ('Morality and needs', 1969, p. 188). These need claims do not refer to ends which are extrinsic to what is needed. But they do refer to extrinsic criteria, and many different kinds of criteria, and it is by virtue of this fact that the concept of need is a relative concept. What is different about needing *to V*, legally, morally, physically, and so on, is not so much a question of the ends being sought which dictate different means, as it is a question of the criteria (not all of which specify 'ends') being appealed to.

My position may seem as arbitrary as White's but it is not, I believe, for three reasons: (1) it does not rule out a whole class of need statements with reference to 'the logic of the concept' as if this were absolute; (2) it does not involve an empirical claim which is false, that is that all need claims are elliptical and need to be completed by 'in order to' explanations; and (3) it covers all the regular uses of the term, the noun form and the verb form, which can equally well be used to make different need claims appealing to different criteria.

We can see how intimately White's case for the proper meaning of need is related to the criteria he elects: the logic of language. Moreover, we can see from the examples that he gives that, so far from the ends involved being extrinsic to the means to attain them, in fact, in many cases of postulating a need, the very existence of the need is logically dependent on accepting the end involved. So, for instance, whether or not my car needs a sun roof depends on whether or not I want it to have one, which may be different from what my car mechanic thinks is reasonable; whether or not I need a visa for Ireland depends on whether or not I want to go there, and so on. It is true, as White points out, that to say that one needs a visa to travel to Ireland is not to say that one needs a visa (1974, p. 163, slightly different example), and this is a case where accepting the means does not entail accepting the ends. But this is in fact a different kind of claim from the claim 'I need a visa for Ireland'. One is a claim about the conditions for satisfying a rule (Taylor's class 1), the other is a claim about means to an end (Taylor's class 2), where the need (means) is logically conditional on the end being accepted.

Although White is right that the term 'needs' is not always synonymous with the term 'ought', or the term 'must' or the term 'lacks', any more than it is always synonymous with the term 'desires', 'wants', and so on, it *can* be synonymous with any of these in different contexts. Thus he is wrong to conclude:

> But whether needs are chosen − e.g., because I want to attain some end − or are imposed − e.g., by physical or legal circumstances − whether they are part of the course of life − e.g., biological or psychological − or merely adventitious − e.g., for a momentary end − makes no difference to the logic of *need*. Hence it is a mistake to suppose that the existence of such various categories of need forms part of the structure of the concept of *need*. (p. 161)

Not only is such a conclusion arbitrary, but it is inconsistent both with his own principle that need is a relative concept and with the accepted uses of the term which the logic of the language seems to sanction. White forces from the accurate distinction that 'to have a need implies to need, whereas to need does not necessarily imply to have a need' the conclusion that the centrality of the concept therefore lies with the verb form 'to need'. If this were the case one could argue the same logic for all cases of words which can be used as both nouns and verbs, for example want, love, care, play, hold, and so on. In each of these cases one can say that 'to have a want, love, care, play, hold, etc. implies *to* want, love, care, play, hold, etc., but to want, love, care, play, hold, does not necessarily imply to have a want, love, care, play, hold'. But does this really prove that the verb form contains the central meaning of the concept, or are they not simply different usages with corresponding restrictions?

H. J. McCloskey (1976, p. 3) in his commentary on White's analysis, for different reasons, reserves the primary use of the term for 'basic' needs − 'the needs of plants, and animals, for water and food' etc., − and sees other uses as parasitic on this. He agrees with White that conditions for self-actualisation, what fell under class 4 in Taylor's classification, as in needs for identity, creativity, esteem, etc., are not properly needs because they refer not to requisites for natural growth, but preconditions for *self*-activity, or *self*-development, qualitatively different from natural or basic needs and to a certain extent both culturally and individually determined. Needs for self-actualisation appeal to the notion of benefit, at once too broad and too relative to encompass needs as such, which McCloskey sees relating to 'what it would be detrimental to us to lack, where the detrimental is explained by reference to our natures as men and specific persons' (p. 6).

McCloskey agrees with White that need statements are elliptical and that 'with talk about needs (noun) the range of reasons that properly can be given is much more limited; and of human needs more limited again than with need (verb) statements' (p. 2). But McCloskey recognises, tacitly at least, that the reasons for the greater restrictiveness of the term in some forms than others refer to the criteria to which the term appeals in these cases: 'human needs', he says, 'can usefully be explained and appealed to only against a background belief in the existence of a common human nature and specific individual natures with certain inherent potentialities (as distinct from mere possibilities), the development of which involves the satisfaction of needs' (p. 1). McCloskey argues, quite rightly I think, that it is because such a human nature is assumed to be naturally given, like the acorn growing into the oak, that many philosophers 'believe that the logical gap between "is" and "ought" statements can be bridged by need statements, that we can move in a logically impeccable way from statements of fact to statements about what we or the state ought to do, where the statements of fact are statements about needs' (p. 1).

I agree with McCloskey that 'the discovery of our needs does not help us to bridge the is-ought gap, to move from fact to value, for the discovery of *human* needs itself involves value judgements that our existence and development are goods or means to or conditions of goods, or of lessening evils of human beings' (p. 2). I agree, in addition that:

> Those who deny that there is some common human nature, and particular natures with inherent potentialities for good development, on the model of the acorn and the oak, or in terms of the teleological model of human nature of Thomistic natural law theory, would do better to drop talk about needs. Instead, I suggest, that they would be better advised to concentrate on the idea of the possibilities of changes in man and men, for the sake of realizing goods, reducing and eliminating evils, for, for such theories, it is the possibility of future goods which may be achieved by what, following Bradley and others, might usefully be called self-realization or self-making, rather than by self-development or self-perfection that is important. (p. 2)

Asserting, as he does, that, 'as against White, it will be argued in this paper that talk of *human needs* does involve value judgments' (p. 3), he goes on, nevertheless, to make his case against certain usages of the term 'needs'. 'Any account of needs which allows luxuries to count as needs, must surely be mistaken', he argues, 'for this is a basic contrast in the context of talk about needs' (p. 3). Is McCloskey arguing that this is a logical distinction or that it is a distinction inherent in the language, and is this claim, whichever it is, itself immune from the value distinctions need talk usually involves? He goes on to claim that: 'It is important, at the conceptual level at least, to distinguish *natural drives, desires, wants, expectations, reasonable expectations, interests, welfare, well-being, luxuries*, from *needs*' (p. 4). His reasons for keeping natural and acquired drives conceptually distinct from needs are (1) because these could be destructive and, unlike needs, undeserving of satisfaction, and (2) because 'it is a matter of empirical inquiry to determine what are our natural and acquired drives, and whether they relate to needs, or whether they relate to some kind of lack of fulfilment, a frustration, a destruction of the self' (p. 4). Here McCloskey seems to be assuming that the concept of needs has a correct use, sanctioned by logic, that stands in contradiction to his earlier assertion that talk of human needs involves value judgements.

McCloskey runs through typical criteria to which various philosophers appeal in arguing for a more or less restricted sense of the term 'need', concluding (p. 6), 'I suggest that harm is too encompassing a word, injury too positive and yet too narrow, and that needs relate to what it would be detrimental to us to lack, where the detrimental is explained by reference to our natures as men and specific persons.' By this criterion food, drink, clear air and basic human needs for survival are deemed genuine needs. Although hedging his bets considerably and talking about 'rejecting the natural law ethics as false, and hence as the proper home of human needs theory' (p. 6), McCloskey nevertheless argues in the same breath that to understand the concept of needs

> . . . we must look to human nature theories which involve the idea that man is born with a nature which has inherent potentialities for development which are good and such that these potentialities can be realized only if certain conditions are realized, where the potentiality to actuality model is that of the acorn to the oak. Where the conditions are such that the possessor of the nature with potentialities would be *impaired, marred, stunted*, as a person if the conditions are not met, we speak of his needs and the talk about impaired, marred, stunted, is to be explained in terms of what is natural to human nature. (pp. 6–7)

Now it seems McCloskey has expanded the reference of the concept of needs back to benefit and well beyond the confines of basic human needs for survival. '. . . talk about human needs', he suggests, 'to be meaningful and useful, must be spelt out in terms of natural goods, goods based on human nature and human ends, where the ends are determined by our natures' (p. 6). It is difficult to see how McCloskey by talking about 'natural goods' himself avoids the naturalistic fallacy which he seems to be upholding. We discover that the real reason why needs, rights and interests are not synonymous 'is in part because the more remote aspects of so-called human development and self-perfection' impress him 'as falling less under the characterisation as development of potentialities on the acorn-oak model, where we (as well as our society) determine within limits set by nature, what we become', than as *'self-making'* (p. 7). *'Self-making'*, he suggests is something other 'than engaging in the activity of making the potential actual, moving from potentiality to actuality as do the acorn which becomes an oak, the tadpole a frog' (p. 7).

All this is very confused: if human nature does develop on the acorn-oak model it is physiologically programmed and there is no room for determination by the self or by society (even within the limits of our nature), which McCloskey gratuitously slips under the oak-acorn model. And yet 'self-making' is said to be something different again. If we dwell on these confusions, it is, however, for the very reason that many supporters of human needs as an objective concept and a way to bridge the is-ought gap, appeal to some such concept of human nature with all its difficulties.

I think that McCloskey is quite right to distinguish rights from needs, but for the wrong reasons. The reason why we cannot move from statements of needs to statements of rights is once again because of the is-ought problem. To establish that something is a need is not *eo ipso* to establish that one has a right to its satisfaction. This would suggest (1) that the authenticity of needs could be established with the same certainty as matters of fact, and (2) that people were thereby entitled to the satisfaction of needs. What offends most against philosophical canons in this way of arguing is less the fact that recommendations are inferred from factual premises, than the fact that the so-called factual premises are themselves nothing but value judgements in disguise. So I cannot agree with McCloskey's conclusion:

> I am therefore suggesting that, *ceteris paribus*, needs are things which ought, where possible, to be available, not withheld, prevented, and indeed, be supplied where necessary; that where needs cannot be met, society or the world [sic!] ought to be reordered so far as possible, so that they are capable of being met, or obtained by the person with the need, provided that greater goods are not thereby lost or jeopardized; that talk of human needs and needs of particular persons involves reference to natures, the perfection, development, non-impairment of which are good. That is to say, needs talk involves reference to a natural good existence and development as human beings from potentiality to actuality; and equally of particular persons; where that, the lack of which leads to a person being impaired, stunted, constitutes a need. If there were no such good nature, we could not indicate human needs. Further, if human existence and the development of the potential into the actual of human and individual natures is not good, talk of needs becomes inapplicable. (p. 7)

McCloskey's arguments for a proper understanding of the concept of human needs refer to an underlying theory of human nature that is metaphysical in character. Such theories of human nature have seen a resurgence with the work of the descriptivists, Anscombe and Foot and others who have pioneered a return to a substantive ethics. Confidence is maintained that inquiry into the nature of virtue, a philosophy of psychology and the emotions, will provide a firm foundation for ethical prescriptions. Some have even hoped to see this assault on the barriers of neo-Kantian formalism produce bridging concepts between facts and values, and the concept of need has been suggested as a candidate.

But not all those who have supported this project have been descriptivists or recognise metaphysics as a legitimate enterprise. For instance, Alasdair MacIntyre in his brilliant article 'Hume on "is" and "ought"' (1971) resuscitates Hume as being, not an advocate, but an opponent of the rigid distinction between facts and values, and one who tried to repudiate a 'religious foundation for morality . . . putting in its place a foundation in human needs, interests, desires and happiness' (p. 121). MacIntyre sees Hume's positive contribution to ethics to lie in his attempt to relate the content of morality to facts about society. The is-ought distinction, the implications of which were not developed in Hume's philosophy, tends in the other direction: to a radical distinction between the content of morality and the facts about existence. Kant, MacIntyre argues, and not Hume was responsible for this tendency which led to 'bourgeois formalism in ethics' (p. 161).

The neo-Kantians have made much of the practical syllogism as a way to reconstruct the logic of statements where on first glance a value conclusion seems to have been derived from a factual premise. Thus such common arguments as 'Soft drugs lead to hard drugs, therefore soft drugs should be banned', can be reconstructed to show that it is not the fact (if it is a fact) that soft drugs lead to hard drugs that supplies the reason for banning them, but the suppressed value premise that hard drugs are harmful. MacIntyre takes the argument another round, however, by suggesting that this value premise is also a fact of a sort, expressing a belief or predisposition, psychological facts about the claimant. He maintains that embracing the value premise constitutes 'wanting', and that it is in terms of 'wanting' that the transition from fact to value, 'is' to 'ought' is made. He argues that 'Aristotle's examples of practical syllogisms typically have a premise which includes some such terms as "suits" or "pleases"', going on to suggest that 'we could give a long list of the concepts which can form such bridge notions between "is" and "ought": wanting, needing, desiring, pleasure, happiness, health — and these are only a few'. Furthermore, he believes 'there is a strong case for saying that moral notions are unintelligible apart from concepts such as these' (p. 120).

MacIntyre has made a long overdue correction to the popular image of Hume's view of morality, distorted as it has been by the emphasis placed on the is-ought distinction, which was, in the context of Hume's thought as a whole, little more than a passing remark. (Kant, for instance, seems to have been unaware of Hume's remark on is-ought, coming close as it did to Kant's own distinction between facts and values, charging Hume in the preface to his *Critique of Practical Reason* for having tried to reduce all *a priori* principles, with the exception of the principles of mathematics, to empirically derived truths.)

MacIntyre follows Hume in trying to establish a 'link between what is good and right and what we need and desire' (p. 120). It takes only a little reflection to see, however, that to reduce needs and desires to psychological facts does little justice to the complexity of those concepts. Only in class 3 of Taylor's classification can needs, like desires, be said to express conative dispositions or psychological facts, and even here, to suggest that these can be empirically established is a claim fraught with difficulties, as we have seen in earlier chapters. In very few cases can the force of need claims be appreciated by assuming them to be descriptions of psychological states. How, for instance, could we differentiate the daughter's claim that she needs a new pair of shoes to keep up with the fashions from the father's claim, for other reasons, that she does not need them, on this basis? Nor can the force of needs as goals, in the sense of needs for rest and relaxation, needs for creativity, and so on, be understood if they are interpreted to be nothing more than descriptions of psychological states. The implications of such claims, factual and normative, are left unexplained by such a transcription.

Charles Taylor, although on different grounds, also argues like Nielsen and MacIntyre, that the is-ought gap can be bridged by concepts of human nature, human needs, wants and purposes (Taylor, 1969). Taylor is concerned, like Hampshire, Anscombe, Foot and others, that the logical distinction between facts and values gives rise to the assumption that values are unrelated to matters of fact, or that values can be set aside when undertaking empirical investigation, a view which he sees supporting the notion of a value-free science. Not only does Taylor show with reference to specific cases that empirical studies almost always end by making recommendations, but he gives an account of the appeal such recommendations characteristically make: this appeal is to basic conceptions about human nature, 'human needs, wants and purposes'. Taylor argues, for instance, against the notion that 'good' simply represents approval or a commitment to principle for which no further grounds can be given. 'Good' is a term itself related to conceptions of human needs, wants and purposes:

> . . . 'good' is used in evaluating, commending, persuading and so on by a race of beings who are such that through their needs, desires and so on, they are not indifferent to the various outcomes of the world process. A race of inactive, godless angels, as really disinterested spectators, would have no use for it, could not make use of it, except in the context of cultural anthropology, just as human anthropologists use 'mana'. It is because 'good' has this use, and can only have meaning because there is a role to fill in human life, that it becomes unintelligible when abstracted from this role. (p. 55)

Why does Taylor introduce the innovation 'godless angels'? Without this qualification one would be forced to disagree with him, since one could risk saying that paying homage to 'the Good' was precisely the function that angels were said to perform – assuming, as one must I think, that they had reasons for deeming God good independent of his authority to command them to do so. Taylor seems to be arguing that 'the good', or values, arise as exigencies of everyday life and the necessity to take decisions. But if the exigencies of action and decision pose, they do not also explain, the problem of values, and it would probably be truer to argue that it is because values are logically independent from the dilemmas of decision in the context of which they arise that these dilemmas are a serious matter.

Having said this, it is important to note that Taylor argues that the role of the concept of the good is such that 'it is supposed to be predicated on general grounds, and not just according to the likes and dislikes or feelings of individuals' (p. 55). He agrees with Moore that we can never say that 'good' means '"conducive to the fulfillment of human wants, needs and purposes"', even though he insists its meaning is 'unintelligible outside of any relationship to wants, needs and purposes' (p. 54). He specifies the relationship between the concept of good and conceptions of human needs, wants and purposes as one in which the appraisal of needs, and so on, *provides the grounds* for the evaluation of something as good, grounds necessary as such for us to take seriously the claim that something is good other than as a merely emotive response, or simply a signification of approval. Thus he concludes that:

> (1) to apply 'good' may or may not be to commend, but it is always to claim that there are reasons for commending whatever it is applied to, (2) to say of something that it fulfils human needs, wants or purposes always constitutes a *prima facie* reason for calling it 'good', that is, for applying the term in the absence of overriding considerations (p. 48).

MacIntyre and Taylor are in fundamental agreement that recommendations in terms of good and bad have as their reference fundamental conceptions of human nature which may be specified in terms of needs, desires, purposes, and so on, although they understand the status of claims about human nature differently. In this respect their position is very similar to that of the descriptivists, Anscombe and Foot in particular, who argue respectively that 'It is not judgement as such that sets us in motion; but our judgement on how to get or do something we *want*' (Anscombe, 1969, p. 181); and that 'a connection with the choices of the speaker is not a necessary condition of the use of the word "good" in its ordinary sense. If a man who calls an *A* a good *A* has reason, other things being equal, to prefer it to other *A*'s, this is because of the kind of a thing that an *A* is, and its connection with his wants and needs' (Foot, 1969*a*, p. 227).

It is not immediately clear that Foot and Anscombe in these passages are arguing the same position. In fact one could be forgiven for thinking that they were at odds, Anscombe arguing we call something good because we want it, Foot that wanting something is a necessary but not a sufficient condition for calling it good. If, however, we supplement Anscombe's statement with her notion of 'desirability characteristics' (Anscombe, 1958, pp. 66 ff.), as explaining the grounds for which we want certain things, we can see that the positions are indeed close.

What the descriptivists, MacIntyre and Taylor have in common is the assumption that the concept of the 'good' is in some way logically tied to other human concepts such as desiring, needing, wanting. This has encouraged them to suggest that the way in which the concepts of good and wants, needs, etc., are related is by virtue of wants, needs, etc., providing the grounds for calling something good. Lest it seem that the position of the descriptivists is no different from that of the utilitarians and emotivists who suggest that 'pro-attitudes' towards things, or the belief that they are conducive to pleasure rather than pain, is a sufficient reason to call them good, let me stress again that the desirability or needworthy quality of such goods is said to inhere in the intrinsic characteristics of the thing needed and its function in satisfying universal human goals such as surviving, 'flourishing', and so on, and not merely in the contingent fact that it is needed or wanted. Even so the argument that the concept of the good is logically related to concepts of need, wants, etc., gives rise, as the descriptivists have formulated it, to two errors that others have pointed out:

(1) It suggests things are good because they are wanted/needed, which means that if we could discover what men universally want or need we could in principle resolve any disputes about the 'good'. The good, if it amounts only to what people want or need, even if those needs and wants are grounded in the intrinsic desirability characteristics of the objects, is not properly a moral concept at all: that is it is a concept that is open to an empirical or scientific treatment, since the criteria by which its meaning can be known are available. Those who want to preserve the concept of good as a moral concept and one which will account for moral disputes as genuine disputes argue not that we call something good because it is the object of our needs or wants, but rather that something is the object of our needs or wants because we deem it good. Phillips and

Mounce making this point against Anscombe and Foot, point out that in trying to convince the Catholic housewife that birth control is justifiable because of the harm that having too many children causes, it will not help to point out that planning their families is what most mothers nowadays want, since 'she believes that what the majority wants is a sign of moral decadence and wants different things. But she does not believe because she wants, she wants because she believes'. (The reasons for which she rejects birth control having to do with her beliefs about the will of God, the honour of motherhood, and so on, which define for her the limits of the concepts of good and bad, harm and benefit) (Phillips and Mounce, 1969, pp. 238–9).

(2) The second mistake of which the descriptivists can be convicted is that of 'supposing that because the word "good" is logically tied in certain contexts to the *word* "needs", it is therefore logically tied to certain concrete *things* which are generally thought to be needs' as Hare puts it (1969, p. 256). (A point that White also made.) Hare goes on to note:

> The two words 'desires' and 'needs' have both misled descriptivists in the same way − and that because there is an intimate logical relation between what is needed and what is desired, so that in many contexts we could say that for a thing to be needed is for it to be a necessary condition for satisfying a desire. It follows that if 'things desired' do not form a closed class, 'things needed' will not either. If, as I said, logic does not prevent us from coming to desire new things, or ceasing to desire old ones, it cannot, either, determine what we do or do not need. (p. 256)

In other words, what Hare is establishing is that what people desire or need is a contingent question and is not logically restricted in the way that the concept of the good is restricted. Thus, as one recent author has pointed out, it is possible for one to act on a desire one desires not to have: for example, the overweight fellow who craves chocolate, but on the other hand, desiring to be thin, and knowing that chocolate contributes to his overweightness, desires not to have the desires for chocolate that he has (Schiffer, 1976, pp. 195 ff.). It is thus possible for us to hold simultaneously conflicting desires in a way that it is not possible for us to hold simultaneously conflicting notions of the good. In elucidating these conflicting desires, for instance, one would not conclude that chocolate was good because I desired it, but bad because I desired not to desire it, as one would have to if 'desire' and 'good' were logically related concepts; one would be more likely to conclude that chocolate, although pleasant, was not good (that is, not conducive to the ends or welfare of him who desires it, 'ends' and 'welfare' obviously being defined in terms other than the desires of the subject − since these are conflicting).

The reason why we object to the concept of the good being defined in terms of human needs, wants and purposes, is twofold: (1) Because human needs, wants and purposes are contingent and not necessarily good in any usual sense of the term, unless that is restricted absolutely to the meaning that someone needs or wants it. (2) Because the whole notion of referring values to facts about human nature, suggests, if one is not very careful, that these are facts in the ordinary sense, and that one is therefore deriving values from facts. While I do not think that Anscombe, or Foot, or Taylor would for one moment mean to suggest that this is so, it does seem that they have lost sight of the fact that by appealing to needs, wants and purposes in the way that they do they merely push back the question of values one step, in that needs, wants and purposes defined in this way have such a strong evaluative element as to constitute values themselves, and therefore belong in the category of metaphysical rather than factual assertions. That this is so we know from the fact that not just any wants, needs or purposes are admissible, but only those which lend themselves to a coherent doctrine of human nature.

Clarification of this point casts some light on Taylor's contentious statement (to be found also in Kai Nielsen's work, as we have seen) that 'to say of something that it fulfils human needs, wants or purposes always constitutes a *prima facie* reason for calling it "good" . . .' (1969, p. 48). What is the force of Taylor's circumlocution 'to say of something that *it fulfils human wants, needs or purposes* . . .'? Would the statement have the same meaning if it was rephrased as, 'to need or want something or find it consistent with one's purposes always constitutes a *prima facie* reason for calling it good . . .'? I think not. And what is the force of the qualification that 'there is a *prima facie* case' for calling things that satisfy human wants, needs or purposes good? Does this mean that there *is* a case for calling them good or only that there seems to be?

The circumlocution suggests that there are *such things* as human needs, wants and purposes, and that they can be decided independently of what people contingently need or want or have as their purposes. The way in which this distinction is made is by tacitly assigning a proper meaning to human needs, wants and purposes such that they are not synonymous with all needs, wants and purposes the people do or could aspire to — since, as we know, some of these are thoroughly bad (for example, the need for revenge, envious desires, designs to kill and other malevolent purposes). In this way Taylor is able to yield the conclusion that to say of something that it fulfils human needs, wants or purposes always constitutes a *prima facie* reason for calling it 'good'. What this amounts to can be summed up in two ways: either one can claim that Taylor has put a surreptitious (and illicit) restriction on what counts as human needs, wants or purposes; or one can argue that Taylor is using the terms needs, wants and purposes so that value assumptions are tacitly (but legitimately) built in. I tend to favour the second interpretation. It seems to me that the term 'needs' at least ('wants' not necessarily) has an unavoidable value dimension, to which Taylor's thesis, more restrictive than most on the status of needs as a value concept, refers.

Nevertheless, I want to deny the assertion, just because: (1) What count as needs, despite the strong value slope of the word, to use Taylor's terminology, is still a contingent matter, and experience tells us that aspirations can fulfil all the usual criteria for the term 'needs' and still be thoroughly bad. (2) 'Wants' lack the value dimension of needs and are not necessarily associated with what is good at all. There is no logical relation between 'needs' and 'wants' ('wants' falling into class 3 of Paul Taylor's classification), and there are absolutely no restrictions on what people might conceivably want (since people are always wanting new things and tomorrow's technologies will undoubtedly produce new and unforeseen wants); the only ones to suggest that there is a connection between wants and the 'good' are those who define 'good' as what people (contingently) want, among whom Charles Taylor certainly does not fall. (3) The same can be said for 'purposes' which can be defined as 'good' only by adding that qualification, since human purposes are also as a matter of fact unrestricted in their scope.

What denying the assertion that 'to say of something that it fulfils human needs, wants or purposes always constitutes a *prima facie* reason for calling it "good"'' at the very least indicates, is that there is no *logical* connection between the concept of 'good' and human needs, wants or purposes. But perhaps the connection that Taylor is trying to establish between them is not a logical one? I am not sure about that, but assuming for the moment that it is not, the options that he is left with are either (1) that this relationship is contingent, which we have already argued it is not, since known needs, wants and purposes can contravene any usual sense of the word good; or (2) this statement is a recommendation in disguise, suggesting that what may be advanced as a human need, want or purpose, assuming that it is seriously advanced as such, is circumscribed by the view of human nature of him who advances it. In other words, this is a recommendation about how to interpret need claims that is, in turn, based on a theory of human nature and how needs, wants and purposes relate to such basic assumptions about man.

Since this seems to be the only viable alternative that we are left with, it seems reasonable to conclude that what Taylor is claiming is this: (1) that empirical theories invariably include either open or tacit recommendations, and that these are not unrelated to the facts under discussion; (2) that the way in which the facts and values relate is in terms of underlying conceptions about human nature, human needs, wants and purposes, which constitute a metaphysical or value framework to which both the facts and recommendations refer, and which they help specify; (3) that this metaphysical or value framework is substantive: that is it does not consist in a list of imperatives, a schedule of rules, or other undefended value axioms, but rather a general theory of the nature of man which establishes the grounds for whatever action-guiding rules the subject subscribes to.

This interpretation of Charles Taylor's position allows us to treat sympathetically his contentious assertion that 'to say of something that it fulfils human needs, wants or purposes always constitutes a *prima facie* reason for calling it "good" . . .' But it means that we can only accept this assertion as true with the provision that what are understood as 'human wants, needs and purposes' are understood in a restricted sense as those needs, wants or purposes seriously advanced as being 'true' wants, needs or purposes; or, needs, wants and purposes consistent with a defensible concept of human nature. In which case, we have reduced the informative nature of the claim to the point where it becomes more or less tautologous. How does this vindicate Taylor's claim (p. 48) that his conclusions tell 'against the well-entrenched doctrine according to which questions of value are independent of questions of fact; the view which holds that before any set of facts we are free to adopt an indefinite number of value positions'? And how does it support the view Taylor claims to be defending that 'a given framework of explanation . . . tends to support an associated value position, secretes its own norms for . . . assessment . . .' (p. 48)?

To begin with let us note that Taylor is not claiming, as it might appear on first glance, that *the facts are secreting the values*: it is the framework that secretes the values. He says (p. 40), 'Thus the framework does secrete a certain value position . . .' He is not deriving values from facts, but from a basic framework of values. It is not altogether certain, however, that Taylor is clear about the implications of this. Although admitting that 'there are wide differences over what human needs, desires and purposes are', he makes reference to 'obvious human wants and needs' (p. 40) as if these were something other than putative. Moreover, if what secretes the value slope is the metaphysical framework, Taylor has not, as he claims, called into dispute the *logical* distinction between facts and values. Early in his essay he noted that those who felt uneasy about the fact-value distinction had not hitherto 'touch(ed) the thesis of the logical separation between fact and value' (p. 26). But nor, I submit, has he, for in relating concepts of the 'good' to conceptions of human needs, wants and purposes, he relates them not to facts, but to specific beliefs about human nature, which belong in the realm of values too. Would Taylor agree, or does he see substantive metaphysical beliefs about the nature of man as a species of fact? We cannot be sure, but this much we can say, that Taylor's thesis, even on the most sympathetic rendering, does not in the least call into question Kant's thesis that values cannot be derived from the facts of existence. One of the ways in which we can see this most clearly is to compare the concept of needs as it is used by Taylor with the quasi-scientific concept of needs that psychologists, concerned to establish the bases of human motivation empirically, put forward. In this case, needs are understood as causes of behaviour and are only differentiated from wants in being (1) a more general category, a generic term that brings wants under its umbrella; and (2) being imputed even where no corresponding wants, or awareness of needs, is present. We see immediately that Taylor's needs are radically different in that (1) they are not understood as the (contingent) causes of behaviour (although they relate to the reasons for, or intentions of, behaviour), and (2) their function for him is not to provide an empirical theory of behaviour, but rather a metaphysical framework.

In conclusion let us note that the criticism of the is-ought distinction advanced by MacIntyre, Taylor, the descriptivists and others has left the logical distinction between facts and values unimpaired. Those who have claimed to bridge the fact-value gap with such concepts as needs, wants, purposes, and so on, have not succeeded in grounding values in facts, as they frequently claim they have. For the way in which they use the terms 'needs', 'wants', 'purposes', indicates that these are not synonymous with all contingent needed or wanted things, but only with wants or needs in a special sense which makes them values, and which mean that they have succeeded only in adducing values from values.

The project of locating a central sense of the term 'need', and showing that other uses are derivative from, or parasitic on, this, is, I think, based on a misconception of the relation between logic and language. The wide range of uses for the term 'needs' does not in any way disqualify it from a justifiable role in a theory of human nature or an ethics. The term 'good' has just as wide a range of uses: 'good' can also be understood as a means or in an instrumental or technical sense; for example, 'these scissors are good (for cutting)'; 'this car has a good engine (i.e., efficient)'. Goodness can also be understood in the sense of beneficial, healthy as opposed to harmful. We can understand the term 'good' in a non-instrumental sense or as an end in more than one way: either as the hedonic good, or pleasure, which is an avowedly subjective concept – goodness being by definition whatever gives pleasure to the individual; or it can be understood in an absolute or objective sense, as that which constitutes the 'good for man', irrespective of the preferences of individuals, that is as man's appropriate end or goal.

Just as in the case of the concept of 'good', the variety of its uses in no way invalidates it as a philosophical concept, so it is with the concept of needs. On the contrary, it is precisely because it has more than one *justifiable* use, or because it is problematic, that the concept is philosophically interesting. If it were simply the case that on investigation only one sense of the term were found to be legitimate and the others were erroneous, then the term would not be problematic and philosophical analysis would end very quickly with something quite conclusive. It is the fact that after linguistic analysis has been completed we are still left with a problem on the question of needs or of goodness that makes them genuine philosophical problems.

Theories about goodness and needs have tended to do this, committing the fallacy of what Whitehead called 'undue concreteness', that is suggesting a conclusiveness and rigour that does not really obtain in this area of inquiry, and ruling out legitimate meanings of the term on questionable grounds. So for instance, G. H. von Wright, in his book *The Varieties of Goodness*, having analysed the various senses of the term 'good', comes down on the side of goodness defined as welfare. Goodness and needs turn out to be closely related concepts on his understanding, and goodness equals what is needed: that is that which is beneficial for man. Von Wright even contends that virtues may in this sense be deemed 'needs' because needs are understood as that which is opposed to the harmful, vices are harmful, and 'virtues are', therefore, '*needed*' (1963, p. 151).

The grounds that the various parties to the needs debate give for seeing the centrality of the concept to lie here rather than there are different. White, for instance, gives priority to the logic of language as he construes it, Paul Taylor to the logic of morals, Nielsen, McCloskey, Anscombe, Foot and Charles Taylor to our fundamental conceptions of human nature as providing a basis for the central meaning of the term 'needs'. One of the cautions against philosophical interpretations of this kind is that they are in every sense stipulative: not only do they give rise to recommendations, but they imply a recommendation that this is the sense in which the term should be understood. But whatever the grounds are that are deemed sufficient to give priority to this understanding of the term over that, they should not appear so conclusive as to rule out the other contenders, or it will turn out that what was philosophically interesting about it to begin with, the fact that it poses a genuine problem and contains inherent ambiguities, is forgotten.

What this reflects at a more general level is an attempt to reduce the very ambiguity and openness which, as we already suggested, characterises man's nature and goals, and of which the paradoxes of everyday life are expressive. Claims that man has an innate nature which prescribes a natural process of self-development, like that of the acorn growing into the oak, are metaphysical claims which cannot be established as matters of fact, setting out no criteria for evidence and specifying in no way how such claims might be established. There are many difficulties with such a notion of human nature, not least of which is how, if man's nature is naturally given, requiring for his part only insight into what his nature requires of him, this notion is to be reconciled with the concept of freedom. This is not to rule out the possibility that human nature *may* be some ontologically existing entity, but only to point out that if it is, we cannot know that it is by any of the usual criteria for knowledge (that is, excluding faith and divine revelation).

Bibliography

Adelmann, F. J. (ed.) (1969). *Demythologizing Marxism: A Series of Studies on Marxism*, Boston Studies in Philosophy no. 2 (The Hague: Nijhoff).

Althusser, Louis (1969). *For Marx* (Harmondsworth: Penguin).

Althusser, Louis (1970). *Lenin and Philosophy and Other Essays* (London: New Left Books).

Althusser, Louis (1972). *Politics and History: Montesquieu, Rousseau, Hegel and Marx* (London: New Left Books).

Althusser, Louis, and Balibar, Etienne (1970). *Reading Capital* (London: New Left Books).

Anscombe, G. E. M. (1958). *Intention* (Oxford: Blackwell).

Anscombe, G. E. M. (1969). 'Modern moral philosophy', in W. D. Hudson (ed.), *The Is-Ought Question* (London: Macmillan), pp. 175–95.

Arendt, Hannah (1959). *The Human Condition* (Garden City, NY: Doubleday).

Arendt, Hannah (1973). *On Revolution* (Harmondsworth: Penguin).

Aristotle (1972). *Politics* (Harmondsworth: Penguin).

Aristotle (1975). *Nicomachean Ethics* (Harmondsworth: Penguin).

Aron, Raymond (1975). *History and the Dialectic of Violence, An Analysis of Sartre's 'Critique de la Raison Dialectique'* (Oxford: Basil Blackwell).

Avineri, Shlomo (1968). *The Social and Political Thought of Karl Marx* (Cambridge: Cambridge University Press).

Avineri, Shlomo (1972). *Hegel's Theory of the Modern State* (Cambridge: Cambridge University Press).

Avineri, Shlomo (1973). 'The instrumentality of passion in the world of reason: Hegel and Marx', *Political Theory*, vol. 1 (November), pp. 388–404.

Avineri, Shlomo (1973). *Marx's Socialism* (New York: Lieber-Atherton).

Babeuf, Gracchus (1967). *The Defense of Gracchus Babeuf before the High Court of Vendôme*, ed. J. A. Scott (Boston: University of Massachusetts Press).

Bailey, Cyril (1928). 'Karl Marx on Greek atomism', *Classical Quarterly*, vol. 22, pp. 205–6.

Barry, Brian (1965). *Political Argument* (London: Routledge & Kegan Paul).

Bartlett, Francis, and Shodell, James (1963). 'Fromm, Marx and the concept of alienation', *Science and Society*, vol. 27 (Summer), pp. 321–6.

Baumann, Zygmunt (1976). *Socialism, The Active Utopia* (London: Allen & Unwin).

Bay, Christian (1968). 'Needs, wants, and political legitimacy', *Canadian Journal of Political Science*, vol. 1 (September), pp. 241–60.

Bay, Christian (1977). 'Human needs and political education', in Ross Fitzgerald (ed.), *Human Needs and Politics* (Sydney: Pergamon), pp. 1–25.

Benn, S. I., and Peter, R. S. (1959). *Social Principles and the Democratic State* (London: Allen & Unwin).

Benthall, Jonathan (ed.) (1973). *The Limits of Human Nature* (London: Allen Lane).

Berki, R. N. (1972). 'Marcuse and the crisis of the new radicalism: from politics to religion?', *Journal of Politics*, vol. 34 (February), pp. 56–92.

Berki, R. N. (1975). *Socialism* (London: Dent).

Blackburn, Robin (1972). *Ideology in Social Science* (London: Fontana).

Bloch, Ernst (1971). 'Epicurus and Karl Marx', in his *On Karl Marx* (New York: Herder & Herder), pp. 153–8.

Boas, George (1948). *Essays on Primitivism and Related Ideas in the Middle Ages* (Baltimore, Md: Johns Hopkins University Press).

Boyers, Robert, and Orrill, R. (1972). *Laing and Anti-Psychiatry* (Harmondsworth: Penguin).

Bravo, Gian Mario (1970). *Les Socialistes avant Marx*, 3 vols (Paris: François Maspero).

Braybrooke, David (1968). 'Let needs diminish that preferences may prosper', in Nicholas Rescher (ed.), *Studies in Moral Philosophy, American Philosophical Quarterly Monograph Series*, no. 1, pp. 86–107.

Braybrooke, Donald (1958). 'Diagnosis and remedy in Marx's doctrine of alienation', *Social Research*, vol. 25 (Autumn), pp. 325–45.

Brennan, Sheilah O'Flynn (1961). 'The meaning of "nature" in the Aristotelian philosophy of nature', in James A. Weisheilp (ed.), *The Dignity of Science* (New York: Thomist Press), pp. 247–65.

Brown, J. A. C. (1964). *Freud and the Post-Freudians* (Harmondsworth: Penguin).

Bury, J. B. (1955). *The Idea of Progress* (New York: Dover).

Cassirer, Ernst (1951). *The Philosophy of the Enlightenment*, (Princeton, NJ: Princeton University Press).

Cassirer, Ernst (1963). *The Question of Jean-Jacques Rousseau* (Bloomington, Ind.: Indiana University Press).

Cassirer, Ernst (1970). *Rousseau, Kant and Goethe, Two Essays* (Princeton, NJ: Princeton University Press).

Caton, Hiram (1972). 'Marx's sublation of philosophy into Praxis', *Review of Metaphysics*, vol. 26 (December), pp. 233–59.

Chamberlain, G. L. (1963). 'The man Marx made', 'A symposium on the young Marx', *Science and Society*, vol. 27 (Summer), pp. 302–20.

Charvet, John (1974). *The Social Problem in the Philosophy of Rousseau* (Cambridge: Cambridge University Press).

Chiodi, Pietro (1976). *Sartre and Marxism* (Hassocks, Sussex: Harvester Press).

Cohen, Gerald A. (1972). 'Karl Marx and the withering away of social science', *Philosophy and Public Affairs*, vol. 1 (Winter), pp. 182–203.

Cohen, Jerry (1969). 'Critical theory: the philosophy of Marcuse', *New Left Review*, no. 57 (September–October), pp. 35–51.

Cole, G. D. H. (1953). *A History of Socialist Thought*, vol. 1: *The Forerunners, 1789–1850* (London: Macmillan).

Colletti, Lucio (1972). 'Rousseau as critic of civil society', in his *From Rousseau to Lenin, Studies in Ideology and Society* (London: New Left Books).

Condren, Conal (1977). 'The quest for a concept of needs', in Ross Fitzgerald (ed.), *Human Needs and Politics* (Sydney: Pergamon), pp. 244–60.

Cooper, David (ed.) (1968). *The Dialectics of Liberation* (Harmondsworth: Penguin).

Cranston, Maurice (1969). 'Herbert Marcuse', *Encounter*, vol. 32 (March), pp. 38–50, reprinted in William P. Gerberding and Duane E. Smith (eds.), *The New Left, The Abuse of Discontent* (London: Bodley Head, 1970).

Crocker, Lawrence (1972). 'Marx's concept of exploitation', *Social Theory and Practice*, vol. 2 (Fall), pp. 201–15.

Crocker, Lester G. (1959). *An Age of Crisis, Man and World in Eighteenth Century French Thought* (Baltimore, Md: Johns Hopkins University Press).

Crocker, Lester G. (1963). *Nature and Culture, Ethical Thought in the French Enlightenment* (Baltimore, Md: Johns Hopkins University Press).

Cunningham, Adrian (1974). 'Objectivity and human needs in Marxism', *New Blackfriars*, vol. 55 (March), pp. 112–23.

Daniels, R. V. (1960). 'Fate and will in the Marxian philosophy of history', *Journal of the History of Ideas*, vol. 21, pp. 538–52.

Davies, James (1963). *Human Nature and Politics* (New York: Wiley).

d'Entrèves, A. P. (1970). *Natural Law* (London: Hutchinson, 2nd edn).

Desan, Wilfred (1965). *The Marxism of Jean-Paul Sartre* (Garden City; NY: Doubleday).

Diderot (1951 edn). *Supplément au voyage de Bougainville*, in *Oeuvres* (Paris: Gallimard, Bibliothèque de la Pléiade), pp. 963–1002.

Diogenes Laertius (1925). *Lives of Eminent Philosophers*, 2 vols (London: Heinemann, Loeb Classical Library).

Duffield, J. (1970). 'The value concept in *Capital* in light of recent criticism', *Science and Society*, vol. 34 (Fall), pp. 293–302.

Duncan, Graeme (1973). *Marx and Mill* (Cambridge: Cambridge University Press).

Easton, Loyd D. (1961). 'Alienation and history in the early Marx', *Philosophy and Phenomenological Research*, vol. 22, pp. 193–205.

Easton, Loyd D. (1970). 'Alienation and empiricism in Marx's thought', *Social Research*, vol. 37 (Autumn), pp. 402–27.

Ellenberger, Henri F. (1970). *The Philosophy of the Unconscious: The History and Evolution of Dynamic Psychiatry* (London: Allen Lane).

Epictetus (1925 and 1928). *The Discourses* and *The Encheiridion*, 2 vols (London: Heinemann, Loeb Classical Library).

Etzioni, Amitai (1968). 'Basic human needs, alienation and inauthenticity', *American Sociological Review*, vol. 33, pp. 870–85.

Fetscher, Iring (1962). 'Rousseau's concepts of freedom in the light of his philosophy of history', in Carl J. Friedrich (ed.), *Nomos IV, Liberty* (New York: Lieber-Atherton), pp. 29–56.

Fetscher, Iring (1973). 'Karl Marx on human nature', *Social Research*, vol. 40 (Autumn), pp. 443–67.

Fitzgerald, Ross (1974). 'Human Needs and Political Prescriptions' (unpublished PhD dissertation, University of New South Wales, Sydney).

Fitzgerald, Ross (1977*a*). 'Abraham Maslow's hierarchy of needs – an exposition and evaluation', Ross Fitzgerald (ed.), *Human Needs and Politics* (Sydney: Pergamon), pp. 36–51.

Fitzgerald, Ross (1977*b*). 'The ambiguity and rhetoric of "need"', in Ross Fitzgerald (ed.), *Human Needs and Politics* (Sydney: Pergamon), pp. 195–212.

Fitzgerald, Ross (ed.) (1977). *Human Needs and Politics* (Sydney: Pergamon).

Flew, Anthony (1964). 'On not deriving "ought" from "is"', *Analysis*, vol. 25 (December), pp. 25–32.

Flew, Anthony (1977). 'Wants or needs, choices or commands', in Ross Fitzgerald (ed.), *Human Needs and Politics* (Sydney: Pergamon), pp. 213–28.

Foot, Philippa (1969*a*). 'Goodness and choice', in W. D. Hudson (ed.), *The Is-Ought Question* (London: Macmillan), pp. 214–27.

Foot, Philippa (1969*b*). 'Moral beliefs', in W. D. Hudson (ed.), *The Is-Ought Question* (London: Macmillan), pp. 196–213.

Fourier, Charles (1971). *Design for Utopia, Selected Writings* (New York: Schocken Books).

Fourier, Charles (1972). *The Utopian Vision, Selected Texts*, J. Beecher (ed.) (London: Jonathan Cape).

Freire, Paulo (1972*a*). *Cultural Action for Freedom* (Harmondsworth: Penguin).

Freire, Paulo (1972*b*). *Pedagogy of the Oppressed* (Harmondsworth: Penguin).

Freud, Sigmund ([1915] 1961). *Instincts and Their Vicissitudes, Standard Edition of the Complete Psychological Works of Sigmund Freud,* ed. James Strachey (London: Hogarth Press), vol. 14.

Freud, Sigmund ([1916–17] 1974). *Introductory Lectures on Psychoanalysis* (Harmondsworth: Pelican Freud Library), vol. 1.

Freud, Sigmund ([1920] 1974). *Beyond the Pleasure Principle* (London: Hogarth Press).

Freud, Sigmund ([1927] 1961). *The Future of an Illusion, Standard Edition of the*

Complete Psychological Works of Sigmund Freud, ed. James Strachey (London: Hogarth Press), vol. 21.

Freud, Sigmund ([1930] 1961). *Civilization and Its Discontents, Standard Edition of the Complete Psychological Works of Sigmund Freud*, ed. James Strachey (London: Hogarth Press), vol. 21.

Freud, Sigmund ([1932] 1973). *New Introductory Lectures on Psychoanalysis* (Harmondsworth: Pelican Freud Library), vol. 2.

Friedenberg, Edgar Z. (1973). *Laing*, Modern Masters Series (London: Fontana).

Fromm, Erich (1942). *The Fear of Freedom* (London: Routledge & Keegan Paul).

Fromm, Erich (1947). *Escape from Freedom* (New York: Farrar & Rinehart).

Fromm, Erich (1949). *Man for Himself, An Enquiry into the Psychology of Ethics* (London: Routledge & Kegan Paul).

Fromm, Erich (1955*a*). 'The human implications of instinctivistic radicalism', a reply to Herbert Marcuse', *Dissent*, vol. 2, pp. 342–9.

Fromm, Erich (1955*b*). *The Sane Society* (New York: Holt, Rinehart & Winston).

Fromm, Erich (1959). *Sigmund Freud's Mission* (New York: Harper).

Fromm, Erich (1966*a*). *Beyond the Chains of Illusion* (New York: Simon & Schuster).

Fromm, Erich (1966*b*). *Marx's Concept of Man*, trans. T. B. Bottomore (New York: Frederick Ungar).

Fromm, Erich (ed.) (1966). *Socialist Humanism, An International Symposium* (Garden City, NY: Doubleday).

Fromm, Erich (1971). *The Crisis of Psychoanalysis, Essays on Freud, Marx and Social Psychology* (London: Jonathan Cape).

Fromm, Erich (1973). *The Anatomy of Human Destructiveness* (New York: Holt, Rinehart & Winston).

Furley, David J. (1967). 'Aristotle and Epicurus on voluntary action', in his *Two Studies in the Greek Atomists* (Princeton, NJ: Princeton University Press), pp. 161–237.

Gay, Peter (1966 and 1969). *The Enlightenment: An Interpretation*, vol. 1: *The Rise of Modern Paganism*, and vol. 2: *The Science of Freedom* (New York: Knopf).

Geras, Norman (1971). 'Essence and appearances: aspects of fetishism in Marx's Capital', *New Left Review*, no. 65 (Janaury–February), pp. 69–85.

Gombin, Richard (1975). *The Origins of Modern Leftism* (Harmondsworth: Penguin).

Gorz, André (1965). 'Work and consumption', in Perry Anderson and Robin Blackburn (eds.), *Towards Socialism* (Harmondsworth: Penguin), pp. 317–53.

Gosling, J. C. B. (1969). *Pleasure and Desire, The Case for Hedonism Reviewed* (Oxford: Clarendon Press).

Gould, Josiah B. (1974). 'Being, the world and appearance in early Stoicism and some other Greek philosophers', *Review of Metaphysics*, vol. 28, pp. 261–88.

Graubard, Allen (1968). 'One-dimensional pessimism, a critique of Herbert Marcuse's theories', *Dissent*, vol. 15, pp. 216–28.

Gross, George (1972). 'The political economy of the unconscious', *Cambridge Review*, no. 17 (November), pp. 53–61.

Habermas, Jürgen (1970). *Toward a Rational Society, Student Protest, Science and Politics*, (Boston: Beacon Press).

Habermas, Jürgen (1972). *Knowledge and Human Interests* (London: Heinemann).

Hammen, Oscar, J. (1953). 'The spectre of communism in the 1840's', *Journal of the History of Ideas*, vol. 14, pp. 404–20.

Hampshire, S. (1949). 'Fallacies in modern moral philosophy', *Mind*, vol. 58, pp. 466–82.

Hancock, Roger (1971). 'Marx's theory of justice', *Social Theory and Practice*, vol. 1 (Spring), pp. 65–71.

Hare, R. M. (1952). *The Language of Morals* (Oxford: Clarendon Press).

Hare, R. M. (1969). 'Descriptivism', in W. D. Hudson (ed.), *The Is-Ought Question* (London: Macmillan), pp. 240–58.

Harris, Abram L. (1950). 'Utopian elements in Marx's thought', *Ethics*, vol. 60 (January), pp. 79–99.

Hegel, G. W. F. (1930). *Logic: Being Part One of the Encyclopedia of Philosophical Sciences*, 3rd edn, trans. William Wallace (Oxford: Oxford University Press).

Hegel, G. W. F. (1949). *The Phenomenology of Mind*, 2nd edn, trans. J. Baillie (London: Allen & Unwin).

Hegel, G. W. F. (1957). *Philosophy of Right*, trans. T. M. Knox (Oxford: Clarendon Press).

Hegel, G. W. F. (1969). *Science of Logic*, Muirhead Library of Philosophy, trans. Arnold Miller (London: Allen & Unwin).

Hegel, G. W. F. (1975). *Lectures on the Philosophy of World History, Introduction: Reason in History*, ed. Duncan Forbes (Cambridge: Cambridge University Press).

Heller, Agnes (1972). 'Towards a Marxist theory of value', *Kinesis*, vol. 5 (Fall) pp. 4–76.

Heller, Agnes (1974). 'Theory and practice: their relation to human needs', *Social Praxis*, vol. 1, pp. 359–73.

Heller, Agnes (1976). *The Theory of Need in Marx*, intro. by Ken Coates and Stephen Bodington (London: Allison & Busby).

Heller, Agnes (1980). 'Can "True" and "False" Needs be Posited?' in K. Lederer et al (eds), *Human Needs: a Contribution to the Current Debate* (Cambridge, Mass: Oelgeschlager, Gunn & Hain), pp. 213–26.

Hirschman, Albert O. (1976). *The Passions and the Interests, Political Arguments for Capitalism before Its Triumph* (Princeton, NJ: Princeton University Press).

Hodges, Donald Clark (1972*a*). 'Marx's concept of value and critique of value fetishism' *Science and Society*, vol. 36 (Fall), pp. 342–6.

Hodges, Donald Clark (1972*b*). 'Marx's theory of value', *Philosophy and Phenomenological Research*, vol. 33 (December), pp. 249–58.

Horne, Thomas A. (1978). *The Social Thought of Bernard Mandeville, Virtue and Commerce in Early Eighteenth Century England*, (New York: Columbia University Press).

Howard, Dick (1973). 'A Marxist ontology? On Sartre's "Critique of Dialectical Reason"', *Cultural Hermeneutics*, vol. 1, pp. 251–82.

Howard, Dick, and Klare, Karl E. (eds) (1972). *The Unknown Dimension, European Marxism Since Lenin* (New York: Basic Books).

Hudson, W. D. (ed.) (1969). *The Is-Ought Question* (London: Macmillan).

Hunt, E. K., and Sherman, Howard (1972). 'Value, alienation and distribution', *Science and Society*, vol. 36 (Spring), pp. 29–48.

Hyppolite, Jean (1968). 'The "scientific" and the "ideological" in a Marxist perspective', *Diogenes*, no. 64, pp. 27–36.

Hyppolite, Jean (1969). *Studies on Marx and Hegel*, trans. and ed. J. O'Neill (London: Heinemann).

Illich, Ivan (1971). *Deschooling Society* (London: Calder & Boyars).

Illich, Ivan (1973). *Tools for Conviviality* (New York: Harper).

Illich, Ivan (1974). *Energy and Equity* (New York: Harper).

Illich, Ivan (1978). *Toward a History of Needs* (New York: Pantheon).

Jay, Martin (1973). *The Dialectical Imagination, A History of the Frankfurt School and the Institute of Social Research 1923–1950* (London: Heinemann).

Jevons, W. S. (1970). *The Theory of Political Economy* (Harmondsworth: Penguin).

Jimack, Peter (1956–8). 'Les Influences de Condillac, Buffon et Helvétius dans *L'Emile*', *Annales de la Société Rousseau*, vol. 34, pp. 107–37.

Jimack, Peter (1960). 'La Genèse et la rédaction de *L'Emile de J.–J. Rousseau*', *Studies in Voltaire and the Eighteenth Century*, vol. 13.

Jouvenal, B. de (1961–2). 'Rousseau the pessimistic evolutionist' *Yale French Studies*, vol. 28, pp. 83–96.

Kamenka, Eugene (1962). *The Ethical Foundations of Marxism* (New York: Praeger).

Kamenka, Eugene (1969). *Marxism and Ethics* (London: Macmillan).

Kant, Immanuel (1949). *Fundamental Principles of the Metaphysic of Morals*, trans. T. K. Abbott (Indianapolis, Ind; New York: Bobbs-Merrill).

Kant, Immanuel (1954). *Critique of Practical Reason and Other Works on the Theory of Ethics*, trans. T. K. Abbott (London: Longman).

Kant, Immanuel (1971). *Political Writings*, ed. Hans Reiss (Cambridge: Cambridge University Press).

Kaufman, Arnold S. (1971). 'Wants, needs and liberalism', *Inquiry*, vol. 14, pp. 191–212.

Kaufman, M. (1879). *Utopias, or Schemes of Social Improvement* (London: Kegan Paul).

Kelly, George Armstrong (1969). *Idealism, Politics and History, Sources of Hegelian Thought* (Cambridge: Cambridge University Press).

Kenny, Anthony (1975). *Will, Freedom and Power* (Oxford: Basil Blackwell).

King, Preston (1976). 'On the Complexity of the Concept of "Need"' (Unpublished paper, University of New South Wales).

Knutson, Jeanne N. (1977). 'Human needs constraining political activity', in Ross Fitzgerald (ed.), *Human Needs and Politics* (Sydney: Pergamon), pp. 96–123.

Kojève, Alexandre (1969). *Introduction to the Reading of Hegel, Lectures on the Phenomenology of Spirit'*, assembled by Raymond Queneau, ed. by Allan Bloom (New York: Basic Books).

Kolakowski, Leszek (1971*a*). 'Althusser's Marx', *Socialist Register*, pp. 111–28.

Kolakowski, Leszek (1971*b*). *Marxism and Beyond* (London: Paladin).

Kolakowski, Leszek (1972). *Positivist philosophy, from Hume to the Vienna circle* (Harmondsworth: Penguin).

Kolakowski, Leszek (1979*a*). 'Anti-utopie utopique de Marx', in *Utopia, Criticism and Enlightenment from the Eighteenth Century*, Proceedings of the Colloquium, 'Utopia, Criticism in the Enlightenment' (Brussels: Free University), pp. 8–40.

Kolakowski, Leszek (1979*b*). 'My correct views on everything', *Socialist Register*, pp. 1–20.

Kolakowski, Leszek (1977). 'The persistence of the Sein-Sollen dilemma', *Man and World*, vol. 10, pp. 194–233.

Kolakowski, Leszek, and Hampshire, Stuart (eds) (1974). *The Socialist Idea, A Reappraisal*, (London: Weidenfeld & Nicolson).

Kovesi, Julius (1967). *Moral Notions* (London: Routledge & Kegan Paul).

Lach, J. (ed.), *Marxist Philosophy: A Bibliographical Guide* (Chapel Hill, NC: University of North Carolina Press).

Laing, R. D. (1965). *The Divided Self* (Harmondsworth: Penguin).

Laing, R. D., and Cooper, David (1964). *Reason and Violence: A Decade of Sartre's Philosophy* (London: Tavistock).

Laing, R. D., and Esterson, A. (1970). *Sanity, Madness and the Family* (Harmondsworth: Penguin).

Lancaster, Kevin (1971). *Consumer Demand: A New Approach* (New York: Columbia University Press).

Leiss, William (1976). *The Limits to Satisfaction: An Essay on the Problem of Needs and Commodities* (Toronto: University of Toronto Press).

Leroy, Maxime (1950). *Histoire des idées sociales en France*, vol. 2: *De Babeuf à Tocqueville* (Paris: Gallimard).

Lichtenberger, André ([1895] 1967). *Le Socialisme au XVIIIᵉ siècle*, (Paris, 1895; New York: Augustus M. Kelley Reprints, 1967).

Lichtheim, George (1969). *The Origins of Socialism* (London: Weidenfeld & Nicolson).

Lindgren, J. Ralph (1973). *The Social Philosophy of Adam Smith* (The Hague: Nijhoff).

Livergood, Norman D. (1967). *Activity in Marx's Philosophy* (The Hague: Nijhoff).

Lobkowicz, Nicholas (1967). *Theory and Practice, History of a Concept from Aristotle to Marx* (Notre Dame, Ind: University of Notre Dame Press).

Lobkowicz, Nicholas (1969). 'Karl Marx and Max Stirner', in F. J. Edelman (ed.), *Demythologizing Marxism* (The Hague: Nijhoff), pp. 65–95.

Locke, John (1959). *Essays on the Law of Nature*, ed. W. von Leyden (Oxford: Clarendon Press).

Locke, John (1967). *Two Treatises of Government*, 2nd edn, ed. P. Laslett (Cambridge: Cambridge University Press).

Locke, John (1975). *An Essay Concerning Human Understanding*, ed. Peter H. Nidditch (Oxford: Clarendon Press).

Long, A. A. (1974). *Hellenistic Philosophy, Stoics, Epicureans, Sceptics* (New York: Scribner's).

Louch, A. R. (1966). *Explanation and Human Action* (Berkeley, Calif.: University of California Press).

Lovejoy, Arthur O. (1948). 'The supposed primitivism of Rousseau's *Discourse on Inequality*', in his *Essays in the History of Ideas* (Baltimore, Md: Johns Hopkins University Press), pp. 14–37.

Lovejoy, Arthur O. (1961). *Reflections on Human Nature* (Baltimore, Md: Johns Hopkins University Press).

Lovejoy, Arthur O., and Boas, George (1935). *Primitivism and Related Ideas in Antiquity* (Baltimore, Md: Johns Hopkins University Press).

Lowenthal, Esther ([1911] 1972). *The Ricardian Socialists* (New York: Columbia University Press, 1911; New York: Augustus M. Kelley Reprints, 1972).

Löwith, Karl (1954). 'Man's self-alienation in the early writings of Marx', *Social Research*, vol. 22, pp. 204–30.

Löwith, Karl (1964). *From Hegel to Nietzsche: The Revolution in Nineteenth-Century Thought* (New York: Holt, Rinehart & Winston).

Lucretius (1937 edn). *De Rerum Natura* (London: Heinemann, Loeb Classical Library).

Lukács, Georg (1971). *History and Class Consciousness* (London: Merlin Press).

McCloskey, H. J. (1976). 'Human needs, rights and political values', *American Philosophical Quarterly*, vol. 13 (January), pp. 1–11.

Mace, C. A. (1953). 'Homeostasis, needs and values', *British Journal of Psychology*, vol. 44 (August), pp. 200–10.

Machiavelli, N. (1950 edn). *The Prince and the Discourses* (New York: Random House).

MacIntyre, Alasdair (1967). *A Short History of Ethics* (London: Routledge & Kegan Paul).

MacIntyre, Alasdair (1970). *Marcuse*, (London: Fontana).

MacIntyre, Alasdair (1971). 'Hume on "is" and "ought"', in his *Against the Self-Images of the Age* (London: Duckworth), pp. 109–24.

McLellan, David (1969). 'Marx's view of the unalienated society', *Review of Politics*, vol. 31 (October), pp. 459–65.

Macpherson, C. B. (1962). *The Political Theory of Possessive Individualism, Hobbes to Locke* (Oxford: Clarendon Press).

Macpherson, C. B. (1977). 'Needs and wants: an ontological or historical problem?', in Ross Fitzgerald (ed.), *Human Needs and Politics* (Sydney: Pergamon), pp. 26–35.

Mandeville, Bernard (1970). *The Fable of the Bees*, ed. Philip Harth (Harmondsworth: Penguin).

Manuel, Frank E. (1956). *The New World of Saint-Simon* (Cambridge, Mass.: Harvard University Press).

Manuel, Frank E. (1965). *The Prophets of Paris* (New York: Harper Torchbooks).

Marcuse, Herbert (1955). 'The social implications of Freudian "revisionism"', *Dissent*, vol. 2 (Summer), pp. 221–40, reprinted as 'Critique of Freudian revisionism', Epilogue to *Eros and Civilization* (1969).

Marcuse, Herbert (1956). 'A reply to Erich Fromm', *Dissent*, vol. 3 (Winter), pp. 79–81.

Marcuse, Herbert (1960). *Reason and Revolution, Hegel and the Rise of Social Theory*, 2nd edn (Boston, Mass.: Beacon Press).

Marcuse, Herbert (1964). *One Dimensional Man, Studies in the Ideology of Advanced Industrial Society* (Boston, Mass.: Beacon Press).

Marcuse, Herbert (1967). 'Thoughts on the defense of Gracchus Babeuf', in J. A. Scott (ed.), *The Defense of Gracchus Babeuf before the High Court of Vendôme* (Boston, Mass.: University of Massachusetts Press).

Marcuse, Herbert (1969). *Eros and Civilization, A Philosophical Inquiry into Freud* (London: Allen Lane).

Marcuse, Herbert (1970). *Five Lectures, Psychoanalysis, Politics, and Utopia* (Boston, Mass.: Beacon Press).

Marcuse, Herbert (1972a). *An Essay on Liberation* (Harmondsworth: Penguin).

Marcuse, Herbert (1972b). *Negations, Essays in Critical Theory* (Harmondsworth: Penguin).

Marcuse, Herbert (1972c). *Studies in Critical Philosophy* (London: New Left Books).

Marcuse, Herbert (1978). 'The need for an open Marxist mind', *The Listener* (9 February), pp. 169–71.

Marsak, L. M. (ed.) (1972). *The Enlightenment* (New York: Wiley).

Marx, Karl (1956). *The Holy Family* (London: Lawrence & Wishart).

Marx, Karl (1964). *The German Ideology* (Moscow: Progress Publishers).

Marx, Karl (1970). *Critique of Hegel's 'Philosophy of Right'*, ed. Joseph O'Malley (Cambridge: Cambridge University Press).

Marx, Karl (1973a). *Grundrisse*, ed. Nicholaus Martin (Harmondsworth: Penguin).

Marx, Karl (1973b). *Surveys from Exile*, vol. 2: *Political Writings* (Harmondsworth: Penguin).

Marx, Karl (n.d.). *Capital*, 3 vols (Moscow: Progress Publishers).

Marx, Karl, and Engels, Frederick (1966), *Marx/Engels Selected Works*, 3 vols Moscow: Progress Publishers).

Marx, Karl, and Engels, Frederick (1975–77). *Collected Works*, vols 1–7, (London: Lawrence & Wishart).

Mascolo, Dionys (1953). *Le Communisme, révolution et communication ou la dialectique des valeurs et des besoins* 2nd edn (Paris: Gallimard).

Maslow, Abraham H. (1943). 'A theory of human motivation', *Psychological Review*, vol. 50, pp. 370–96.

Maslow, Abraham H. (1948a). '"Higher" and "lower" needs', *Journal of Psychology*, vol. 25, pp. 433–6.

Maslow, Abraham H. (1948*b*). 'Some theoretical consequences of basic need-gratification', *Journal of Personality*, vol. 16, pp. 402–16.

Maslow, Abraham H. (1954*a*). 'The instinctoid nature of basic needs', *Journal of Personality*, vol. 22, pp. 326–47.

Maslow, Abraham H. (1954*b*). *Motivation and Personality* (New York: Harper).

Maslow, Abraham H. (1956). 'Criteria for judging needs to be instinctoid', in M. R. Jones (ed.), *Human Motivation: A Symposium* (Lincoln, Nebr.: Nebraska University Press), pp. 33–48.

Maslow, Abraham H. (1963). 'Fusions of facts and values', *American Journal of Psychoanalysis*, vol. 23, pp. 117–31.

Mepham, John (1972). 'The theory of ideology in *Capital*', *Radical Philosophy*, no. 2, pp. 12–19.

Merleau-Ponty, Maurice (1964). *Signs* (Evanston, Ill.: Northwestern University Press).

Mészáros, István (1970). *Marx's Theory of Alienation* (London: Merlin Press).

Meyer, William J. (1974). 'Democracy: needs over wants', *Political Theory*, vol. 2 (May), pp. 197–218.

Mill, John Stuart ([1909] 1976). *Principles of Political Economy*, ed. William Ashley (London: Longman, 1909; New York: Augustus M. Kelley Reprints, 1976).

Mins, Henry F. (1948). 'Marx's doctoral dissertation', *Science and Society*, vol. 13 (Winter), pp. 157–69.

Mitchell, Juliet (1975). *Psychoanalysis and feminism* (Harmondsworth: Penguin).

Moore, Stanley (1963). 'The metaphysical argument in Marx's labour theory of value', *L'Institut de Science Economique Appliquée, Cahiers*, series S., no. 7, Supp. no. 140 (August), pp. 73–95.

Moore, Stanley (1971). 'Marx and the origin of dialectical materialism,' *Inquiry*, vol. 14 (Autumn), pp. 420–9.

Morel, Jean (1909). 'Récherches sur les sources du *Discours de l'Inégalité.*' *Annales de la Société Jean-Jacques Rousseau*, vol. 5, pp. 119–98.

Morrow, Glenn R. ([1923] 1969). *The Ethical and Economic Theories of Adam Smith* (New York: Longman, 1923; New York: Augustus M. Kelley Reprints, 1969).

Murdoch, Iris (1970). *The Sovereignty of the Good* (London, Routledge & Kegan Paul).

Murray, Henry, *et al.* (1938). *Explorations in Personality* (New York: Oxford University Press).

Myrdal, Gunner (1953). *The Political Element in the Development of Economic Theory* (London, Routledge & Kegan Paul).

Nasser, Alan G. (1975). 'Marx's ethical anthropology', *Philosophy and Phenomenological Research*, vol. 35 (June), pp. 484–500.

Nell, Edward, and Nell, Onora (1972). 'On justice under socialism', *Dissent*, vol. 19 (Summer), pp. 483–91.

Nichols, James H., Jr (1976), *Epicurean Political Philosophy, The 'De rerum natura' of Lucretius* (Ithaca, NY: Cornell University Press).

Nielsen, Kai (1963). 'On human needs and moral appraisals', *Inquiry*, vol. 6, pp. 170–83.

Nielsen, Kai (1969). 'Morality and needs', in J. J. McIntosh and S. Coval (eds), *The Business of Reason* (London: Routledge & Kegan Paul), pp. 186–206.

Nielsen, Kai (1977). 'True needs, rationality and emancipation', in Ross Fitzgerald (ed.), *Human Needs and Politics* (Sydney: Pergamon), pp. 142–56.

Ollman, Bertell (1971). *Alienation: Marx's Conception of Man in Capitalist Society* (Cambridge: Cambridge University Press).

O'Malley, Joseph J. (1966). 'History and man's "nature" in Marx', *Review of Politics*, vol. 28, pp. 508–27.

O'Malley, Joseph J. (1970). 'Methodology in Karl Marx', *Review of Politics*, vol. 32, pp. 219–30.

Owen, Robert (1836). *The Book of the New Moral World, Containing the Rational System of Society, Founded on Demonstrable Facts, Developing the Constitution and Laws of Human Nature and of Society* (London: Effingham Wilson Publishers).

Owen, Robert (1970). *A New View of Society* and *Report to the County of Lenark*, ed. V. A. C. Gatrell (Harmondsworth: Penguin).

Packard, Vance (1957). *The Hidden Persuaders* (London: Longman).

Parekh, Bhikhu (1972). 'Utopianism and manicheism: a critique of Marcuse's theory of revolution', *Social Research*, vol. 39, pp. 622–51.

Passmore, John (1970). *The Perfectibility of Man* (London: Duckworth).

Paterson, R. W. K. (1971). *The Nihilistic Egoist, Max Stirner* (London: Oxford University Press).

Pelczynski, Z. A. (ed.) (1971). *Hegel's Political Philosophy, Problems and Perspectives* (Cambridge: Cambridge University Press).

Peters, R. S. (1960). *The Concept of Motivation* (London: Routledge & Kegan Paul).

Peters, R. S. (1974). *Psychology and Ethical Development* (London: Allen & Unwin).

Phillips, D. Z. and Mounce, H. O. (1969). 'On morality's having a point', in W. D. Hudson, (ed.), *The Is-Ought Question* (London: Macmillan), pp. 228–39.

Pilling, G. (1971). 'The law of value in Ricardo and Marx', *Economy and Society*, vol. 1, pp. 281–306.

Pire, Georges (1953–5). 'De l'influence de Sénèque sur les théories pédagogiques de J.-J. Rousseau', *Annales de la Société Jean-Jacques Rousseau*, vol. 33, pp. 57–92.

Plato (1945). *Plato's Examination of Pleasure (The Philebus)*, ed. R. Hackforth, (New York: Bobbs-Merrill, from Cambridge University Press edn).

Plato (1970). *The Laws* (Harmondsworth: Penguin).

Plato (1974). *The Republic*, ed. H. D. P. Lee (Harmondsworth: Penguin).

Pocock, J. G. A. (1975). *The Machiavellian Moment* (Princeton, NJ: Princeton University Press).

Poster, Mark (1975). *Existential Marxism in Postwar France, From Sartre to Althusser* (Princeton, NJ: Princeton University Press).

Poulantzas, Nicos (1969). 'The problem of the capitalist state', *New Left Review*, no. 58, pp. 67–78.

Poulantzas, Nicos (1972). 'On social classes', *New Left Review*, no. 78, pp. 27–54.

Proudhon, P. J. (1970). *Selected Writings*, ed. Stewart Edwards (London: Macmillan).

Reich, Wilhelm (1975). *The Mass Psychology of Fascism* (Harmondsworth: Penguin).

Renshon, Stanley (1977). 'Human needs and political analysis: an examination of a framework', in Ross Fitzgerald (ed.), *Human Needs and Politics* (Sydney: Pergamon), pp. 52–73.

Rieff, Philip (1961). *Freud: The Mind of the Moralist* (New York: Harper).

Rieff, Philip (1966). *The Triumph of the Therapeutic* (New York: Harper).

Rist, J. M. (1969). *Stoic Philosophy* (Cambridge: Cambridge University Press).

Robinson, Paul (1972). *The Sexual Radicals* (London: Paladin).

Roche, Kennedy F. (1974). *Rousseau, Stoic and Romantic* (London: Methuen).

Rosen, Frederick (1977). 'Basic needs and justice', *Mind*, vol. 86 (January), pp. 88–94.

Rotenstreich, Nathan (1963). 'On the ecstatic sources of the concept of "alienation"', *Review of Metaphysics*, vol. 16 (March), pp. 550–5.

Rousseau, Jean-Jacques (1913). *The Social Contract and Discourses* (London: Dent, Everyman).

Rousseau, Jean-Jacques (1962). *Political Writings of J.-J. Rousseau*, ed. C. E. Vaughan (London: Oxford University Press).

Rousseau, Jean-Jacques (1964). *Ouvres Complètes*, vol. 3: *Ecrits Politiques*, vol. 4: *Emile*, etc. (Paris: Gallimard, Bibliothèque de la Pléiade).

Rousseau, Jean-Jacques (1972). *Emile* (London: Dent, Everyman).

Rycroft, Charles (1971). *Reich*, Modern Masters Series (London: Fontana).

Saint-Simon, Henri de (1952). *Selected Writings*, ed. F. M. H. Markham (London: Oxford University Press).

Saint-Simon, Henri de (1975). *Henri de Saint-Simon, 1760–1825, Selected Writings on Science, Industry and Social Organization*, ed. Keith Taylor (London: Croom Helm).

Sartre, Jean-Paul (1955). *Literary and Philosophical Essays* (London: Rider).

Sartre, Jean-Paul (1960). *Search for a Method* (New York: Vintage Books).

Sartre, Jean-Paul (1969). *Being and Nothingness, An Essay on Phenomenological Ontology*, Trans. by Hazel E. Barnes, with an intro. by Mary Warnock (London: Methuen).

Sartre, Jean-Paul (1974). *Between Existentialism and Marxism* (London: New Left Books).

Sartre, Jean-Paul (1976). *Critique of Dialectical Reason*, vol. 1: *Theory of Practical Ensembles*, Trans. Alan Sheridan Smith (London: New Left Books).

Schaar, John H. (1961). *Escape from Authority, The Perspectives of Erich Fromm* (New York: Basic Books).

Schacht, Richard (1971). *Alienation* (London: Allen & Unwin).

Schiffer, Stephen (1976). 'A paradox of desire', *American Philosophical Quarterly*, vol. 13 (July), pp. 195–203.

Schumpeter, Joseph A. (1954). *History of Economic Analysis* (New York: Oxford University Press).

Searle, John (1964). 'How to derive "ought" from "is"', *Philosophical Review*, vol. 73 (January), pp. 43–58.

Sekora, John (1977). *Luxury, The Concept in Western Thought, Eden to Smollett* (Baltimore, Md: Johns Hopkins University Press).

Seneca (1969 edn). *Letters from a Stoic* (Harmondsworth: Penguin).

Shklar, Judith N. (1969). *Men and Citizens, A Study of Rousseau's Social Theory* (Cambridge: Cambridge University Press).

Singer, Peter (1973). 'The triviality of the debate over "is-ought" and the definition of "moral"', *American Philosophical Quarterly*, vol. 10 (January), pp. 51–6.

Skinner, Quentin (1978). *The Foundations of Modern Political Thought*, vol. 1: *The Renaissance*, vol. 2: *The Age of the Reformation* (Cambridge: Cambridge University Press).

Smith, Adam (1812). *The Theory of Moral Sentiments*, in *The Works of Adam Smith*, vol. 1, (London).

Smith, Adam (1973). *An Inquiry into the Nature and Causes of the Wealth of Nations*, Modern Library edn (New York: Random House).

Sombart, Werner (1967). *Luxury and Capitalism*, trans. W. R. Dittman (Ann Arbor, Mich.: Michigan University Press).

Springborg, Patricia (1978). 'Ideology and the Fact Value Distinction', unpublished paper presented at the Australian Philosophy Association Conference, Canberra, August 1978.

Springborg, Patricia (1977). 'Karl Marx on human needs', in Ross Fitzgerald (ed.), *Human Needs and Politics* (Sydney: Pergamon).

Stafford-Clark, David (1967). *What Freud Really Said* (Harmondsworth: Penguin).

Steinkraus, Warren E. (1971). *New Studies in Hegel's Philosophy* (New York: Holt, Rinehart & Winston).

Stirner, Max (1971). *The Ego and His Own*, ed. John Carroll (London: Jonathan Cape).

Sullivan, Roger J. (1974). 'The Kantian critique of Aristotle's moral philosophy, an appraisal', *Review of Metaphysics*, vol. 28 (September), pp. 24–53.

Talmon, J. L. (1952). *The Origins of Totalitarian Democracy* (London: Secker & Warburg).

Talmon, J. L. (1960). *Political Messianism, the Romantic Phase* (London: Secker & Warburg).

Taylor, Charles (1964). *The Explanation of Behaviour* (London: Routledge & Kegan Paul).

Taylor, Charles (1966). Marxism and empiricism', in Bernard Williams and Alan Montefiore (eds), *British Analytical Philosophy* (London: Routledge & Kegan Paul).

Taylor, Charles (1969). 'Neutrality in political science', in Peter Laslett and W. G. Runciman (eds), *Philosophy, Politics and Society*, 3rd series (Oxford: Basil Blackwell) pp. 25–57.

Taylor, Charles (1975). *Hegel* (Cambridge: Cambridge University Press).

Taylor, Charles (1978). 'Marxism, the science of the millennium', *The Listener*, 2 February, pp. 138–40.

Taylor, Paul (1959). '"Need" statements', *Analysis*, vol. 19, pp. 106–11.

Thompson, Clara, and Mullahy, P. (1951). *Psychoanalysis, Evolution and Development* (New York: Hermitage House).

Tucker, Robert C. (1963). 'Marx and distributive justice', in C. J. Friedrich and J. W. Chapman (eds), *Nomos IV, Justice* (New York: Aldine-Atherton Press), pp. 306–25.

Van de Veer, Donald (1973). 'Marx's view of justice', *Philosophy and Phenomenological Research*, vol. 33 (March) pp. 366–87.

Veblen, Thorstein ([1899] 1975). *The Theory of the Leisure Class* (New York: Macmillan, 1899; New York: Augustus M. Kelley Reprints, 1975).

Venable, V. (1946). *Human Nature: The Marxian View* (London: Dobson).

Von Wright, G. H. (1963). *The Varieties of Goodness* (London: Routledge & Kegan Paul).

Walton, P., Gamble, A., and Coulter, J. (1970). 'Image of man in Marx', *Social Theory and Practice*, vol. 1 (Fall), pp. 69–84.

Wasserman, Earl (ed.) (1965). *Aspects of the Eighteenth Century* (Baltimore, Md: Johns Hopkins University Press).

Weisskopf, Walter A., 'The image of man in economics', *Social Research*, vol. 40 (Autumn), pp. 547–63.

White, Alan R. (1974). 'Needs and wants', *Proceedings of the Philosophy of Education Society of Great Britain, Supplementary Issue*, vol. 8 (July), pp. 159–80.

Wittgenstein, Ludwig (1968). *Philosophical Investigations*, 3rd edn (Oxford: Basil Blackwell).

Wollheim, Richard (1971). *Freud* (London: Fontana).

Wood, Allen W. (1972a). 'The Marxian critique of justice', *Philosophy and Public Affairs*, vol. 1, pp. 244–82.

Wood, Allen W. (1972b). 'Marx's critical anthropology: three recent studies', *Review of Metaphysics*, vol. 26 (September) pp. 118–39.

Index